GENERAL VIEW OF THE AGRICULTURE OF THE COUNTY OF SUFFOLK

GENERAL VIEW of the AGRICULTURE of the COUNTY OF SUFFOLK

A Reprint of the Work Drawn up for the Consideration of the Board of Agriculture and Internal Improvement

by

ARTHUR YOUNG

Secretary of the Board

DAVID & CHARLES REPRINTS

7153 4676 8

This book was first published in 1813

This edition published in 1969

Printed in Great Britain by
Clarke Doble & Brendon Limited Plymouth
for David & Charles (Publishers) Limited
South Devon House Railway Station
Newton Abbot Devon

MAP
of the SOIL *of*
SUFFOLK

Nele sculp! Strand.

GENERAL VIEW

OF THE

AGRICULTURE

OF THE

COUNTY OF SUFFOLK.

DRAWN UP FOR THE CONSIDERATION OF

THE BOARD OF AGRICULTURE

AND INTERNAL IMPROVEMENT.

BY

THE SECRETARY OF THE BOARD.

LONDON:

PRINTED FOR SHERWOOD, NEELY, AND JONES,
PATERNOSTER-ROW:
SOLD BY G. AND W. NICOL, PALL-MALL.

1813.
[*Price* 10*s.* 6*d. in Boards.*]

London: Printed by B. M'Millan,
Bow Street, Covent Garden,

ADVERTISEMENT.

THE great desire that has been very generally expressed for having the AGRICULTURAL SURVEYS of the KINGDOM reprinted, with the additional communications which have been received since the ORIGINAL REPORTS were circulated, has induced the BOARD OF AGRICULTURE to come to a resolution of reprinting such as may appear on the whole fit for publication. It is proper at the same time to add, that the Board does not consider itself responsible for any fact or observation contained in the Reports thus reprinted, as it is impossible to consider them yet in a perfect state; and that it will thankfully acknowledge any additional information which may still be communicated: an invitation of which, it is hoped, many will avail themselves, as there is no circumstance from which any one can derive more real satisfaction, than that of contributing, by every possible means, to promote the improvement of his Country.

N. B. *Letters to the Board may be addressed to* LORD SHEFFIELD, *the President, London.*

INTRODUCTION.

IT is not easy to conceive an undertaking more difficult, than to give such an account of a province, as shall on one hand be minute enough to convey satisfactory information ; and on the other, shall not be so minute as to include matter either of insufficient importance, or that is more calculated for a general treatise or report than for a local and appropriated one.

The first edition of this memoir was drawn up under the idea that the Board of Agriculture wished for such a return from the several counties, as should answer the various purposes, 1. Of describing the most interesting features of the local practices, and noting the most remarkable deficiencies ; the one as an example to other counties, the other for attaining the knowledge that might prove useful to this ; 2. Of receiving such a report of the statistical circumstances of the county, as might enable the Board to combine, from various sources, the real state of the kingdom. These objects I fulfilled to the best of my ability, touching very lightly on those articles which must necessarily be common to every county, and dwelling particularly on such as had something more local in their merit.

Such I conceived to be the wish of the Board; and after above fourscore reports have been received, I remain clearly of opinion, that this is the true idea of a county report.

If I am right in this idea, any chapter, section, dissertation, &c. that might be taken from the account of one county, and with equal propriety inserted in another; is not properly a part of the return of a particular district. If such a distinction be not adhered to, the report of a single county might swell into a complete body of husbandry. I trust that those who may have any opinion of the little talents I possess, will believe that I could have expatiated largely in various divisions of this work; but I am apt to hold, that the next evil to writing badly on a good subject, is attempting to write well when the opportunity is improper; and I still conceive, that in treating of any subject locally, all general deviations, however ably treated, are liable to the *non erat his locus*.

In the first reports, the surveyors were at liberty to make their returns in whatever manner and form they pleased; but since the President of the Board has drawn up and distributed a particular arrangement of the subjects on which he wished for information, and to be adhered to in the corrected reports, it has become necessary to cast anew the materials, which will necessarily be favourable or the contrary, to the reporter, proportionably as the new arrangement coincides with the intelligence afforded by the county. The reader will observe, in various sections of the following papers, treating of practices the same in Suffolk as every where else, that brevity has been the principal object in view; and that the chief additions have been under those heads in which the practices of the county are not found in many others, as in carrots, cabbages, hemp, the polled breed of cows, &c. If in consequence of the Board having surveyed the kingdom, such a practice as cultivating carrots for horses should be established in other light land districts, and every county contributes some useful practice in the same way, there will not long remain any question of the benefits which have resulted from the institution; without having in contemplation those greater and more general advantages which must flow from an establishment singularly calculated to direct the attention of mankind to the first and greatest field in which human industry can be exerted; which, like similar institutions, when duly supported, and availing themselves of the progress of their own experience, promises to move with that accelerated effect which results from corrected views, and improved means of attainment.

Some of the communications which have been received in consequence of the first edition

being distributed, might have been interwoven
in the text in a manner to have left the work
more uniform; but as I think the gentlemen
who have had the goodness to give their attention thus to furnish assistance, should have the
credit of it, I have annexed their communications with their names.

CONTENTS.

CHAPTER VIII.—GRASS.

CHAPTER IX.—GARDENS AND ORCHARDS.

CHAPTER X.— WOODS AND PLANTA-
TIONS.

CHAPTER XI.—WASTES.

CHAPTER XII.—IMPROVEMENTS.

CHAPTER XIII.—LIVE STOCK.

CHAPTER XIV.—RURAL ECONOMY.

CHAPTER XV.—POLITICAL ECONOMY.

CHAPTER XVI.—OBSTACLES TO IMPROVEMENT.

CHAPTER XVII. — MISCELLANEOUS OBSERVATIONS.

AGRICULTURAL SURVEY

OF

SUFFOLK.

CHAPTER I.

GEOGRAPHICAL STATE.

SECTION I.—SITUATION AND EXTENT.

By the new map of Mr. Hodskinson, an oblong of almost unindented form may be measured, of 47 miles long by 27 broad. The land stretching beyond it, in the N. E. and N. W. parts, will more than fill the deficiency in the S. W. That form indicates a surface of 1269 square miles, or 812,160 acres. In Templeman's survey from old maps, he makes it 1236; but, as he computed by geographic miles, his estimation was confessedly erroneous, and of no other use than that of comparing one country with another. Suffolk, therefore, may be computed at about 800,000 acres.

SECT. II.—DIVISIONS.

THE two grand divisions of the county, are, 1. The liberty of Bury St. Edmond's. 2. The body of the county, as it is termed; for each of which there is a separate grand jury. The subdivision is into hundreds.

SECT. III.—CLIMATE.

IT is unquestionably one of the dryest climates in the kingdom ; with which circumstance two others unite : the frosts are severe, and the N. E. winds, in the spring, sharp and prevalent. In these northern latitudes, and insular situations, the most humid countries are the most free from frost and snow, till you arrive on the western coasts of Ireland, where the rains are incessant, and frost almost unknown. Severe winters and dry springs have a strong influence on agriculture : the former render turnips a precarious dependence, and the latter lengthen the winter, to the great expence of the keepers of live-stock. On the whole, however, the climate of this county must be reckoned favourable.

SECT. IV.—SOIL.

THERE is not, perhaps, a county in the kingdom which contains a greater diversity of soil, or more clearly discriminated. A strong loam, on a clay-marl bottom, predominates through the greatest part of the county, as may be seen by the map annexed ; extending from the south-western extremity of Wratting Park to North Cove, near Beccles. Its northern boundary stretches from Dalham, by Barrow, Little Saxham, near Bury, Rougham, Pakenham, Ixworth, Honington, Knattishal, and then in a line, near the river which parts Norfolk and Suffolk, to Beccles and North Cove ; but every where leaving a slope and vale of rich friable loam ad-joining the river, of various breadths. It then turns southward by Wrentham, Wangford, Blithford, Holton,

Bramfield, Yoxford, Saxmundham, Campsey Ash, Woodbridge, Culpho, Bramford, Hadleigh; and following the high lands on the west side of the Bret, to the Stour, is bounded by the latter river, with every where a very rich tract of slope and vale from thence to its source. Such is the strong land district of Suffolk taken in the mass; but it is not to be supposed that it takes in so large an extent without any variation: a rule to which I know few exceptions, is, that wherever there are rivers in it, the slopes hanging to the vales through which they run, and the bottoms themselves, are of a superior quality; in general composed of rich friable loams: and this holds even with many very inconsiderable streams, which fall into the larger rivers. The chief part of this district would in common conversation be called clay, but improperly. I have analyzed many of these strong loams, and found them abounding with more sand than their texture would seem to imply; so that were they situated upon a gravel, sand, or chalk, they would be called *sandy loams;* but being on a retentive clay-marl bottom, are properly, from their wetness, to be termed *strong,* or *clayey loam.*

The district of rich loam being much less clearly discriminated, will leave more doubts on the minds of persons acquainted with it. From the river Deben, crossing the Orwell, in a line some miles broad, to the north of the river Stour, to Stratford and Higham, there is a vein of friable putrid vegetable mould, more inclined to sand than to clay, which is of extraordinary fertility: the best is at Walton, Trimley, and Felixtow, where, for depth and richness, much of it can scarcely be exceeded by any soils to be found in other parts of the county, and would rank high among the best in England. As the position recedes northward to the line from Ipswich to Hadleigh, it varies a good deal; in many places it approaches sand,

and in some is much stronger, as about Wenham and Raydon : the general complexion, however, of the whole of Samford hundred is that of good loam. I was much inclined to class the hundreds of Lothingland and Mutford, that is, all to the north of a line drawn from Beccles to Kessingland, in this division of soil ; the rent of much would confirm such an arrangement; but on reconsidering the quality of the soil in various parts, and palpable sand so often intervening, especially along the coast, I think it, upon a general scale, safer to let it pass as part of the sandy maritime district.

Of that district I must observe, that my arrangement will startle many persons, who speak of *clay* in a loose and indefinite manner. I was told of large tracts of clay near Pakefield and Dunwich*, and particularly on the farm of Westwood Lodge ; but when I examined them I could not find a single acre : I found rich loamy firm sand worth 20*s.* an acre, but nothing that deserved even the epithet *strong*. I was assured that there was little or no sand in Colness hundred, where I saw hundreds of acres of buck-wheat stubbles. All these expressions result from the common ideas of soils being not sufficiently discriminated. Land of 15*s.* or 20*s.* an acre, in the eastern parts of the country, is never called sand, though deserving the epithet as much as inferior ones. The error has partly arisen from the title of *sandling* being given peculiarly to the country south of the line of Woodbridge and Orford, where a large extent of poor, and even blowing sands is found ; but speaking with an attention to the real quality of the soil, and not at all regarding the rent, the whole of the maritime

---

* There is not an entire acre of clay near Pakefield or Dunwich; but almost all the corn lands thereabouts have been made by opening pits, and laying from 60 to 120 loads of clay per acre. That is what in Suffolk is called *clay*, though more properly marl.

district may be termed sandy ; towards the north, much inclining, in various parts, to loamy sands, and in others to sandy loams ; but so broken, divided, and mixed with undoubted sands, that one term must be applied in a general view to the whole. This district I take to be one of the best cultivated in England ; not exempt from faults and deficiencies, but having many features of un-questionably good management. It is also a most pro-fitable one to farm in ; and there are few districts in the county, if any, abounding with wealthier farmers, nor any that contain a greater proportion of occupying proprietors, possessing from one hundred to three and four hundred pounds a year.

The under stratum of this district varies considerably, but in general it may be considered as sand, chalk, or *crag;* in some parts marl and loam. The crag is a singular body of cockle and other shells, found in great masses in various parts of the country, from Dunwich quite to the river Orwell, and even across it in Wolver-ston Park, &c. I have seen pits of it from which great quantities have been taken, to the depth of fifteen and twenty feet, for improving the heaths. It is both red and white, but generally red, and the shells so broken as to resemble sand. On lands long in tillage the use is discontinued, as it is found to make the sands *blow* more.

The western district of sand is a much poorer country, containing few spots of such rich sands as are found on the coast, but abounding largely with warrens and poor sheep-walks : a great deal under the plough *blows,* and consequently ranks among the worst of all soils, black sand on a yellow bottom perhaps excepted. Parts of the district take, however, the character of loamy sand ; the whole angle, for instance, to the right of the line from Barrow to Honington (see the map), in which no blowing, or even very light sand is found. A more striking exception, though of small extent, is found at Mildenhall, where there is an open field of arable land of capital value, dry yet highly fertile, and friable without being loose ; its products almost perpetual, and its fruitfulness almost unvaried. The under stratum, through almost all the district, is a more or less perfect chalk, at various depths, but I believe uninterrupted; and it may be received as a rule, that the whole of it, low vales on rivers only excepted, is proper for sain-foin.

Of the fen district it is only necessary to observe, that the surface, from one foot to six, is the common peat of bogs, some of it black and solid enough to yield a considerable quantity of ashes in burning; but in other places more loose, puffy, and reddish, and consequently of an inferior quality; the under stratum generally a white clay, or marl. Part of these fens is under water, though subject to a tax for the drainage, which has failed; but in Burnt Fen, by a late act of Parliament for improving the banks, 14,000 acres are completely drained, and under cultivation.

SECT. V.—MINERALS AND FOSSILS.

THERE are no mines in the county; nor other fossils connected with agriculture, except such as are necessarily mentioned under the titles of *soil* and manure.

SECT. VI.—WATER.

SUFFOLK may be esteemed a well watered country : its boundaries to the north and south are rivers partly navigable; and it is every where intersected by streams which would be invaluable, was that most beneficial of all practices, irrigation, understood : but unfortunately, these waters have from the creation ran in waste, to an incalculable loss. There are, however, some thousands of acres which might easily, by this improvement, be advanced to a state infinitely more productive.

CHAPTER II.

PROPERTY.

SECT. I.—ESTATES.

THE state of property in Suffolk may be considered as beneficial in its division. The largest estate in the county is supposed not to exceed 8000 or 8500*l.* a year ; and it is a singular instance of the rise in the value of land within the period of forty or fifty years. There are three or four other estates which rise above 5000*l.* a year ; and I have a list of thirty others which are about 3000*l.* a year and upwards. Under this, there are numbers of all sizes ; but the most interesting circumstance is of a different complexion—I mean the rich yeomanry, as they were once called, being very numerous, farmers occupying their own lands, of a value rising from 100*l.* to 400*l.* a year. A most valuable set of men, who, having the means and the most powerful inducements to good husbandry, carry agriculture to a high degree of perfection.

SECT. II.—TENURES.

THE great mass of the county is freehold property, but copyholds are numerous, and some of them large. Of college leases, scattered in various parts, nothing particular is to be noted.

Under this head, however, may not be improperly
arranged some customs which are very great impedi-
ments to the due cultivation of the soil ; these are the
rights of commonage and pasture, which exceed the
ordinary cases. At Troston, on the borders of the
western sand district, I found open field lands in which
the course is one crop to two fallows ; and these consist
in leaving the land to weeds for the flock of one farmer,
who, by prescription, is the only person that can keep
sheep in the parish! Nothing can be imagined more
beggarly than the husbandry and crops on these lands ;
the same farmer has even the right of sheep-feeding
many of the inclosed pastures and meadows after the
hay is removed. In return for such privileges, he is
bound to fold a certain number of acres for the other
farmers. It is not difficult to trace the origin of such
customs ; but wherever found, they ought to be abo-
lished, by giving an equivalent.

CHAPTER III.

BUILDINGS.

SECT. I.—HOUSES OF PROPRIETORS.

I WISH it was in my power to insert an account of houses so singularly adapted to the residence of country gentlemen of a certain property, as to merit a particular attention. This branch of architecture has been strangely neglected: great exertions have been made for the convenience of men of large fortunes, but none that are adapted to the mode of living which takes place by reason of smaller incomes.

SECT. II.—FARM-HOUSES, AND REPAIRS.

THE farm-houses are much improved within the last twenty years; but they are still very inferior to what, it is to be hoped, they may become in some future period. They are too often built, even at present, of lath and plaster, which decaying in a few years, occasions repairs being so heavy an article of deduction from the annual receipt of an estate, as to lessen considerably the net profit resulting from landed property. The extent to which this evil operates in the eastern part of the kingdom in general, may be conceived from a curious fact; that the repairs on one estate of about 15,000l. a year, came in eleven years to above 40,000l.

This is partly owing to houses, and still more, to barns being larger, and more numerous than necessary; as the farmers of this county are in respect of barn-room not easily satisfied. The advantages, and even the mode of stacking corn, are not well understood.

It is very much to be regretted, that the durability of brick and stone, upon comparison of lath and plaster, or wattle and clay, for all buildings, should not induce proprietors universally to use those superior materials, and they would find the difference of expence not material.

SECT. III.—COTTAGES.

Some very respectable individuals have distinguished themselves most laudably, by building neat and comfortable cottages for the poor; but such instances are not general, and can only be effected by persons of a certain income; as unfortunately the rent commonly yielded by them will not pay more than two to four per cent. at the utmost, for the money invested, reduced considerably by repairs, especially if of lath and plaster, or wattle and clay. Were the reward of labour sufficient to enable the poor to pay a higher rent for their habitations, it would contribute greatly to the improvement of cottages. In Suffolk, they are in general bad habitations; deficient in all contrivance for warmth, and for convenience; the door very generally opening immediately from the external air into the keeping-room, and sometimes directly to the fire-side; the state of reparation bad, and the deficiency of gardens too general. In this respect, which is nearly connected with the comforts of a poor family, there is a want of attention amongst many of the poor themselves; for I have

seen small plots of garden ground contiguous to their
cottages, in a wretchedly neglected state ; and in the
parish where I live, there is an instance of a cottager
who owns his own dwelling, letting about a quarter of
an acre contiguous to his house to a neighbouring
farmer, at the common value of such land ; yet the man
is sober, saving, and industrious. He is, I should apprehend, a bad calculator.

The general rent of cottages is from 40s. to 3l. with
or without a small garden.

Mr. Davenport, of Bardwell, remarks, " that it must
in a pretty good degree benefit the poor, if their cottages
were not to be annexed to the hirer of the farm, but to
be let to them immediately by the landlord, or his
agent, who must have particular orders for that purpose.
The farmer often lets them as dear as he can, and
beyond their value, in order to lower his own rent ;
whereas the landlord would let them at a proper price,
and not suffer the rich farmer to take a mite for his
further bulk from the poor starving labourer ;" which
observation is certainly just, and has been well elucidated by the Earl of Winchilsea, in his valuable
Memoir on Cottages.

CHAPTER IV.

OCCUPATION.

SECT. I.—SIZE OF FARMS.

THESE, in Suffolk, must, in a general light, be reckoned large ; and to that circumstance, more perhaps than to any other, is to be attributed the good husbandry so commonly found in the county. In the district of strong wet loam, there are many small ones from 20*l*. to 100*l*. a year ; but these are intermixed with others that rise from 150*l*. to 300*l*. and some even more. In the sand districts they are much larger, many from 300*l*. to one of 850*l*. or 900*l*. ; that of West Wood Lodge, near Dunwich, in the occupation of Mr. Howlett, and belonging to Sir John Blois, Bart. consisting of above 3000 acres, is without exception the finest farm in the county. Agriculture is carried on to great perfection, through much of these sand districts, owing not a little to these large occupations in the hands of a wealthy tenantry. But this is a point that calls for an observation relative to the profit of cultivating different soils, which is, that there is no comparison between the wealth of our farmers on dry and on wet land. On the former, the occupation of a farm of 200*l*. or 300*l*. a year, has been throughout the county, generally found attended with a very handsome profit, visible in various circumstances, and ascertained on the death of the farmers. But on the wet land, though numbers are very much at their ease, yet the advantages, and fortunes made, have been exceedingly inferior, and mixed with many instances that will not allow the idea of considerable profits *. Conclusions may be drawn from this not unimportant : it should seem to mark what I have many years observed, that the management of light soils is vastly better understood than that of heavy ones ; and it may possibly be found, that the latter are higher rented than the former, and also the expence of stock and cultivation much greater. The fact is probably owing, also, to the arable land being, on wet soils, in too great proportion to the grass †. These are circumstances much deserving the attention of landlords.

In some parts of the county, the farms continue very small. The Rev. Mr. Nesfield, of Wickhambrook, writes me, that " the parish of Wickhambrook contains about 3000 acres of arable and meadow land, besides pasture, of which I can give no accurate account. It is all strongly inclosed ; the fields in general are exceedingly small, and divided into 59 farms : the largest, including Bansfield-Hall Park, rated at 133*l.* per annum ; one at 118*l.* one at 112*l.* and one at 110*l* ; nine between 60*l.* and 100*l.* three at 60*l.* The rest are of all sizes, from 60*l.* down to 5*l.* per annum."

---

* The second solution of this difficulty seems more adequate than the first, though certainly, for a number of years, the management of light soils was better understood than that of heavy ones. Yet the considerable improvements that have lately been made, give reason to believe that the comparison will not long remain in favour of the former.—*Note by J. R.*

† Notwithstanding this opinion, which is in a great measure well-founded, the constant request from the heavy land farmers to their landlords is, to be allowed to break up more land, and they will pay more rent accordingly —*Note.*

SECT. II.—RENT.

To ascertain as nearly as possible, the rent of land in every county of the kingdom, is an object of great utility in an agricultural view. In many cases, for want of other authorities, the produce of the soil cannot be calculated but by means of the fair rent of it*; and it is unnecessary to explain the variety of lights in which a knowledge of the gross produce is of material consequence, being in truth the greatest and most solid foundation of the national wealth and power. There is, however, some delicacy necessary in treating, under the authority of a public board, a subject which has been apt to excite jealousies, as if it were probable that ascertaining rent was one step to the imposition of certain taxes. The idea seems to me unfounded: Government hath such a variety of methods of acquiring knowledge of that nature, that it could derive very little assistance from any possible enquiries made through the medium of a Board of Agriculture. And it might further be observed, that in all questions of taxation, ascertaining the national amount of any object, is of less importance, than deciding upon the principles and effect of the imposition, which must ever determine such questions ; and by no means the fact of a rental being 20 or 26 millions, or any other sum to be supposed. In an agricultural light, a knowledge of the rent is an essential article, for there are low rents paid by certain modes of management, with more difficulty to the tenant than would attend much higher ones, under a change of conduct. Such a difference is a very strong argument, applicable equally to both landlord and tenant.

---

* Which may perhaps be generally allowed to be one-fifth nearly of the produce.—*Note by J. C.*

1803. An observation should be added here, which the two scarcities, experienced since the former edition of this work, have broughr powerfully to the minds of many farmers. The great and rich ones profited considerably by the high prices of corn ; but the little ones suffered more by poor rates than they were benefited by prices. Rent should always be calculated (for private use) in union with rates and tithe ; for it must be evident at the first blush, that a farmer can pay more rent where rates are 5s. in the pound, than where they are 15s. The only safe and unobjectionable way of estimating the rent of land is to deduct the expences per acre (including 10 per cent. on his capital for his own profit) from the acreable produce ; and the remainder is for rent, rates, and tithe, (where not taken in kind,) from this sum deduct rates and tithe ; the remainder is the landlord's rent, and the farmer cannot afford to pay one penny more. By extraordinary capital ; or by uncommon skill or exertions, he may make more than 10 per cent. and in that case the difference is the fair remuneration for such capital, skill, or exertions.

The following calculation will shew this, perhaps, more clearly. Let us suppose the land of that quality which has been denoted good loam.

Course 1 Turnips.
        2 Barley.
        3 Clover.
        4 Wheat.

	£	s	d
Produce. Turnips - -	2	0	0
Barley, 4 quarters at 25s. - -	5	0	0
Clover - - - -	2	10	0
Wheat, 3 quarters, at 52s. - -	7	16	0
Carried forward -	£17	6	0

Brought forward -	£17	6	0
Straw 10s. - - -	1	0	0
	18	6	0
Per acre -	4	11	6

Expences. Wear and tear, per acre,	0	2	6
Labour - - - -	1	5	0
Seed - - - -	0	8	0
Team - - -	0	12	0
	2	7	6
Farmer's capital £7. per acre, and allowing him 10 per cent. it makes - -	0	14	0
	3	1	6

Produce - -	£4	11	6
Expences - -	3	1	6
	1	10	0
Suppose tythe gathered; it takes *	0	8	9
	1	1	3
Suppose rates - -	0	5	0
Remains for rent - -	0	16	3

Yet land that will, on an average, produce these crops lets at 20s.

* Allowing 4s. for food to the team not tytheable.

Again, - -	£1	10	0
Suppose tythe compounded at 5s.			
an acre - - -	0	5	0
	1	5	0
Suppose rates - -	0	5	0
Remains for landlord -	1	0	0

Hence it appears, that if he pays 20s. rent, and 5s. rates, and his tythe is gathered, he has 3s. 9d. an acre less than is necessary to give him 10 per cent. on his capital.

It appears that four rents and an half are nearer the fact than five.

I do not see how the farmer can live if he makes less than 10 per cent. on his capital ; for it is to be remembered, that every shilling of produce is here brought to account, and though the clover and turnips may by some be thought low, yet it must not be for-gotten that both are extremely apt to fail, wholly or partially ; so that many crops of these plants must produce far beyond this estimate in order for the ave-rage to rise to the sums I have noted.

To ascertain the rent of the several districts is impos-sible ; nothing more is to be expected than to guess, with some degree of approximation, to the truth. On the foundation of as correct information as I could, from residence and examination, procure, I am inclined to believe, that the several soils are at present rented as under, the whole country included, sheep-walk, waste, commons, &c. which are very large deductions from the rate of the cultivated land.

	£.	s.	d.
The strong or wet loam, at per acre, -	0	13	0
The rich loam, - - -	0	14	0
The maritime district of sand, -	0	10	0
*The western ditto of ditto, -	0	5	0
The fens, - - - -	0	2	6

1803. In the ten years that have elapsed since the former survey was made the proportions have suffered some change, so that I am inclined to estimate the particulars in the following manner.

	£.	s.	d.
Strong loam at per acre - -	0	16	0
Rich loam - - - -	0	18	0
Maritime district of sand - -	0	12	0
The western ditto - -	0	6	0
The fens - - - -	0	4	0

It should be noted, that there are in all these districts, except the fen, tracts that let at 20s. and 25s. and even higher rents, and meadows higher still; but the rents here minuted are those of the whole county, as viewed in the map.

GENERAL VIEW OF THE RENTAL OF THE COUNTY.

Dividing the county according to the soil in the annexed map, and weighing each division accurately, I

* In the western sandy district, there is a very large proportion of heath, which will probably reduce the average value of the district below 5s. per acre. There are also extensive heaths in the neighbourhood of Ipswich, so unfavourable to sheep, that they are of very little value in their present state.—*Note by T. L.*—— I was aware of these circumstances, and do not conceive them to reduce the rent below 5s. —*A. Y.*

find the proportions are, to the total of 800,000 acres,
as under; to which I have added the rent and totals.

ACRES.		£.	s.	d.
30,000 fen, at 2s. 6d. -	-	3750	0	0
*46,666⅔ rich loam, at 14s. -		32,666	13	4
156,666⅔ sand, at 10s. -		78,333	3	4
113,333⅓ do. at 5s. -		28,333	6	8
*453,333⅓ strong loam, at 13s.		294,666	13	4
800,000, average rent, 10s. 7d.		£437,749	16	8

ACRES.		£.	s.	d.
30,000 fens, at 4s. -	-	6,000	0	0
46,666₂ rich loam, at 18s. -		42,000	0	0
156,666⅔ sand, at 12s. -		93,999	0	0
113,333⅓ do. at 6s. -		33,999	0	0
453,333⅓ strong loam, at 16s.		362,666	0	0
800,000		£538,664	0	0

SECT. III.—TYTHES.

THERE is as great a variety in the circumstance
attending the receipt of tythes in Suffolk, as in most
other districts of the kingdom. They are gathered in

---

* Quere.—Is the difference of 1s. per acre between rich and strong
loam sufficient? I should rather suppose 2s. or 3s. nearer the value and
truth. *J. C.*—I am of the same opinion as to *real* value; but I state
here simply what I conceive to be the fact.—*A. Y.*

NOTES COMMUNICATED BY CORRESPONDENTS.

Rent of common field land in Bardwell, 10s. to 20s.

In Barningham, arable 16s. pasture lower.

In Hopton, arable 14s. 6d.

Fornham St. Martin, 9s. on an average; the greatest part common
    field.

kind by some ; and the compositions admitted by others, vary in proportion to the liberality, and situation in life of the possessors.* In the mass, they must certainly be considered as favourable to the occupier, and to do credit to the moderation and feelings of the gentlemen, who, having the power to require what would be a very heavy payment from the farmer, content themselves with compositions under the real value.

These are, in some parishes, by the acre, and in others by the pound of rent. They vary too much to allow of general description, consistent with accuracy.

Mr. Nesfield, of Wickambrook, informs me, that for 75 years they have been there invariably 3s. an acre for corn, when a fore crop ; 2s. the after crops ; and 11d. an acre for hay.

1803. Tythes have been considerably advanced since the first edition of this work ; and they would have been carried higher, had it not been for the check of poor rates. The compositions are not often rated more than nominally ; but when taken in kind, they pay a proportion of that burthen, but in bad times not often a fair proportion. It seems undeniably equitable that the poor rate should be paid in exact proportion to the neat profit made by every occupier of the land. A pound rate is taken as the nearest practicable approach to a real ascertainment of such profit : suppose an acre of land let at 20s. and rated at 20s. and that the farmer makes for himself a profit of 20s. exclusive of rates : suppose, on the contrary, that his profit from a low price of corn is, on the same acre of land, 10s. and that

* The present mode of the payment of tythes is as little liable to objection in Suffolk as in most parts of the kingdom, as they are generally compounded for at a very reasonable rate. Yet it is readily admitted, that the mode, even thus qualified, is liable to great objections, but not particular to this county.—*Note.*

he is still rated at 20s. It is evident that the burthen of the rates should vary with his capacity of paying them, and that this variation should extend to the neat profit of the rector from his tythe. If any person will calculate the effect of this principle extended to tythe taken in kind, he will find the result different from that of the common tythe valuations.

SECT. IV —POOR RATES.

IT has long been an object of considerable consequence, not only in a political light, but with a view to the better administration of the poor law, to ascertain with some degree of correctness, the progressive rise of rates. The House of Commons have more than once called for returns from all the parishes in the kingdom, but for want of such being complete, and also from their not being periodically renewed, so much use has not been derived from them as might on a different plan have attended such wise exertions. The rise in Suffolk, during the last ten years, has been very considerable, and in some cases enormous I wish my correspondents had enabled me to give a proper number of details on this progression ; at present, I have it in my power to insert but one or two striking instances.

Progress of rates in the parish of Glemsford, containing 2400 acres, rated at 1800l. a year, and has 40l. a year estate for the poor.

					£.	s.	d.
1772	-	-	-	-	678	5	8
1773	-	-	-	-	590	16	6
1774	-	-	-	-	404	5	8
1775	-	-	-	-	343	14	5
1776	-	-	-	-	456	7	4
1777	-	-	-	-	482	18	3

					£.	s.	d.
1778	-	-	-	-	516	16	8
1779	-	-	-	-	610	3	5
1780	-	-	-	-	482	11	10
1781	-	-	-	-	549	16	8
1782	-	-	-	-	645	7	11
1783	-	-	-	-	586	3	6
1784	-	-	-	-	496	5	4
1785	-	-	-	-	570	11	4
1786	-	-	-	-	607	17	6
1787	-	-	-	-	783	8	6
1788	-	-	-	-	948	11	2
1789	-	-	-	-	1039	6	4
1790	-	-	-	-	1062	6	4
1791	-	-	-	-	1113	5	$10\frac{1}{2}$
1792	-	-	-	-	1100	8	$6\frac{1}{2}$
1793	-	-	-	-	1703	5	0
1794	-	-	-	-	1594	4	$5\frac{1}{2}$
1795	-	-	-	-	1594	4	$5\frac{1}{2}$
1796	-	-	-	-	2129	12	$11\frac{1}{2}$

The gentleman who favoured me with this account
(the Rev. Mr. Butts), adds, " I forbear to comment on
the causes of the rapid increase in the rates during the
last six years; I shall only observe, that in the first seven
years of the period above-mentioned, a worthy magistrate, now no more (who was then resident in the
parish), gave unremitted attention to all the *minutiæ*
of parochial business ; and that from 1788, there has
been no *justice* nearer that four miles from the scene of
action.

" I am of opinion that there is a radical evil in our
present poor-laws, which, if not speedily removed, will,
in many populous villages in this kingdom, be attended
with utter ruin to the small farmers. The evil I mean

to point at, is the almost irresistible power of the overseers in their respective parishes, who, in many
instances, which come under my own immediate observation, are landholders, who have received no advantage
from education, and who are by routine put into office,
from their large occupations.

" In all public business, much of private interest
must frequently be sacrificed to the general good : with
men of this description there may not exist a sufficient
idea of foregoing profit for articles with which the
parish work house is to be supplied.

" Experience (the only test of theory) in my own and
a neighbouring parish, has evinced that the attention of
gentlemen to parochial business has effected a saving of
300*l.* or 400*l.* per annum in the poor-rates. As soon
as they ceased to attend, the stream returned into its
former muddy channel, and the lost time to the selfish
contracters, who winked at each others exorbitant bills,
was amply compensated by a rise in the rate , increasing
nearly in an arithmetical progression ; as the abstracts
from the rate-books of these parishes will irrefragably
demonstrate.

" The only remedy that appears to me to be in the
least likely to check the progress of this growing evil,
is to incorporate the hundreds, and to appoint men of
liberal educations, and independent fortunes, to super-
intend all matters relative to the poor. As a proof of
the necessity of such incorporations, I must observe,
that in many populous villages, there is only one man
of this description to combat a different tribe : of what
avail can his systems of reform be, with those who never
look beyond the term of their leases, for the welfare of
the present, much less of the rising generation ?

" The recent direful events of a sister kingdom
cannot fail of conv cing every man, not utterly bereft

of his senses, what must be the inevitable consequence of entrusting an illiterate multitude with power. I am far from arraigning the farmers of this country ; the majority of whom are no doubt a very respectable body of men, who would not abuse the power given them by the 43d of Elizabeth, over the poor.

" But if it can be proved, that *one* in *three* is actuated by selfish motives, and that in some parishes, the majority may be of this class, I apprehend that it will be readily admitted, that in such parishes, an incorporation of the hundred of which they constitute a part, is necessary ; and that it would most probably provide an effectual remedy against the evil. Parish politics, and alehouse councils, would then lose their effects ; the complaints and necessities of the paupers would be impartially attended to ; private interest, or local connections, would not decide on the merits of the respective claimants,

" The very salutary effects arising from such incorporations, are evident, from the almost incredible reduction of the poor-rates in several hundreds in this county, which are incorporated ; which have gradually decreased since the acts granted for the union of the interests of the parishes. In some instances, a reduction has taken place of full one-half of the former rates, and the paupers in every respect better provided for ; and what is of equal, if not of greater consequence, the rising generation brought up in habits of industry, and a knowledge of their duty both to God and man ; and not left in total ignorance and indolence, as is most frequently the case in parishes where the children of the paupers are suffered to remain totally unemployed to the age of sixteen or seventeen : the natural consequence of this long leisure is, that they contract habits of idleness and vice, and become noxious members of society, annually adding to the enormous burthen of rates, which in such cases can have no limit.

" It has been urged, in objection to this plan, that if gentlemen do not attend to the business in the hundred houses of industry, that the evil is increased, and iniquity is established by a law : but if it were allowable to argue from the abuse against the use, no law or government could exist for a day ; and if men of enlightened minds and disinterested hearts (and such, we cannon doubt, are to be found in *every hundred* of every county of this much-envied island) are not to be entrusted with power, where can it with safety be placed? Experience has sufficiently proved the fallacy of this argument.

" It may be said, that if magistrates attended properly to their duty, such incorporations would be needless, as every abuse of the poor laws might be immediately remedied on an application to them. No doubt, were a sufficient number of active and intelligent men appointed by the Lord Lieutenants in every county, to fill the most important and useful office in which it is possible that any member of the community can be employed, much might be done towards correcting the growing abuses ; but where the residence of a justice is at the distance of six or seven miles from the existing grievance, there is but little chance of its being removed : ignorance, and want of leisure, in the small occupier and pauper secure the overseer from any interruption in his inattention to those laws which were enacted for the benefit of society ; but which, I am confident, without the intervention of the magistrate, become, in many instances, oppressive.

" The following extract from the rate-book of an adjacent parish, will render every thing that can be further said on the subject, to prove that the evils complained of arise from the causes I have mentioned, entirely needless.

					£.	s.	d.
Easter 1770 to Easter 1771	-	-	1091	17	5
Ditto 1771	ditto	1772	-	-	1320	5	7
Ditto 1772	ditto	1773	-	-	1886	1	3
Ditto 1773	ditto	1774	-	-	1276	1	8
Ditto 1774	ditto	1775*	-	-	848	2	3
Ditto 1775	ditto	1776*	-	-	817	9	10
Ditto 1776	ditto	1777*	-	-	966	7	9
Ditto 1777	ditto	1778	-	-	1113	6	11
Ditto 1778	ditto	1779	-	-	1151	17	3
Ditto 1779	ditto	1780	-	-	1202	19	5
Ditto 1780	ditto	1781	-	-	1146	10	11"

Amount of money raised by assessment for the relief of the poor in Woodbridge:

				£.	s.	d.
1791	-	-	-	1021	14	0
1792	-	-	-	890	13	2
1793	-	-	-	833	3	7
1794	-	-	-	889	8	3
1795	-	-	-	1175	0	0

The voluntary contributions of the inhabitants of the parish, towards purchasing coals, and reducing the price of flour, in the years 1794 and 1795, amounted to upwards of 300l.

At Bildeston, Mr. Cooke informs me, the rates during the scarcity were at 5s. in the pound, per quarter!

At Lavenham, they have been 7s. 6d. in the pound, per quarter!!

* During these three years, a committee of gentlemen attended to the parish business.

At Brome, near Eye, rates, the Rev. Mr. Negus informs me, are about three shillings in the pound.

1803. In addition to the preceding accounts I have procured the following:

An account of the several sums of money raised by rates for the maintenance of the Poor of Lavenham, Suffolk; commencing at Easter, 1790 to Easter, 1803.

					£.	s.	d.
Easter 1790	to Easter	1791	-	-	1480	4	1
Ditto 1791	ditto	1792	-	-	1451	6	0
Ditto 1792	ditto	1793	-	-	1274	3	0
Ditto 1793	ditto	1794	-	-	1724	11	1
Ditto 1794	ditto	1795	-	-	1610	13	8
Ditto 1795	ditto	1796	-	-	2663	15	3
Ditto 1796	ditto	1797	-	-	2231	15	9
Ditto 1797	ditto	1798	-	-	1863	16	6
Ditto 1798	ditto	1799	-	-	1969	0	3
Ditto 1799	ditto	1800	-	-	2656	1	9
Ditto 1800	ditto	1801	-	-	4110	12	3
Ditto 1801	ditto	1802	-	-	3021	8	0
Ditto 1802	ditto	1803	-	-	1564	9	9

Collection by rates at Hadleigh.

				£.	s.	d.
1790	-	-	-	604	9	0
1791	-	-	-	614	14	0
1792	-	-	-	694	17	3
1793	-	-	-	1999	18	7
1794	-	-	-	1021	8	3
1795	-	-	-	1105	0	0
1796	-	-	-	1220	2	1
1797	-	-	-	967	5	8
1798	-	-	-	1097	0	3

				£.	s.	d.
1799	-	-	-	2059	0	9½
1800	-	-	-	4646	17	10
1801	-	-	-	2437	18	8
1802	-	-	-	1303	19	6

Sums raised every year by Rates, at Cockfield, from 1790 to 1802 (both years inclusive), as appears by the Parish accounts.

				£.	s.	d.
1790	-	-	-	333	12	1
1791	-	-	-	361	2	10½
1792	-	-	-	299	14	5
1793	-	-	-	337	14	10
1794	-	-	-	343	16	6
1795	-	-	-	609	4	6½
1796	-	-	-	840	7	2
1797	-	-	-	615	15	6
1798	-	-	-	540	3	2½
1799	-	-	-	586	1	9
1800	-	-	-	1089	4	7
1801	-	-	-	1600	14	11
1802	-	-	-	792	17	5½
13 years				8350	9	10
Per year				642	6	10¼

Calling the new rent roll 2600*l.* and the average expence of poor per year 640*l.* the rates would be 4*s.* 11*d.* in the pound per year; and, on the old rent roll (2120*l.*), 6*s.* 1*d.* per year.

The present (1803) rent roll, including houses, cottages, and tythe, 2628*l.*

SECT. V.—LEASES.

In Suffolk, the more common terms for leases are
seven, fourteen, and twenty-one years; much land is
occupied by men who are tenants at will. There are
few counties that have been more improved by leases
of twenty-one years than this has been. The tracts in
the sandy districts, which have been converted from
warren and sheep-walk into cultivated inclosures, by
means of clay, marl, and crag, have seen these improvements effected by means of such leases giving the tenant
that security in the investment of his money, which
induced him to lay it out: nor have they operated only
in such capital undertakings; they have caused large
tracts to be hollow drained, and have occasioned an
improved cultivation in almost every respect where it
depended on larger sums being expended than common
to farmers who are not able or willing to make such
exertions.

Leases, however, are not absolutely necessary on
lands so rich, or so fully improved, as to want no such
exertions; but even in this case, the general management is more likely to be spirited, when the tenant has
a *certainty* of reaping the benefit of his expenditure for
a long term.

In all cases of long leases, great attention should be
paid to the clauses that respect the three or four last
years; for want of this, we sometimes see lands that
have been well improved, left in so exhausted a state,
that the landlord does not reap that portion of the benefit
which his confidence merited.

SECT. VI.—EXPENCES AND PROFIT.

INQUIRIES into these circumstances of the national husbandry, can only be suggested by the Board of Agriculture with a view to excite a spirit of industry, and to shew the importance of investing in agriculture pursuits a sufficient capital to ensure to the cultivator of the soil a fair return for his exertions and skill. There may be nothing improper in stating, that it is conceived that the usual farming capital is estimated to amount from 3*l.* to 6*l.* per acre, according to soil, and other circumstances: and certainly, the farmer who has skill and experience, ought to make at least ten per cent. on his capital. He must in many cases make much more. The old estimate, here as elsewhere, was, that the produce amounted to three rents; but for many years past, that idea has been utterly erroneous— was he now to make no more, he would soon be in goal.

1803. The calculation here given of 3*l.* to 6*l.* per acre, for stocking farms, will no longer hold good. By stock, is understood not only things purchased, but the first year's expences provided for; and labour has risen so enormously, with a corresponding increase in poor rates, tythes, and every article of wear and tear— not forgetting rent itself; with an increased price of horses, sheep, and lean cattle, that I cannot estimate it at less now than from 4*l.* to 8*l.* per acre; and I have known some cases in which it has risen to 10*l.*

CHAPTER V.

IMPLEMENTS.

_____

PLOUGH.

THE Norfolk wheel plough, and the little light swing plough of Suffolk, are the common implements. The latter is a good tool for depths not exceeding four inches, but there is scarcely a worse for more considerable depths.

A very ingenious blacksmith, of the name of Brand, who has been dead some years, improved the Suffolk swing plough, and constructed it of iron. I have been informed, that the copse, in its present state, was an improvement of his; if so, it is much to his credit, for there is no other in the kingdom equal to it.

WAGGON.

Waggons are universal in the county; the modern, and greatest of all improvements, that of substituting one horse carts or cars, being, generally speaking, unknown; the usual load is ten quarters of wheat to four horses, on turnpikes, and five on bye-roads.

CARTS.

Carts are much too heavy and ill-constructed; they usually contain from 36 to 40 bushels, and are drawn by three, four, or five horses, according to weight of load.

HORSE RAKE.

This is common : it is drawn by one horse, for clearing spring-corn stubbles, instead of the corn dew rake drawn by a man. It is a very good tool ; but to substitute the sickle, and bind in sheaves, is a superior practice.

THE DRILL ROLLER.

This tool, invented in Norfolk, has been much used in Suffolk. Its object is to save the expence of dibbling, by making little channels four and a half inches asunder, across a clover lay after ploughing ; the wheat seed is then sown broad-cast, and is covered by a bush harrow. For light soils, that require pressure, it is a good implement, but inferior to dibbling. Another use to which it is applicable, is that of pulverizing a fallow on stiff lands in a dry season, in which it is incomparably effective ; more so than any spike roller that I have seen.

NEW DRILL.

Mr. Brettingham, of St. John's, near Bungay, informs me, that a new drill plough, supposed to be invented by Mr. Stanton, of Weybred, is, in reality, the invention or improvement of Mr. Henry Balding, of Mendham, who has been bringing it to perfection by ten years application, and at no small expence. He had some thoughts of applying for a patent for it, but dissuaded from that by Mr. Brettingham, as he thought that any monopoly of useful machines must be of general disservice to the community, and that it might possibly turn the attention of a good farmer from a good farm.

THRESHING MILLS.

At the time of my drawing up the first edition of this Report, there was not, I believe, one threshing mill in the county. They are now considerably multiplied, principally by reason of the accuracy with which they have been constructed by Mr. Asbey, of Blyborough, who has made them for the following persons, among many others ; Mr. Press, of Wetheringset ; Mr. Freeman, of Occold ; two for Mr. Howlett, of Westwood ; Mr. Gabbiter of Bruisyard ; Mr. Fillpot, of Walpole ; Mr. Moss, of Crettingham ; Mr. Tye, of Sibton, near Yoxford ; Mr. Battram, of Hoo, near Wyckham Market ; Mr. Pipe, of Peasenhall ; Mr. Manby, of Sibton ; Mr. Samuel Howlett of Frossington ; Mr. Augur, of Beccles ; Mr. Coates, of Hinton, &c. They are worked by three horses ; the price of one with a fifteen feet wheel, 100 guineas ; an eighteen feet wheel, 120 guineas, but not including a winnowing machine. They do the work exceedingly well, and much to the satisfaction of those who have had them. I was present at the working of one in Norfolk, with which the owner, Mr. Reeve, was well pleased. They thresh barley as clean as any other grain, unless the straw is very short indeed, and then so well, that the difference is but trifling. Mr. Reeve and Mr. Howlett thought them in a very great state of perfection. The diameter of the drum wheel is 4 feet 10 inches, and it moves 130 revolutions in a minute. But Mr. Asbey has lately made a very great improvement in them, at the instigation of Mr. Howlett, by constructing a moveable machine, which may be wheeled a mile, and set to work in one hour. I saw his first on this construction with much pleasure, as it promises to be equally powerful with the fixed ones, and much more generally useful. It is moveable on wheels to any single stack, and does not demand any building whatever. The price (a winnowing machine included) 160 guineas.

THE EXTIRPATOR.

Of this tool, the Rev. Mr. Lewes, of Thorndon, writes: " A Mr. Hayward, of Stoke Ash, in this neighbourhood, has invented a machine for destroying weeds, and clearing ploughed lands for seed, which, by the experience of four years, is found more effectual than any other instrument hitherto used for that purpose. Having lately the opportunity of speaking to Mr. Hayward concerning it, I inquired whether he would apply for a patent, or take any method to make it public? Upon his replying in the negative, I requested his permission to take a plan and description of it, which I have herein inclosed, and beg leave to submit it to the inspection of the Agricultural Society, as the speediest mode of introducing to universal practice an instrument so essentially serviceable to farmers. The extirpator, or the scalp plough, as it is generally termed, is drawn by two or three horses, according to the quality of the soil, and the depth you put it to. The land should be once ploughed over, before this instrument be used. If it has laid a summer fallow, the usual way is to work it twice over with the extirpator, about two inches deep at the first, and about four inches deep, and crossways, at the second time, which, with running a harrow once over, will not only effectually destroy all weeds, but also render it very fine, and ready for the drill, or sowing. Lands being ploughed in autumn, and intended for spring crops, are by this instrument prepared for seed better than any other method ever tried in this country.

It will work in all lands, and may be handled by any person that knows how to manage a plough. It will *easily* plough one acre per hour, and not in the least distress the horses. A farmer assured me, that he could with three horses work up sixty acres per week with it ; and that a person having the extirpator, may, with only three horses, farm as much land as would, without it, require six horses. It is not customary in this part of the country to work oxen, but I am confident it will answer the same purpose where oxen are used. It is advisable to work all lands that are over-run with weeds, twice over. Some lands may possibly require three times dressing. Some time should elapse, for the weeds that are cut to die before it is ploughed a second time. It is now adopted by most farmers in this neigh-bourhood ; and its great utility will be attested by every person that has used it. Many, whose prejudice against every novelty induced them at first to ridicule the idea, are now as warm in praising it, and acknowledge it to be the greatest improvement in agriculture they have ever witnessed."

Fig. 1. Represents a back view of the machine, when put together ready for work.

A, The shares, eight inches broad and nine inches long, which are fixed to stalks, rising ten inches. The distance between them is eleven inches.

B, The hind ledge, six feet long, and about four inches square.

C, The fore ledge, five and a half feet long, four inches square. The distance of these ledges is twelve inches.

D, The beam, seven feet long; its elevation is three feet three inches. Vide Fig. 2.

E, The handles.

Fig. 3. Represents a share with its stalk.

This instrument is fixed to the wheels, &c. of a common wheel plough, and made to go shallow or deep in the same manner.

SCARIFYERS AND SCUFFLES.

The introduction of the drill husbandry has brought with it many of these tools, which however are almost equally applicable to the broad-cast system. Mr. Cook's are very good tools, and his fixed harrow deserves much commendation, being so contrived, that by a diagonal variation in the position in which it is used, one, two, or three teeth may be worked in a nine-inch interval. All these tools are of great use ; and, indeed, indispensable in the system of rejecting spring ploughings. Scuffles are various, and the invention and improvement of many different persons.

CHAPTER VI.

INCLOSING.

SUFFOLK must be reckoned amongst the earliest inclosed of the English counties, but there are very large tracts yet open, that want the benefit of this first and greatest of all improvements. Some modern inclosures have been made by act of parliament, but the spirit is not active; the examples have not been well followed, though the success has been great.

PARISH OF CONEY WESTON, IN SUFFOLK,

contains about 1260 acres; the rent about 192*l.* Inclosed in 1777, by act of parliament.

REGISTER.

	Births.	Burials.		Births.	Burials.
1761,	6	6	1778,	4	3
1762,	4	0	1779,	3	3
1763,	1	6	1780,	6	5
1764,	2	4	1781,	5	5
1765,	3	3	1782,	4	6
1766,	6	2	1783,	5	3
1767,	3	2	1784,	4	0
1768,	3	1	1785,	7	5
1769,	2	4	1786,	6	4
1770,	8	3	1787,	9	1
1771,	0	1	1788,	3	3
1772,	4	2	1789,	13	4
1773,	4	5	1790,	6	4
1774,	3	3	1791,	6	4
1775,	3	2	1792,	8	4
1776,	6	2	1793,*	10	2
	58	46		92	56
	46			56	
	12 Increase.			43 Increase.	

* Year ending June 3, at the Generals.

Rents greatly raised since the inclosure; and the farmers at the same time far richer than before.

RENT.

£.

In 1774	Valuation	590
1760	——	336
1764	——	506
1769	——	539
1782	——	877
1793	——	898

Poor rates 1s. 3d. in the pound, rack rent.

21 houses, poor-house included.

36 families, containing 212 souls.*

BARNINGHAM.

Inclosed 1796. Allotted 1798. Second Crop 1800.

Quantity.—About 400 acres of common

180 —— of open field arable.

Soil.—The common, strong wet land; the open arable, turnip and barley land: will give wheat, but not fair wheat land.

Rent.—Of the open field arable, before inclosing, about 15s.; now about 17s.; the common allotments now 16s. or 17s.

Course.—Open field; it was all turniped by agreement; and managed nearly as the inclosed. Now it will be 1. Turnips. 2. Barley. 3. Clover. 4. Wheat.

---

* From the case here inserted (which is, in truth, a copy of what has been done in many places in the county of Norfolk), the Board of Agriculture may see clearly, that in no one object that comes under their consideration, are their exertions more beneficially employed than in procuring bills of inclosures.—*Note by T. E.*

Tithe.—It remains subject to tithe.

	Acres.	Rent. £.	Tithe. £.	s.
Farms.—Now, No. 1.	375	602	52	0
2.	157	128	19	0
3.	79	65	10	0
4.	154	115	18	0
5.	115	102	17	0
6.	165	152	29	0
7.	52	52	10	0
8.	1c9	92	11	0
9.	5	5	0	14
10.	84	87	16	0
11.	22	22	4	0
12.	17	18	4	0
13.	24	22	4	0
14.	7	7	0	14
15.	36	36	8	0
16.	4	4	0	19
17.	2	3	0	14
18.	4	3	0	16
19.	8	8	2	0
20.	3	3	0	13
21.	2	3	0	11
22.	2	2	0	9
23.	5	5	1	4
24.	11	13	3	0
25.	21	21	4	0
26.	9	6	0	4
27.	7	8	1	15
28.	1	1	0	5
29.	1	1	0	7
30.	2	2	0	8

By the inclosure there was no alteration, except that the farms were lessened one.

	£.	s.	d.
Expences of passing the Act through Parliament - -	213	12	0
Surveyor's bill, mapping, &c. -	179	0	0
Commissioner's Bill for roads, fences of glebe, poor's allotment, &c.	320	0	0
Five Commissioner's Fees - -	235	14	0
Solicitor's Bill, including interest of money, and all other expences to the final inrollment of the award	375	5	0
	1323	11	0

Poor.—Twenty acres allotted for their firing; furze on part, and will sow the rest so as to cut one-fifth every year.

Improvement.—The common was in general ploughed once, and either sown or dibbled with oats; the produce about 5 coombs an acre. Then sown again with oats, and the appearance very bad; probably 2 or 3 coombs. Some wheat on the oat subble. Mr. Patterson pared and burnt in 1799 time enough to get in a very late crop of turnips. The expence, 40s. an acre paring and burning, spreading and fuel 10s. more: the turnips stood better than any in the parish, and worth 5l. an acre from all others having failed. Sowed oats after, and the crop 14 coombs an acre. The year 1800 pared and burnt 54 acres more, at 50s. an acre expence, and sowed oats on 16 acres; they were late, and will produce 12 coombs an acre; on the rest turnips and cole: 11 acres very good turnips, far better than common, this year, in which so many have failed entirely.

Cows.—Not more than two cottagers kept cows; but a few of them, two or three, had a mare for breeding a foal, but others had geese. The benefit of the common little, for it was fed by two flocks of sheep, which swept nearly the whole.

Sheep.—There were 400 kept; now very few, upon account of the fences.

Corn—Will be very greatly increased for 400 acres brought into productive cultivation.

Rates.—About 2s. in the pound, before the inclosure.

PAKEFIELD AND GISLAM, 1798.

Quantity.—330 acres of common; no open field.

Rent.—Quality price 13s.

Corn.—250 acres to be ploughed.

Sheep.—None kept before. A rotten common.

Cattle.—Now much more.

Tithe.—Remains subject.

Rates.—An incorporated hundred.

Poor.—Only three cottages, except those belonging to farmers.

WOLLINGTON, 1799.

Quantity.—860 acres; 250 of it warren, 992 open-field arable.

Rent.—The open field, before, was 8s. per acre; now, 12s. all round.

Corn.—The increase very great; about 500 acres may be ploughed, and 360 pastured.

Cattle.—The 360 will keep much more than the commons did before.

Sheep.—Not decreased, but added to.

Poor.—To every cottage, allotments according to right, by act; they claimed for 2 cows, and allotted for them 2½ acres of the best land.

BARTON MILLS.

Quantity.—About 300 acres of common fen, 30 or 40 of which were subject to inundations ; and 500 of common sheep walk ; 800 in all ; 1900 acres in the parish.

Rent of the parish has been nearly doubled by the inclosure ; but the farmers are well satisfied.

Improvement.—Nothing very great, if expences are considered ; the common fen was very unequal in surface, and required very great labour to bring it to a cultivable state. Some was pared and burnt, but the success has not hitherto answered ; so that a proprietor assured me that it would have been more advantageous never to have meddled with the common. Some things were not well managed ; 300*l.* expended in a tunnel under the river, to drain 30 or 40 acres, which have been very often under water since. But the division of the heath answered greatly ; 300 acres of it have been broken up, and are under corn, &c. The first year they generally dibbled in oats or peas ; the second, oats or wheat ; the third, turnips ; the fourth, oats ; and now, layer. But Mr. Archer on one piece began with turnips, and he thinks that has answered better than any.

Corn.—Certainly increased much.

Sheep.—Lessened greatly ; there were 40 score ; now about 20.

Cows.—Annihilated, was the answer.

Poor.—There were 28 common-right houses ; and 8 acres, worth 8*l.* a year, were assigned to each. The poor people of all did not suffer, but little owners of 20*l.* or 30*l.* or 40*l.* a year, very severely. A few such, who by means of the common, summer-fed 7, 8, or 10 cows, and wintered them on the straw of their arable, having 15 to 20 acres in a *shift*, found themselves with allotments of 20 or 25 acres of good land, which would neither feed a team, nor half the cows (had they attempted it) which they kept before. They were forced to sell immediately.

Tithe.—Land was allotted.

Rates.—Last year 13*s*. in the pound on the commissioner's valuation. A few years ago 4*s*. in the pound on old rental.

Expences.—2500*l*. besides fences.

TUDDENHAM.

Quantity.—Above 3000 acres in the parish; part of which a very extensive common, and about 1500 acres of arable.

Corn.—Greatly increased.

Sheep.—Fewer k pt than before.

Cows.—Little difference.

Poor.—They did not keep one cow, only asses and geese. 100 acres of upland, and 30 of low common allotted for fuel; and in this respect they assured me themselves that they were very well supplied. The herbage is let at 19*l*. a year, which is divided among them. There were 28 common rights. Poor rates are very high; one family with only five children had in the scarcity 18*s*. a week allowed.

POPULATION.

			Baptisms.			Burials.
1780	-	-	2	-	-	2
1781	-	-	9	-	-	8
1782	-	-	7	-	-	10
1783	-	-	11	-	-	9
1784	-	-	9	-	-	8
1785	-	-	7	-	-	4
1786	-	-	8	-	-	11
1787	-	-	11	-	-	12
1788	-	-	7	-	-	5
1789	-	-	8	-	-	5
			79			74
1790	-	-	8	-	-	5
1791	-	-	18	-	-	11
1792 } 1793	-	-	13	-	-	17
1794	-	-	6	-	-	4
1795	-	-	12	-	-	5
1796	-	-	8	-	-	7
1797	-	-	10	-	-	8
1798	-	-	9	-	-	4
1799	-	-	9	-	-	8
			93			69

First period, Baptisms   -   -   -   79
Burials   -   -   -   74

Increase   -   5

Second ditto, Baptisms   -   -   -   93
Burials   -   -   -   69

Increase   -   24

CHAPTER VII.

ARABLE LAND.

Though the dairy district of Suffolk is extensive, and the number of sheep great, yet the arable part of the county is much the most considerable.

SECT. I.—TILLAGE.

Ploughing.—In every part of the county this is done with a pair of horses, conducted with reins by the ploughman ; and the quantity of land usually turned in a day, is an acre upon stiff soils, and from one and a quarter to one and a half on sands.

The ploughmen are remarkable for straight furrows ; and also for drawing them by the eye to any object, usually a stick whitened by peeling, either for water cuts, or for new laying out broad ridges, called here *stitches* ; and a favourite amusement is ploughing such furrows, as candidates for a hat, or pair of breeches, given by alehouse-keepers, or subscribed among themselves, as a prize for the straightest furrow. The skill of many of them in this work is remarkable.

1803.—Under this head of ploughing I should here note the greatest of all modern improvements in the management of wet arable land, and an improvement which, till very lately, was confined to this county, that of avoiding all, or nearly all, spring ploughings. It is astonishing that certain writers, some of whom have been in this county, and even farmed in it, who have been warm advocates for drilling, should not have pointed out this practice almost as the *sine quâ non* of drilling on strong land ; it has spread that husbandry here in ten years more than ten centuries would have spread it without this important discovery. It is the hinge upon which spring drilling turns upon such soils, and in travelling near 1000 miles in Norfolk I met with not one instance of it, though the drill occupies near 30 miles of a sandy district. This most interesting management will be particularly explained in the following sheets.

Rolling and Harrowing.—In general, there is nothing in the practice which demands particular attention ; but I found in the hemp district a management in working clover lays for wheat, which ought to be noted. A heavy roller follows the ploughs, then a spike roller. This prepares well, especially in a dry season.

1803.—The introduction of the drill husbandry, which has spread rapidly in the county, has depended very much on harrowing being made a part of the system of drilling. The stitches are drawn out with as great accuracy as possible, in order that all successive operations may be executed, the horses walking only in the furrows of the stitches, and the harrows made to fit them. This attention is the more necessary, as every thing in the drill husbandry depends on a new system of rejecting spring ploughing as much as possible, and the same reasons which have governed this system, have extended to every operation for avoiding all poaching and trampling, by keeping the horses off the stitches with the most attentive caution.

Ridges.—The form of laying arable lands upon dry soils, is, on the flat, with finishing furrows ; alternate gathering and splitting ; but on wet lands, the three-foot Essex ridge of two *bouts* is most common.* In some districts, six, eight, and ten feet *stitches*, a little arched, are used.

1803.—The new improvement in tillage of discarding spring ploughings, has changed almost all the ridges of the strong land district; they are now adapted to the size of the drill machines, either for one stroke of it or for a bout. Suppose the drill sows six rows at nine inches, this takes five spaces or forty-five inches, and if the farmer allows twelve inches for the *stitch* or ridge furrow, this adds six on each exterior beyond the rows, or twelve to forty-five, being fifty-seven inches for the ridge for *one* movement of the machine, but if he drills at a *bout* of the machine he then reckons on twelve rows, which demand eleven spaces or ninety-nine inches, to which add twelve for the two outsides, and the ridge must be one hundred and eleven inches, or nine feet three inches ; but if the farmer wishes for a wider furrow as a freer path for the horses, and that the outside rows may not be on the very edge of the furrows, he adds as many inches to the ridge as answers his purpose. If he makes his ridge 10 feet, it gives him twenty-one inches in each furrow ; eighteen however are amply sufficient, or a ridge of nine feet nine inches. Whatever tools are worked upon the land are made with a view to this circumstance, so that the horses may always walk in the furrows.

* It may be worth noticing, that on many of the poorest and driest sands, rye is sown on four furrow ridges, which, to persons accustomed to a wet soil, appears absurd; but it is done in order to lay a greater depth of mould (if such it may be called) together, for the corn to strike root in. The poorer the land, the more necessary is this mode thought to be.—*Note by T. L.*

SECT. II.—FALLOWING.

There is no question of the merit of fallowing, when compared with bad courses of crops. If the husbandry is not correct in this respect, the fallowist will certainly be a much better farmer than his neighbours : but there are courses which will clean as well as summer fallow, by means of plants, which admit the best tillage of a summer fallow. Cabbages planted in June or July : winter tares admit three months tillage if tillage be wanted. Beans well cultivated will preserve land clean,* which has been cleaned by cabbages. And, in any case, two successive hoeing crops are effective in giving positive cleanness. These observations are not theory, they are practice ; and it is high time that mankind should be well persuaded that the right quantity of cattle and sheep cannot be kept on a farm, if the fallows of the old system be not made to contribute to their support.

SECT. III.—COURSE OF CROPS.

THE management of the arable land, in the four distinct soils, is essentially different, and merits a description as particular as can be given in the short compass of a report.

* They should be drilled at thirty inches distance, and ploughed between : if any quickens are found, or remain, two or three ploughings in spring for barley, will eradicate them. I have had forty bushels of wheat after beans, drilled as above.—*Baillie.*

STRONG LOAM ON A CLAY-MARL BOTTOM.

Common exertions in common practice, diverge into
such endless variations, that to note the methods pursued by individuals, would fill a volume. In a work of
this nature, which must be considered but as a sketch of
the subjects to be treated more particularly by those
whose situation enables them locally to give the authority denied to others, it is only practicable to seize the
most prominent features, such as best discriminate the
system pursued.

In the strong soils of Suffolk, the more general course
of crops, into whatever variations it may usually be
thrown, includes summer fallow as the common preparation for the rotation of corn products; the old system,
very general about forty or fifty years ago, was the
uniform husbandry of unenlightened Europe.

The fallow to prepare for wheat ; the wheat succeeded by oats or barley ; and that again by the return
of fallow. This husbandry is still found even in inclosed
lands.   But, generally speaking, it is changed for one or
two other courses, either to make the fallow still the
preparation for wheat, or to change that crop for barley.
In one case it is thus:

1. Fallow,
2. Wheat,
3. Barley,
4. Clover,
5. Wheat ;

or the same principle governing many variations. This
principle is, that a fallow when once given, will enable
the farmer to omit it the second return, and even the
third also, by means of clover, tares, pease, &c. Thus
improving a little upon the old system of a dead fallow
every third year.

The other method is a later improvement ; to change the principle of relying on a year's tillage as the preparative for wheat, and substituting clover. Thus,

1. Fallow,
2. Barley,
3. Clover,
4. Wheat ;

which for lands (if such there be) that really demand fallowing, is a correct mode, and seldom practised except by good farmers. Others not of equal intelligence, continue it by the addition of a crop of barley or oats after the wheat ; or by sowing clover with that crop, taking pease after the clover, and wheat after the pease. Where manures sufficient can be raised or purchased, a still better course is followed :

1. Beans,
2. Barley,
3. Clover,
4. Wheat,

Or, 1. Fallow,
2. Wheat,
3. Beans,
4. Barley,
5. Clover,
6. Wheat,

manured on the surface after the clover is mown and prepared for a repetition of the same course. Fallowing in the second course should be rejected ; and ever afterwards.

The note of these courses is sufficient to give the general idea of common practice on this soil. Variations cannot be attended to ; a notable one is, planting cabbages instead of fallow : but, as that will be mentioned elsewhere, I omit it here.

RICH LOAM AND SAND.

On this soil the management is more uniform. The rotation, called the Norfolk husbandry, is very generally introduced, which is making turnips the preparation for barley, and clover that for wheat, in the course of,

1. Turnips,
2. Barley,
3. Clover,
4. Wheat ;*

which is certainly one of the best systems that ever was invented, and, indeed, nearly unexceptionable. There are two common variations, but both for the worse : to take a second crop of barley or oats after the wheat, and then recommence : the other, to sow clover with that second barley, and then wheat again on that clover : this is very bad, for it fouls the land.†

---

* I apprehend that the course of cropping here mentioned cannot be improved upon, except, perhaps, by substituting in the second round, oats for barley ; and sometimes other grass seeds in lieu of clover, every second or third round, for I believe clover will not stand on lands constantly laid down therewith every fourth year. *Note by J. R.*—There is reason in this observation, and other plants, instead of clover, would be found to answer. —*A. Y.*

† Upon a deep rich soil, such as is described by Mr. Young, in Walton, Trimlies, and Felixtow. 1. Turnips. 2. Barley. 3. Beans. 4. Wheat. 5. Barley. 6. Clover. 7. Wheat.—This will appear, at first sight, a very extravagant rotation of cropping ; therefore the tillage given to each crop should be explained. The land intended for turnips, should be ploughed soon after wheat-sowing, or at any rate before Christmas : in the spring, when the barley-sowing is finished, should be ploughed back again, and have at least three earths more, with proper harrowing and rolling, before the sowing-earth. At the time the turnips are sown, a small one-horse roller should follow the plough, close after the seed, and the harrows close after the roller ; by this method the surface will be smooth, and have a neat appearance ; the land will retain its moisture ; the young plants sooner receive the benefit from the wind, and of course there will be no clods to obstruct the progress of hoeing, which should be performed twice. *I am*

But the longer clover is persisted in, the more the
land becomes *sick* of it, to use the common expression ;
this has long been observed in Suffolk, but of late the

convinced *the fly never destroys the young plants, where the surface is made
fine, as it does when suffered to remain coarse and uneven.* After the turnips
are fed off, the land should be ploughed a good depth, and have, at least,
three earths, with proper rolling and harrowing to each earth, before sown
with barley, which should be as early in the spring as the season would
permit : when the barley is up to a proper height, let it be rolled, and
afterwards properly weeded. In the winter following, manure the barley
stubble with about sixteen chaldron per acre, of good rotten compost ; and
the spring following, plant with beans at one ploughing ;* taking care to
make the land fine, by rolling and harrowing ; when the beans are all
come up, roll them with a two-horse roller, and about a fortnight after,
harrow them, and let them be properly hoed twice afterwards. When the
beans are harvested, and every thing cleared off the land, sow wheat at one
ploughing ; when the wheat is likewise harvested, and the stubble-feed is
fed off, which will be in November, clear off the stubble, and manure
with about twelve chaldron per acre ; immediately plough the land, but
not too deep ; early in the spring, plough again, and take care to plough
deeper, so as to bring the manure all upon the surface ; then give proper
harrowing, and plough twice more before you sow with barley ;† with which
sow from twelve to sixteen pounds of clover-seed per acre. In the summer
let the barley be carefully weeded; feed the young clover in the autumn, but
not long after Michaelmas ; in the spring following, look the young clover-
layer over, and take out every weed that may be an impediment, and when
the clover is off, sow with wheat in the autumn, as usual. This is the rotation
of cropping with the tillage, manuring, &c. &c. as practised by very intelligent
farmers, upon as good arable land as any in the county ; and I will venture
to say, no country is more productive, or kept cleaner ; and from the tillage that is given to every spring-crop ‡ of corn, the lands have the neatest
appearance possible. Where the lands are too wet, and not so proper for
turnips, winter-tares are sown in September, and either fed off the land in
May, or mowed till the middle of June, or beginning of July, to be given
to the cart-horses in the farm yards : In this case, the land should have
all the tillage possible, till after Michaelmas, when it is properly laid up to
keep it dry during the winter; in the spring it is ploughed and managed
the same as if turnips were fed off. Upon lands of nearly the same quality
as before described, but where the the under-stratum is a gravel, their
management is as follows : 1. Turnips. 2. Barley. 3. Beans. 4. Wheat.
5. Turnips. 6. Barley. 7. Clover. 8. Wheat. The first four crops are

* No spring ploughing by any means.—*A. Y.*
† Luter practice is quite different.—*A. Y.*
‡ All different now, 1803.—*A. Y.*

evil has forced a variation, by omitting it one round, by substituting pease, tares, or some other crop, and so having clover once only in eight instead of four years. Or, by breaking the rotation differently, once only in six years.

managed as before described; and the turnips in succession to the wheat, are generally manured for with light muck, out of the farm-yard; this, with the feeding them upon the land, and the tillage given for the barley, almost ensure a plant of young clover. In the first rotation of cropping, I ought to have given my reason for planting beans after a crop of barley in succession to turnips, because it is generally understood, that clover should be sown with barley, after a summer-land-crop of turnips; but whoever understands the tillage of strong rich land, knows that they do not work so fine after turnips, as when the land has been cropped longer; of course, the young crop of clover is not so likely to plant, and will be subject to May-weed: now by manuring the wheat-stubble for barley, and giving the tillage as described, the land not only works finer, but is, by being manured, rendered more kindly to receive the young clover; and it will be found to have fewer weeds, and be more productive, than if sown after a summer-land-crop of barley. In the second rotation of cropping, where the land is not so strong, beans succeed the barley in the first instance, and clover in the second, where the turnip crop is manured for; of course the young clover comes into a share of manure to encourage it; and by being kept at a distance by the aforesaid rotations, the land is not so likely to be tired of it. In land that has been tired of growing clover, by the rotation of turnips, barley, clover, and wheat, I have sown with the barley, half the usual quantity of clover, a quarter of a peck of trefoil, and a sack of hay-seeds per acre; mowed the next summer for stover, and the winter following manured for beans, which should be hoed twice; and in the autumn sowed wheat. I have known the above method answer beyond expectation; for the hay-seeds, with the clover and trefoil, are sure to produce a good crop of stover, and yield a fine piece of seed afterwards. Beans are very kindly after a layer of this sort, and when the land is ploughed for wheat, will be in the best possible state to receive it, and less subject to slugs or worms. Some farmers sow ray-grass with the clover; but I do not approve it; for amongst the hay-seeds there always is found a proportional quantity of the narrow-leaved plantain, and Dutch clover; and it is well known hay-seeds are of a better quality than ray-grass, spread close to the ground, and not run up to bents like it; and if suffered to remain two years, will increase upon the land, when ray-grass is known to decrease the second year. I confess myself no friend to ray-grass, and think it never should be sown, but upon land of the lightest and worst quality imaginable; for sheep feed, there is no comparison. Where the plant of clover fails in a small degree, the farmer should never attempt to sow wheat next following; but to manure for pease or

SAND.

On the sand districts, the management varies proportionably with the badness of the soil; but in one feature it is universal, that turnips are every where the

beans, and give them proper hoeing, and then to sow wheat in succession; for I believe it is generally understood, that wheat never plants kindly after a thin crop of clover; but is subject to the worm, and to be root fallen.— In the sand land or eastern district of Suffolk, where the soil is light, and principally manured and fed with sheep, the practice with the best farmers is to break up their layers at two years, and to plant pease, and if the pea-stubble is free from grass, to sow ray, which is generally folded as soon as the seed is deposited; the next year give a summer tillage for turnips; fold them off with sheep and lambs, and baulk the land in the spring, to prevent the fold from drying away: give one ploughing for barley, and sow with it half a bushel of ray grass and half a peck of trefoil, and let the layer continue two years. Layers should never be suffered to continue more than two years, except upon very poor land; in that case, the farmer gives it what is called a ris-baulk in the winter after the second year, which causes it to yield a good deal of sheep-feed the following summer; it is ploughed up again after Christmas, and sown in the spring with oats, or with buck-wheat the beginning of June. The turnip-crop follows, which is generally folded for. Some years since, it was the common practice to let the layers continue for four or five years, which practice is now generally exploded. It is well known, a layer upon poor land is never so productive as in the first and second years; after which time the artificial grasses will be worn out. Where a layer is clayed at about sixty loads per acre, a good crop of pease are expected the following summer; and if the farmer can manure after them, at about twelve loads per acre, he has a chance, upon a tolerable good walk, to grow two or three quarters of wheat per acre, and is sure, by good tillage, to have good turnips afterwards, and his land in fine condition to sow with barley and seeds. I should in this case recommend the turnips to be fed off with oxen and sheep, because of mixing the clay properly with the soil. Modern practice is the growing a crop or two of corn at breaking up a layer; but the old practice was to ris-baulk and break up the following year, and to fallow for turnips; but then they kept the land in tillage for several years afterwards; nor did they sow a sufficient quantity of seeds, and very often deferred sowing till the second crop after turnips; that their layers were very full of quitch-grass, when broke up, and in no condition to receive a crop of corn. A walk that is laid down with plenty of seeds for two years, never grows so much corn as when first broke up again. Upon a walk with a cold bottom, Dutch clover is sown

preparation, the basis for both corn and grass. There
is no sand so light that it will not yield, by means of
dung or fold, this crop.

with trefoil, and half a bushel of ray grass, which make very fine sheep-
feed : formerly a bushel of ray grass, and a quarter of a peck of trefoil;
now the practice is reversed to half a bushel of ray grass, and half a peck
of trefoil upon a poor walk. Upon the strong loamy wet lands called High
Suffolk, which was formerly *chiefly* pasture, and appropriated to the dairy,
but of late years have been converted into arable, the management is dif-
erent to any thing I have treated about: here a fallow for wheat, then
beans; wheat, and then a fallow again; or a summer-tillage for turnips,
which are drawn off the land for cows, or in their stead cabbages; where
they are not grown a summer-fallow for oats or barley. This is a better
practice than fallowing for wheat; but I should recommend, where they
do not grow cabbages or turnips, the sowing of tares in September, and
either mow or feed them, and give proper tillage till Michaelmas; then to
lay the land upon small ridges to keep it dry during the winter, and in the
spring to sow with barley, and clover, and then wheat following. The soil in
this country is so exceedingly strong, and wet in winter, that it will scarce
admit any thing to go upon it; and in summer, when dry, will not yield
to the heaviest roller; which makes it one of the worst counties in the
kingdom to cultivate; but of late years has been very much improved by
under-draining, which seems to be well understood by the occupiers: The
roads too have been much improved. These considerations have induced
the farmers to offer greater rents, to have the liberty of converting more
pasture into arable, and their request has been too generally complied with;
but I fear, the landlord, instead of increasing his rental, will, in a few years,
find it decreasing. Many of these lands are now tired of growing corn;
and in my opinion can only be recovered by the following method of
farming them, viz. Tares fed or cut early, good summer-tillage, and laid up
dry for the winter; in the spring sow barley, and with it two sacks of hay-
seeds, half a peck of clover, and a quarter of a peck of trefoil; mow for
stover the first year, and feed the second; manure for beans and then sow
wheat. By this method, the land will have the advantage of two years rest,
and will have but two exhausting crops of corn in six years; the farmer
will be enabled to keep a larger stock without turnips, which always cause
more hurt to the land in getting them off, than the service it receives by
growing them; and as the labour will be less, consequently fewer horses
will be required upon the farm. As the plough in this country has prevailed,
the cows have decreased in number, and it is said in the neighbourhood of
Debenham, and Earlsoham, there are fewer cows than were kept ten years
since, by a thousand: hence the advanced price of butter and cheese is ac-
counted for. Ask the farmer concerning fire-wood, and he tells you it is
become so exceedingly scarce, they have not a sufficiency for large dairies

After turnips, barley is generally sown ; then grass seeds succeed, but with variations. On bad sands trefoil and ray grass are chosen, because their duration equals the views of the farmer: they are left two or three years, and when broken up, a *bastard* fallow given for rye. The discrimination between good and bad farmers, in this arrangement, depends entirely on this point ; good ones consider every thing as subservient to sheep, consequently leave their grasses as long as possible ;* but bad ones, in a hurry for corn, and an immediate advantage, plough too soon. All these sandy districts are invariably sheep farms (rabbits only excepted) ; the flocks feed in winter on turnips, and in summer on these *layers.* On the better sands, frequently the layers are broken up, and pease planted to great advantage by hand dibbles, and this is succeeded by a better crop of wheat than when sown on such layers kept bare by feeding all the summer. Two rows are dibbled on each flag, and they come up so regularly as seldom to want hoeing.

as formerly. A lease of one of these farms came into my hands lately, wherein there were two clauses that unravelled the secret: the first, leave to convert into arable, any quantity of old pasture land ; but to lay down the same quantity of arable land with grass seeds ; and the second, to have liberty to take down every pollard-tree that stood in the way of the plough ; this seems a most effectual way of clearing the country of old pasture-land and fire-wood : I suppose this is not the only existing lease of the kind.

In the western district, the management of land is similar to that of the eastern part of the county, except that the farmers grow tares to mow, and give green to their flocks of sheep in dry pinching weather, which is not the practice in the eastern district ; this accounts for the lambs bred in the neighbourhood of Bury, being in general better than those bred on the other side of the county. I have always considered the lamb-growers on the eastern side to be but in an infant state of managing their flocks of sheep, compared with the flock-masters on the other side of the county.— The under-stratum in some parts of the western district, is a sharp flinty chalk, and seems well calculated for the growth of sain-foin, yet very few farmers have attempted to cultivate it.—*Anthony Collet, Esq.*

* This is a true system for improvement, and a just remark.—*Baillie.*

Buck wheat forms in some very poor spots a variation; and small pieces of tares are sometimes seen; but the system I have described holds good in general.

In Sampford hundred, on their poorer soils they are excellent farmers, as well as on the richer loams: their course is,

  1. Turnips,
  2. Barley,
  3. Trefoil and ray-grass,
  4. Peas dibbled,
  5. Barley;

which is admirable management.

FEN.

The course of crops generally pursued in this district, is to sow cole-seed on one ploughing, after paring and burning; which is for sheep-feed or seed, according to circumstances; then oats twice in succession; with the last of which crops they lay down with ray grass and clover, for six or seven years, and then pare and burn, and repeat the same husbandry.

Such are the courses of crops which are usually practised in the four predominant soils of Suffolk; and I should remark, that they are found indiscriminately on the fields of men who have worked no improvements, and those by whom considerable ones have been effected.

SECT. IV.—CROPS COMMONLY CULTIVATED.

I. WHEAT.

PREPARATION.

Tillage.—Wheat in this county is usually sown on summer fallow, or on clover land; in the former case, after three or four ploughings; in the latter, upon one. Fallows are generally thrown into the three foot or two *bout* ridge the last earth but one, which is reversed in the sowing earth. The seed ploughed in; but on clover lays it is of course covered by the harrow, a method very inferior to dibbling.

1803.—Such was the old management, but the modern improvements have effected through the heavy land district a considerable change. This has been partly explained under the article Tillage, and will be more particularly treated when I come to detail the practice of individuals.

Manure.—It is common with many farmers to manure their clover lays for wheat with the farm-yard compost of the preceding winter. The same husbandry is common in parts of Norfolk, where they do it with a view to the turnips which follow; but in Suffolk it is too often spread with a view to a crop of barley to follow the wheat. There is scarcely any doctrine in husbandry more orthodox, than the propriety of spreading all the dung of a farm for the turnip or bean crops; a practice on which depends not inconsiderably, the progressive amelioration of a farm, since, by making the turnips as productive as possible, the live stock is increased, which increases dung, and goes round in that beneficial circle which makes cattle the parents of corn.

Sort.—The sorts of wheat are not numerous, they consist chiefly of the common red, the white, and the bearded, called also *rivets*, and which is sown chiefly on wet cold lands. I introduced, some years ago, and with considerable success, the white velvits ; and other kinds, not of general note, have been cultivated. Burwell is so famous in Suffolk for its wheat seed, that I am happy to insert the following communication from Mr. Turner.

" Burwell is in Cambridgeshire, on the border of Suffolk, near Newmarket Heath, a considerable part of which lies in Burwell parish, and where the greatest number of racces are run : but as it is a place famous likewise for producing the best seed wheat in the kingdom, I shall take a pleasure in executing the task you have set me, in giving the best description of it I can. Burwell, then, is a large parish, containing within bounds nearly 7000 acres, 3000 of which are arable, 500 are pasture, and the rest are fen grounds. The arable land is divided into three shifts, two of which produce corn every year, viz. wheat and barley, and the third is fallow. The greatest number of acres under the plough are called white lands, as the appearance of the land in dry weather is white, on account of its being a shallow soil, lying near the white stone, and not being a spit deep in many places. There is another sort of plough land in the parish, which is called red land, lying down towards Newmarket Heath ; but the quantity of this is very small, when compared with the white land, and its quality is far inferior. It is the white land which produces the true seed wheat which is in great request in the north, on account of its becoming ripe much sooner than any other seed that is sown, and consequently makes an earlier harvest in a cold climate. This wheat bears the highest price in the market, and is threshed as soon as it is got into the barn ; that is, it is only topped out, not threshed to straw, and the sheafs are tied up again, and laid up for some time before they are threshed again to straw, so that it is the ripest and best part of the ear from which the seed is obtained in the early threshing. The reason why this white land wheat is so beneficial for seed, I humbly think, is owing to the saltpetre with which the soil is impregnated, arising from the white stone underneath it ; and what has confirmed me in this opinion is, that my house is built with the same stone, dug out of the pits, and the walls, in damp weather, are always wet with saltpetre, and produce a great deal of moisture after a frost. With regard to the method of cultivating the land here, there has been no alteration in that particular for these twenty-three years, the time of my residence in this parish."

Steeping.—This operation, as a preventive of the smut, is universal. The modes vary, but there are many farmers that will sow the smuttiest seed without apprehension, having from experience perfect confidence in their methods of dressing the seed ; the most common is to make a brine strong enough to bear an egg, and to steep the seed in it rarely long enough, and some only swim it ; all dry with lime. The following mode has been also found absolutely effective : make about half a hogshead of strong ley, by running water through wood ashes several times, and put it into a copper with half a pound of arsenick ; let it boil about five minutes, which will so far take off the poisonous quality of the arsenick, as to prevent the destroying of fowls or birds that may pick up the uncovered seed : after the ley is boiled, put it into a deep tub (an old wine pipe cut will make two) and let it stand until it is cold ; then get a strong close made basket, that will hold about two bushels, and set in the ley, and put half a bushel of wheat into the basket at a time, stirring it well several times, and skimming off the light dross that will rise ; then drain the ley from it, and lay it on a brick or clay floor, and sift as much lime upon it as will prepare it for sowing ; about a quarter of a peck of lime will dry four bushels of wheat sufficiently, if mixed the night before it is used. This quantity of ley will swim about 50 bushels of wheat.*

1803.—The most important variation that has been introduced has been that of using seed of the last year, which is not subject to the smut, nor demands any steeping : and a valuable effect attending it, is, that the cups of Mr. Cook's drill machine, which many farmers have changed for larger, thus deliver seed enough ; as steeping and liming lessens the quantity of seed per acre by about two pecks.

Quantity of Seed.—Two bushels an acre, are the common allowance of seed ; some will sow a peck more, and if late in the season, even to three bushels ; and some will, on good land, trust to seven pecks ; but even in dibbling, that quantity is oftentimes put in.

Time of Sowing.—October and November are the months in which this crop is sown in Suffolk : experiments have been made in the county, which shew that September is, if wet enough, a better time ; but very few farmers are so early.

Putting in.—Observations on sowing clover land wheat, by Mr. William Macro, of Barrow, Suffolk.

* The method of R. Andrews, Esq. and various others.

" From upwards of twenty years experience, I am of opinion that the best way of sowing clover lands with wheat is as follows :

" To plough the land ten days or a fortnight before you sow it, on to stitches of thirteen or fourteen yards in breadth, unless the land is very heavy, and not under-drained, in that case two or three yards are better ; but in both cases let the land be ploughed some time to get dry, and after rain enough to make it dress well, lay on the seed, at the following rates : if in the month of September, two bushels per acre is enough (except on chalky soils, which will at times require near a bushel per acre extra) ; in October, sow three bushels per acre ; and in November four bushels per acre will seldom be found too much.

" The furrows should by no means be more than eight or nine inches in breadth, less is better, if the plough turns them well ; and the two first furrows should not be lapped one on to the other, as is common with most farmers, but ploughed so as to leave a space of about two inches between them, for some seed to fall in, as in the other case the seed must of course harrow off in dressng the land, and leave the best part naked. Some farmers object to so much land being left whole under the first two furrows ; but I never saw any disadvantage from it, but the contrary.

" Another thing I have observed in some farmers, and have paid very dear for it myself ; that is, drawing the land over with a heavy harrow when only one cast, or half the seed is sown, which never should be done, for the seed can never be laid in too deep with harrows, and by harrowing before all the seed is sown, what you sow afterwards, especially if late in the season, might almost as well be thrown on the highway, for by being laid in so fleet, the mildest winter will kill it. I tried only one breadth of a harrow so the last season, and it is plainly to be seen (notwithstanding this favourable winter) as far as I can see the land.

" I own I am at a loss to account for the wheat thriving better on lands that have been ploughed some time, than it does on fresh ploughed lands which dress as well, or better : but I have often tried both ways on the same lands, and always found the former answer best. I have often tried dibbling in of wheat, upon both clover and ray grass lands, and both have answered very well, but best on the former. It cost 8s. 6d. per acre (covering included). And when wheat is so high as 6s. per bushel, the saving in seed will about pay the expence, as one bushel per acre is as much as can well be got in. But this never answers so well, after about the middle of October."

1803.—A very great improvement has taken place amongst the enlightened cultivators of beans, tares, &c. which is that of putting in the wheat without any ploughing. They scarify and scuffle, rake, clear, and burn, till the surface is fine enough for the drill to work ; and then leave it till rain comes for drilling. Thus the roots of the wheat have a firm bottom to root in, which this crop much affects. The success has been very great ; in the Appendix I give the observations I made on many farms on my re-survey of the county, and where this management is mentioned. I have practised the husbandry myself, in the same field wherein the plough was used, and found the method superior to the common practice.

Dibbling.—This practice, which there is every reason to denominate excellent, is well established in the county,

and increases every year.* In the maritime sand district,
many thousand acres are thus put in. One farmer near
Dunwich, the year before last, dibbled 258 acres, and
this year above 250, that is, his whole crop ; and many
others apply the same method also for their whole crop.
The ground being rolled with a light barley roller, a
man walking backwards on the *flag*, as the furrow slice
is called, with a dibber of iron, the handle about three
feet long, in each hand, strikes two rows of holes, about
four inches from one row to the other, on each flag ;
and he is followed by three or four children to drop the
grains, three, four, or five in each hole. In this way,
from six to seven pecks of seed are deposited, at very
equal depths, in the centre of the flag. A bush-harrow
follows to cover it : the expence eight to nine shillings
an acre. There are several circumstances which tend
to render this method superior to the common. The
treading so equally, is very beneficial upon light soils ;
and in dry weather hurtful upon none. The seed is
laid in at an equal and good depth ; and it is all in the
flag itself, and not dropt in the seams, where weeds, if
any, will arise : and there is some saving in seed. The
fact is, that the crops are superior to the common, and
and the sample more equal. It is not common to hoe,
except only one row be put in instead of two. Some use
a frame which strikes many holes at a time ; but the
work is not so well done, and I found the practice not
equally approved. The vast system of well-paid employment for the poor, which this practice carries with
it, is a point of immense importance. I heard of families

* Pease, particularly white ones, are very generally dibbled on ray-grass
layers, and followed by wheat, upon light lands where wheat was formerly
little cultivated. Even barley and oats are sometimes dibbled, but rarely.—
Note by T. L.

who had received, father, mother, and children, among them, two guineas a week for six weeks.*

Drilling—is practised with great intelligence and success, by individuals, in several parts of the county ; † The kinds of drills are various ; Mr. Cook's; variations of Mr. Ridge's ; and a new one, which promises to be an improvement on all, now made by Mr. Brock, a millwright at Harlstone.‡

* Dibbling and drilling are very admirable improvements in modern husbandry, and carry with them all the advantages enumerated. If drilling be rather the cheapér mode, the consideration of the excellent employment dibbling and setting affords to a poor family, more than counterbalances that advantage.—*Note by J. R.*

† Instead of bush-harrowing after drilling, I recommend rolling the land across the drills with a roller of a weight according to the state of the land, so as to close the drills and press the land pretty flat. This has very much the same effect as the treading of the children who drop the corn after the dibblers, to which many attribute the superiority of dibbling. This observation particularly respects mixed soil, and light lands, which cannot lie too close.

‡ *Dibbling.*—This practice has been introduced into the county but few years ; it is every where tolerably well understood ; but within two years has been very much improved upon. For wheat, a narrow set plough of only seven inches width at bottom, is used to plough with ; then follows a one-horse roll to level the flag, or furrow, for the dibblers, who strike only one row upon each when the wheat is deposited, *two or three kernels in each hole*, a two-horse roll follows, afterwards the harrows twice in a place ; when the field is finished in this manner, it is harrowed up again obliquely ; by this method the wheat is deposited in the middle of the flag, at nine inches distance in the rows; and when come up, has the appearance of being drilled ; the two-horse-roller is of material use in closing up the holes, and preventing the wheat from being disturbed by harrowing ; the land is made so solid by rolling, that very little apprehensions are entertained about the slug or worm. If there should be occasion to hoe in the spring, how easy and cheap the operation ! Bush-harrowing is of very little use ; it can only sweep the dust or light mould over the holes, and the first shower of rain that follows, most of the holes will be seen, and much of the wheat swelled out of them. Six pecks of wheat per acre are deposited.

Beans are in general dibbled one row upon a furrow, and the same distance should be kept so as to plant them square, at nine or ten inches;

On drilling, the Rev. Mr. Hill, of Buxhall, writes ; " I still prefer the drill method of husbandry, and that because I am from frequent trials convinced I get much

a two-horse roll should follow the ploughs, to level the land for the dibblers, which should be harrowed twice after the beans are deposited ; when the beans are all up, they are rolled, and in ten days or more, harrowed with heavy harrows : In hoeing them, the best method is to hoe across the land the first time, and length-ways the steatches the second; the work will then be better performed, both in respect to destroying the weeds, and moulding up the beans, which, when planted as above directed, will have more air, and certainly stand a better chance for a crop, than when housed together, by the old manner of planting them too thick ; besides, here is a saving of seed. Formerly three bushels per acre, or more, were deposited; now not two bushels. Pease are likewise planted by the dibble, in the same manner as wheat.

Oats—upon land that is stiff and unkindly to work in the spring, no way is equal to dibbling them ; and where old pasture-land is broke up for oats, it certainly is preferable to any other method; an instance I will mention : a farmer in the village I live in, broke up two acres of pasture-land in February, 1794; in March he planred it with oats, by dibbling two rows upon a flag ; the quantity of seed deposited upon the two acres was exactly one coomb ; the land was several times rolled with a two-horse roll, and often harrowed, to cover the seed ; the produce was forty coombs and one bushel, of the best oats I saw any where last season. This was the greatest quantity I ever knew produced from a coomb of seed.

Barley is seldom dibbled, by reason the land is so dry in April, that the holes will run in, and not stand open to receive the seed ; for which reason, and the want of expedition, it can never be the general practice.

Drilling—Is very well understood by individuals, and has succeeded when done properly ; but the general deficiency of the drill-machines, and the saving of seed, which has been recommended by drill venders, in order to introduce their drills to the public, have in fact, been the causes why many of them have been laid aside. One and the same drill can never answer in a large and a small occupation, any more than one man can dibble in the corn upon a large, as well as a small farm. This is the case with Mr. Cook's drill. I use a drill which Mr. Young saw at work when he surveyed the county, and can speak to its utility ; it has nine coulters ; goes with two horses, and will keep pace with six ploughs : In barley sowing, it finishes ten acres every day, with ease to the horses, and can never be affected by rain or wind, and will deposit the corn the same, whether the land is hilly or level. In all drilling, the land should be well ploughed, and made fine, before the drill comes upon it, by rolling and harrowing ; a one-horse roll should follow the drill, to close the land upon the seed, and then the more the land is harrowed, the better ; very little seed is saved by

better crops from it, and save at least one half of my
seed; and particularly so in wheat, as I have found
from repeated trials, that I get more at harvest from
wheat planted at eighteen inches asunder, than from
that which is planted nearer; indeed this year (which
you know has not been favourable to thin plants) my
eighteen inch wheat has the advantage, even in quantity
of straw producing 666 sheaves, from exactly the same
quantity of land, in the same field, and of the same kind
of land. That planted at nine inches asunder, has produced only 564 sheaves; and I believe as little difference
in the size of the sheaves as possible. But I must tell
you my bailiff dislikes all experiments, and therefore if
it was in his power, he would certainly lean towards the
old method of drilling at nine inches asunder; but notwithstanding all this, the account he brings me of the
produce of my experiment this year, is still more in
favour of the eighteen inches than ever it has been before, that having yielded 8 c. 1 b. 1 p. the nine inches
7 c. 1 b. 2 p. I should likewise inform you, that this
same experiment has been tried on the same land several
years, always having the eighteen inch on the same side
of the field, to shew which would have the advantage
in a length of years: the eighteen inch has always had

drilling, for it is found by experience, that corn drilled at nine inches
asunder, requires thickness in the rows; in that case they will nearly touch
before harvest, and appear as if sown broad-cast. Farming should come as
near to gardening as possible; but nothing will accomplish it like drilling.
Let any judicious agriculturist examine the row of pease, or kidney beans
in a garden, and see which are the most productive, the thick, or the thin
ones: let him examine the young plants of clover in drilled barley, and in
barley that is sown broad-cast; and it will soon be distinguished which
has the preference.—Dibbling and drilling corn, have been attended with
the best consequences to the poor, by encouraging the farmer to weed it,
in a ten-fold degree to what he did when sown broad cast: and as the
ploughing, rolling, and harrowing, are more attended to by the farmer, the
land is in a better state of tillage, than ever was thought necessary, before
they were introduced.—*A Collet, Esq.*

the advantage in corn, though never before in bulk of straw."

Noted by Correspondents.—Mr. Davenport observes, that at Bardwell, wheat, beans and pease, are generally dibbled.—Mr. Brettingham, near Bungay, says, that " dibbling wheat, beans and pease, has been practised many years, and latterly barley and oats, which are thought to answer well; the expence 10*s.* 6*d.* an acre without any allowances, which is, I think, in a great degree saved by *planting* on the first earth instead of *sowing* on the third, which was frequently the case, and some saving in the seed, suppose from one to one and an half bushel per acre."—Mr. Banks, of Metfield, observes, that the poor find much employment for themselves and children, in planting almost all kinds of grain, both in spring and autumn.—Mr. Moore, of Finingham, writes, " Dibbling wheat maintains its reputation and increases it—price 9*s.* per acre, and beer. People are foolishly captivated with the green appearance of their wheat in winter, when thick-set, and put in six, and even seven pecks per acre, which, I am persuaded, is a waste of one or two. Many people dibble even their barley and oats, which, if it in any degree answers, must be beneficial, by finding employment for the children, now spinning earns so little. Our plants of clover are very hazardous ; the farmers consider the land as *tired of it.* A substitute seems to be wanted for a time."

1803. Since the first edition of these papers, a revolution has taken place in the agriculture of the strong land district ; for drilling in many parishes is become universal, except in the south-western angle of the county ; and promises to spread every where. And it is a most singular circumstance, that though the practice has much extended in the sand districts, yet, at present, it is more general on the strong and heavy soils. Whereas in the neighbouring county of Norfolk this practice has extended itself very considerably in the north-western district of sand, but I found only one driller upon clay. The success in Suffolk has been very great indeed ; and it has originated (particularly in the case of all spring corn), as I conceive, from a most admirable improvement, in praise of which too much can scarcely be urged—that of avoiding as much as possible all spring ploughings. By means of this most decisive stroke of true and enlightened practice, the strong land farmer has placed himself, comparatively speaking, on velvet. His difficulties formerly were dreadful. His ploughs often moved in mire, or amongst hard clods, or his right season lost by waiting for better weather. He turned down the dry friable surface which frosts had given him, and he rarely regained it. Drillers were forced upon the new system ; and their neighbours, who saw the beneficial effects, adopted the whole system, taking the drill as well as the rejection of tillage ; and thus it has spread with unexampled rapidity. The idea was extended to autumnal sowings, so that many have pea and bean stubbles, and are drilled without any ploughing, by means only of scarifying and scuffling; and this practice, also, by leaving a firm bottom for the roots of wheat, has precluded the common malady of root fallen crops, and the success has been very satisfactory. This general rejection of tillage by the plough whenever circumstances permit, I consider as one of the greatest, if not THE greatest improvement of modern husbandry : it has changed the face of the greatest part of this country, and will change the face of others as fast as it is introduced with skill and intelligence.

Culture while growing.—When wheat is dibbled one row on a flag, or furrow, it is always well hand-hoed; but if two rows, it is too thick to admit that operation conveniently. Sometimes, however, such is also hoed; and there are many good farmers who make it a rule to hand-hoe their broad-cast crops; but the practice cannot be said to be general. The price is usually from 6s. to 8s. an acre. Cutting out thistles with weeding hooks, is universal.

Harvest.—They are more careful and attentive in many parts of the kingdom, in harvesting all sorts of corn, than they are in Suffolk. The wheat sheaves are generally made too large, which is a heavy evil in a wet harvest. Very attentive husbandmen are apt to think all too large that are made by tying two handfuls to form a a band, one length of straw not very short, being esteemed sufficient. In forming the *shocks*, or stooks, also, they use no precautions against rain, merely setting ten or a dozen together, without capping or other attention, a method that is found in other counties very useful.

Threshing.—I do not know of any threshing-mill in the county, which is rather surprizing, for one abounding so greatly in corn.

1803. A noble change has taken place in this respect, for there are at present above twenty.

Produce.—The crops of wheat vary considerably: from one quarter and a half on the poor sand, when substituted for rye, and at that small produce answering better, to three and an half on the rich and strong loams. Upon the finest soils in the county, specified elsewhere, four, and even five quarters are not uncommon. Probably the general average of the whole may be estimated at twenty two bushels per acre, on a medium of seven years.

In the answers I have been favoured with to my circular queries, there are a few minutes that merit being noted.

At Bardwell, Mr. Davenport remarks, that five coombs, is an indifferent crop.

At Brome, Mr. Negus mentions the produce to be five coombs.

At Hopton, by Mr. Stone's account, four coombs. At Barningham, five.

II. BARLEY.

PREPARATION.

THE preparation for this grain, is very generally a crop of turnips, which being eaten on the land by sheep, or drawn off for cattle, three spring earths are given by good farmers, and the seed on sands ploughed in ; on heavier soils harrowed in. The rule, however, of giving three ploughings is much more invariable in Norfolk than it is in Suffolk. On wetter soils, and in wet springs (which have not been common of late years), it some-times happens that the lands break so friably under the plough after sheep feeding, that it is better to put in the barley on one, than on more earths ; but that is merely an exception, and not to be followed as a rule. It is to be regretted, that the use of scufflers is not more known, as they would in various instances be more effective than the plough. Soils too heavy for turnips, are in many places summer fallowed for barley ; and if fallows are applied, this is certainly one of the bes applications, in which case the grain is sowed on one spring earth, and the earlier the better.

1803. In putting in the barley crop, the greatest of modern improvements in tillage has taken place, to a degree that I had little expectation of seeing in ten years, when I wrote the above recommendation of scufflers for this crop. They are now, in the heavy land district, very generally substituted for the plough, and the effect is as great as can be conceived. Whatever the preceding crop of preparation, whether fallow, tares, pease, or beans, the stitches being ploughed in autumn to the breadth that suits the drill machine and scufflers, in the spring, as soon as the soil is dry enough, it is scuffled, the horses walking only in the furrows, and drilled without any more ploughing. Even turnip land, the crop fed early to receive some pulverization from frosts, is treated in the same manner, and with very great success.

Sort.—The common barley, *hordeum vulgare*, is the only sort I have known cultivated in Suffolk.

1803. Winter barley for sheep feed has been lately introduced.

Quantity of Seed.—On very light sandy lands in the western district, so small a quantity as two bushels, and two and a half, are sown; but the common practice on all soils in general, is to sow from three to four bushels.

Time of Sowing.—April is the season most common; but varying with many circumstances from the beginning of March to the beginning of May. I have known farmers wait by reason of drought, to the last week in May, and even the first in June.

1803. *Drilling.*—This husbandry is very generally introduced, and with such success, that it is certainly spreading ; the usual distance is 9 inches, many at 6, and some few at 12. The success has been greatly arising from the practice of substituting the scarifyer and scuffle for the plough, thereby preserving the friable surface left by the frosts.

Harvest.—Barley is every where in Suffolk mown, and left loose : the neater method of binding in sheaves, is not practised. The stubbles are dew raked, by men drawing a long iron-toothed rake ; but this is better, and much quicker performed, by a horse-rake, a very effective tool.

Produce.—The produce of barley varies greatly ; from two quarters to six. I am inclined to think the average, so difficult in all cases to calculate, may be estimated at four quarters.

Products, noted by Correspondents.—At Bardwell, Mr. Davenport observes the average produce to be seven coombs. At Brome, Mr. Negus notes eight coombs as the average. At Hopton, Mr. Stone calculates it at three quarters.

III. OATS.

PREPARATION.

It is not common to give more than one ploughing for oats, whether on a stubble or lay.

Sort.—The black, the white, the Tartarian, and the light oat, are the sorts cultivated in Suffolk; but the two first only are common. The Tartarian are very productive, and have been brought to a good weight per bushel. The light, called also *flight* oats, are known only on the poorest sands, and in the fen district.

Quantity of Seed.—Four bushels an acre are the general allowance of seed.

Time of Sowing.—Oats are sown throughout the spring, generally before barley; whereas in Hertfordshire, white oats are rarely sown till after all the barley is in the ground.

Dibbling.—When oats are put in on a layer, it is not uncommon in every part of the county to dibble them, and if it is upon a stale furrow, and escape the red worm, good crops are gained; much better than from merely covering the seed by harrows.

Drilling.—Oats are now (1803) commonly drilled in various parts of the county, and with a success equal to that which attends drilled barley.

Harvest.—Oats are mown, and gathered loose, as barley. But I have known some very great crops on new land, reaped and bound in sheaves; a practice that ought to be more common.

Produce.—The average produce of this grain may be estimated at four quarters and an half. Instances of extraordinary products are not uncommon. The Rev. Mr. Kedington, in three successive crops of Tartarian on an old pasture, the soil good loamy sand, gained thirty quarters. Mr. Negus, of Brome, mentions ten coombs as the average produce. At Hopton, Mr. Stone estimates it at four quarters.

IV. RYE.

THIS grain has gradually given way to the culture of wheat, by means of those improvements which in the last fifty years have taken place in so many parts of the kingdom. It is now found only on poor sands, and from several observations I have made on the crops of both on the same soil, I am much inclined to think that wheat will generally pay better. To see a year's summer fallow, and a folding, bestowed on any land, in order to reap three or four coombs of rye, is mortifying. Assuredly the same expence to procure an improved sheep-walk, would, where one part of a farm is sacrificed to another in folding, produce even more corn by giving the fold to soils that would pay better for it.

Preparation.—Fallow is the general preparation : by some a whole year ; by others a bastard fallow.

Seed.—Six pecks an acre, the usual quantity.

Time of Sowing.—The end of September and beginning of October the common time.

Produce.—Good crops of this grain are rare in the sands of Suffolk ; on better soils, three quarters an acre are sometimes gained ; but the common produce does not exceed two.

V. BEANS.

It is difficult to cultivate rich moist soils to full advantage, without the assistance of this plant, which has two qualities of singular importance ; first, that of extracting very little from the fertility of the land ; and second, preparing better, perhaps, for wheat, than any other crop. They are not generally cultivated in Suffolk, but yet are in sufficient quantity to shew the importance of a more extended use.

1803. A considerable extension has taken place since the former edition of this work. I have seen many crops that for cleanness would not have disgraced Kent. The culture is still increasing.

Preparation.—It is uncommon to give more than one earth for beans, and generally improper, for they love a whole firm furrow, and never thrive better than on a layer.

In Kent, they find that no plant pays better for dung, but it is uncommon in Suffolk to afford them any ; yet dunging fallows for wheat is found in all parts of the county, and is a most barbarous practice. Where this husbandry is pursued, there could be no improvement more obvious than giving the dung to beans, and then taking the wheat.

1803. One of the greatest of improvements is fast spreading in Suffolk ; that of giving the one ploughing for this crop in autumn, and drilling in the spring without further ploughing. The success very great ; I have done it on my own farm, and can recommend it as an excellent system.

Sort.—The little common horse-bean, ticks, and Windsor ticks, are the sorts generally cultivated ; and about Clare, mazagans are sown. The first is the most saleable, and usually at the highest price.

Seed.—If broad-cast, three bushels an acre ; by some persons, with a view to very good hoeing, only two. And in dibbling or drilling, two bushels are the common quantity.

Dibbling.—Beans have been dibbled a row on every flag ; by others, on every other flag. I have found it more advantageous to plant in clusters four or five beans in every hole, and eight or nine inches from hole to hole, which admits much better hoeing than when more thickly set. Dibbling is the best and most effective method of cultivating beans.

Time of Sowing.—This is guided by the season : as soon as the land is dry enough in the spring to work well, is the right time ; and February, in that case, a proper time ; but they do well all through March.

Culture while growing.—Hoeing, and incessant cleaning, are essential to this culture ; but in this respect the Suffolk farmers are behind their brethren in Kent, where both horse and hand-hoes are for ever at work, and the crops kept in a degree of garden cleanness. In Suffolk, it is not uncommon to give two good hand-hoeings, but after that, the crops are left to themselves ; yet, with no other attention, the culture is found profitable on good soils.

Harvest.—I have seen beans mown, and gathered

loose in Suffolk, which is abominable management: they are, however, usually reaped, and bound in sheaves; splint yarn for bands, or made of straw.

Culture of the Stubble.—The Kentish method of shimming the stubbles of beans, which cannot be too much commended, is unknown in Suffolk: whatever may have been the hoeing, there will remain some weeds; these ought not to be ploughed in, but cut shallow on the surface, harrowed out, and burnt, or removed to the compost dunghill. By repeating this operation to absolute cleanness, the land is left in garden order for wheat.

1803.—In this point also the husbandry of the county is greatly improved; scarifying and scuffling are now well executed, so well that we go beyond the Kentish practice, and put in the wheat without any ploughing; and I have seen as fine or finer crops thus managed, than where ploughing has been added. If the culture is by ploughing, still these preparatory operations should take place, in order that no weeds or stubble be turned down, which only gives a loose bottom where the roots of the wheat require a certain degree of firmness and solidity, which is much lessened by green or dry unrotting vegetables. It is this circumstance which causes such various accounts of the effect of ploughing in buck wheat. If done in time to be quite rotten before the wheat roots take possession of the bottom of the furrow, it is beneficial; but if so late as to prevent a solid bottom, it often fails: and by *bottom*, is not meant an unstirred steril subsoil, but the lower portion of that surface which has been stirred by the plough. Much however depends on soil, for in some cases where if you loosen at four inches, the earth is good enough at six; if you lighten at six, the roots will establish themselves at eight. No rule is of universal application. Does not this reasoning imply, that when dung is spread for wheat, it ought to be ploughed in very shallow?

Produce.—Beans are every where an uncertain crop, consequently the average produce difficult to estimate : in Kent they probably exceed four quarters; but in Suffolk I should not estimate them at more than three nd an half, yet six or seven are not uncommon.

Application of the Crop.—The quantity given to horses is not very considerable ; and the consumption by hogs, or ground for fattening cattle, is still less. If the culture was more general, and the crops consumed at home in fattening cattle, sheep and hogs, it would have a more powerful tendency to improve a country, and promote the growth of wheat, than most other measures that could be pursued ; but for this the price of meat must be high.

1803.—In this respect also the Suffolk farmers have been moving; many beasts are now stall-fed with bean flou.

VI. PEASE.

PEASE are more common in Suffolk than beans, as they are not equally confined in point of soil.

Preparation.—The best preparation that is practised in Suffolk, is that of a ray-grass layer, one earth being given to a lay of two years ; it is more beneficial for this grain than any other method pursued, for dry soils; but they should always be dibbled, which is the method pursued by our best farmers.

Sort.—The sorts of pease are various; we have white, blue, grey, and dun, with the names of their respective colours.

Seed.—Two bushels an acre are the common allowance of seed; but three are sown broad-cast by some farmers.

Time of Sowing.—March and April are the common seasons.

Culture while growing.—The dibbled crops being close planted, neither want nor admit of hoeing. Those who drill their crops, both hand and horse hoe, but the method is not common.

Harvest.—They are generally cut with what is called a pease *make*, which is the half of an old scythe fixed in a handle, with which they are rolled into small bundles, called *wads*, as they are cut.

Produce.—Of all crops, this is the most uncertain; it varies from three to ten sacks; perhaps the average may be estimated at five. Mr. Stone's account for Hopton, makes it five or six.

Application of the Crop.—Hogs are fattened with some, but the quantity not considerable.

VII. BUCK WHEAT,

Is, in this county, on the very poorest sands, more common than in many other parts of England; and is, for such soils, a very valuable crop.

Preparation.—I never knew manure bestowed for this crop ; but the time of sowing admits so much tillage, that any land may be perfectly cleaned for it.

Seed.—One bushel an acre is the common quantity.

Time of Sowing.—The end of June the usual time ; but the whole of that month is proper ; and it is some-times sown the first week of July.

Harvest.—Mown, and gathered loose.

Produce.—Crops vary, from four to eight sacks ; five probably the average.

Application of the Crop.—It is found good for feeding and fattening hogs and poultry ; and some farmers have given it to their horses with success.

Ploughing in for Manure.—This is not a common practice ; but one gentleman has with great skill applied a peculiar husbandry to it, which deserves reciting. The Rev. Mr. Moseley, of Drinkston, has the the merit of planning and executing a system of tare husbandry which deserves considerable attention. The following is his own account of it.

" When I had the pleasure of seeing you at Drink-ston, you expressed a desire of hearing from me, as soon as I could ascertain the effects of ploughing in buck wheat as a vegetable manure for wheat, after having previously taken a crop of tares for fodder. In compli-ance with with your request, you receive the following imperfect account.

" Your excellent method of managing light lands I generally adhere to, viz. turnips, barley, clover, and wheat; but finding, from a failure of clover in my two last crops after barley, that the succeeding ones were not equal to my expectation, I determined to try something as a substitute for that excellent preparation. Tares, I was aware, were frequently sown, and excellent crops of wheat have succeeded; but, as there were near three months between the time of cutting tares and sowing wheat, I thought that something might be done in the interim, in order, not only to keep the land clean, but to improve the succeeding crop.

" It was necessary to consider what would answer this end, that would not be attended with considerable expence; buck wheat claimed the preference, as it was of quick growth, and had been recommended as a strong and lasting manure. I, therefore, determined to try the effects of it, and have reason to think that my expectation was not too much raised; for, although I cannot with that certainty ascertain the real produce of the land as I can wish, as a considerable quantity of the wheat has been destroyed by vermin, yet, still have I had the satisfaction of lodging in my granary as much as I usually have done in the common method of husbandry. The loss I sustained, was, indeed, very considerable, and almost incredible, from such small animals as mice, for there was not a rat in the barn, and will be a standing memorial to me for thrashing my corn in the proper season. It was computed at one fourth of the whole crop. But, even deducting the loss, and allowing the increase to be equal to former years, will it not be right sometimes to alter the usual course, and substitute a preparation equally profitable as clover for the farmer's grand crop, wheat?

" The land upon which this experiment was made, was light, and produced excellent turnips and barley, but seldom more than a moderate crop of wheat; twenty

bushels per acre, were as much as might be expected in
a good season.

" But, although I cannot speak with precision in regard to the wheat crop, yet I can thus far affirm, that
the additional profit from the rye, as spring feed, which
succeeded the wheat, was more than equal to the original price of the buck wheat. How long the effects of
this manure will continue, I cannot possibly say ; but,
from the luxuriance of the rye, should not have made
the least doubt of its operative qualities to the ripening
that crop. The expence is trifling, for you cannot find
any manure, even for a single crop, equal in all respects
to this for five shillings, which is, in general, the price
of two bushels, and is sufficient for one acre.

" But a material advantage there certainly is from
two vegetable crops, the one immediately succeeding
the other, in cleaning the land ; for although the rye
was sown as soon as I could conveniently plough after
the haulm was carried off, yet, upon breaking up the
land after the rye was fed off, it was much cleaner than
it was after the last fallow.

" I wish I could have drawn a more accurate conclusion from this experiment, as I find that it is the first
that has been made in this manner ; and would not have
troubled you with this, had it not been by your particular desire, it being impossible to ascertain precisely the
loss I sustained, consequently, from mere presumption
to offer any thing as certain from it.

" I hope hereafter to be more accurate, as I have six
acres, which have produced this season twelve waggon
loads of tares, and are now sown with buck wheat, to
be ploughed in the latter end of the month as a preparation for wheat. The produce of these you shall be
acquainted with, as I wish to give you a fair account of
this, as I think, valuable vegetable manure."

And in a succeeding letter:—" I am now able to ascertain the real product of my field of wheat after my tare and buck wheat system ; and it gives me peculiar satisfaction to assure you that the increase has exceeded my expectation.

" The field contained near six acres, including borders, and the produce was twenty-nine coombs two bushels of clean wheat, so that it may reasonably be set at five coombs per acre, which is a much larger crop than I expected.

" The appearances at different times were such, as sometimes to promise a large crop, at others, a very moderate one. At first, vegetation seemed to be very luxuriant; this continued till April, when it changed much for the worse, and from that time till harvest, appearances were against it. For this, I believe, I can in some measure account. The tares and buck wheat were both in too forward a state ; the one not to exhaust the land in some degree, the other, to afford that food for the succeeding crop which might have been expected, had the tares been cut a fortnight sooner, and the buck wheat turned in before it had formed the seed. Delays from frequent storms occasioned the latter.

" However, upon the whole, I am so well satisfied with my success, that I shall try several methods of applying this useful manure, sometimes to assist my crop with others, and sometimes, as the only manure that can conveniently be procured.

" One observation I have made in watching the tare and buck wheat system, and which every cultivator ought to have primarily in view, viz. that in order to ensure the succeeding crop, it will be necessary to mow the tares as early as possible, that the buck wheat may be sown and ploughed as soon as it is in blossom. By this management, much time will be gained, the land

little exhausted, and the buck wheat in a state to afford
the strongest vegetable manure to the succeeding crop :
and could this be performed early enough in the autumn
to allow three weeks or a month for the buck wheat to
rot, I would then adopt Mr. Ellis's mode of harrowing
the land, and then plough and sow the wheat in broad
lands, under thorough. This way, he says, in his treatise
upon buck wheat, will dress the ground for three years;
whereas clover, vetches, or turnips, ploughed in, will,
only for half the time. My grand object, in adopting
this preparation, has been hitherto to secure a crop of
tares as a substitute for clover-hay, and it has answered
the intended purpose ; the crops of tares having been
uniformly good, and the succeeding crops of wheat
equal, if not superior to former years.

"If what Mr. Ellis has asserted be fact, in respect
to the strength of buck wheat as a manure, surely it
would be well worth considering, wherein this comparative difference of buck wheat, and other vegetable
manure consists. This only can be brought to the test
by a chymical operation, and, according to my opinion
well deserving a serious trial. If you think it of that
consequence in the general system of husbandry as I
really do, I am persuaded that you will favour us with
some experiments to ascertain the reality of this asser-
tion. and point out the respective properties of the
manures, from that and other vegetables.

" I find in your experiments upon the best preparation for a crop of barley, that beans claim the preference,
and that the buck wheat land, with all the apparent
advantages of the crop for manure, did not answer so
well as the fallow. Having thought much of this preparation, I think that I can point out a method by which
it would have answered better, and that is, by sowing
the wheat stubble with tares, immediately after carrying

on the muck, and then upon one earth throwing in the buck wheat. If this had been done, I question whether the crop of barley would have been worse, as the muck would have forced that, and the creditor side would have made no despicable appearance.

" If we treat this article in this manner, we must adjust our calculations in the following way :*

	l.	s.	d.	Creditor.	l.	s.	d.
To manure - -	1	9	9	2 Loads of tares, 1l. 15s.	3	10	0
1 Ploughing - -	0	6	0	By 4 quarters, 2 bush. and 1 peck barley, at 20d.	4	5	7½
Tares for seed, 2 bushels	1	5	0				
Sowing, harrowing, and rolling	0	6	3	By straw - -	0	12	4
Mowing, &c. - -	0	5	0				
1 Ploughing, harrowing, &c.	0	7	3		8	7	11½
					8	5	5
2 Bushels of buck wheat	0	5	0				
Rent - - -	0	18	0	To profit £.	0	2	6½
Sundries -	0	2	1				
3 Earths - -	0	18	0				
Harrowing and rolling	0	0	10				
Seed and sowing -	0	10	3				
Harvest - - -	0	5	10				
Threshing - -	0	4	6				
Rent, tithe, and rates -	0	18	0				
Sundry expences - -	0	3	8				
£.8		5	5				

" I think that I have not placed the tares at too high a rate to the credit account, as I really think that the fodder is well worth 1l. 15s. per load ; nor do I think two loads per acre too much, as, upon moderate land, I have seldom had less : I have therefore estimated the profit accordingly.

" If we allow, according to my mode of treating your * land, the same quantity of barley per acre, it will

* Mr. Mosely here alludes to an experiment published in the Annals of Agriculture. The observation and the calculation are perfectly fair ;

then, instead of being the most unprofitable of all the preparations, be found infinitely the most profitable. But even deducting something from the barley crop, or throwing out the crop of tares entirely, if it be true that this vegetable manure will continue to improve a crop for three years, your experiment of a single year is by no means complete, as, according to the common course, the succeeding crops might be expected to derive much benefit from this manure.

" I have never sown buck wheat upon wet cold lands, consequently cannot ascertain the effects of it as manure upon them: what I have hitherto done, has been upon a light sandy soil, and from experiments upon that, my mite of information has been drawn."

I may call for the attention of farmers anxious to become acquainted with real improvemements in agriculture, to this account of Mr. Moseley's system; which is one of the best imagined arrangements that has been discovered. One ploughing puts in the winter tares; that earth is given in autumn, and consequently opens the soil to the influence of frosts; as the spring advances, and the sun becomes powerful enough to exhale the humidity, and with it the nutritious particles of the land, the crop advances and screens it from the action of his beams. Whatever weeds are in the soil, vegetate with the young tares, and are either strangled by their luxuriance, or cut off with them before they can seed. A crop is gained at a very moderate expence, which is usually worth from 40s. to 3l. an acre; oftentimes much more. But this crop is cleared so early from the land, that it would remain exposed to the sun through

and had the trial been a part of my design, I have no doubt but the result would have been correctly as this very ingenious correspondent states it. —A. Y.

the most burning part of the summer for three months, as that ingenious gentleman rightly observes ; if left so, there would be a call for three ploughings to do mischief, except in the point of killing some weeds. To give one earth immediately, and harrow in buck wheat, spares that expence, and covers the earth when it most wants to be so protected. But a great deal more is done ; for according to this comparison, a coat of manure is gained at absolutely no expence ; and the year is carried through from Michaelmas to Michaelmas, and three crops put in on only three ploughings, viz. the tares, the buck wheat, and the wheat. It is not easy to invent a system more complete. Let me go further, and remark, that Mr. Moseley in this husbandry is original : many have sown tares ; and many have ploughed in buck wheat ; and most have given a year to each ; but it is the combination of the two that forms the merit, and is a plan not before registered ; and therefore, we are to pronounce (as far as the advancement of the art is concerned), not yet practised.

When we see the universal eagerness and anxiety expressed by the experimental philosophers of the present age, to secure to themselves priority of discovery (an anxiety fair and honourable, as speaking a noble emulation in the path of fame), ought we not to do justice to those who in a less brilliant, but more useful walk, invent new combinations of old practices that have the merit, because the advantages, of novelty ?

VIII. TARES.

THIS plant is generally cultivated to the extent of a
few acres; the scale applicable to soiling the horses of
the farm; it is not, however, as it ought to be, a universal
practice.

Preparation.—It is not common, though an excellent
practice, to manure for tares; and one earth only is
given for them.

Sort.—The winter and the spring tare are the only
sorts cultivated. I once saw white tares in the county,
but they were not found equal to the common sort.

The following experiments were made by the Rev.
Mr. Laurents, of Bury, to ascertain the distinction of
winter and spring tares.

" Whether there subsists an essential difference between the spring tare and the winter tare, is a question,
about which husbandmen are not unanimous. Some
assert the distinction which is made between the two,
real, and grounded in the nature of the plants themselves;
whilst others conceive it imaginary, and to lie merely
in the difference of the seed time. With a view to
decide this question, have the following experiments
been made.

" *Experiment* I.—Sept. 30th, 1783, I sowed seeds of
the winter tare and of the spring tare near one another
in the same soil and exposure; and covered both with a
coat of crumbled mould one inch deep. The weather

proving mild, the spring tare soon made its appearance; and two days after came up the winter tare. This ascendant the former did not fail to maintain over the latter until the middle of December; for at this time that was about six inches high, and this not above four. They both were in a vigorous and thriving condition, when a frost came on and continued for some weeks. When a thaw took place I found the spring tare lying on the ground slimy, and putrified to the very root. The winter tare had received no damage. This grew up afterwards, and was ripe before the middle of August.

" The circumstance of the different fates they had experienced from the frost, led me into the fields to view the state of tares in a more open situation. There I found, that in some grounds scarce any plants had failed; in others were patches of something in a state of putrefaction, resembling the dead tares in my garden.

" *Experiment* II.—On 6th of March, 1784, both sorts were sown in the manner above described; and in their springing up and growth, observed a progress similar to that which I had remarked in autumn. Near a week later than the winter tare of the autumnal sowing, the spring tare of the vernal sowing arrived to perfect maturity. But the winter tare of the vernal sowing was mildewed, nor did a single pod of it ripen.

" From these two circumstances there appears a material difference in the constitution, if I may so call it, of the two tares in question. I shall say nothing to the trifling difference in the colour and size of their seeds, but pass on to the only visible marks of distinction I was able to trace in watching the process of the two experiments. And this is a disparity in the first leaves of the upright stalks above *(a)* in the annexed plate. The figures in this plate, delineated from specimens gathered about the end of November, render a technical description unnecessary.

" N. B. The leaves on the branches, which afterward issue below *(a)* and in time form the bulk of the plants, resemble one another in the two vetches. This is all I am able to offer toward the decision of the question. Let the reader judge.

" The purpose of curiosity thus far answered, let us see what may redound from these enquiries to the interests of agriculture. And here it requires no great degree of penetration in the husbandman to discover the necessity of keeping the seeds of the two tares separate and unmixed; since sown out of season neither is found to prosper. Hence the seedsmen too may learn a lesson. What the practice may be in other places I cannot tell; but in the course of last summer, wishing to compare with our winter tare that which is cultivated in the Pays de Caux, and called there by the farmers *hyvernache*, I searched almost every shop in Rouen, where it was likely to be found, in vain. And the reason assigned for my disappointment was, that the time of sowing it was over. So very nice and exact a proportion between the wants of the farmer and the stock at market, struck me as a case somewhat remarkable; the solution of which is this: after the autumnal sowing, the remains of the *hyvernache* are thrown in among the other vetch. Now this practice stands condemned by the result of the second experiment.

" Some winter tares, self-sown in August, were so forward as to suffer from the severity of the winter more than what I had sown in experiment the first. It appears to me, that if the shoots below *(a)* in the plate are coming out before the winter sets in, they are sufficiently forward. They will then stand ready to start at the genial summons of returning spring."

Seed.—Two bushels to three, are the portion of seed commonly allotted to an acre.

Time of Sowing.—September is the usual season for sowing winter tares; but continued by some through October: March and April for the spring sort.

Harvest.—When left for seed, they are cut and wadded as pease, with a *make.*

Produce.—From three to six sacks an acre.

For Soiling.—This is the best and most general application of the crop. Winter tares, if sown in September, are in Suffolk ready to mow, that is, pretty full in blossom, by the first week in June. Upon rich soils, or manured, they will be earlier; but the loss is considerable by mowing too soon, and it depends on the time of sowing having been varied in a succession, to procure them for several weeks consumption.

For Hay.—They are found to make excellent hay, if the season is good to save it; they bear rain, however, worse than any other sort of hay.

IX. COLE-SEED.

THERE is a considerable quantity of cole-seed sown in all parts of this county; but in the fen district, it is one of the principal crops.

Preparation.—The preparation is the same as for turnips, but manure not commonly bestowed for it; in the fens it is generally sown on one thin ploughing, on pared and burnt land.

Seed.—A quarter of a peck is the common quantity of seed; but I have known half a peck sown by many.

Time of Sowing.—If for sheep feed only, it is sown in the turnip season; but if for seed, in the beginning of August,

Harvest.—It is reaped, and left on the *gravel* till fit to thresh.

Threshing.—Threshed in the field on cloths, and the straw burned, which is wasteful management, for there is no vegetable substance, however apparently dry, that will not rot, and make manure, when bedded in a farm-yard for the urine and dung of cattle to mix with it.

Produce.—Various; from four to ten sacks an acre; five coombs, or two quarters and a half an acre, probably the medium; and as it sells from thirty shillings even to fifty shillings a sack sometimes, it is a very profitable crop to the farmer.

For Sheep.—The application most important, and most beneficial *to a farm*, is this ; it is excellent for sheep, and exceeds turnips both in fattening and giving milk.

Succeeding Crop.—When seeded, it is commonly succeeded by wheat, which farmers are fond of representing as excellent, in order to convince their landlords that the crop is innocent, in not exhausting : I have seen very good wheat after it ; but it is certainly an exhausting crop. When fed, it is followed by barley or oats.

X. TURNIPS.

THE culture of this plant, may justly be esteemed the greatest improvement in English husbandry that has been established in the present century. In Suffolk, it has changed the face of the poorer soils, and rendered them more productive to the landlord, the tenant, and the public, than any other system of management, perhaps, that could be devised. The culture has been accurately described by a considerable and practical Suffolk farmer, in the *Annals of Agriculture*, from which I shall extract the material heads.

Soil.—The right soil for this root is a deep sand, such as has adhesion enough to make it of the value of from 5*s.* to 15*s.* an acre ; if the land is wet or stiff, such as yield good wheat crops, the culture may not be advantageous, especially if used, as it should be, as a preparation for barley : on such a soil, it would lessen

the crop; I should sooner prefer blowing sands of 3s. 6d.
and even 2s. 6d. per acre, which, when folded, and the
season happens to be wet, yield profitable crops; indeed,
such lands can be farmed no other way, for, if no turnips
are gained, no corn will be had ; and a mere sheep-walk
is then the only use that can be made of them. Where
a farmer has no proper soil for turnips, I think it would
be prudent to give up the winter feeding of more cattle
than his hay and straw will do for, unless he depends on
buying turnips, which may sometimes be advantageous,
and sometimes the contrary. I will just observe, that I
have a neighbour upon a wet soil, with about 30 score
very fine sheep, who, one year with another, cannot
grow 20 acres of turnips, but depends on buying of
his neighbours.

Preparation.—*Tillage.*—The first earth should be
given before Christmas, of a common staple depth ; and
if before the spring seed-time a second earth can be
given, it will be very useful ; for, if there should be any
spear-grass in the land, that pernicious weed is apt to
get too great a hold before barley-sowing is over ; immediately after the barley is in, the third earth should
be given ; this will be in May ; the fourth about the
second week in June ; and the fifth, or seed-earth, the
latter end of the same month, unless the soil is subject
to the mildew, in which case Old Midsummer will be
full soon enough. And let it be observed, that harrowing
with every earth is very necessary, for the surface should
always be kept in fine friable order, that the seed-weeds
may grow, otherwise, if that is omitted till the seed-
earth, they will then grow so powerfully as to smother
many of the young plants.

Manure.—For manure we depend on the fold or
farm-yard, usually both ; of farm-yard dung not less
than 12 loads should be spread on an acre, such as was

made the preceding winter, and once turned over. In respect to the length of dung, it should neither be long nor quite rotten; the best condition is, when it is in such a state that the labourers say, it will neither spit nor fork. I never tried any other manure for this root, except once an experiment on shell marl from Wood-bridge-side, called there *crag*. I had seen such great effects there from it, that, through curiosity, I brought a waggon load (back carriage) and tried it on a light turnip soil, and also on a good strong loam, and it was with great surprize I found that it did scarcely any good on either: the advantage was, if any thing, rather greater on the former, but not sufficient to induce me to carry it a single mile, had a crag-pit been found on the farm. When the dung for turnips is rather long, and ploughed in with the seed-earth, the seed should only be rolled in.

Sort.—The white round Norfolk is preferred; the red round, and the small green round, are known, but the tankard sorts are uncommon.

Seed.—The quantity of seed depends on the soil; upon a naturally good turnip sand a pint an acre, evenly delivered by a good hand, or sowing engine, will be enough; no soil demands so much seed as chalky land, when the chalk comes quite to the surface; upon such soil, a quarter of a peck an acre will seldom be too much; the reason of the difference is, that the fly is sure to attack the plants upon this soil much more voraciously and with greater certainty, than on any other. I do not, therefore, recommend this soil for turnips in general, but where it so happens, that one end, or one side of a piece of turnip land is of this sort (which is often the case) to be careful to lay the seed thick enough on those parts.

Having mentioned the sowing-engine, I should remark, that though it is, with care, a good tool, yet it is liable to have the holes stopped by two seeds sticking in them, so that if the seedsman is not very attentive, he may go some distance without a regular delivery.

Time of Sowing.—The season for sowing extends from New Midsummer to the end of July : this variation is necessary for two reasons ; first, because the land cannot be all manured to sow early : and, secondly, because the late sown will last much longer than the early ones, which are apt to mildew, and consequently more likely to be rotted by hard frosts afterwards, for which reason all farmers should take care to have some late sown ; I have had them from a sowing the first week in August, which proved the most profitable crop on my farm, owing to the frost killing others while these escaped.

Culture while growing.—Hoeing is so essential towards getting a good crop, that I am surprized a farmer should think of sowing them with any other view.* As soon as the plants are stout enough, they should be harrowed with a light harrow once in a place ; this assists the hoeing ; it is not easy to describe the state of the plants when they are ready for the hoe ; age will not discriminate, because the season will vary from three weeks to eight, and even nine, from the the time of sowing ; but a better rule is, to begin when the plants in general

* I have been informed, by gentlemen that I am sure would not deceive me, that there are parts of the kingdom where all hoeing is unknown; but certain I am, that if one of those farmers would come into this country, and compare our crops with his own, he would return with a determination to change his practice.

spread a circle of about four inches diameter. If any of the fields, after the hoeing begins, are getting too forward, which in a wet season is often the case, a second harrowing (the contrary way) may safely be given.

I find, by sowing my turnips at different seasons, that six men will hoe an hundred acres twice; but those who do not equally vary their seasons, must of course proportionally increase the number. The second hoeing is given about a fortnight or three weeks after the first, at half the expence, that is, 2s. an acre; this is sometimes omitted, but it answers exceedingly well.

Accidents.—It is necessary to say something on the failures that turnip crops are liable to, which are the fly, the mildew, the black canker, and to rotting from frost. I calculate that the frost destroys half the crop once in six or seven years; the fly not only destroys some crops entirely, but even when a second or third sowing yields something, it is gained at the expence of one or two ploughings, harrowings, and seed, when no tillage is wanting for the land: this may, on an average, be calculated to amount to the loss of a whole crop once in five or six years; the mildew is rather connected with the rot, and the black canker has not yet been so common with us, as to demand a particular calculation.

I would, for the above reasons, notwithstanding all the praise that is due to this most useful root, recommend to all sheep-masters, especially those with breeding flocks, not to trust singly to them. I have found very great advantage from having certain breadths of cole-seed, rye, and winter tares, sown early on the first stubbles that were cleared the preceding autumn; indeed, supposing no failures, it is absolutely necessary to have

some provision for the couples, by the time the lamb;
begin to feed, as it will put them on a great deal faste;
than the best turnips that can be given.

Application of the crop.—In regard to consuming the
crop, I would recommend feeding sheep with them upon
the land, as by far the best preparation for barley, provided the soil is true turnip-land, that is dry. The
benefit will, however, vary with the time of eating off,
for those that are eaten early in the winter, will not by
any means, give so good barley as those which are eaten
later, provided the plants do not run for blossom, for
then they exhaust the land, and the succeeding crop
suffers. Carting off is common, but the expence,
allowing for the damage done to the succeeding crop,
is too great, and I should never recommend the culture
with that view.

Preservation.—On this subject, the Rev. Mr. Orbell
Ray, of Tostoc, thus expresses himself:—" Your ad-
dress, requesting information of the measures pursued
for preserving turnips, and relieving the land from the
exhausting effects of their very rapid vegetation, during
the spring, determined me to send you the following
account of my treatment of this root, the advantages of
which I have experienced for many years, and which,
with a few variations, is, I believe, the general practice
of the Suffolk farmers. About the middle of February,
I began to draw my turnips, cutting off the tap-root at
the same time, and carried them to a pasture field, adjoining to my farm-yard, where they were unloaded,
and labourers employed to take the roots, one by one,
and set them upon the grass, in as upright and close a
manner as possible. I pursued this method through the
month of March, until I had collected above an hundred

loads; always availing myself of dry windy weather, when the tops are less brittle, and the roots in the cleanest state. The expence varies with the distance of carriage; the setting up about three halfpence per load of 40 bushels. The growth of the top is not much interrupted by the loss of the tap-root, and is an ample compensation for the waste of the bulb. I carried about two loads per day to nine bullocks which were confined in a farm-yard with suitable binns; and do not recollect that I ever experienced so profitable an expenditure of my turnips. The cattle did not leave the yard till the second week in May; when they were turned into a field of fresh luxuriant ray grass; I observed that the succulent quality of the turnip-top was more acceptable to their palates than the grass. And I am moreover convinced of this very important circumstance, that the quantity of nutritious food is increased by this method. The turnip-rooted cabbage appears to me to be highly deserving the attention of flock-masters. The singular mildness of the last winter rendered its resistance to the severity of seasons, an unnecessary quality. That it possesses this in a perfect manner, appears from the testimony of many who seem inclined to confine its excellence to this single point. If the preference given by animals to any sort of food, be a sure way of judging of its excellence, I had an opportunity of marking that predilection in the case of sheep, in a manner highly to the advantage of this root. I had a rood of these cabbages in my orchard, which I took up in the month of March, with little expectation, from their singular hardness, that any part except the top would be consumed. I repeatedly offered them to my bullocks; but after an unsuccessful effort to break them, they devoured the top and left them. I sliced them and offered them to my hogs, and they rejected them. I had, at that time, some wether hoggets feeding off turnips, with an allowance, by hurdles of a fresh piece, as occasion required. I directed my bailiff to carry a load of these cabbages every day to the sheep, spreading them upon the land already cleared. The sheep immediately gave them the preference ; and though they seemed to make very slow progress with their teeth, their perseverance, till all was consumed, convinced me that these cabbages rank high in the list of winter resources."

On this account I may remark, that a method somewhat different from the foregoing, has been practised with great success in the neighbourhood of Bury. The turnips, when running for blossom, have been topped and tailed in the field as they were pulled, carted home, and laid under cover for stall-fed bullocks, which have thriven perfectly well upon them throughout the whole month of May. The stalks have been ploughed in, and have proved a dressing for the barley crop ; which has been found good, but not equal to that which followed the turnips fed off by a flock of sheep.

The difficulty of feeding off turnip-rooted cabbages clean with sheep, has prevented many persons from cultivating that useful plant ; but Mr. Ray has found that it answers very well to cart them off the land for sheep ; and Mr. Le Blanc carts off the fragments left by his flock into his farm-yard, and finds himself well paid for the labour of doing it, by the sustenance they afford to his lean hogs, at a season when threshing is just over, and, consequently, hog's-meat scarce.

Value.—The value is exceedingly various, rising from 10*s.* to 50*s.* per acre, with many entire failures, that upon a general medium of all lands and all seasons, sink the product greatly. I do not conceive they can be estimated at more than 35*s.* an acre.

XI. CLOVER.

AFTER the culture of turnips, the introduction of this plant, as a preparation for wheat, must be esteemed the greatest of modern improvements upon arable lands. It has been cultivated in Suffolk largely beyond the memory of the oldest man ; and is, in every branch of its management, perfectly well understood by good farmers.

Preparation.—The due preparation for clover, consists chiefly in its right arrangement in the course of crops. It ought invariably to be sown, and is so by the best and most accurate husbandmen, with the first corn crop after a fallow one, such as turnips, &c. ; when two white corn crops are sown in succession, and clover with the second, it is an error, and doing an injustice both to the plant and the land. The land, after turnips are consumed, should be made fine for the barley and clover.

Seed.—Ten or twelve pounds an acre, are the common quantity ; but fifteen are better.

Feeding.—It is upon clover that the generality of farmers depend for the summer support of their teams ; which in common management graze it in the fields. Sheep, also, are fed on it with the greatest success.

Hay.—Clover hay, so valuable at London, is hardly saleable in Suffolk ; but it is sometimes made for home use. From one and an half to two tons per acre, on good land, are the usual produce.

For Soiling.—It is not commonly applied to this use, which is more generally seen in Hertfordshire. No plant, except lucerne, chicory, and tares, is better adapted to it.

For Seed.—Great quantities are seeded in Suffolk, it being a favourite, because sometimes a very profitable crop. But there are farmers that have been injured by repeating it too often.

Failure of Clover.—By repeating clover too often, as every fourth or fifth year, the lands in this county have become tired of it. Though the plant rises well, and has a good appearance in autumn, after the spring corn is removed, yet it dies in the winter ; and there is nothing more mischievous to the soil than half a plant of clover, as weeds are sure to supply its place.

On this subject, Mr. Williams, of Marlsford, writes me, " that it would be desirable and valuable, if the Board could point out an artificial grass as a substitute for clover; of which, from long use, the lands are wholly tired. Indeed, for some years, they have been obliged to use trefoil and ray-grass. This parish is critically situated at the junction of the two soils, the strong and light ; the substratum of one a clay, the other gravel and red sand ; and the remark of one, that he finds it necessary to sow more seed on the light soil than he did, gives some reason to apprehend that the lands may in time reject it also ; and this he knows to be the case with others on light soils. One more opulent, of concern more extensive, and of course more apt to experiment, was a few years ago informed by a Durham gentleman, that in that district a grass called cow-grass was well thought of and used ; understanding it to be very similar to clover, only that the stem is solid instead of tubical. He endeavoured in London, and the North, to procure the seed, but was disappointed by their sending clover-seed, and has not been able to come at it since."

Chicory is this great desideratum, and will answer on all soils: it may be managed in every respect like clover.

XII. TREFOIL.

SOMETIMES sown for a single year's crop, when intended for seed ; but more commonly substituted when the land is meant to rest two or three years, and ray grass usually mixed with it.

Seed.—The same quantity as of clover.

Application of the Crop.—When not seeded, generally fed with sheep.

Duration.—Trefoil, though a biennial crop, will, by seeding itself, last several years in the land. It is generally left two or three.

XIII. WHITE CLOVER

Is a very valuable plant for soils on which it will abide ; but it lasts a short time on wet ones. On sands and dry loams, it is excellent husbandry to add a few pounds to trefoil and ray grass. In some parts of the county, 10*l.* and 12*l.* per acre has been made of the seed.

XIV. SAINFOIN.

THIS noble plant, the most profitable of all others on the soils it affects, is much cultivated in Suffolk. In the sandy districts, especially the western, it is every where found, though not in the quantity that ought to be sown of it. The culture, however, has increased of late years.

Soil.—The peculiar land for this plant, is that which has chalk under it; but many dry sound loams and gravels will do for it. The Rev. Mr. Mosely, of Drinkston, has had it some years, and now in good perfection on a gravelly loam without any chalk ; and on soils that are dry, the crop is in proportion to the goodness of the land.

Preparation.—As sainfoin remains many years on the land, the preparation by good farmers, is that of a very complete turnip fallow. Two crops of that plant in succession, form the perfection of management.

Seed.—Four bushels an acre, alone, are the usual quantity, and the price generally a guinea the coomb of four bushels. Some have sown only three, and five or six pounds of clover with it, to form a crop the first year, as the sainfoin is weak till the second, but it is not a practice to be recommended.

Time of Sowing.—Generally sown with barley or oats, in the spring ; but Mr. Fairfax, of Bury, tried it in September, with rye, and with great success.

Mowing for Hay.—They find in Suffolk what has been observed elsewhere, and first publickly noted, I believe, by Tull, that there is a great convenience in being able to mow sainfoin almost with equal advantage either early or late, as the weather may suit. The hay, all the world knows to be excellent. It requires no other making than once turning the *swaths*.

Produce.—About two tons per acre on tolerable soils, may be estimated as the average crop : on poorer land, one and an half.

Crop of Seed.—The seed amounts to about four and an half, or five coombs per acre; and the straw is good fodder for cart-horses.

Value.—Two tons an acre, of hay, cannot be valued at less than 4*l.* used at home, and much more if sold. The seed is a guinea a coomb. The after-grass excellent for cows, calves, oxen, &c. and may be lightly fed by weaned lambs, without damage to the plant ; though it should never be hard fed by sheep, and especially in the spring. What immense advantages at so small an expence, seed alone excepted !

Duration.—About twelve or thirteen years may be considered as the mean duration in Suffolk.

Breaking up.—Paring and burning for turnips, is unquestionable the best mode of breaking up a sainfoin layer, but not practised here. It is usual to give one earth for oats.

SECT. V.—CROPS NOT COMMONLY CULTIVATED.

UNDER this head it is necessary to note the following articles of cultivation :

1. Hops,
2. Cabbages,
3. Carrots,
4. Lucerne,
5. Chicory,
6. Potatoes,
7. Hemp.

I. HOPS.

AT Stowmarket and its vicinity, there are about 200 acres of hops, which deserve mention, as an article which is not generally spread through the kingdom. The average produce, six cwt. at 5*l.* or 30*l.* per acre, and expence in labour only 7*l.*

Eighteen or twenty acres are grubbed up and turned to meadow within a few years, owing to bad times. The soil they plant on, is a black loose moor, on a gravelly bottom, very wet and boggy, lying on a dead level with the little river that runs by the town; the more boggy and loose it is, the better the hops thrive, especially if the gravel be within three feet; the neighbouring grounds rise in such a manner as to shelter them very well. Before planting, these morassy bottoms were coarse meadow, worth about 20*s.* an acre, and some much less. In preparing for hops, they form them into beds sixteen feet wide, by digging trenches about three feet wide, and two feet or two feet and an half

deep, the earth that comes out being spread upon the
beds, and the whole dug and levelled. Immediately
upon this, they, in March, form the holes six feet asunder every way, twelve inches diameter, and a spit deep,
consequently, there are three rows on each bed.—Into
each hole they put about half a peck of very rotten dung,
or rich compost, scatter earth upon it, and plant seven
sets in each, drawing earth enough to them afterwards
to form something of a hillock. Some persons in the
first years sow French beans, or beans, and plant cabbages; but not reckoned a good way by Mr. Rout, to
whose obliging communication I owe the particulars
from which I draw this account: in about two or three
weeks, but according to the season, they will be fit to
pole with old short poles, to which they tie all the shoots
or vines, and then keep the land clean by hoeing and
raking; at Midsummer they hill them. The produce
the first year will be three, four, and even five hundred
weight of hops per acre. After this they reckon them
as a common plantation, and manage accordingly.

Manure is not always given regularly; but amounts,
upon an average, to ten loads a year, value 5s. a load in
the plantation. They keep it till it would run through
a sieve, which they prefer to a more putrid state.

The labour of forming the beds for a new plantation,
by digging the drains, &c. amounts to 4l. an acre. That
of the annual work, picking excepted, is put out to the
men at 4l. an acre per annum, for which they dig, strip,
sack, clean drains, hoe, rake, hole, tie, &c.

Three poles are put to each hill, consequently, there
are 30 hundred (at 120) to the acre, at 24s. a hundred
delivered. They are generally of ash, and the length
they prefer is 24 feet. But in addition to this regular
poling, when a hop raises much above a pole, they set
another to take the shoot to prevent its falling, preventing

the circulation of air, and entangling with the poles of other hills.

A hop garden will last almost for ever, by renewing the hills that fail, to the amount of about a score annually; but it is reckoned better to grub up and new plant it every twenty or twenty-five years.

The only distempers to which they are subject, are the fly and honey-dew ; they know the blast and the red worm, but they are rare ; the latter chiefly on dry land. The lightning they think favourable, as it kills flies and lice.

Mr. Rout has raised a bank against the river about three feet high, to lessen the force of floods ; but does not wish to keep them entirely out : as he finds, that if the water comes in gently, and does not wash the earth away, it is rather beneficial. And he is clear, that if he was to let the river into his drains to a certain height, in very dry weather, it would be of service to the crop.

Relative to the expence of forming a new plantation, they had, many years ago, an idea that it cost 75*l.* an acre ; and Mr. Rout is clear that it cannot now be done under 100*l.* Among other articles, he named the following :

	£.	s.	d.
Preparing the beds, - - -	4	0	0
Manure, - - - -	2	10	0
Planting, - - - -	1	5	0
Sets, if bought, or the labour in raising and cutting, - - - -	1	15	0
Hoeing, raking, and moulding, -	0	10	0
Tying, - - -	0	10	0
Poling, - - - -	0	10	0
30 hundred poles, at 24*s.* - -	36	0	0
Shaving and knotting, 6*d.* per hundred,	0	15	0
Carrying to the ground, 2*s.* per hundred,	3	0	0

				£	s	d
Picking, drying, and bagging, 20s. per cwt. 4 cwt. }				4	0	0
Duty 10s.	-	-	-	2	0	0
Two bags,	-	-	-	0	10	0
Two years rent, 20s.	-	2	0	0		
Tythe,	-	2	0	0		
Rates, 7s. in the pound,	-	0	14	0		
				4	14	0
				£.61	19	0

The gross calculation, therefore, includes some articles not noticed here, or takes a considerable portion of the expence of building the kiln. The annual expence they reckon :

				£.	s.	d.
Rent, when the land is in order,	-	2	0	0		
Tythe,	-	-	-	1	0	0
Rate 7s.	-	-	-	0	14	0
Labour, by contract,	-	-	4	0	0	
Manure,	-	-	-	2	10	0
Picking, drying, and bagging, 20s. per cwt. 8 cwt. }				8	0	0
Duty 10s.	-	-	4	0	0	
Three bags, at 5s.	-	-	0	15	0	
Annual renewal of poles, suppose	-	4	4	0		
Interest of money	-	-	3	2	0	
Ditto kiln,	-	-	1	0	0	
				£.31	1	0

Mr. Rout's crops have varied from 1 cwt. which was the lowest he ever had, to 13 cwt. which he thinks was the greatest produce he ever received ; on an average, 8 cwt. and the mean price 4l. per cwt.

				£	s	d
Eight cwt. at 4l.	-	-	-	£32	0	0
Expences,	-	-	-	31	1	0

This account nearly resembles many others I have taken in different counties.

Another minute of the expence and produce of Stowmarket:

EXPENCES.

	£.	s.	d.
Stock, 25*l.* for poles, the interest of which -	1	5	0
Rent, · - - 2 0 0			
Tithe, - - - 1 0 0			
Rates, - - - 0 14 0			
	3	14	0
Rent total per annum, - -	4	19	0
Three load of poles, at 22*s.* annually -	3	6	0
Manure, four loads a year, - - -	0	16	0
Labour, - - - -	3	10	0
Carriage of poles, and sharpening, -	0	3	0
Picking 6 cwt. and drying and carting, 10*s.* } per cwt. - - -	3	0	0
Bagging, - - - -	0	3	0
Kiln, - - - -	0	5	0
Duty, at 1*d.* and 15 per cent, - -	3	4	0
Carting to Sturbitch fair, 1*s.* 6*d.* -	0	9	0
Fences, and draining, - -	0	10	0
	£.20	5	0
Interest of that sum, -	1	0	0

PRODUCE.

The average price, 5*l.*

	£.	s.	d.
Six cwt. at 5*l.* - - -	30	0	0
Expences, - -	21	5	0
Profit, - - -	8	15	0

	£.	s.	d.
Replenishing may be reckoned one-sixteenth annually, - - - }	2	0	0
Remains, - - -	6	15	0
Still to be deducted for a farm impoverished by the manure being taken for hops, }	2	0	0
Neat profit, - - - £.	4	15	0

Where they pick latest are the best hops next year.

The two hundred acres of hops in this neighbourhood, are spread in the following proportion, through these parishes :

In Stowmarket,	-	-	50 acres.
Combs,	-	- -	30
Newton,	-	- -	20
Dagworth,	-	- -	8
Finborough,	-	- -	20
One-House,	-	-	20
Shellan,	-	- -	5
Buxhall,	-	- -	15
Stow-Upland,	-	-	10
Haughley,	-	- -	8
			186, &c.

The expences of forming a new plantation, given at page 110, are now (1803) higher than they were when the former edition was printed.—The account may now be stated thus :

	£.	s.	d.
Preparing the beds, - - -	4	10	0
Manure, - - - -	3	0	0
Planting, &c. sets, - - -	1	15	0
Hoeing, &c. - - -	0	10	0
Tying, - - - -	0	10	0
Poling, - - -	0	10	0

	£.	s.	d.
30 hundred of poles, at 38s. - -	57	0	0
Shaving, &c. 6d. per hundred - -	0	15	0
Carrying to the ground, 2s. 4d. - -	3	10	0
Picking, drying, and bagging, 25s. per cwt. } 4 cwt. - - - -	5	0	0
Duty, 21s. 3d. per cwt. - -	4	5	0
Bags, - - - -	0	10	0

	£.	s.	d.			
Two years rent, - -	6	0	0			
Tythe, - - -	2	2	0			
Rates, - - -	2	2	0			
				10	4	0

	£.	s.	d.
	91	19	0

ANNUAL EXPENCE.

	£.	s.	d.
Rent, - - - -	3	0	0
Tythe, - - - -	1	1	0
Rates, - - - -	1	1	0
Labour, - - - -	4	0	0
Manure, - - - -	3	0	0
Picking, &c. 8 cwt. - - -	8	0	0
Duty 21s. 3d. - - -	8	10	0
Three bags, - - - -	0	15	0
Renewal of poles, - - -	5	0	0
Interest, - - - -	4	0	0
Ditto kiln, - - - -	1	0	0

	£.	s.	d.
	39	7	0

The produce or price must therefore have risen, or the cultivation would be abandoned.

II. CABBAGES.

THE culture of cabbages,* is another article which adds not inconsiderably to the agricultural merit of Suffolk. The most approved method is, to sow the seed in a very rich bed, early in the spring ; to prepare the land by four ploughings, the last of which buries an ample dunging, and forms the land a second time on three feet ridges, along the crown of which the plants are set in a rainy season, about Midsummer. They are kept clean by horse and hand hoeing. The produce rises to above thirty tons per acre. A gentleman near Bury carried this husbandry very near to perfection, and on so large a scale as to seventy acres in a year ; but he sowed more than half the seed in August, and pricked out at Michaelmas ; planting in the field the first heavy rains in May : his crops always great, and their use in fattening oxen distinguished.

On this subject, Mr. W. Green, of Bradfield, thus communicates :—" Sow the seed on a very rich bed the beginning of March ; one pound of seed on ten rods of ground for three acres ; the sort, drum-head, from its flat top, and as hard as a stone ; price of the seed 2s. 6d. per pound ; this better than the tallow-loaf, heavier and harder. The land where they are to be planted, to be

* Cabbages certainly produce, in some seasons, a great quantity of food, which is very excellent ; but if the season for pricking them out be very dry, they are attended with inconceivable trouble. They must all be watered by hand ; and even this will not always succeed. They cannot, therefore, be grown on a large scale by common farmers, and not at all on light soils. The subsequent crop of corn is materially injured by the growth of cabbages. *Note by J. R.*--I must think otherwise ; and have seen from forty to seventy acres on a farm every year or several years.—*A. Y.*

ploughed up at Michaelmas ; let it lie till spring ; plough four or five times ; dung before the last ploughing ; fifteen load (three horses) an acre dung, or twenty dung and earth ; plough it in on three feet ridges, the latter end of June ready to plant, that is to wait for rain. Much depends on having large stout plants ; the seed-bed is therefore drawn, when rain comes, all hands to work. The expence is about 3s. an acre planting. In about a month, plough between, by drawing the lands into baulks, and then shut up, after which hoe with hand-hoes ; but do not hand-hoe before shutting up, for by the hoe following the plough, the clods which roll on to the plants are easily removed ; another reason is, the space of land on which the plants stand after drawing out, being too narrow to bear a hoeing. Hand-hoeing thrice, each time 2s. an acre, 6s. in all. I have cultivated them six years, and never lost a crop but once for want of rain.

About three weeks after planting, taking the opportunity of rain, replant the vacancies from failure.

Begin to use them a month after Michaelmas for milch cows, and keep using them so till the end of March ; but they ought to be off the land the middle of that month, as they then shoot, and *draw* the land. Three good acres will do for my dairy of twenty cows, with straw and some hay ; but if absolutely no hay, then five acres of cabbages. For weanling calves they are most excellent. Turnips are apt to give them the garget, by which they very commonly die ; but in six years I have lost only one calf in above forty, by feeding them on cabbages, nor can any calves thrive better.

In fattening beasts, I find that a middling crop will fatten in proportion of three fourths of an acre for two beasts of 50 stone that have had the summer grass.

Hogs prefer them exceedingly to turnips ; of this I

have a striking instance the present season ; for having a field part under turnips and part cabbages, my sows, &c. have at various times this winter got into the field, and I do not think they have begun ten turnips in the whole field, but constantly got to the cabbages.

In regard to value, I have no positive data to calculate on, for it is not easy to keep accounts accurate enough to ascertain it, but in a general way, reckon a good acre worth from 4*l.* to 5*l.* ; or, more generally, to be double the value of turnips.

I am sensible, that this practice leaves the farmer without cabbage assistance for a month or six weeks in the spring ; part of this time may be supplied by drawing cabbages for about a fortnight, and the remainder by a practice which I have followed many years with success. It is, to keep about twenty acres of my meadow rouen (after-grass) till April, never turning any thing in from the scythe till that time. This is excellent for cows, for ewes and lambs, especially crones ; and I believe it will be found (it has proved so with me) that any piece of rouen that is worth 5*s.* at Michaelmas, will be worth 10*s.* in April, and so in other proportions ; but the value will depend a good deal on the weather ; in a dry time it goes very far, but in a wet season it is much spoiled. Let it also be remembered, that this grass is saved from a season (autumn) when food is exceeding plentiful, and of little value to those who do not sell.

EXPENCES OF AN ACRE OF CABBAGES.

	£.	s.	d.
Rent, - - - -	0	10	0
Tythe, - - -	0	1	6
Poor-rates, - - -	0	1	3
Five ploughings, - - - -	1	0	0
Two harrowings, - - - -	0	0	6

	£.	s.	d.
Manuring, - - - - -	2	0	0
Seed-bed seed, &c. - - -	0	1	6
Planting, . - - -	0	3	0
Deficiencies, - - -	0	0	6
Hand-hoeings, - - - -	0	4	0
Horse-work in hoeing, - - -	0	4	0
Cutting, and carting quarter of a mile, -	0	15	0
	£.5	1	3

This is giving the total expence of the manure to
the cabbages ; but if the advantage is divided, as it certainly is, then not more than 15s. should be laid to the
crop, which will make the total expence 3l. 16s. 3d.

The barley or oats that follow cabbages, have been
thought by some to be inferior to that which succeeds
turnips, but in my experience I have not found it so ;
for I have several times had turnips and cabbages in the
same field equally dunged, and the soil and management
the same, but I have found that that crop gives the best
barley which is taken off earliest."

The heavy part of Suffolk is the only district in
England, that, to my knowledge, has the culture of
cabbages established among common farmers, and is in
that respect curious. It may be remembered, that on
the publication of my *Northern Tower*, in 1770, in
which this culture was for the first time fully explained,
in the practice of many very spirited gentlemen in Yorkshire, &c. it gave rise to a sort of farming controversy,
concerning the utility of that cultivation, many persons
declaring it to be an unprofitable article, and that when
large crops were gained, they were found to be good for
little. I saw enough of it in that and some succeeding
journies, to be fully convinced of the great benefit of the

crop; and declared expressly in favour of it. To find a branch of cultivation fixed here, and to have found that it had established itself since the period of that publication, could not but make me solicitous to inquire into every circumstance that related to it.

They do not have recourse to either turnips or cabbages as a necessary article in any course of crops, but merely in subservience to the dairy. On the contrary, they are very generally of opinion, that the husbandry with any other view is disadvantageous. The wetness of their land is such that carting off these crops poaches the soil to an extreme, so that the barley which succeeds them is damaged considerably. This point goes to both; or rather, cabbages being much easier got at, and standing clear above the ground, have, in this respect, a considerable advantage. But the idea among them is very general, that cabbages exhaust the land much more than turnips. I saw few farmers who were not of this opinion; and as it is an interesting point in the cultivation, I made numerous inquiries; and repeated them with such attention, that I believe I brought away the truth very correctly.

The point, that they exhaust more than turnips, seemed upon the whole to be well ascertained; but some circumstances, even in this respect, deserve attention.

Several were inclined to attribute this fact to the common practice of cutting off the cabbages, and leaving the shanks and roots in the ground, which throw out sprouts, and *draw* the land when the effect of the crop ought entirely to have ceased. The remark is sensible, and some effect must certainly flow from the neglect of not extracting them root and all. It seemed to be a general opinion, that barley after turnips was better by two coombs an acre than after cabbages; but it was admitted as generally, that the cabbages were superior to the turnips in quantity and value of food, by more than the amount of two coombs of barley. The opinion most common is, that one acre of cabbages is equal to an acre and a half of turnips: several farmers assured me, that it was equal to two of turnips. Mr. Garneys of Kenton, that an acre of his cabbages has been better than any two of turnips he ever grew; and farther, that though his barley after turnips has had the longest straw, yet he thinks the quantity of corn little superior, and the sample of it not equal. I met with several whose cabbages were done, who thought turnips superior as a preparation for barley; but who wished very earnestly they had planted more cabbages.—Mr. Dove, of Euston-Hall, thought that barley after a summer fallow without dung, would give more, by three coombs an acre, than cabbage or turnip land would, though dunged for that crop. John Fairweather has had part of a field turnips and part cabbages, equally dunged for, and the barley as good after one as the other.

The Rev. Mr. Chevallier has cultivated them with attention for several years; and has found them so very convenient in frost and snow, that he would never be without some, were there no other reason for it. He lays forty loads an acre (three-horse ones) of dung for them; and has observed very generally that they give more, and better milk and butter, than turnips. I found him feeding four cows and seven hogs with them; and that they ate (besides some hay) two three-horse loads of cabbages a week, which was in the proportion of an acre lasting that stock eighteen weeks: if hay had not been given, the calculation of value would have been easy; but suppose the cows at 1s. a week, and 1s. more for the hogs, it is 5s. a week, and for the acre 4l. 10s. Thirteen fat wethers were also supplied with them, and except what they picked up in open weather on a bare grass field, had nothing else to eat ; these consumed one load a week ; this is the proportion of an acre (as I found in both cases, by counting the rows of an acre, and seeing the cart loaded) keeping 26 sheep 120 days, or more than 16 weeks, which, at four-pence a head per week, amounts to 6*l*. 18*s*. 8*d*. for the acre. I have no doubt but the value of an acre will be found very generally in this country to vibrate between 4*l*. 10*s*. and 7*l*.

It was universally agreed among all the farmers I conversed with, that cabbages and straw were by far better food for milch cows than any quantity of hay : if this point is well considered, it will be entirely decisive of the question of their merit, and put their exhausting qualities almost out of the inquiry. A circumstance that proves their goodness for butter, is, the veal carts which go regularly from this county to London, taking large quantities thither, which is sold and eaten as hay-butter as long as the cabbages remain sound ; but when they rot, there is an end of this laudable deceit, for by no management can the same thing be done with turnips.

The culture here given to this crop, nearly resembles that for turnips ; the land is ploughed three, four, and sometimes five times. In May, or the beginning of June, it is manured very amply with a compost of earth and dung: some cart them separate ; 30 or 40 loads of earth, and spread it, and then 20 of dung. But the quantities vary proportionably to the plenty the farmer has, and to the richness of the soil. The land is immediately ploughed on to the three feet ridge, and left for rain, when the planting is executed as fast as possible ; distance of the cabbages in the rows two feet. The seed is 3*s*. the pound, sown the latter end of February, on a seed-bed very well dunged at Michaelmas. A great object is to get fine large plants; their superiority to others in the end being very considerable.

I shall, upon the whole, observe, on the general features of the intelligence I received on this branch of culture, that as far as the experience of this country extends, they are more exhausting than turnips. In some instances it has not proved so; but in general it has. The degree of this exhausting quality is not well ascertained. It is said to amount to about two coombs an acre in the barley crop: but the *same authority* also ascertains, that the value of the crop exceeds that of turnips by *more* than this superiority of the turnip-land barley. I must confess, that this is not a point on which I am well satisfied, and wish much that Mr. Chevallier would experiment it with the most decisive care. He is so remarkably attentive and accurate in every thing, that if he would undertake it, I am sure the event could be depended on. Will he allow me to recommend to him to choose two acres (not more) one exactly on each side the gateway of the field where the trials are made; and to order a load of dung alternately to each, in order that the manure may be positively the same? Let the same tillage be given to both acres, and no difference allowed, but planting one with large cabbage plants, and sowing the other with turnip seed. Cultivate both, in respect to hoeing, in the completest manner possible. The cabbages to be thrice horse-hoed. In carting them off, as well as in carting the dung on, let each acre bear no more than its own poaching, which is easy when the gate is between both. Let them be consumed at the same time, which is essential to the experiment; and in order that this circumstance may not be troublesome, a load of turnips might be drawn for every load of cabbages used (roots to be taken as well as the rest) and set close to each other in the corner of a grass field, where they will keep well, should it be inconvenient to consume them at the same time with the cabbages. It would farther be necessary to weigh some rows of the cabbages, and some square rods of the turnips, to compare the produce of each ; and carefully to register the cattle supported by each, provided they were equally fed, but no hay to be used in the consumption of them. Such an experiment in such hands, would throw great light on this question ; and by a few repetitions, would absolutely ascertain it.

From what I observed, and I examined the land carefully under both crops in many fields, both must damage the land considerably. The carting them off poaches this soil in a dreadful manner ; but the turnips worst, because they are on steatches nearly flat, and the cabbages on three feet ridges, where the poaching is chiefly in the furrows : nor have I the least doubt, for this reason, of the great superiority attributed to summer-fallow barley.

In the consumption of these crops, the farmers of this district are in one instance exceedingly reprehensible.—There is no idea of confining cows to a farm-yard. They are universally open to two, three, or more pastures, so that the cattle have the barn-door at pleasure, and range over the fields almost where they please. The cabbages and turnips are scattered about on lands so wet, that the cattle at every step are up to the fet-lock, and they walk regularly backwards and forwards to the farm-yards, poaching in such a manner, that if the soil was not very fertile, it would never recover, but harden with the summer sun into knobs of steril mortar. I know not a more pernicious custom, nor one more ruinous to a farm. It is doubly so ; for the poaching not only injures the land, but the dung is at the same time lost, which, accumulated with the litter of the yard, would add greatly to the value of the dung-hill. Every farm is well furnished with neat-houses, where the cows have standings, and are tied up, from three feet to three feet six inches allowed to each ; but they are used only for suckling, milking, and baiting with hay.

1803. The culture of cabbages has declined in Suffolk, in the cow district, since the former edition of this work, more even than the number of cows has lessened. But they retain a scattered establishment in most parts of the county. I may, however, venture safely to assert that they do not receive the attention which is unquestionably due to their merit. I can attribute the decline to nothing but ill management. Men who will cut off the cabbages for expedition, and leave the stalks in the ground to exhaust it for no purpose whatever, must necessarily injure the following crop. While a man with ease draws up a cabbage by the roots, they have done little harm by exhaustion, but when it will not come up without difficulty, there are to be seen from every root millions of fine white fibres shooting out in every direction, from that moment they certainly exhaust considerably—but they should be removed to a grass field previously to this happening. There are no crops that do not require some appropriate attention ; and if it be not given, no wonder that full success is not the consequence.

III. CARROTS.

The culture of carrots in the *Sandlings*, or district within the line formed by Woodbridge, Saxmundham, and Orford, but extending to Leiston, is one of the most interesting objects to be met with in the agriculture of Britain. It appears from Norden's Surveyor's Dialogue, that carrots were commonly cultivated in this district two hundred years ago, which is a remarkable fact, and shews how extremely local such practices long remain, and what ages are necessary thoroughly to spread them. For many years (generally till about six or seven past), the principal object in the cultivation, was sending the carrots to London market by sea; but other parts of the kingdom having rivalled them in this supply, they have of late years been cultivated chiefly for feeding horses; and thus they now ascertain, by the common husbandry of a large district, that it will answer well to raise carrots for the mere object of the teams.

Not to enter very minutely into the cultivation, I shall note here, that the most approved method is, to leave a barley stubble (which followed turnips) through the winter, and about Lady-day to plough it by a double furrow as deep as may be, and to harrow in 5lbs. of seed per acre. About Whitsuntide they hoe for the first time, thrice in all, at the expence of 18s. an acre.* The produce on good land, of 10s. to 15s. an acre, 400 to 500 bushels, but sometimes 800 are gained; on poorer soils, less; even to 200 bushels. They are left in the field during winter, and taken up as wanted; by which means in severe winters, they suffer by the roots rotting,

* Near Bury, they never cost less than 25s. and sometimes 30s. per acre, for three hoeings.

unless well covered by snow. In feeding, they give
about eighty bushels a week to six horses, with plenty
of chaff, but no corn ; and, thus fed, they eat very little
hay. Some farmers, as the carrots are not so good to
Christmas as in the spring, give forty bushels, and four
of oats, a week, in the fore part of the winter ; but in
the spring eighty, and no corn. By long experience
they find, that horses are never in such condition as on
carrots, and will, on such food, go through all the work
of the season better than on any other in common use ;
fed only with corn and hay, even with a great allowance,
they would not be in néar such order. If oats and carrots are given at the same time, they leave the oats and
eat the carrots ; but for horses that are rode fast, they
are not equally proper. They begin to use them before
Christmas, and continue it sometimes till Whitsuntide ; those used in the latter part of the season being
taken up and housed, to have the land clear for sowing
barley.

There is scarcely an article of cultivation in any
county of England, that more demands attention than
this of carrots in Suffolk, for it is applicable to all sands,
and dry friable sandy loams, of which immense tracts
are found all over the kingdom, but this application of
them unknown. The subject is so important, that I
think it deserving the further attention of here adding
the notes I took in a journey, the chief object of which
was to ascertain the value and other circumstances of
the crop.

Carrots, Mr. Kirby has cultivated for some years ;
never less than four acres, and generally more. His
culture is to sow them broadcast after clean barley or
turnips, in order to lessen the difficulty and expence of
hoeing. He has tried them in drills fourteen inches
asunder, but they would not do, and is clear they cannot

be cultivated to advantage that way. He approves much of the crop by way of improving land, provided it is clean ; but if foul, cannot be cleaned from spear grass (couch) while under carrots.—He is decidedly of opinion, that they are not an exhausting crop ; for, supposing them to be sown on one part of a field, and turnips on the other, neither part dunged, the turnips fed on the land ; and the carrots carried off, as good barley will succeed the carrots as the turnips. But when he sows them after turnips, and then barley, he gets two coombs an acre more barley than would be yielded if that crop was to follow turnips without the carrots intervening. All which is, upon the whole, very much in favour of the culture. The expence and produce as follow, on poor sand of 5s. an acre :

	£.	s.	d.
One ploughing, deep, - -	0	7	0
Seed and sowing, - - -	0	4	6
Hoeing, - - - -	1	1	0
Taking up, 1s. a load of forty bushels topped, that is, on two hundred, -	0	5	0
Carting home, - - -	0	5	0
Rent, tythe, and rates, - - -	0	7	0
	£.2	9	6

Produce.—Two hundred bushels per acre ; but the value used at home not ascertained. The prime cost, at the above expence, is just three-pence a bushel.

Of all other applications, the most advantageous is that of fattening bullocks, in which he thinks them very profitable ; has given them to his flock, and the ewes gave much milk ; but the hardness of the root

made them crones too soon, by breaking their teeth,
on which account he left off that use of them. He kept
eighteen horses a whole winter on carrots, with the
common allowance of chaff and corn, substituting the
carrots for much of the hay.—That winter they ate only
twelve tons of hay, whereas, in other winters, they ate
forty tons ; the saving was therefore twenty-eight tons,
or above one ton and an half per horse. The allowance
of oats was two bushels per horse per week. They
were constantly worked, and *never were in so good
order*.

About Woodbridge, they have been in the habit of
selling the greatest part of their crops for the London
markets, from which it has been conjectured, that the
profit of the culture resulted not from the use of them
in feeding their horses, but from the sale alone.
Another point in dispute also arose concerning even
that application : it has been contended that the utility
is only when used in small quantities for the health, but
not for the entire support of a team. These points are
all of considerable importance ; for it is in vain to recommend a great extension of the culture, if we cannot
ascertain, beyond a shadow of doubt, the value of the
crop when it is produced. In all such disquisitions I
never, in one moment of my life, had any other object
than that of ascertaining the truth : and, therefore, my
only regret was, that of having viewed the country without sufficient attention ; the moment was now come
when I could repair that error, and, by a more minute
examination, satisfy myself on a point so interesting to
the national agriculture.

The first place we came to beyond Woodbridge in
this excursion, was Sutton, on the farm of Mr. Gerrard,
where we received the following information : that
they ploughed for them but once, which was a double

furrow as deep as possible ; but Mr. Gerrard put them in on one very deep furrow, the plough drawn by three stout horses. They sow five pounds of seed per acre about Lady-day. Begin to hoe at Whitsuntide ; three hoeings in all, at from 15s. to 18s. an acre. Ten loads (each 40 bushels topped clean) an acre upon good land, a middling crop ; but upon walk-land (poor sheep-walks ploughed up) less. I was assured, by the workmen that hoed them, that Mr. Gerrard had once twenty loads an acre. I viewed his field this year of ten acres, which the hoers guessed at six or seven load ; they appeared to the eye to be about half a full crop. Last year Mr. Gerrard had seventeen acres which produced nine loads an acre ; he sold an hundred loads clean roots to London, consequently he had fifty three of refuse ; that is, two-thirds saleable ; the standing price 1l. 1s. a load. Respecting the use for horses—they are sold not uncommonly for that use at 15s. a load. In feeding, they give two loads a week to six horses, with plenty of chaff, without any corn ; and thus fed, they will eat very little hay. The horses are never in such condition as on carrots, and will, upon such food, go through all the work of the season, being the best that can be given to a cart-horse ; but will not do for horses that are rode fast. They begin to feed with them before Christmas, and continue it sometimes till Whitsuntide ; those used in the latter part of the season being taken up and housed, to have the land clear for barley sowing. After carrots, they sow either pease or barley ; both do well. The ten acred piece I saw, was a blowing sand, which they said would produce probably about two quarters an acre of barley ; the course being, 1. carrots ; 2. barley ; 3. trefoil and ray grass, two or three years ; 4. pease, dibbled in with a frame ; 5. rye.

Advanced next to Shottisham, where I viewed Mrs.

Curtis's field of carrots, of eight acres, very fine. Sowed five pounds an acre on a double furrow ; hoed thrice at 18s. The product guessed at six or seven loads ; the average ten (each 40 bushels). More than half the crop is saleable. Last year many rotted on the ground ; for their practice is to take them up as wanted, except having a store for their own use before hand, in case of frost. In feeding, they give six horses a load a week, and a coomb of corn ; this, in the fore part of the winter, when they do not reckon them so good as they are in the spring ; then two loads a week, and no corn ; fed only on corn, even with a great allowance, they would not be in near such order ; if oats and carrots are given at the same time, they leave the oats and eat the carrots. Till lady-day they have straw, and after that hay, but eat very little of it, if they have a proper quantity of chaff with the carrots. They could be supported on chaff and carrots only, without either corn or hay, and would be as fat as moles.—The expression used was, " That the country could not be supported without them, for they had not hay for such a number of horses, if corn was the food, as in other countries." This is not the only application ; Mr. Linn fatted his bullocks last winter on them, late in the spring, to great profit. Others have tried it, and found that they do exceedingly well on them. Respecting the effect of the culture as a preparation for corn, they get very clean and good barley after them ; but carrots must not be sown in land that is foul. They choose a clean barley stabble ; if the land is very full of weeds they are too difficult to hoe.

Proceeded to Ramsholt, where, on repeating our inquiries concerning carrots, we found that they sow five pounds of seed, at 1s. a pound, upon a double furrow fourteen inches deep, worth ploughing 7s. an acre ; hoe thrice at 15*s*. to 21*s*. an acre. Take up at 14*d*. to 16*d*. a load, topping included. Mr. Weeden, on eighteen acres last year, had eight loads an acre nett for London, and two loads for himself; which crop is an average one. I viewed his field this year, it is nineteen acres, a regular and fine crop, without a weed to be seen. Barley is always sown after them, and is as good as that after turnips, though fed off, which they attribute to the depth of tillage bringing up old manure to the surface. In regard to the use in feeding horses, Mr. Weeden used carrots all last winter, and gave no oats, yet they never did better: five horses are allowed one load and a half (always forty bushels to the load) a week; they begin to feed after Christmas, and continue till the end of April: plenty of chaff is given, and the horses do not eat above half the hay they would do if they had no carrots. Mr. Weeden assured me, that if he was obliged to buy his horse provender, he would purchase refuse carrots at 15*s*. a load, rather than oats, unless the latter were so low as 7*s*. a coomb, then part carrots and part oats. Mr. Bennington, at the Dock, would rather buy carrots at 15*s*. a load, than oats at 10*s*. a coomb. Has found them also of admirable use for hogs.

Proceeded next to Alderton, where we found that Mr. Abblet had eight acres of carrots; but last year twenty. He thought that six horses should not have more than one load a week; one bushel per horse a day a proper allowance; but they keep the horses so fed in such health, that he thinks the saving of hay is not considerable. The food he should prefer would be both oats and carrots, one peck of oats to a bushel of roots. If he was forced to buy horse-food, he would prefer carrots at 15*s*. to oats at 10*s*. Culture and produce as before described.

Called next on Mr. Wimper, a gentleman-farmer of

the same place, very sensible and intelligent, who
obligingly informed us, that he generally gives oats to
his horses as well as carrots; not because they would
not do upon the roots and chaff, but because he has
usually a greater stock of horses, &c. than breadth of
carrots, and therefore he limits the use of them. If
forced to buy his horse-food, he would prefer refuse
carrots at 12s. to oats at 9s. Fortunately I put to this
gentleman a question which I had before omitted:
would you cultivate carrots if there was no sale for
them? To which he replied, that he would undoubtedly
have a few; as many as his consumption demanded;
not only for his horses, but for his weanling calves, to
whom he gave as many as they would eat; and also for
pigs, and sows with pigs, in which application they are
particularly useful. That calves must thrive greatly on
them, I have not a doubt, for I saw many young cattle,
oxen, and fat beasts of Mr. Wimper's breed, which
were in every respect very noble beasts, and proved, from
their age, how well they must have been fed when
young.—Respecting the produce, the average on land
of 10s. an acre, &c. is about nine or ten loads; and four
or five on walk-land. The total expence of an acre
about 3l. 3s.: if nine loads the crop, the prime cost is
7s. a load. Sometimes he has seen as good barley after
them, as after turnips fed, but it is not common.

From hence to Hollesley, where repeated our inquiries; they choose the best land they have, which is
the red soil; double furrow it fourteen inches deep;
sow five or six pounds of seed at Lady-day, the price
from 9d. to 18d.; hoe thrice at from 18s. to 21s. but if
the land is very clean 16s. The common price of taking
up, 1s. a load; sometimes up to 1s. 4d. topping included;
it is done with spades. On good land, average produce
ten or twelve loads; but on heath not more than five or

six. Three-fourths of the crop clean roots for sale. As good barley after them as after fed turnips, but not always: generally good. In the application of the crop not sold, they give them to horses with plenty of chaff, but in general no corn while on carrots ; nor will they eat so much hay as if they were fed on oats: calculate the saving at more than a fourth. Some farmers give as many carrots as they will eat ; but in general about two bushels each horse a day. The selling price 12s. to 14s. a load for the refuse roots.

Next we went to Capel St. Andrews. Mr. Gross's great farm of 2,700 acres ; of whom, repeating our inquiries, we found, that he had been accustomed to cultivate carrots, even to last year, but his crops were so eaten up by the innumerable number of hares which his landlord, Lord Archibal Hamilton, preserved, that he has determined to sow no more. In these cases, the tenant, doubtless, has his recompense in the rent, but the public has none. The profusion of game in this and another of his Lordship's farms, Buttley Abbey, Mr. Chandler's, which are together above 5000 acres, puts a barrier to good husbandry, and prevents one of the best articles of culture in the kingdom from spreading. It is not only the hares that do the mischief, but their preservation nurses up a breed of rabbits which add to the evil. The reflection I have added is my own, and not the farmer's, who seemed very well inclined to second his landlord's wishes.

When Mr. Gross did use carrots, he gave his horses each one bushel a day with chaff, but no oats ; and assured me, that he had much rather feed on carrots than on oats; also, that they save more than half the hay ; he has known his horses, after feeding on this root, refuse their hay entirely.

The culture of carrots, was, some years ago, more

common about Orford than at present, supposed to be owing to the great improvements in the sands near the Woodbridge river, which have rivalled them in the supply of the London market.

About Leiston are many carrots : few farmers of any consideration but have ten or twelve' acres every year ; they have, however, a bad custom of continuing them on the same field for four or five years. The carrot culture improves the soil so much, that two years are the most they should be continued, by which means the larger track receives the benefit, I have no doubt, from the situation of their consuming all themselves.

Passed over some poor land, commons, and uninteresting husbandry, till we came to Wantesden ; where, on making farther inquiries, we found that Mr. Curteen, of the Hall, has four acres of CARROTS FOR HIS OWN CONSUMPTION ONLY, giving them to his horses. Mr. Simpson was, for many years, on the same farm, and constantly in the same practice ; always had a crop for his horses, and neither he nor Mr. Curteen ever sold a load to London. Here then we have found this clear fact : the intelligence was from a labourer that worked with Mr. Curteen ; it was soon after confirmed by a neighbouring farmer, who said there were some others in the practice as well as Mr. Curteen.

It will not be improper here to review the several particulars we have gained. Without recurring to every article of the culture, it will be sufficient to touch only upon the principal objects which have been the subject of doubt and disquisition.

At Sutton, six horses two loads a week ; no corn ; and eat little hay.

At Shottisham, six horses one load a week, with corn ;

in the spring two loads, without corn; eat little hay.

At Ramsholt, six horses seventy-two bushels a week; no oats; and half the hay saved.

At Alderton, six horses forty-two bushels a week; oats given; and saving of hay not considerable.

At Alderton, oats given because not carrots enough.

At Hollesley, six horses two loads a week; no corn; more than a fourth of the hay saved.

At Capel, six horses one load a week; no corn; save more than half the hay.

Upon reviewing these circumstances, it appears that two loads a week are a very large allowance, probably more than are necessary; seeing that with seventy-two bushels at one place, which is one and three quarters, and one load at another, all the corn is saved; let us therefore decide, that when six horses eat eighty bushels of carrots a week, which is thirteen bushels a week for one horse, they want no corn whatever, and will eat only half the hay of corn-fed ones. This will enable us to ascertain the value tolerably, though not exactly, because we do not know what would be the fair allowance of oats to balance such feeding with carrots. The whole turn of the intelligence ran upon the vast superiority of condition in which horses are kept by carrots, to that which is the result of corn-feeding, for this evident reason, carrots are given nearly, if not quite, in as large quantities as the horses will eat; but oats are never given in such a manner, they are always portioned out in an allowance very far short of such plenty. A quarter and an half of oats, would, I am persuaded, from the general turn of every man's conversation, be inferior to two loads of carrots; this at 20s. is 1l. 10s.; there is to be added the saving of half the hay, which may be called ten pounds per horse a day, or seventy pounds per week, which at 50s. a ton, is 1s. 4d. per horse, and 8s. for six ; which, added to 1l. 10s. for corn, makes in all 1l. 18s. against eighty bushels, or 19s. a load : and that this is a moderate calculation, appears from the decided preference given by several farmers in favour of carrots at 15s. a load, against oats at 20s. a quarter, not reckoning the carrots by any arbitrary estimation, but supposing themselves forced to *buy* the one or the other.

The prime cost is calculated at 7s. a load ; and that this is fair, will appear by the following articles :

	£.	s.	d.
Rent, tythe, and poor-rates, - -	0	15	0
Ploughing, - - - -	0	7	0
Harrowing, &c. - - - -	0	1	0
Seed, and sowing, - - -	0	6	0
Hoeing, - - - -	0	18	0
Taking up ten loads, at 1s. 2d. - -	0	11	8
	£.2	18	8

The tenth of which is 5s. 10d. or per bushel one penny three farthings ; call it, however, 2d. per bushel, or 6s. 8d. per load ; and if, to square with one article of intelligence, it is made 7s. it will not amount to two-pence farthing the bushel. Here, therefore, another view opens upon us, which is the farmer's *profit* : the carrots are worth in feeding his team 15s. but they cost him only 7s. he has therefore the advantage of 8s. a load as the grower, on all his horses consume, and on an average 4l. an acre.

Another way by which a friend made his calculation, was this :

At one load and a half of carrots, nine loads a moderate acre, lasts six horses six weeks (N. B. He was

inclined to think, from the intelligence, that one load
and an half ought to be esteemed the proper quantity)
and save six quarters of oats, which, at 20s. is

	£.6	0	0
Three and a half cwt. of hay a week saved : }			
21 cwt. at 2s. 6d. - - -	2	12	6
	8	12	6
The carrots may cost - -	3	3	0
Farmer's profit per acre, by feeding horses,	£5	9	6

It admits of various calculations ; but view it in any
light you please, the result is nearly, though not exactly,
the same.

Two facts result most clearly from this intelligence ;
that horses will do upon them as well as upon oats ; and
that this application will not only pay the charges of
culture, but leave a *profit*, nearly as great as the *gross
produce* of a common crop of wheat. No wonder, therefore, the farmers cultivate them for their own use alone,
without any view to a sale.

It should farther be remarked, that this result takes
place, not in a district where the horses are poor mean
animals, that betray a want of good food, but, on the
contrary, amongst the most useful teams that are to be
found in England ; and that these teams are fattest, and
in the highest condition, when they are supported by
carrots. No greater proof of the excellency of the food
can be wished for, than the horses going through the
barley-sowing upon it, and the root doing better at that
season of hard labour than earlier in the winter ; this
seems to speak the heartiness, as well as wholesomeness
of the food. One conclusion very naturally arises from
this part of the intelligence, that the crop, or a considerable part of it, ought to be taken up in autumn, and

packed in a barn ; in which they would much sooner
loose their juciness, and acquire that more withered
state, in which they are found to yield the best nou-
rishment.

The next circumstance to be attended to, is the
advantage of the plant as a preparation for corn ; all the
preceding minutes agree, that the barley after them is
good and clean ; several persons were inclined to think
it equal to that after turnips fed on the ground ; but the
fair result is evidently, that if carrots were so fed, the
barley would be much superior ; of this the intelligence
will not permit us to doubt. It is, however, fair to
observe, that they one and all declare for putting them
in upon clean land, and in this course, 1. turnips ;
2. barley ; 3. carrots ; 4. barley, &c. ; from which it
appears, that on these sandy soils they are not to be
depended upon, for cleaning them when foul with
couch.

I cannot conclude the subject, without earnestly calling on all persons who have sands, or light sandy loams,
to determine to emancipate themselves from the chains
in which prejudice, or indolence, have bound them. To
cultivate this admirable root largely and vigorously ; to
give it the best soil they have ; to plough very deep ; to
hoe with great spirit ; and to banish corn from their
stables, as a mere luxury and barren expence that ought
to be extirpated ; an effect that flows very fairly, from
the preference which the instinct of the four-footed
inhabitant generally gives to carrots.

1803.—In the detail of fresh intelligence on other
objects which is inserted in the appendix, there are some
further articles respecting carrots. A fact extremely
interesting is the very great extension of the culture
since the former edition of these papers ; they have
extended themselves above twenty miles, to near Loestoff;

and this extension is for home consumption, none being sent thence to London. By degrees I doubt not but they will travel to Yarmouth and into Norfolk, where there are great tracts of country very well adapted to the culture.

———

IV. POTATOES.

THIS root has not been cultivated in Suffolk till within a few years. I have had them on a large scale; and Mr. Mure, of Saxham, on a still larger; but in general they are not much attended to; not so much as they ought to be by cottagers. I have, however, the satisfaction of observing, that they increase, and promise to be much better established.

Mr. Nesfield, of Wickhambrook, writes—" The recommendation of the culture of potatoes from the Board of Agriculture, has afforded me particular pleasure; the more, perhaps, for its coincidence with the advice which I have been earnestly pressing upon my parishioners for near forty years, with as little effect as if it had been delivered from the pulpit. They begin, however, I think, to listen to it now with some degree of attention: and, were it pursued in this part of the country with the spirit which its importance deserves (the plan of which I have repeatedly pointed out), I have no doubt but in a very short time the parish rates would be reduced lower than they have been for the last fifty years. I would observe, however, that unless potatoes are universally cultivated by every farmer in a quantity proportioned to the number of his labourers, from a rood, suppose, to an acre, (and there is, I believe, hardly any farm in any part of this kingdom, which will not afford such a quantity of suitable land, upon which, with proper management, they might be planted any number of years in succession) ; until this, I say, is done, the culture of them, even in large patches here and there, will not prove of any *general* utility."

1803.—This branch of cultivation has spread largely into every part of the county ; the two scarcities operated powerfully in this respect, so that I question whether there be not at present ten times as many acres as there were ten years ago.

V. LUCERNE,

NOT cultivated, to my knowledge, by any farmers ; but some gentlemen have it in small pieces. I have had many acres ; enough to prove it an object deserving great attention.

1803.—The Earl of Albemarle has tried it on a large scale at Elden ; but the experiment is not of sufficient standing yet to ascertain how far it will succeed on a rather poor sand.

VI. CHICORY.

THIS plant I introduced some years ago into the husbandry of England. I have had as far as ninety acres of it, and cultivate it still very largely for sheep. The accounts I have given of it in the Annals of Agriculture, are ample. The reader will allow me to refer him to that work, for a variety of information on the subject.

VII. HEMP.

THE district of country in which this article of cultivation is chiefly found, extends from Eye to Beccles, spreading to the breadth of about ten miles, which oblong of country may be considered as its head-quarters.

It is in the hands of both farmers and cottagers; but it is very rare to see more than five or six acres in the occupation of any one man. With cottagers, the more common method is, to sow it every year on the same land : there is a piece at Hoxne, which has been under this crop for seventy successive years. The soil preferred, is, what is called in the district, *mixed land*, that is, sandy loam, moist and putrid, but without being stiff or tenacious; in one word, the best land the country contains; and does well, as may be supposed, on old meadow, and low bottoms near rivers. They manure for it with great attention; so that it may be taken as a maxim, that hemp is not often sown without this preparation : of dung and moulds, twenty-five three-horse loads per acre; of dung alone, sixteen loads. This is done directly after wheat sowing is finished.

The tillage consists in three earths, with harrowing sufficient to make the soil perfectly fine; and it is laid flat, with as few furrows as possible.

Time of sowing, from the middle to the end of April; but will bear being sown all May. It is often found, that the early sown yields hemp of the best quality.

Quantity of seed, eleven pecks per acre, at the price of one shilling to two shillings a peck, generally from sixteen to eighteen-pence. Much is brought from Downham, and the fens; the seeded hemp is not so good by eighteen-pence or two shillings the stone.

No weeding is ever given to it, the hemp destroying every other plant.

It is pulled thirteen or fourteen weeks after sowing ; the wetter the season the longer it stands ; and it bears a dry year better than a wet one ; they make no distinction in pulling, between the male and female ; or femble and seed hemp, as denominated in some places. In the Cambridgeshire fens they are frequently separated, which may arise from their hemp being coarser, and the stalk larger. The price of pulling is one shilling a peck of the seed sown, or eleven shillings an acre, and beer ; but if it comes in harvest, the expence is higher. It is tied up in small bundles called *baits*.

It is always water-*retted* ;* clay pits preferred to any running water, and cleaned out once in seven or eight years. An acre of three small waggon loads are laid in one *bed*. They will water five times in the same hole ; but it is thought by some too much. If necessary to wait, they pull as the hole is ready, not choosing to leave it on the land after being pulled.

It is generally four days in the water, if the weather is warm, if not, five ; but they examine and judge by feeling it. The expence is twelve to fifteen shillings an acre.

The grassing requires about five weeks ; and if there are showers, constantly turned thrice a week ; if not,

---

* Generally ; but in a circle of about six miles round Thilnetham, the greater part is never put into the water at all, but is dew-retted which is done by laying it on pasture ground, for from three to six weeks, according to the season, and turned five or six times. This, process costs about one shilling per stone per acre, including pulling, spreading, turning, and getting up ; and the hemp at market is not worth so much by two shillings per stone, as that which hath been water-retted, and therefore probably the custom of dew-retting is only followed to any considerable degree where there are not pits sufficient to water-ret what grows in a district —*Note by a Correspondent of the Board.* Thilnetham is in Norfolk. *A. Y.*

twice a week. This is always on grass land or layers. It is done by women; the expence ten shillings an acre. It is then tied up in large bundles of eight or ten *baits*, and carted home to a barn or house to break directly.

Breaking is done by the stone, at one shilling. There are many people in the district who do it, and earn fifteen or sixteen-pence a day, and beer. The offal is called hemp *sheaves*, makes good fuel, and sells at twopence a stone.

It is then marketable, and sold by sample at Dis, Harling, Bungay, &c. price 5s. 6d. to 8s. a stone; generally 7s. 6d. In 1795, 10s. In 1801, 14s.

The buyer heckles it, which is done at 1s. 6d. a stone; he makes it into two or three sorts: *long strike*, *short strike*, and *pull tow*. Women buy it and spin it into yarn, which they carry to market, and sell at prices proportioned to the fineness. This the weaver buys, who converts it into cloth, which is sold at market also. The spinners earn better and more steady wages than by wool: a common hand will do two skains a day, three of which are a clue, at nine-pence; consequently she earns six-pence a day; and will look to her family and do half a clue.—Nor is the trade, like wool, subject to great depressions, there being always more work than hands; the consequence of a brisk demand. They begin to spin at four or five years old: it is not so difficult to spin hemp as wool; but best to learn with the *rock*. For very fine yarn, one shilling a clue is paid for spinning. About Hoxne, the yarn is half whitened before weaving; but in other places, weave it brown, which is reckoned better. The weavers of fine cloth earn 16s. or 18s. a week, middling 10s.

The fabrics wrought in this county from their own hemp, have great merit. They make it to 3s. 6d. and

4s. 6d. a yard, yard wide, for shirts: and I was shewn sheets and table linen, now quite good, after twenty years wear. Huckabacks, for table linen, 13d. to 7s. a yard, ell wide.

The produce of an acre may, on an average, be reckoned forty-five stone, at 7s. 6d. Some crops rise to fifty-five, and even more ; and there are bad ones so low as twenty-five. If sold on the ground as it stands, generalty 1s. a rod, or 8l. an acre.

The account of an acre may be thus estimated:

EXPENCES.

	£.	s.	d.
Rent, tythe, and rates, - - -	1	10	0
Manure, 25 loads, at 1s. 6d. - -	1	17	6
Three earths, at 4d. harrow included, -	0	12	0
Seed, - - - - - -	0	16	6
Sowing, - - - - - -	0	0	6
Pulling, - - - - - -	0	12	10
Watering, - - - - -	0	12	0
Grassing, - - - - -	0	10	0
Breaking, - - - - -	2	12	6
Carriage and delivery, - - -	0	5	0
	£. 9	8	10

PRODUCE.

	£.	s.	d.
Forty-five stone, at 7s. 6d. - -	£. 16	17	6
Expences, - - - - -	9	8	10
Profit, - - - -	£. 7	8	8

All accounts of this sort must be received with due allowances for many variations. The preceding was taken at Hoxne; but at Beccles (where, however, the quantity cultivated is not equally great) a very different mode of calculation takes place, and rent is *valued*.

EXPENCE.

	£.	s.	d.
Rent, tythe, and rates, - - -	4	0	0
Manure, - - - - -	3	0	0
Tillage, - - - - -	1	4	0
Seed, twelve pecks, - - - -	1	16	0
Pulling, - - - - -	0	19	0
Watering, - - - - -	0	12	0
Grassing, - - - - -	0	10	0
Breaking, - - - - -	2	10	0
	£. 14	11	0

PRODUCE.

	£.	s.	d.
Fifty stone, at 8s. - - -	£. 20	0	0
Expences, - - - - -	14	11	0
Profit, - - - -	£. 5	9	0

The common method is to sow turnips on the land immediately after the hemp is cleared: this is for producing, among the little occupiers, some food for a cow and the family. With good management, one ploughing and one hoeing will carry them to the value of 30s. But an evil arising from the practice is, that the land must for the next crop, be mucked in the spring, when carting does more damage. When corn is sown after the hemp, it is wheat; and these are the best crops in the country, as nothing is esteemed to clean land like this plant. After the wheat, barley or oats, and this great also.

Finding the profit so great, I demanded why the culture did not increase rapidly ? I was answered, that its coming in the midst of harvest was embarrassing, and that the attention it demanded in every stage of its progress was great ; being liable to be spoiled if the utmost care was not perpetual.

It is considered, and with great justice, throughout the district, to be of infinite consequence to the country ; and especially to the poor, who are entirely supported by it, and are now earning six-pence a day by spinning, with more ease than three-pence is gained in the other side of the county by wool.

The culture has increased considerably in the last ten years.

A manufacturer at Stowmarket, thus communicates to me on this subject, from whose account it appears that there are variations :—" Hemp may be grown, with success, on the same land, many years, by manuring annually. The quantity of seed usually sown, is from nine to twelve pecks per acre; varying with the strength of the soil, and the custom of the country. In those places where the finest and best hemps are grown, twelve pecks is a common quantity.

" The soil and season make a very material difference in the produce and quality. An acre will produce from 25 to 60 stone ; an average crop may be estimated about 36 or 38.

" Hemp, when left for seed, is seldom water-retted, from the additional trouble and expence ; but I am of opinion, it would be better if so done. It is generally stacked and covered during the winter, and is spread upon meadow-land in January or February. If the season suits (particularly if covered with snow) it will come to a good colour, and make strong coarse cloths. It is much inferior to hemp pulled in proper time, and water-retted.

" The custom of some places is to dew-ret their hemp ; that is, to spread it on meadow-land as soon as pulled, and turn it frequently ; but this is a very bad method of retting it ; the bark will not come off completely—it therefore requires more violent means of bleaching the yarn, and consequently diminishes the strength.   It is likewise much sooner injured in rainy seasons than hemp water-retted : water-retting is performed by binding the hemp in small bunches, with the under hemp, when pulled, and as soon as may be, placed in rows crossing each other in the water, and immersed. Stagnant water is deemed the best: it requires four, five, or six days steeping, till the outside coat easily rubs off, and is then spread on meadow-land, and turned frequently until finished   The same water will not be proper for receiving hemp more than three times in a season, and the first water always produces the best colour, in the least time.

" But I do not pretend to give exact directions for managing hemp ; it can only be acquired by practice. When the hemp is retted, it is bound up in sheaves or large bunches, and with a machine called a brake, the cambuck is broken in pieces, and with a swingle is cleared from the small remaining pieces of the cambuck, and then bound up in stones. In Suffolk 14½ pounds of hemp are deemed a stone. The hemp which breaks off in the operation, and called shorts, is bound up by itself, and is about half the value of the long hemp.

" The price of breaking hemp varies with the length, and the ease or difficulty with which the cambuck separates from it : from 12*d.* to 18*d.* or 20*d.* is paid :

12*d.* and 14*d.* are the most common prices. The refuse is only fit for burning, and is sold from one penny to two-pence per sack.

" I have been informed that there are mills erected for breaking flax ; and as the mode of breaking is similar, I imagine they might be applied to hemp. In some parts of the country, where much hemp is grown, this might prove a considerable saving. But as hemp is very bulky before it is broken, and small quantities only are grown in each village, in general, I fear it would not answer the expence to erect many of them.

" When the hemp is broken it is fit for market, and is purchased by hecklers. Dis, Harleston, and Hales-worth, are considerable markets for hemp ; but the greatest quantity is sold to neighbouring hecklers, with-out carrying to market.

" The prices vary very much : dew-ret hemp sells from 1*s.* to 18*d.* or 2*s.* lower than water-ret, The pre-sent price of the best water-ret is about 8*s.* 6*d.* per stone: this price is very high. Dew-ret hemp is proper for coarse yarns only : and if that were made from water-retted hemp, it would be stronger and of a better colour.

" The first operation of the heckler, is bunching or beating the hemp ; this was formerly, and is still, in some places, done by hand ; but in Suffolk, is now always done by a mill, which lifts up two, and some-times three heavy beaters alternately, that play upon the hemp, while it is turned round by a man or boy to receive the beating regularly. This mill is sometimes worked by a horse, and sometimes by water ; but I think a machine might be contrived to save the expence of either. In this I may be mistaken.

" The time requisite for beating the hemp, varies according to the quality of it, and the purposes it is intended for ; the finer the tow is intended to be, the more beating the hemp requires. When bunched, it is dressed or combed by drawing it through heckles, resembling wool-combers tools, only fixed. The prices paid the heckler vary in different places, and with the different degrees of fineness to which it is dressed; from three farthings to two-pence per pound is paid ; and the earnings are from 15*d*. or 16*d*. to 2*s*. per day.

" In the hemp trade there are no fixed rules for combing, as in the wool trade. The same hemp is dressed finer or coarser, to suit the demands of the purchasers. It is sometimes divided into two or three sorts of tow, and sometimes the whole is worked together for one sort.—The prices of tow vary, from about 6*d*. to 18*d*. per pound.

" The heckler either sells the tow to spinners and to weavers, or puts it out to spin himself, and sells the yarn to the weavers. The prices of spinning vary with the fineness of the yarn :

		d.	*d.*
1 clue from a pound is worth spinning, about		7 or	$6\frac{1}{2}$
$1\frac{1}{2}$ clue from a pound, - - -		$8\frac{1}{2}$ or	8
2 clues from a pound, - - -		$9\frac{1}{2}$ or	9
$2\frac{1}{2}$ clues from a pound, - - -		$10\frac{1}{2}$ or	10
3 clues from a pound, - - -		12	

" The spinners who buy the tow, sell their yarn to neighbouring weavers, or at the nearest market. The yarn is reeled, in many places :—2 yards, 1 thread ; 40 threads, 1 lea ; 20 leas, 1 skain ; 3 skains, 1 clue, 4800 yards : in others—3 yards, 1 thread ; 40 threads, 1 lea ; 20 leas, 1 skain ; 2 skains, 1 clue, 4800 yards. The former is the most convenient method for the bleacher and weaver.

" Weavers, in general, purchase their yarn from spinners in the neighbourhood, or at markets, and deliver it to the whitester, as he is sommonly called, who returns it, bleached, to the weaver ; receiving 20 or 21 for bleaching 120 clues.

" Bleaching the yarn is performed by laying it in large tubs, covered with thick cloths, upon which ashes are placed ; and pouring hot water daily through it, turning the yarn frequently, until the bark comes off. It is then rendered whiter, by spreading it on poles in the air. This is a difficult part of the business ; the art consisting in procuring the best colour with the least diminution of strength.

" Weaving is, in general, conducted in the manner I have stated ; that is, by purchasing the yarn at market, and after bleaching, making it into cloth of various degrees of fineness and breadth. The breadths are half-ell ; three quarters wide ; three quarters and a nail ; seven-eighths and yard-wide sheeting ; yard-wide ; seven-yards one-eighth wide ; and ell-wide. Prices from 10*d.* per yard, half-ell-wide, to 4*s.* or 4*s.* 6*d.* ell-wide.

" Exceeding good huckaback is also made from hemp, for towels and common table-cloths. The low priced hemps are a general wear for husbandmen, servants, and labouring manufacturers ; the sorts from 18*d.* to 2*s.* per yard, are the usual wear of farmers and tradesmen ; the finer sorts, seven-eighths wide, from 2*s.* 6*d.* to 3*s.* 6*d.* per yard, are preferred by many gentlemen, for strength and warmth, to other linen.

" The largest quantity of hemp is sold as it comes from the loom, and bleached by the purchasers ; but some quantity is bleached, ready for weaving, either by the weaver or by a whitester : this is done by boiling it in lye (made from ashes), and frequently spreading it on the grass till it is white.

"Many weavers vend their cloths entirely by retail, in their neighbourhood; others to shopkeepers, principally in the counties of Norfolk and Suffolk, and in part of Essex; and others at Dis, where there is a hall for the sale of hemp cloth, once a week; and at Norwich, where there is a street occupied by weavers, from different parts of the country, who have shops in it.

"The earnings of the journeyman weaver vary considerably, from the season; frosty, windy, and very dry weather being unfavourable; and they vary, also, from the great difference in skill, and the quality of the materials to work upon: they may earn from about 1s. to 1s. 6d. per day; in extra cases, more.

"I think, Sir, you will perceive, from the statement I have given of the manner in which the hemp trade is conducted, the difficulty of ascertaining, with any certainty, the profits arising from an acre of hemp, converted into cloth.

"I will now, agreeably to your request, proceed to mention a few hints, which may tend to the improvement and extension of the trade:

"Although I have stated hemp, in the process of manufacturing, to pass through the hands of the breaker, heckler, spinner, whitester, weaver, and bleacher of cloth, yet many of these different operations are frequently carried on under the direction of the same person. Some weavers bleach their own yarn and cloth; others their cloth only: others heckle their tow, and put it out to spinners; others buy the tow, and put it out; and a few carry on the whole of the trade themselves. This latter is the plan which I pursue, the advantages appearing to me considerable.

" When the trade is conducted by different persons,
their interests often clash : by under-retting the hemp,
the grower increases the weight ; by slightly beating it,
the heckler increases the quantity of tow, but leaves it
fuller of bark ; by drawing out the thread beyond the
staple, the spinner increases the quantity of yarn, but
injures the quality ; by forcing the bleaching, the
whitester increases his profit, but diminishes the strength
of the yarn. The whole should, therefore, be checked
and regulated by the weaver, with a view to his
ultimate profit ; which, in the hemp trade, should
ever be deemed inseparable from the strength of his
cloths.

" It appears to me, that in manufacturing cloth, in
general, in Ireland, Scotland, and elsewhere, strength
has been sacrificed to fineness and colour.—Flax is
pulled too early (being finest before it acquires its full
strength), and drawn beyond its staple, to render the
cloth finer, at the price ; and although there never was
a time when the linen manufacture excelled so much in
colour and in fineness, yet the want of strength was
never so universally complained of.

" The hemp manufacture cannot rival that of flax, in
fineness ; nor is it desirable :—in colour, it is by no
means deficient, and possesses this advantage over Irish
and all other linens, that its colour improves in wear-
ing, while theirs declines. But the article in which
English hemp, properly manufactured, stands unrivalled,
is the strength ;—flax will not bear the least comparison
with it, in this respect ; and I can assert, from experience, that it is far superior in strength to Russian—the
strongest known hemp next to the English.—Every regulation made in the trade should, therefore, be done with a
view to improve it in this respect ; and one of the most
beneficial, I conceive to be an increased bounty on the

growth of hemp ; if it could be procured, the additional bounty to be paid for hemp water-retted only. If large farmers could be induced to grow it, as they became habituated to the management of it, the trouble would decrease, and the bounty might in time again be discontinued.

" The necessity of keeping up the quality of the cloths, should be strongly impressed on the weavers ; perhaps if premiums were given for the best manufactured hemp cloths, it might be serviceable, under proper regulations I think the public would be found very much disposed to encourage a strong manufacture of cloth ; and there are facts which induce me to think so.

" Considerable quantities of Russian sheeting are sold in England, merely for their strength ; as they are coarser, at the price, than any other foreign linen.

" Suffolk hemp, if known, would always be preferred, being stronger than Russian, from the quality of the thread, and at the same time, lighter in washing ; which is often an objection to Russian.

" The quantity of good hemp being gradually increased, would insensibly increase the number of spinners, and extend the trade. Some regulations are wanting respecting reeling the yarn. The same method the wool trade has adopted would not, I think, succeed ; as the spinners often buy the tow, and therefore it would be impracticable for an inspector to examine the yarn. But if the punishment were similar, and the owner of the tow, the putter-out, or the person to whom it was offered, were permitted to prosecute, it might answer the purpose.

" In Ireland and in Scotland, I am informed, there is a board, or committee of gentlemen, entrusted with powers by government for the regulation of the linen trade : if some plan of this kind were adopted, I think it would be very serviceable, as they would acquire in time, a complete knowledge of the trade, in its different branches ; and apply such rewards and regulations as the different times and situations would require ; and might extend these to circumstances which general regulations by parliament could not effect.

" In Scotland and in Ireland, each piece of cloth is stamped by an officer, with the length, breadth, and number of one hundred threads contained in the warp.

" If a similar practice were obtained here, it would have a beneficial tendency ; as the length, breadth, and rate (or number of threads in the warp) being given, it is easy to ascertain what should be the weight. If then a certain mark were put on each piece of hemp manufactured agreeably to the best rules, it would improve the quality of the cloths, by exciting competition rather in goodness than in fineness. This would also prevent a practice which, I fear, prevails greatly ; the selling other cloths, made up to imitate hemp, in lieu of it.

" If the method I have hinted should be found impracticable, some means should be devised to prevent this imposition on the public, which, if suffered to proceed, will discredit, and perhaps ruin the manufactory.

" You will perceive, Sir, that these are, many of them, hazarded thoughts, which it would require much reflection to mature and reduce to practice.

" You inquire if Suffolk hemp is used for ropes ? I believe, never. It is too fine and dear ; and sacking is principally made from Russian hemp, although the offal of English is sometimes used.

" I hope, Sir, you will find the above account in some degree satisfactory : if you wish any further information, I shall be happy to give it you, as far as in my power. You will be pleased to make any use of these hints you think proper—concealing my name. I have inclosed a few specimens of hemp cloth, of different degrees of fineness."

The Rev. Mr. Mills, of Bury, also writes thus :— " Hemp delights in a black rich mould, the richer * and stronger † it is, the better. It has sometimes been sown upon the breaking up an old lay, and where there has been sufficient depth, with success. Let the land be well worked and manured with 30 loads per acre, about a fortnight before seed time, which is from the beginning to the end of April: if sown earlier, as the plants are almost as tender as French-beans, the frosts would greatly injure, if not totally destroy them ; the sooner (the season permitting) it is sown, the better, though it has been sometimes deferred to the 15th of May. Three bushels and an half of good bright seed are sufficient for an acre, which should be gently and lightly harrowed in—the birds must be kept off the land till the plants appear ; the time of pulling is about the beginning of August, or, more properly speaking, thirteen weeks from the time of sowing : the leaves turning yellow and the stalks white, are signs of its maturity ; the male and female hemp are pulled together : indeed when the crop is thick, it is impossible to separate them. The expence of pulling is generally estimated at one shilling per peck, according to the quantity originally sown.

" When it is all taken up and bound in small bundles, with bands at each end, to such a bigness as you can grasp with both hands, it is conveyed to the pond of

---

* A rich black strong soil is best for every thing ; but it would too much discourage the culture if it was supposed to be essentially necessary ; I have seen it thrive well, sown after turnips fed off on good common friable loams ; manure will make it thrive on any except very dry and sterile soils.—A. Y.

† A good and friable clay, well manured with mould, will answer; the soil cannot be too rich.

standing water (if a clay pit the better), where it is laid bundle upon bundle, direct and across, thus, this is termed a bed of hemp, and after it is piled to such a thickness as to answer the depth of the water (which cannot be too deep) * it is loaded with blocks and logs of wood, until all of it is totally immersed : after remaining in this state four or five days, as the weather shall direct, it is taken out and carried to a field of aftermath, or any other grass, that is clean and free from cattle ; the bundles being untied, it is spread out thin, stalk by stalk ; in this state it must be turned every other day, especially in moist weather, lest the worms should injure it ; thus it remains for six weeks or more, then it is gathered together, tied in large bundles, and kept dry † in a house till December or January, when the stalks are broken and the bark wholly freed from them, by an instrument called a breaker. The art of breaking it by a labourer of common capacity, would be learnt in a few hours, and the swingling of it, which follows, requiring some sleight as well as labour, though more difficult, might in a little longer time, be acquired. After breaking and swingling, it is sent to the heckler and hemp-dresser, to be prepared for spinning, according to the fineness desired.

" Should the hemp stand for seed, the yarn of it will never be so white, as it is not watered, but only spread on the grass for the benefit of the dews ; it will not be improper to observe in this case, after it is tied in bundles, it is set up like wheat in shocks, till the seed will freely shed, and then threshed out.

* This deserves experimental inquiry; watering hemp is a partial rotting through fermentation ; the vicinity of the atmosphere must for that purpose be necessary. The best hemp ponds I have seen, have not exceeded the depth of six feet.—*A. Y.*

† It might do as well stacked, if kept perfectly dry.

" In the state hemp comes from the brake, it will fetch from 6s. to 7s. 6d. per stone ;* in the year 1787, it sold as high as 9s. The produce is so variable and uncertain, that in one season a rood and six perches of land has produced 17 stone, and another with the same culture and manure, only twelve.

" The expences of cultivation may be thus estimated :

	£.	s.	d.
Rent of an acre of land, - -	1	0	0
Ploughing, sowing, &c. - -	0	10	6
Three bushels and ½ of seed (sold from 1s. 4d. to 2s. 6d per peck) at 1s. 6d. per peck, }	1	1	0
Boy keeping birds a week or more, -	0	1	6
Pulling, at the rate of 1s. per week, according to the seed sown, - - - }	0	14	0
Getting it in and out of water, turning, and laying up, - - - - - }	1	1	0
Tythe and town charges† not estimated,			
£.4		8	0

* The hemp is tied up in stones, when it comes from the brake.

	£.	s.	d.
† To continue this account : - - -	4	8	0
Tythe and rates, suppose - - - -	0	6	0
The lowest crop mentioned, is 48 stone per acre, let us suppose only 40, breaking, at 1s. 3d. - - - }	2	10	0
Total, - - - - - -	7	4	0

PRODUCE.

	£.	s.	d.
Forty stone, at 7s. - - - - -	14	0	2
Parliamentary bounty, 3d. a stone, - - -	0	10	0
	14	10	0
Expences, - - - - - -	7	4	1
Neat profit per acre - - - -	£.7	6	0

A. Y.

" The expence of breaking hemp, is from 1s. to 1s. 6d. per stone ; the dressing at the hecklers 1s. 6d. per stone ; and the spinning (according to the fineness) from 7d. to 1s. per clue. A clue is three skains, a skain is 20 leas, a lea is 40 threads, a thread is two yards when reeled. The weight of a clue varies with the fineness or coarseness of the thread.

" There cannot be much difficulty in a wool-spinner's learning to spin hemp ; the usual stint of a woman, is two skains per day, or from four-pence half-penny to eight-pence, according to the fineness ; from this there are no deductions ; and the price has been nearly the same for some years.

" As you requested, I inquired if a rich sand would answer for the cultivation of hemp ; and whether wheat might be sown after it. Both these questions were answered in the negative.* And the reason assigned against the wheat was, the richness of the land would make it run to straw. Oats is the general crop after hemp.— Turnips sown immediately after it, have answered tolerably well."

---

* It is common to sow wheat after hemp in various parts of this kingdom, and also in France; and it is reckoned one of the best preparations for that grain; but upon a rich black mould, the observation of this gentleman is probably very just. I have seen very fine hemp on good sands.—*A. Y.*

CHAPTER VIII.

GRASS.

SUFFOLK is not famous for its grass lands, either in respect of fertility or management. Coarse pastures, though of considerable value, are found to a large extent in the cow district.

SECT. I.—MEADOWS AND PASTURES: THEIR CULTURE AND PRODUCE.

THE management of meadows and upland pastures, in this county, in general, can scarcely be worse. Upon the same farms, where almost every effort is made upon the arable, the grass is nearly, or quite neglected. A little draining is sometimes, though rarely, bestowed. Manuring them is almost unknown in the hands of tenants ; and as to mole and ant hills, bushes, and other rubbish, immense tracts of what is called grass, are over-run with them. Rolling is seldom performed. Things wear rather a better aspect upon farms occupied by the owners ; but, speaking generally, I allude principally to tenants. As to lands in the hands of gentlemen, they are managed, in many cases, in a much superior stile, but not always.

The arable lands of the county are so much better managed than the grass, that an improvement in the latter would be attended with great private and national advantage. Our sister county of Norfolk is, if possible, yet worse in this respect. The reason of this general neglect, results not from inattention, but an erroneous calculation. In the farmer's estimate, and he is right, there will be a considerable benefit remaining to the landlord at the end of a lease, from all improvements of grass land; whereas upon arable there may not be one penny left from the expenditure of a pound. This is true, but the conclusion, that what the landlord gains is at the expence of the tenant, is a very great error; both may gain considerably, but not at the expence of each other. One reason why improvements of grass are so rarely seen, and also why most tenants would, if their landlords allowed it, plough up every acre of grass on their farms, results, in some measure, from their making no fair experiments of the value, which is not to be done in ordinary rough land, except by sheep only. If they would lock into such a field, a certain lot of sheep, suppose two, two and a half, or three to an acre, and keep them there the whole year, registering the hay given in deep snows, and on no account folding those sheep on other lands (as in that case little improvement results from sheep-feeding), they would find the return of such lands not contemptible; and if they continued the trial for a few years, they would see such lands constantly improving; so that the more sheep were kept, the more might be kept in future. These are experiments very easily made with a quiet breed, and there are not many more important ones.

Feeding.—I have not met with any practices in the feeding of grass lands, that would mark a peculiarity of management.

Mowing.—Towns must every where be supplied with hay, which, with the necessary consumption of the farms, universally occasions large tracts to be mown.

Hay-making.—This branch of the farmer's business is but imperfectly practised in Suffolk : the grass is left too long after the scythe, nor is there sufficient attention to grass cocks, and those of the second size. Too much is left to the hazard of weather; nor is there sufficient care taken to tread the stacks enough in making; they are rarely pulled, but left loose and rough on the surface ; and the practice of trussing is but now coming slowly in.

A gentleman in this county has invented a stage, which he uses for building the upper parts of stacks of hay or corn : it consists of two parts, one of which is a frame, eight feet wide, made of two fir balks twenty-two feet long, braced together in a parallel position, and having several holes bored in them, about fourteen feet from the ground, for the reception of the hinges of the stage ; and an hook in each of them, to hang the chains on which support the outward edge of the stage, and serve to raise it or lower it at pleasure. The other part is a moveable stage, eight feet long, and three feet eight inches broad, having an hinge under each end, at the hinder, or edge nearest the stack ; one end of the hinges is made like a bolt, to enter the holes in the balks ; the stage likewise has an iron plate under each end, with an hole in it to receive an hook on the chain.

The stage is set against the stack when it becomes so high that it is inconvenient to pitch on to it from the buck of a waggon. The holes in the balks most commonly used, are fourteen feet from the ground, about the height of a waggon load of hay; should the stage be fixed lower, it would be of no use, not being wanted whilst a man can conveniently pitch from the buck of a waggon on to a stack ; and should it be fixed much higher, it would be found too high for a man to pitch on to, when the waggon is nearly empty.

A stage like this is not expensive, and might be used for nailing up weather-boarding, painting, plaistering of walls, and other purposes.—*(See the plate.)*

Produce.—The produce of mowing lands is various ; but there are few fields reserved for hay, that will not yield a ton on an average ; low meadows, and uplands well improved, produce one and an half, and two tons ; and it may not be far from the fact, to estimate the fair rent at 1*s.* per cwt. of the average crop.

Improving.—Gentlemen here, as elsewhere, improve their grass lands, but it is not common to see farmers do it. There are large tracts in the county, which would pay well for draining, smoothing, clearing from bushes and rubbish, and manuring; but attention is given almost exclusively to the arable land.

Laying down to Grass.—This is a part of husbandry little practised, and not much understood in Suffolk. The common method has been, to sow hay seeds, as they are called, which must be good or bad, according to the plants in the fields that are mown. Twenty sacks an acre, at 2*s.* 6*d.* a sack, have been sown, and not with bad success ; but the expence is high, and bad plants propagated as well as good ones. I have been for some years collecting separate grasses gathered by hand, and have several fields sown with them : they promise to be successful.

1803. There is no point in husbandry that has been

so well and so fully explained as this has been in the communications to the Board of Agriculture ; the great value of the information thus laid before the public shews the right way of ascertaining any questionable point, and of giving an authority to practices no otherwise attainable. In the memoirs on breaking up and laying down grass lands, there are various opinions, and some counter to each other ; but a careful reader will find little difficulty in extracting the knowledge applicable to any case.

Breaking up Grass.—Whatever is expended upon arable land, the tenant can, in the course of a lease, get back again. Upon grass this is not the case : he may make as large a profit ; but still he will leave something at the end of a term for the landlord. If this idea be not the cause of the ill management noted, I know not what is. But the conduct ought to be a lesson to landlords, to be very careful indeed, of the clauses in a lease by which they allow grass lands to be broken up : instead of which, it has been common in various parts of the county, to let great tracts be ploughed, to the unquestionable damage of the farms.

1803. Since the former edition of this work much larger tracts of grass have been broken up, and the number of cows very much lessened. When the mischievous variations in the price of corn by means of most inefficient corn laws are considered ; and that the price of dairy products has been more regular than that of any other farming produce, this must be attributed to a want of foresight in landlords, which they will probably by and by repent.

CHAPTER IX.

GARDENS AND ORCHARDS.

THERE is nothing in this branch of culture, that has come to my knowledge, that seems to claim particular attention ; without doubt, there are practices in the county which would be worthy of insertion had they been communicated. I have only to observe one practice, not common elsewhere, which is, that of building garden walls no more than the breadth of a common brick in thickness, by means of waving the line. The saving is considerable. In regard to the effect, both in point of duration and fruit, accounts are various ; and the introduction of this method is not of sufficient date, to ascertain it satisfactorily.

CHAPTER X.

WOODS AND PLANTATIONS.

THE woods of Suffolk hardly deserve mentioning, except for the fact, that they pay in general but indifferently. By cuttings at ten, eleven, or twelve year's growth, the return of various woods, in different parts of the county, have not, on an average, exceeded nine shillings per acre per annum ; the addition to which sum, by the timber growing in them, but rarely answers sufficiently to make up for the difference between that produce and the rent of the adjoining lands. There cannot be a fact more clearly ascertained, than that of every sort of wood being at a price too low, to pay with a proper profit for its production ; and nothing but the expence and trouble of grubbing, prevents large tracts of land thus occupied, from being applied more beneficially.*

Timber.—The strong loams of Suffolk formerly contained considerable quantities of large oak ; these, as in every other part of the kingdom, have been much lessened, and the succession that is coming on, bears no proportion to the growth that preceded it. Improved cultivation of the lands, is the cause of this fact, which is so general in England. Rough pastures, over-run with thorns and

* Many of the woods might be converted to tillage, with much more profit than they at present produce. But perhaps this practice might be found gradually to reduce the growth of oak timber, and on that account, it would be good policy to let them remain in their present state.— *Note by J. R.*

briars, and broad hedge-rows, were nurseries of timber.
As land became valuable, these have been cleared; and
with this obvious and valuable improvement, timber has
of course declined; a circumstance not at all to be regretted, for corn and grass are products much more
valuable.

Copses.—Underwoods are not generally productive in
this county. The net return from such as I am acquainted with, is much less than that of the adjoining
lands under other products: I know various woods
which yield little more than half the net rent; and I
have observed in various instances, that the soil is much
inferior to that of the contiguous lands.

Grubbing up.—If the soil be dry, few operations answer
better than grubbing up woods; for on such, the exclusion of the sun, united with the fall of leaf for centuries have formed a good depth of vegetable mould; but
in wet tenacious soils, that have not been drained, I have
know them grubbed in this county with very inconsiderable profit; yet the roots have paid for the work of
extracting them. This is one of the many titles of subjects which I have inserted in this work, not for the
value of the communications I am possessed of, but in
hope that my readers who may have experience, may be
induced to send an account of their experiments.

Planting.—In most of the instances with which I am
acquainted in Suffolk, planting has been performed more
with a view to ornament than profit; how far they are
made to unite, is a subject worthy of attention; and
when it is seen that I have no Suffolk communications
on it, I may hope the deficiency will be supplied by those
gentlemen who have it in their power.

CHAPTER XI.

WASTES.

IF there be one object more important than another in
the examination of the agriculture of a province, with
a view to the improvements that are practicable in it,
it certainly is this of wastes.* No person who has reflected seriously on the state of the soil of England, but
must be convinced that there want few instigations to
cultivate wastes, but the power to do it, without those
very expensive applications to parliament, which are at
present necessary even for the smallest objects. If the
Board of Agriculture be able to accomplish this desideratum, it will merit greatly ; and the national interests
find themselves advanced in a degree which no other
event whatever could secure. The magnitude and importance of this design cannot be understood, without
discovering the extent of these wastes, which will,
without doubt, be effected by means of the surveys going
on in every part of the kingdom.†

* The importance of this subject cannot be too much enforced ; and
it were an object worthy the Board of Agriculture, to obtain a Bill from
Parliament, permitting a general inclosure throughout the whole county,
of waste lands. Where the commons consist of good lands, the advantages of converting them to private property, would be prodigious ;
and the poorest, by being so converted, would, I am persuaded, produce double their present value ; whereas, at present, the profit is
extremely small indeed. And whenever a landlord lets a farm with a
common-right, which is valued with the rest of his premises, I believe
every good farmer who makes use of it, would be a loser instead of a
gainer—Note by J. R.

† The importance of inclosing waste lands, is evident too from
another consideration, supposing an equal profit only would be the

I have calculated from much information, of different kinds; and from comparing and combining various data, conclude that there are in Suffolk wastes to the amount of nearly, perhaps quite, 100,000 acres, or $\frac{1}{8}$ part of the whole; comprehended under the terms sheep-walk, common, warren, &c.

It is, however, to be noted, that none of these are, strictly speaking, absolutely *waste*, if by that term is understood land yielding nothing: I include all lands uncultivated, which would admit of a very great improvement, not always profitably to the tenant, who may, on a small capital, make a great interest per cent. by a warren, for instance, but in every case to the public.

Commons fed bare, may seem to yield a considerable produce, but there is often a great deception in it: the cattle and sheep should be followed through the winter, and whenever it is found that there is no adequate winter provision, so often the case with poor men's stock, there are large deductions to be made from the apparent produce of the summer.*

In Bardwell, Mr. Davenport observes, that " Bobec Heath, in this parish, contains about a thousand acres. It affords a walk to five hundred breeding ewes, but their chief support, and that of their lambs, must be artificial

result: the men who usually reside near a common, are the depredators of the neighbourhood: smugglers, sheep-stealers, horse-jockies, and jobbers of every denomination, here find their abode.—*Note by J. R.*

* In this case, the poor man's stock ought to be, and generally is, sold to those who abound in winter provision. If a poor man buys a cow in May, and keeps her on a common through the summer, he sells her again in the autumn at a considerable loss. If he buys hay to maintain her over the winter, his loss is increased; and it frequently happens that dry cattle (bought in early in the summer), are sold in the autumn for less than prime cost. Hence, the small advantages resulting to the poor from their right of common.—*Note by H.*

grasses on the inclosed lands of their owners. There may be also somewhat more than an hundred bullocks in it, with a few mares and colts, and colts from two to three years old. If a beast is put on the heath about old May-day, and is taken from it at Michaelmas in much the same order in which it was sent, it is supposed to have done pretty well. The farmer, meanwhile, has had his home-feed for his cows, and the beast is kept in tolerable order till it can be put to turnips. There are several inclosures which have been formerly taken out of heath, which are now under the plough, and, having been clayed, produce well.

Sapiston is a small parish, and all of it the property of the Duke of Grafton. The greater part of the heath was inclosed a few years ago, and what remains of it, with other rough pasture whereon are many timber trees, makes a walk for about three hundred ewes.

1803. The Duke has made very considerable exertions in breaking up sheep walks in Euston, Pakenham, Bardwell, Sapiston, &c. ; on some land in his Grace's own hands, and on others by encouraging his tenants. These lands have all been inclosed carefully, clayed or marled, and requisite barns, &c. erected. The improvement has been great, and of real national importance, as well as highly beneficial to the estate.

SHEEP-WALKS.

Many farmers think these desart wastes necessary for their flocks, which is very questionable. They are undoubtedly useful, and, if they were converted to corn, the number kept upon a farm might, in a few cases, decline ; but good grass adapted to the soil would be abundantly more productive for the flock. Whoever has viewed the immense wastes that fill almost the whole country from Newmarket to Thetford, and to Gastrop-gate, and which are found between Woodbridge and Orford, and thence, one way, to Saxmundham, not to mention the numerous heaths that are scattered every where, must be convinced, that their improvement *for grass*, would enable the county to carry many thousands of sheep more than it does at present.*

Some wastes that have been noted to me by correspondents, are these : in Hopton, four hundred and ninety acres. In Barningham, five hundred acres : the

* The following observations will perhaps induce us to believe we are not under so very egregious an error. 1st, Upon newly broken up lands, the lambs are subject to the rickets, and other pernicious maladies; and the effect lasts for numbers of years. Of this I can speak from experience. 2dly, Upon examination, it will be found that the wastes complained of are extremely poor, and not worth the cultivation. The rage for ploughing up has been so great within these late years, that except in a few instances, within the places mentioned (between Newmarket and Gastrop) no waste land remains worth cultivating. Several instances which have come under my observation, renders this position of the author extremely doubtful to me. Within a few miles from me, several heaths which were broken up and improved under skilful occupiers, about thirty years since, have within these last ten years been laid down again, and re-converted to heath lands. And this, from a practical proof, that neither so many, nor so good sheep, could possibly be reared without them. And it may be observed, that the new heath will not be so good as the old one for more than twenty years to come. *Note by J R.*——All this is founded on the supposition of their being broken up for corn ; in which case the remark may partially be right ; but they ought to be cultivated for grasses and sheep.—Heaths that are broken up for corn, and in the common way of two successive crops of oats being taken, when relaid are not so good as before they were broken up at all—granting the fact (which however deserves enquiry, and especially into the seed sown, which was probably ray grass) what has it to do with my proposition ? The object of which is not corn, but good grass.—*A. Y.*

quality very good.* In Brome, one hundred and twenty
acres. Mr. Hayward, of Lakenheath, informs me, that
that parish contains five thousand acres of fen; two
thousand five hundred acres of warren; one thousand
acres of open-field arable, and a common of three hundred acres.

Mr. Page, of Beccles, observes, that the grand division
of commons in that vicinity is into rated and unrated;
and even the rated are of disservice, by being generally
over-stocked to such a degree as to render cattle, after
a long grazing, of sometimes less value than when
turned on at first. A custom is also prevalent among
farmers, of skinning the turf from the commons, for
foundations to their manure heaps; and among the
poor, of gathering the manure of the stock partly for
fuel and partly for sale, and thus the commons decline
every year.

* Since inclosed and broken up.

CHAPTER XII.

IMPROVEMENTS.

Among the improvements which have been communicated to me through the liberality of the clergy, in
their replies to my circular letter, I may note that of
wheat being substituted for rye. Mr. Davenport observes, that in Bardwell, he finds from the rector's
books, that a century ago, there was but little wheat
grown in the parish, but much rye ; now the reverse.

Mr. Greaves informs me, that at Lackford one-third
more corn is annually raised than some years ago ; 300
acres of sheep-walk heath having been broken within
12 years ; and that a large tract of heath is broken up
in West Stowe.

Of 4000 acres in Downham, near Brandon, the whole
some years ago was warren, but now a large quantity is
under the plough.—*Mr. Wright.*

Of 1200 acres in the parish of Dunwich, one-half is
waste ; but agriculture on waste sands and black heaths
has advanced rapidly in the last 20 years, by means of
clay marle.

SECT. I.—DRAINING.

HOLLOW-DRAINING.

This most excellent practice is general on all the
wet lands of the county : it is too well known to need a

particular description. I shall only observe, therefore,
that the distance between the drains is usually from $5\frac{1}{2}$
to 8 yards; the common depth is 24 inches, from 20 to
26;* the breadth at top, just wide enough to admit a
man to work in; and at bottom, as narrow as possible,
not more than two inches. The materials used for
filling, bushes covered with straw, sometimes straw or
stubble only; and the expence, if with bushes, amounts,
on an average, every thing included, to two guineas, or
forty-five shillings an acre, the men being paid three
shillings a score rods for the work. The duration varies,
according to the goodness of the work and materials,
from 12 to 25 years; and some filled with straw only,
have been known to last much longer. It will not be
improper to hint, that there are two errors very common in the performance of this improvement. The
first is, making the drains in, or nearly in, the direction
of the declivity; whereas, they ought always to be made
obliquely across it. The other is, that of marking
out, and making numerous drains across the sides of
springy hills, which might, in many cases, be drained
completely with a single drain, judiciously disposed,
according to those obvious principles upon which the
celebrated drainer, Mr. Elkington of Leicestershire,
proceeds.

1803. Mr. Simpson of Witnesham, and Captain
Wootton of Rattlesden, contend, that, in drawing out
hollow drains, it is right to mark them *with* the declivity,
and not across it, as the drains then draw both ways,
whereas, when across the slope, they can draw only on

---

* In this article of draining, from 20 years practical experience, I
have found 30 inches of much more advantage in the depth than what is
here mentioned, as it will draw the land drier, and the drain is much
more secure from being stopped up by carting or treading over it in wet
weather. The price of labour to have this work properly done, cannot
be less than four shillings per score.—*Note by J. P. Denham.*

one side. These gentlemen have tried it, and assure me they speak from the effect on their farms. *See the Appendix.*

No improvement can have greater or more immediate effects than this of draining; none that pays the farmer with more certainty. Its importance is perfectly well understood, and the practice general.

About twenty years ago, a Mr. Makins, of this county, invented a plough for cutting these drains, which was rewarded by the Society of Arts; but, on various attentive trials, it was found to work at a greater expence than the spade, and has long since been totally laid aside.

James Young, Esq. of Clare, in this county, has thus described the method common in that vicinity, but improved by himself:

" The forcible arguments you made use of when I had last the pleasure of meeting you, have determined me to communicate to you the mode of land-draining I have practised these several years.

" Little use or advantage would be derived from my enumerating the failures and disappointments I met with in many of the experiments which I have made; suffice it to say, I have every reason to prefer my present method; and I will endeavour to give it to you in such plain terms as shall be within the comprehension of every common farmer: my grand wish is to remove that dread of the expence which has prevented many from land-draining their farms, and to impress on the minds of farmers the same opinion I have of it: I know from experience, that in clayey soils it will answer perfectly, that it is the least expensive and the most expeditious, as well as most durable improvement of any in the whole system of agricultural economy.

" I have a field that used to be so wet and poachy in

the winter, as not to be able to bear the weight of a sheep ; I land-drained and fallowed it, then sowed it with wheat, without any manure, and had a crop equal to half the value of the land.

" During the wet weather, about the middle of last April, I examined a field of six acres, which I land-drained in the month of November in the year 1773, and had the satisfaction to find every drain in the field (except one) running.

" I do not pretend to determine what sort of soil will be most benefited by land-draining ; in my opinion, there is scarce any land in a clayey country, but will be greatly improved by it, and in particular, wherever the horse-tail *(Equisetum Arvense)* abounds, a man will be very seldom disappointed in expecting to be repaid the expence by the first crop.

" I hold it right never to draw the drains straight down a hill, but obliquely across it, with a descent just sufficient to give the water a fall into a leading ditch ; there are some fields where a leading ditch must be co-vered. I contrive almost every method to have as few covered as possible ; I like to have every drain inde-pendent ; and have carried it so far as to have open ditches cut on purpose.

" When I have marked the drains in a field (usually a rod asunder) I draw two furrows with a common foot plough, leaving a balk betwixt them, about 15 inches wide ; then with a strong double-breasted plough, made on purpose, I split that balk, and leave a clean furrow, 14 or 15 inches below the surface ; but where the depth of soil requires it, for I like to touch the clay, by a se-cond ploughing I sink it to 18 or 20 inches ; it is then ready for the land-ditching spade, with which I dig 15 inches deep, a drain as narrow as possible. It is an invariable rule with me, never to suffer the man who

digs to cover up the drain, but it is left open for me or
my bailiff to examine, and then it is well filled up to the
shoulder with wheat-stubble, cut and stacked for the
purpose immediately after the harvest, and a small stick
or two at the outlet, to prevent its being stopped by any
external accident. Lastly, with a common plough I turn
a furrow of the upper soil, or mould, upon the drain,
taking care not to turn in any of the dead soil raised by
the land-ditch spade, which ought always to be laid on
the outside, and scattered over the land.

" It is right not to let the drains lie open any length
of time, lest they get injured by wet or frost ; my general
rule is to fill them up every day.

" It is not easy to ascertain the price of carting the
wheat-stubble to the place where it will be wanted, and
stacking it, because the value must depend upon the
distance ; it is equally difficult to say, what the work of
the ploughs ought to be valued at, for though several
acres may be drawn out in a day, with one plough, yet,
I never choose to do above two or three hours work at a
time ; therefore, I shall leave every farmer to fix his
own price upon these parts of the business, only desiring
him to consider, that it is work that will wait for a
leisure time, and frequently, if the horses were not so
employed, they would earn nothing.

" I pay for digging the land-drains, one shilling and
eight-pence, and for filling them up with stubble, four-
pence, per score rods, without any beer whatever : an
active man, used to the work, where the soil is not
stony, will dig 23 or 24 rods in a day, within working
hours.

" The state of the expence, that is, the money a
farmer will pay out of his pocket for land-draining an
acre of land, will stand thus :

	£.	s.	d.
For cutting and raking together, an acre of wheat-stubble, generally sufficient for an acre of drains, - - - - -	0	2	0
Digging eight score rods of drains, -	0	13	4
Filling them up with stubble - -	0	2	8
Extra-work with the common spade, on an average, a day's work of a man, -	0	1	4
	£.0	19	4

" Thus, in as plain and concise a manner as possible, I have given you the whole process, to be disposed of in whatever manner you shall think proper. I have not ventured to broach a single idea on the theory of land-draining; let time and experiment ascertain its effect; you know it wants not philosophy to encourage the trial."

REPLY TO QUERIES.

Question I. Were the failures and disappointments mentioned, owing to sinking the drains deeper than mentioned, or to filling with other materials?

Answer. The failures and disappointments I met with at first, were not owing to any of these causes, but to drawing the drains with too steep descent, carrying too many into one covered leading ditch, using a spade too wide at the bottom, not digging the drains a sufficient depth, and not paying a proper attention to the examining and filling them up: I never did use any other materials than wheat straw, stubble, and wood.

Question II. Clay and clayey soil mentioned.—Has Mr. Young tried his method in such as have the clay to the surface? At what depth is it found on his farm in common?

Answer.—I never knew my method used on any land that has clay to the surface; the depth of my surface soil is below the common sweep of the plough.

Question III. " A crop of wheat equal to half the value of the land."—Has Mr. Young observed that fields early after draining, are more fertile than they are after some years have elapsed; such remarks have been made elsewhere; query, if so, to what does Mr. Young attribute it?

Answer. Such remarks and observations, form a powerful argument in favour of land-draining, for as the drains gradually become impaired and fall into decay, the lands will consequently return to their pristine state and nature.

Question IV. Were the drains in the six acre field of 1773, filled with stubble only?

Answer. They were all filled with stubble only, except a little wood at the mouths, and empty themselves singly into an open leading ditch or drain cut for the purpose.

Question V. What is meant by a *leading ditch?* A drain, or a fence ditch? If open drains are cut across borders, how cart on them? Does not Mr. Young throw several drains into one carrier or master drain?

Answer. By a leading ditch, I mean a carrier or master drain, into which all the single drains empty themselves, and may be covered or open as situation suits; in many instances, the fence ditch of the field will serve the purpose. I strongly recommend these carrier ditches to be open, though at the expence of a whelm at the bottom of a field where a cart-way is necessary; the leading many drains into one carrier ditch, that is covered, must be more liable to accidents and injuries, than where every drain empties itself singly into an open ditch.

Question VI. How many horses to plough the furrows fifteen inches deep? Is it necessary to plough into the clay? It seems from this expression, that Mr. Young's surface soil is 18 or 20 inches deep; are the drains, as implied, 30 inches deep?

Answer. I never use more than four horses, generally but three, to draw the drains; I do not mean the surface soil of my land is 18 or 20 inches deep, but my rule is to touch the clay, though obliged to go that depth, and the spit taken with the land-ditch spade is always 15 inches deep.

Question VII. What is the duration of the stubble? Has Mr. Young drained any fields a second time? In cutting across old drains, if done, what was the appearance? Does the stubble partially rot and the clay arch? Or does the rotten subble keep an open vein? Is it common, or do others fill with stone or wood? Would Mr. Young recommend those materials in any particular cases?

Answer. I have never been able to ascertain the duration of the stubble with any degree of exactness, neither have I ever drained a field a second time; but a drain will sometimes be stopped by carting on the land in the wet, or some other accidental cause, in which case, as soon as it is discovered by the wetness of the place, my practice is, to make one or more fresh drains in different directions to the old ones; and I have many times observed old drains, when cut across, though there was not the least appearance of any vegetable substance remaining

in them, but full of of a loose porous earth, at once run
freely, or, according to my workmen's phrase, bleed
afresh.—As I hold cheapness to be one of the first re-
commendations of any plan of improvement in agriculture, I can say nothing in favour of stone ; in some
cases, particularly across an horse or foot path that is
much frequented, the use of wood may be adviseable,
but I use it very sparingly.

Question VIII. Has Mr. Young applied his method
to draining grass fields ; if so, in what manner does he
take the first spit ? And is this draining found equally
beneficial as on arable ?

Answer. I have had but little experience in draining
grass lands, having only two upland pastures that required it, and only a small part of them ; my method
there, was to take a deep spit with the common spade,
hen one of 15 inches with the land-ditch spade, fill up
with stubble, shovel in the mould only, and lastly, to
lay on the turf neatly, so as to make as little blemish as
possible ; it has been done eight years, and continues to
answer perfectly.

We re I to drain grass fields on a larger scale, I should
pursue the same process I have hitherto done in arable
lands ; the turf may very easily be first raised by a
common foot plough.

Question IX. Does Mr. Young ever drain in summer ? Which is the better season, that, or winter ?

Answer. I never land-drain in summer ; two inconveniences attend it ; the increase of labour in a clayey
soil, when hard and dry, is very considerable, and the
want of leisure, where good labourers are scarce : there
are, who land-drain through the whole summer, but I always find something more material to do at that season.

" What shall I say in answer to your last request, that I would particularize my soil ? There are so many technical terms used in agriculture, which are merely provincial, I am fearful lest I should not be understood by farmers at a distance ; I will, therefore, just state the general properties and qualities of my land, sufficient to enable the farmer of every country to judge of it by comparison :—In a tract of 200 acres of inclosed arable land, mostly broken ground, yet by no means steep, it is natural to suppose a variety of soil, but mine varies remarkably little, except in the depth of the surface soil, which is universally shallowest and wettest on the highest grounds, and consists of moderately heavy brown moulds, mixed with different proportions of clay ; the under stratum is every where white, or grey tender clay, abounding with calcareous earth, except here and there patches particularly wet, which in this country, are called galts ; these consist of stone and gravel, and sometimes loose sand, are never of a large extent, and are effectually laid dry by land-draining.

" I have no land so light, but that the succeeding crop of barley will be injured by feeding off turnips by sheep in wet weather ; neither have I any so stiff or heavy, as to require three horses in a plough : my constant practice is to plough with two horses a-breast, one man holding the plough, and guiding his horses with rope reins. It has been advanced, that we have not a particle of clay in this parish ; in answer to which, give me leave to subjoin the best definition of clay I have ever yet met with : " Earths firmly coherent, smooth to the touch, not easily breaking between the fingers, heavy, viscid and ductile to a great degree while moist, not readily diffusible in water, and when mixed with it, not readily subsiding from it : this genus is the most unctious of any of this series, and hardens by fire, into a kind of stony substance."—*Vide Da Costa's Natural History of Fossils.*

SECT. II.—PARING AND BURNING.

THIS husbandry, which, properly managed, is the most admirable of all improvements, and improperly, the most mischievous,* is known only in the small angle of fen. In that district they could not cultivate without this capital assistant. It is scarcely possible, profitably, to bring boggy, moory, peat soils, from a state of nature into cultivation, without the assistance of fire, which is the most effective destruction of the spontaneous growth, and never fails, but because the men employed do not pare deep enough. In these fens, the original surface is rough and unequal, from great tufts of rushes, &c. called there *hassocks.* Some persons cut them with spades, at the expence of five or ten shillings an acre; others with the plough. Paths for the horses were, in that case, to be cut by hand, and the plough made on purpose, and called a hassock plough, cut laterally much beyond the line of its draught. But opinions are, in general, that hand work is the cheaper; in either case the hassocks are dried, heaped, burnt, and the ashes spread. After this they go over it again with a very complete and effective tool, called a fen-paring plough, the furrow of which is burnt. Coleseed is then sown on one shallow ploughing; never harrowed, in order not to disturb the

---

* This is the remark of a man of science and observation, and very unlike the declamation of many reporters, who know nothing about it. —*Baillie.*

whole furrow, but rolled, or lightly bush-harrowed. This cole-seed is either for a crop of seed or for sheep food; in the latter case, sells for a guinea an acre; in the former, for two or three guineas. Oats are then sown; the crop productive; and the land, if well laid down to grass, becomes good meadow. But the management in this respect is very bad, for they sow only clover and ray grass; and after six or seven years, pare and burn again; instead of which, if proper seeds were sown,* the land would be ever after in an improving state.

Whatever objections have been made to the husbandry of paring and burning, have either been the result of theoretical reasonings on false principles, or else founded on facts furnished by very bad farmers. The common conduct is to make this operation the preparation for successive corn crops, and perhaps in a bad rotation. If a dunghill were given to a bad farmer, and it was used on similar principles, it would almost equally exhaust the soil; yet who has found out that dunging land is bad husbandry? Paring and burning gives a dunghill also: it is bad management alone that converts it into an evil. Make it the preparation for grass, and all is safe.

It is very rare to find such instances of sudden improvements as have been made in Burnt Fen. Forty years ago five hundred acres were let for a guinea a year; but in 1772 an act was obtained for a separate drainage,

* Quere—What are proper seeds?—Perhaps marl grass, with meadow foxtail grass, may be found beneficial. A small mixture of the finest ray grass, or darnel, is found to answer well. Marl grass, though resembling red clover in appearance, is quite different in its effects. Clover is found unfriendly to all natural grasses, and marl grass the reverse. I find this fact established by extensive experience upon my own farm in Pembroke-shire. One very material advantage resulting from the culture of marl grass is, that neat cattle are not so liable to swell by eating it in moist weather, as they are with red clover; nor is its hay so dangerous to horses wind, as clover.—Note by H.

and one shilling and six-pence an acre levied for the
expence of embankment, mills, &c. In 1777, the bank
broke, and most of the proprietors ruined. In 1782, on
the success of the machine called *the bear*, in cleansing
the bottoms of the rivers, and other reasons, occasioned
some persons to purchase in this neglected tract. The
banks were better made, mills erected, and the success
great. Servants of the former proprietors bought lots
for 200*l.* with almost newly erected buildings on them,
that cost 3, 4, and 500*l.* Such lots now let at 100*l.* per
annum. An estate of Mr. Jones, bought of ———
Chitham, Esq. for 200*l.* would now sell at 2000*l.* A
Mr. Cash bought eight hundred acres for 25*l.* he since
sold half of it to Edward Gwilt, Esq. of Icklingham, for
100*l.* the other half he sold for 300*l.* which has been re-
sold for 800*l.* ; and Mr. Gwilt could now sell his for
1600*l.* Three farms sold for 600*l.* would now let for
300*l.* a year. Mr. Foote of Brandon, in 1780, bought
three hundred and ninety acres for 150*l.* a considerable
part of which is now let at 10*s.* an acre. All these
improvements have been very much owing to paring
and burning.

The application of fire is as useful and effective to
land as that of water. There are in Suffolk many thousands of acres of poor, wet, cold, hungry pastures and
neglected meadows, over-run and filled with all sorts of
rubbish, and abounding with too few good plants to
render their improvement easy without breaking up :
all such should be pared and burnt ; not to keep under
the plough to be exhausted and ruined, which is infal-
lible, and the land left in a worse state, beyond all comparison, than it was before ; but to be laid *immediately*
to grass, that is, as soon as the course of husbandry
necessary will admit. This ought to be without variation, under any pretence whatever, in this course of

crops : 1. pare and burn for turnips,* which fed on the land by sheep. 2. oats ; and with these oats the grass seeds sown. The oats and the turnips would more than pay all the expence of a previous hollow draining, should that be necessary ; of the paring and burning, and every other charge : and the change, from a very bad pasture to a very fine one, would all be neat profit. The tenant would be greatly benefited, and the landlord would find his estate improved, if let, as farms ought to be let, if not in the vicinity of great cities, with an absolute exclusion of selling a lock of hay under any pretence whatever.

The dry rough sheep-walks covered with ling, furze, broom, &c. should also be broken up in the same manner ; but universally to be laid down again with the grasses suitable to the soil and to sheep. On weak thin stapled land, two crops of corn, after paring and burning, would be pernicious. *Perhaps* they might be well laid down without a single one, which would be so much the better.†

* In moist bottom lands, rape will often succeed better than turnips ; and the sheep feed better with rape upon such lands.—*Note by H.*

† It is humbly presumed, that it would be better to take two or three successive crops of turnips, in order to completely eradicate all the seeds of ling, furze and broom, before the land be laid down to grass, as otherwise those plants will appear with redoubled vigour. These observations on paring and burning are very excellent, being founded on common sense, reason and *experiment*, and confute the absurd doctrine of other surveyors, who condemn one of the first of agricultural improvements, as productive of an injury which is entirely occasioned by a covetous and slovenly culture.—*Note by Mr. Boys of Kent.*——There can be no objection to repeated crops of turnips, if fed on the land. They form excellent husbandry.—*A. Y.*

SECT. III.—MANURING.

UNDER this head the Suffolk husbandry furnishes some information in the several articles of

1. Marl, chalk and clay.
2. Crag, or shell marl.
3. Town manures.
4. Farm-yard composts.

CLAY, MARL, &c.

Claying—A term in Suffolk which includes marling; and indeed the earth carried under this term is very generally a clay marl; though a pure, or nearly a pure clay, is preferred for very loose sands.

The extent to which this improvement has been carried, in both the sand districts,* is very considerable, there being few farmers of any note, on very light land, that have not carried large quantities. Mr. Rodwell near Bury, though not on a very large farm, has carried 140,000 loads. The operation of this manure, acting

---

* Clay is thought to be nearly as good a manure for heavy land as for light land; and it is a constant practice to lay clay upon clay land, especially if the land has been laid down with grass-seeds for some years.

In the eastern part of Suffolk, if the clay pit be not very distant, the price of *digging*, *carrying*, and *spreading*, is 50s. for 120 loads, which is really cheaper than a farmer can do it with his own men and teams.

I must here observe, that the clay of Suffolk will answer a second time; viz. Suppose the first coat of 100 loads per acre, to last 20 years, at the expiration, 50 loads per acre will make the land in good heart again; and the best mode of doing it is, to lay down the land with grass-seeds for a couple of years, and then lay the clay upon the turf the latter end of the summer, and break up the land in the spring following, to set with pease, if the land be proper for that crop—*Note by a Correspondent of the Board.* It should be a year above ground.—*A. Y.*

both chemically and mechanically, is so obvious on very light soils, that it wants no explanation. But when the *clay* is not of a good sort, that is, when there is really none, or scarcely any clay in it, but is an imperfect, and even a hard chalk, there are great doubts how far it answers, and, in some cases, has been spread to little profit. The quantity usual is from 60 to 80, and sometimes 100 loads an acre, the load containing about 32 bushels. Many experienced farmers prefer carrying 40 or 50 loads only, and repeating it after the first course. The land receives more immediate benefit, and double the number of acres may be clayed in the first years of the lease, without any additional expence. The men are paid from 27*s*. to 30*s*. per 120, for filling and spreading, earning 10*s*. or 11*s*. a week ; and the expence of teams is about as much more.* When this manuring is done, therefore, on very poor land, the expence is equal to the value of the fee-simple of the estate. The duration, and indeed the whole effect, depends much on the course of crops pursued. If the plough is too freely used, and corn sown too often, it answers badly, and the effect is

---

* In consequence of the impossibility of the occupiers being always with his men, and the opportunities they perpetually have of deceiving him, in regard to filling the loads, the best way seems to be, to put out the claying at two-pence or two-pence farthing per square yard, measuring the content of the pit after all is carried out. At this rate, I have found that the men earn from 9*s*. to 12*s*. per week.—With respect to the expence of teams, I have never given less than four-pence per square yard, measured as above, and found, moreover, tumbrils, wedges, &c. With respect to the quantity of loads per acre, 100 perhaps is not too much for newly cultivated heaths or warrens ; but for other fleet soils, which have been for a long time under cultivation, 50, or at most 70 loads, are quite sufficient.—On such soils, to lay on too much is attended with great loss.—*Note by J. R.*

						l.	*s.*	*d.*
4 Men, at 11*s*. per week,	-	-	-	-	-		2 4	0
6 Horses,	-	-	-	-	-	3 12	0	
Driver,	-	-	-	-	-	0 9	0	
Tumbrils, &c.	-	-	-	-		0 3	0	
							4 4	0

soon lost; but, with good management, it lasts 20 years. Where the management is good, and the clay well adapted to the land, the profit is very great. In many cases, a course of fallow and rye, or *light* oats, is converted to fine barley, clover, and wheat, and the produce of the soil multiplied twenty-fold; but, on the contrary, the cases in which the return has been inadequate, are not a few. And I believe it will be found, that on soils that will yield sainfoin, it is more profitable to cultivate that grass, than to clay the land for corn.

In the carrying on of clay,* or marl, they have made, of late years, in the maritime district, especially about

* *Clay.*—There are various sorts of clay; some so exceedingly strong and loamy, that it will not mix with the soil; others strong and full of particles of chalk; and another sort very tender, and has a mixture of sand; the second is the best; the use of it prevails very much at this time, in the strong wet lands in high Suffolk, even where clay is ploughed up. Within a few years, the mixing clay with maiden earth, and muck out of the farm yards, is very much practised; and a good farmer will tell you, that muck should never be carried upon the land alone; his reason assigned is, muck produces straw with little corn; but to grow a full crop of corn, you must use compost. Claying was performed formerly with tumbrils, drawn by five horses; but is now done with small one-horse carts, as described by Mr. Young in his *Annals*, at one-third less expence; these carts had three wheels, which added much to the expence of them, and have been found very inconvenient, and often out of order; to remedy this evil, the third wheel, with the frame, has been taken off, and a pair of shafts substituted; the horse now goes nearer to his work, and from the small weight thrown upon his back, much steadier. These carts are getting into general use in the county: they are drove by little boys, of from ten to twelve years old, and will be of the most essential service in training them to use horses at so early an age: an old man, incapable of hard labour, generally superintends the unloading them. Some farmers have thought they do not carry a sufficient quantity, and have set up tumbrils; these go with two horses, and must have a large lad to drive them; they are not equal, or not to be compared to the one-horse carts.

In Colness and Sampford hundreds, chalk-rubbish is brought back-freight by the corn-hoys, from Kent and Essex, and stands the farmer in 4s. per chaldron, besides the expence of unloading, and is then carried two or three miles to the land. The method is, to mix it with maiden earth and muck out of the farm-yards, at the rate of five or six chaldrons per acre; after laying two months or more, the heaps are turned over to ferment: in

Blithborough and Dunwich, one great improvement,
which is, substituting the one-horse cart for the common tumbril. Thirty of these small carts have been at
work in a single field, while the great tumbrils were all
left idle at home; having been found, on careful trial,
much inferior to them. A sketch of this nature does
not admit the detail of economical management ; but
new and important features it is right to touch on.

—— Kirby, Esq. of Kesgrave, has made considerable
exertions in this husbandry. I found his clay carts hard
at works claying an old sheep-walk in order to break it
up. He laid 80 loads an acre, of about 36 to 40 bushels
each, and the pit at such a distance that he can carry
but eight loads a day ; the expence therefore is heavy.
It is a clay marl; left a year on the walk before breaking
up, and then ploughed for pease, which is excellent
husbandry. On the poor parts of the farm his course of
crop is, 1. turnips ; 2. white oats ; but if the turnips
are left late in the spring, then buck-wheat sown the
first week in June ; 3. ray-grass, one bushel per acre,
and if the land is not of the worst sort, one-fourth peck

the winter this compost is laid upon the land for beans, at the rate of 16
loads per acre, and is, without exception, the first manure that is to be met
with. In some parts of Suffolk and Essex, *near the chalk-pits*, the farmers
are very extravagant in the use of it ; and in Essex they are said to have
injured their cold wet lands very much by it. Chalk certainly gives to the
land a solidity, and is a great check to weeds in general ; but in a few years
will settle down lower than the land is ploughed ; for which reason it
should be used sparingly, and renewed again in eight or ten years. Chalk
being so expensive, and difficult to procure in Colness and Sampford hundreds, has been the cause of a frugal use of it ; for I doubt not, had it been
found in the country, the farmers would have split upon the same rock as
the Essex farmers have done, *by using too much of a good thing.* This
manure has been used *mixed*, as before described, more than thirty years
in this country with success ; and it is a saying at this time amongst the
oldest occupiers, " Leave off buying chalk, and you leave off selling corn."
Land certainly has been found to plant better with turnips and clover, since
the introduction of chalk; and the wheat and barley to be of a better colour
and quality.—*Anthony Collet, Esq.*

of clover; seeds it the first year, and leaves it two, three, or four. Upon this lay clay for, 4. pease; 5. rye; on one earth. But upon the good loam, his course is the common and excellent one of 1. turnips; 2. barley; 3. clover; 4. wheat. He finds upon the poorest sands, that he can get white oats where barley would fail.

The late Mr. W. Macro, thus examined the question of the profit of claying by a tenant:—" As a well-wisher to all improvements in agriculture, I am sorry to find that it is now out of fashion for the proprietors of lands to bear any part of the great expence that attends claying and marling, and which on that account, falls heavy upon the common farmer that has a taste and spirit for improvement, and who, after spending a sum of money nearly equal to the value of the lands he improves, lies under a probability of not enjoying the benefit for more than fifteen years,* without due return for all his labour and industry, with the chance of being obliged to pay an advanced rent for his own improvements.

" To begin with the expence: the first is the *filling*, which (including spreading) is 25s. a hundred, or 2½d. a load, with an allowance by some farmers, of 2s. 6d. by others, of 5s. for opening the pit, and 1s. a load for all the large stones they throw out at the time of filling; the farmer to find drifts and stakes for letting down what they call the *falls*.

" The team must consist of four strong traice horses,

---

* I say little more than 15 years, because, if a farmer lets his lands lie a proper time after claying, and allowing a proper time likewise for threshing and going to market, it will be near three years before he gets any of his money into his pocket again from the first year's claying, and allowing him six or seven years to get over a large tract of land: he will then enjoy the first improvement about 18 years, and the last about 12 or 13 years, the medium of which will be about what I have above stated.

and two shaft ditto, which, for such strong work, must have very high keeping; I cannot, therefore, lay their labour at less than 2*s.* a day each,* and the carter at 1*s.* 6*d.* a day, which, supposing they carry one day with another (allowing for wet weather, and hindrance by accidents, &c.) 30 loads a day, will be about 5¼*d.* per load more, making in the whole 7¾*d.* a load, for filling, carting, and spreading.

" As farmers differ in opinion about the quantity that should be laid upon an acre, some preferring 80 loads, and others 70, I will take the medium, and say 75 loads, which at 7¾*d.* a load is,

	£.	s.	d.
per acre	2	8	5¼
Harrowing and rolling several times, to pulverize and spread it equally on the surface, per acre - - - -	0	1	6
Picking the stones up, and carting off, where used for the highways, per acre -	0	0	0
Loss by the stones thrown out by the labourers in the pit, the farmer seldom making half the money of them again, about a load to 70 loads of clay -	0	0	0
Wear and tear of carts and harness, including accidents, at a farthing per load, per acre	0	1	6¼
Drifts, stakes, &c. &c. per acre -	0	0	0
Loss of seed, as it should always be laid upon a layer, and lie some months before it is ploughed in, per acre - - -	0	1	0
	£. 2	12	6

* Two shillings a day for a cart-horse may be thought a high price, but when it is considered that he is, or ought to be worth 20*l.* I believe no person in his senses would lend another such a horse, pay keeping, shoeing, and farrier, and run the hazard of his being spoiled, by being whipped and strained thirty times a day out of clay-pit, for less money.

		£.	s.	d.

Interest of the above sum for two years and
a half, as it will be so long before the
farmer gets any of his money into his
pocket again   -   -   -   -   0 6 6¼

£. 2 19 0¼

" The next expence the farmer has to encounter (and
which must ever be a deduction from improvements in
agriculture in this kingdom, as the laws now stand) is
the *tythes;* for no sooner has he been at the expence of
carrying a thousand or two thousand loads of clay, or
marl, than his rector may demand a larger *composition*.

" The farmer's argument, that he has been at all the
expence, and has not yet any of his money into his
pocket again, is of no avail; for he tells him that the
tenth of all his past, and future improvements, are, by
law, as firmly vested in him, and his successors, as if
a tenth part of the expence had been taken from his
(the rector's) own pocket; therefore, if he will not give
him ten or fifteen pounds a year more, he must draw
his tythes. And thus, on some improved farms in
Norfolk (as I have been informed) before the first lease
is expired, they have paid nearly as much in tythes as
they did in rent.

" To return to the 2*l.* 19*s.* 0¼*d.* which sum, being
money sunk upon another person's estate, the interest of
it is not only an additional rent to the farmer, of about
3*s.* an acre, but he is in all fairness, in the course of
his term, to be reimbursed the principal likewise; and
which sums added together, allowing for the decrease of
interest, as the principal is paid off, I calculate to
amount to 5*s.* 6*d.* an acre per annum, which, supposing
the rent to be 5*s.* an acre when the farmer enters upon

his farm, more than doubles it, from the time of improving till the lease expires.

Mr. Brettingham, near Bungay, writes me, that the lands at Ilketshall are much clayed, often to the amount of eighty to one hundred and twenty loads an acre, twenty-four bushels each, which makes it necessary to cart off the turnip crops.

Mr. Parlby, of Stoke, by Nayland, remarks, that " that parish is six miles by three ; the soil generally light This large area formerly grew very little wheat or barley, but chiefly rye, buck-wheat, or oats ; many of the gravelly hills were covered only with broom, which now, by proper composts with chalk, produce fair crops of the finest wheat and barley. The method of chalking the land was introduced about sixty years ago ; since which time the agriculture of the parish has been constantly improving, and the general surface of it is now covered with very fine crops of wheat, barley, oats, &c."

In Sampford hundred, the soil rich loamy sand ; they buy Kentish chalk at Manningtree, at seven shillings a five-horse load, with which they form composts for turnips ; they do this while London dung may be had at ten shillings a load.

CRAG.

In a part of the maritime sand district called *the Sandlings*, which are south of Woodbridge, Orford, and Saxmundham, they formerly made a very great improvement, by spreading shell marl on the black ling heaths, with which all that tract was once covered. But as the marl, called there crag, is all dry powdered shells, like running sand, without any principle of adhesion, the effect was good only once ; for, after cultivating those heaths, on trying the crag a second time, it was found to do little or no good ; and, in some instances, even to make the sand *blow* the more. It seems, therefore, to have acted in this respect like lime, which has been frequently found to have great effect on the first application, upon lands long in a state of nature ; but on repetition, that effect has been found to decline.

TOWN MANURES.

In the neighbourhood of all the towns in this county, the farmers have for thirty years past been very assiduous in purchasing all sorts of manures ; so that the price has been gradually rising to 5s. or 6s. a waggon load, for even the inferior sorts : at five miles distance, a load of dung is estimated to cost, by the time it is on the land, from 12s. to 15s. ; an expence so enormous, as to leave it a question whether it answers. In the neighbourhood of Bury, farmers neglect soot, which is carried to others at Isleham, Burwell, &c. at a more considerable expence, eight-pence and nine-pence a bushel, besides many miles of carriage.

1803. The expence of town manures has since risen considerably. Dung, &c. to 7s. 6d. and 8s. a waggon load, and soot to 1s. a bushel. I have heard it calculated that dung is now spread at the expence of 21s. a waggon load.

In Sampford hundred, the soil a rich sandy loam, they buy large quantities at Manningtree, which come from London, and for which they give 10s. for a five-horse load at the quay, and which costs 20s. when on the land ; all spread for turnips. There is great vigour in such an exertion.

FARM-YARD COMPOSTS.

The methods of this county are those general in the kingdom, and extremely deficient. The dung and refuse straw is turned over in the spring, and thrown into heaps, where it lies some time to dry ; or carted on to hedge rows upon earth turned up to receive it, often remaining exposed to the sun and wind before it is covered up with earth, gaining nothing by the mixture; whereas, had the earth been carted into the yards in autumn, as a foundation for the dunghill, it would in the course of the winter be well saturated with urine, and in the spring be ready to cover the dung immediately in turning, or to be carted without.

It is an almost general error, to be too inattentive to the quality of the dung thus made. It is scarcely credible how many farmers, good ones in other respects, manage their farm yards in such a manner, as would impress a belief that they thought the sun, air, wind, and rain, extracted nothing valuable from a dung-hill ; and that the washings running into a ditch, a river, or a pond, did not carry off the most valuable part. Landlords, however, are much to be condemned, when they form farm-yards, not to prepare conveniencies so obviously adapted to the right practice, as to force an adherence to it.

CROPS TO WHICH MANURE IS APPLIED.

Upon this subject a question in practice arises in Suffolk, whether the dung and composts of various kinds should be spread for turnips, or upon clover lays and fallows for wheat? I have attentively remarked the practice in various parts of the county, and it appears,

that in the best cultivated districts, manure is applied
for turnips: this is the case in Sampford hundred, on
the rich loams and sands, and with great success. There
are many good farmers who are in different habits, but
the balance, on an accurate examination, would be
against them.

<hr>

SECT. IV.—IRRIGATION.

Of all the improvements wanting in this county,
there is none so obvious, and of such importance, as
watering meadows. The rivers, streams, and brooks,
in every part, are numerous; few countries are better
watered with small streams; yet is there not a well-
watered meadow in the county;* at least, not one to
my knowledge. Some individuals have been so struck
with the benefit of partial flooding by accident, that
they have thrown water over meadows, but never have
done it in a manner to be highly beneficial, and usually
without any attention to take it off again But of all
improvements, this is perhaps the most unquestionable
and important. To view large tracts of poor and un-
productive arable land, below those levels in which
water might be made to flow, is a spectacle that wounds

* After reading Mr. Boswell's Treatise on watering meadows, and
conversing with a gentleman well acquainted with him, and with the
directions necessary to be given for the proper management of the
work, I have, since the beginning of November last, completed such
works as to be able to lay the greatest part of three meadows, containing
more than 20 acres, completely under water at any time, when there is
a stream running; and I have very little doubt, but the practice will
become general in a few years, where it can be done.—*Note by J. P.
Denham.*

every feeling of a man that looks about him with the eye of an irrigator; and yet this horrid sight is to be found almost in every parish of the county, at least in the vicinity of every stream, and in lands kept in the hands of gentlemen who call themselves farmers, and are really fond of husbandry. It would be idle to enter at large into the means of effecting this improvement. It is understood and practised, in great perfection, in many of our counties, and men to perform the operation easy to be had.*

1803. In ten years something has been done, a little; but sorry I am to say, that the county still continues liable to just condemnation for the extreme slowness with which this improvement moves. Joshua Grigby, Esq. at Drinkstone, has watered a meadow, and is about to extend the irrigation to others.

* The mode of sending for men from other counties to irrigate the meadows, has been embraced by a few individuals in the county within these last two or three years; and it is most sincerely to be wished that it may become general.—*Note by J. R.*

CHAPTER VIII.

LIVE STOCK.

THIS object is perhaps the most important in the whole range of rural economies. The poorest and most backward nations contrive to raise bread for their consumption, equal to the demand; and to increase the quantity with the increase of their mouths. Their wheat, in the most miserable husbandry, is nearly equal, and much of it superior, to that of our highly cultivated fields; and we feel constantly in our markets the effect of their competition; but with all that concerns live stock, the case is abundantly different; it is by great exertions only, that a people can be well supplied, and for want of such exertions, many nations are forced to content themselves with such meat as others would not touch. Look at a sample of French and Swiss wheat, no difference is found; but examine the cows of Swisserland and of Lorraine, what a difference! Compare the mares of Flanders with the ponies of Bretagne, the sheep of England and of France; reflect on the wool in competition; examine the fleeces of Segovia and of Italy, in the same parallel of latitude.

Next to the cultivation of waste lands (which, by the way, much depends on the well ordering of live stock), this is the greatest desideratum in the agriculture of Britain. The sheep, cows, hogs, and horses of Suffolk, demand attention.

SECT. I.—CATTLE.

The cows of Suffolk have long been celebrated for the great quantity of their milk, which, I believe, much exceeds, on an average, that of any other breed in the island, if quantity of food and size of the animal are taken into the account.

The country, which is more peculiarly, but not exclusively the seat of the dairies, is marked out by the parishes of Codenham, Ashbocking, Otley, Charlsfield, Letheringham, Hatcheston, Parham, Framlingham, Cransford, Bruisyard, Badingham, Sibton, Heveningham, Cookly, Linstead, Metfield, Wethersdale, Fressingfield, Wingfield, Hoxne, Brome, Thrandeston, Geslingham, Tenningham, Westrop, Wyverston, Gipping, Stonham, Greting ; and again to Codenham, with all the places within, being a tract of country of 20 miles by 12. The limits cannot be exact, for this breed of cows spreads over the whole county ; but this space must be more peculiarly considered as their head quarters.

The breed is universally *polled*,* that is, without horns ; the size small ; few rise, when fattened, to above 50 stone (14lbs.). The points admitted are, a clean throat, with little dewlap ; a snake head ; clean thin legs, and short ; a springing rib, and large carcass ; a flat loin, the hip bones to lie square and even ; the tail to rise high from the rump. This is the description of

---

* The breed is in general polled; but a certain proportion of the calves would have horns, if reared : the inconvenience of horned cattle among horses, and the damage they do to fences, are an inducement to the farmers to sell all the calves as veal to the butchers, or to the sucklers, which would have horns, and to keep for stock only the polled ones. The horns are to be felt at a very early age

some considerable dairy-men. But if I was to describe
the points of certain individuals, which were very famous for their quantity of milk, it would vary in several
points ; and these would be such as are applicable to
great numbers: a clean throat, with little dewlap; a
thin clean snake head ; thin legs ; a very large carcass;
a rib tolerably springing from the centre of the back,
but with a heavy belly ; back-bone ridged ; chine thin
and hollow ; loin narrow ; udder large, loose, and
creased when empty ; milk-veins remarkably large,
and rising in knotted puffs to the eye. This is so general, that I scarcely ever saw amongst them a famous
milker that did not possess this point. A general habit
of leanness, hip-bones high and ill-covered, and scarcely
any part of the carcas so formed and covered as to please
an eye that is accustomed to fat beasts of the finer breeds.
But something of a contradiction to this, in appearance,
is, that many of these beasts fatten remarkable well, the
flesh of a fine quality ; and in that state will *feel* well
enough to satisfy the touch of skilful butchers. The
best milkers I have known, have been either red, brindle,
or yellowish cream-coloured.*

The quantity of milk given is very considerable indeed. There are few dairys of any consideration in the
district, that does not contain cows which give, in the
height of the season, that is, in the beginning of June,
eight gallons of milk in the day ; and six are not uncommon for a large part of the season. For two or

* Several farmers in the parish of Hoxne, have found great advantage
from a cross between the true Suffolk polled cow, and the short horned
Yorkshire. The calves have been better either to fat young, or to keep
for stock. A steer of this breed, barely three years old, was killed last
Christmas, and weighed more than 69 stone. Cows from this cross,
upon good land, give a great quantity of rich milk.—*Note by T. M.*——
I cannot recommend any crosses for the Suffolk breed, with a view to
the dairy.—*A. Y.*

three months a whole dairy will give, for all that give
milk at all, five gallons a day on an average, if the season
is not unfavourable, which, *for cows of this size*, is very
considerable.—When the quantity of milk in any breed
is very great, that of butter is rarely equal. It is thus
in Suffolk ; the quantity of milk is more extraordinary
than that of the butter. The average of all the dairies
of the district may be estimated at three firkins ; and
three-fourths of a wey of cheese per cow, clear to the
factor's hands, after supplying the consumption of the
family. The hogs are very generally laid at a guinea
per cow, and a calf, at a fortnight old, half-a-guinea.

	£.	s.	d.
Three firkins, at 38s. average price of last seven years,	5	14	0
Three fourths wey, at 36s.	1	7	0
Hogs,	1	1	0
Calf,	0	10	6
£.	8	12	6

(1803.—The rise of prices has carried this sum to
12l. 12s.)

About 2s. or 3s. may be deducted from this, on account of the calves reared to keep up the stock ; and if
something more is struck off on account of a few ill-
managed dairies, that do not properly come into the
account, it may reduce it to eight guineas. Instances
are numerous, that raise it higher. The cows of a farm
at Aspal, have paid more than once 8l. per cow, when
butter and cheese were at 32s. Another of nine cows,
produced thirty-one firkins. The butter and cheese of
a farm of 90l. a year, let nearly at its value, produced
(price at 32s.) 140l. and there are 40 acres under the
plough. A farm of 185l. a year, that has near 100 acres

of arable, produced 121 firkins of butter, and 65 weys
of cheese. In another instance, 20 cows made 80
firkins, besides cheese ; and another, in which the cows
made four firkins of butter each, but no cheese. The
common calculation is, that a cow in milk eats in summer two acres of grass ; and that on an average of twenty
miles by twelve, there is one cow to every five acres of
the whole country.

In regard to the expences, the dairy-maid earns to
the full amount of her wages, by spinning hemp or
wool ; and as she is fed pretty much from the dairy,
the charge is very small. Interest of the capital invested
in the cow is 7s. 6d. or 8s. as much more for losses.
Fuel, and wear and tear, add something. Hay is from
one-half to three-fourths of a ton per cow ; or, as they
calculate by expence to the farmer, and not value in the
market, 15s. The profit left, much exceeds what any
other application of the soil would yield, which, though
good for cows, is not rich enough for fattening oxen
beneficially.

In feeding these cows, the most singular circumstance
is, the use of cabbages,* an article of culture which gradually established itself within about twenty five years
past, each farmer usually having a small field merely
for the use of his cows ; and turnips are cultivated on a
small scale for the same purpose. Opinions are much
divided concerning the profit of the practice. Carting
off these crops on such wet land, is very prejudicial to
the succeeding corn ; consequently, those who make

---

* The practice of growing cabbages in this neighbourhood, about ten
years since, amongst the dairy farmers, was almost general ; and some
were grown by graziers ; the food was much approved of ; but the damage done to the succeeding crops was looked upon as very great. This
seems confirmed by there not being one acre growing within six miles
this year.—Note by J. P. Denham.

corn the first object, do not approve them; but the more
intelligent men, who consider the dairy as the principal
point to attend to, approve cabbages. The value of an
acre rises from 4*l.* to 7*l.* In respect to their utility for
cows, there is but one opinion : every one agrees, that
cabbages and straw are by far better food for milch cows
than any quantity of hay; and a circumstance that
proved the goodness of the food for butter, was, the veal
carts, which go regularly from this district to London,
taking large quantities of butter, which was sold and
eaten as hay-butter as long as cabbages remained sound;
but when they rot, there is an end of this laudable deceit, as no management can do the same thing with
turnips.*

Another circumstance in the management of their
cows deserving notice, is, that of tying them up in the
fields, without house, or shed, or roof to cover them.
With rails and stakes they form a rough manger ; and
the cows are tied to posts about three feet from each ;
at their heads is a screen of faggots. Litter is regularly
given, and the dung piled up in a wall behind. They
find this better than letting them range at will, for cows
before calving; and that the shelter of the hedge and

* To obviate the inconvenience of carting cabbages or turnips from
heavy land, I recommend a small cart on a roller ; but in every instance
where turnips can be fed upon ground where they grow, I strongly
recommend it, being convinced that the barley crop following fed turnips, will be from four to eight bushels per acre more than where the
turnips have been drawn. Cabbages should at all times have the outward decayed leaves stripped off before they are given to cows, otherwise the butter must be bad. I have tasted butter made from turnip-fed
cows, equal to any spring grass butter, which was effected by scalding
the milk; it would not answer for carrying any distance, because the
perfect sweetness of it does not remain above two days; but for eating
quite fresh made, nothing can be better.—*Note by a Correspondent of the
Board.*

dung, and the warmth of their bodies, are enough without any cover.

The greatest fault to be found with their management, is the carelessness with which they breed. There is no such thing in the country as a bull more than three years old; two years the common age. The consequence of this is inevitably, that, before the merit can be known of the stock gotten, the bull is no more. It must be obvious, that such a system precludes all improvements. It springs very much from the want of the spirit of breeding getting into this country; but this cannot originate here, while the price of a bull is 4*l.* or 5*l.* If a very attentive breeder was to arise, who bred merely for quantity of milk, and procured a breed better than any of his neighbours, and could attain the price of guinea for covering a cow, something would gradually be done; for this purpose, there should be premiums given, or some other method taken, to excite a spirit of emulation.*

On the management of Suffolk dairies, Mrs. Chevallier, of Aspal, thus communicates :—" In the visit we had lately the pleasure of receiving from you, your inquiries concerning cows, and the management of our dairies, were, I believe much more numerous than very easily to be satisfied. Your request that I would make up the deficiency, by sending you such particulars as have occurred to me, was dictated, I am afraid, rather by your partiality than your judgment; for I assure you, there is nothing in my own management peculiar, nor does it exceed that of any well-conducted dairy in this county. And I request you will observe, that my only inducement for throwing a word of the subject on

---

* The quantity of butter supposed to be sent from Suffolk to London, annually, is about 40,000 firkins.

paper, is your opinion that there are circumstances common here which are not so in other counties ; but which may be useful if better known : should this not be the case, remember that you are more answerable for this letter than myself.

" In the conversation I heard on your purchasing cows, I observed that you inquired after large and hand-some ones ; but I have often known little cows not at all remarkable for beauty, give more milk than the greatest; for instance, at present, the smallest cow we have, a cream coloured polled one, gives more milk than any of the rest, though some are almost double the size. This cow last summer, for some time in the height of the season, gave four gallons of milk at a meal, twice a day; three gallons for the rest of the summer, and has given more than two gallons within two months of calving. This vast quantity of milk is not uncommon in this country.

" But I recollect an observation you made, on the product in money of cows being nearer a par through the kingdom than the quantity of milk ; and it may be said, that the milk of cows which give so much, is not so rich as when the quantity is less. Mr. Chevallier having some horned cows from Mr. Toosey's breed, and originally from Mr. Bakewell, which do not give so much milk as our Suffolk breed, I tried an experiment lately for comparing the quality of the milk. Three quarts from a Suffolk polled cow, and the same quantity from a horned one of Mr. Toosey's breed, were set in separate bowls ; stood thirty-six hours, and then skimmed ; the Suffolk milk gave two and one-third ounces more cream than the horned one; it was put into two clean quart bottles and churned : the quantity of butter exactly one-fourth more from the cream of the polled than from that of the horned cow. Then

added to each bowl of milk an equal quantity of hot
water, and after twelve hours skimmed them a second
time ; when the milk of the horned cow yielded four
ounces more cream than that of the polled. As in the
first experiment the superiority of butter was more than
that of cream, we may conclude from this trial, that
the quality of the milk was very nearly equal. I repeated the experiment to try the weight of an equal
quantity of the cream of each : the milk stood thirty-
six hours ; the quantity was about one-sixth more from
the polled than from the horned cow ; the weight of
the same measure of each, equal. I do not offer these
experiments as decisive, nor by any means sufficient to
draw conclusions from ; but they seem to deserve attention for varying and repeating them with more care and
accuracy, that if any material difference is found, it may
be known. All I can conclude at present is, that the
milk of the polled cows appears to be as rich as that of
the horned ones ; but the quantity they give in summer
is greater ; and that will be the proper season for
repeating these trials.

" By similar experiments it would be easy to ascertain
whether the milk of cows that are generally in good
order or fat, is not superior in quality to that of others
of the same polled breed, that are poor and lean.

" Certain it is, that the product of our polled breed
is very great. In the year 1784, I made from five cows
to the amount of 42l. besides the milk and cream consumed by a family of fourteen in number ; nor was that
a more productive year than common, for I have done
it more than once : and I am informed that 7l. per cow
is very common in this country, large dairies through,
on an average.

" The following is the product of one with which I
am well acquainted :

	£.	s.	d.
3 Firkins of butter, at 32s. - -	4	16	0
1 Wey of cheese, - - -	1	12	6
Hogs, - - - - -	1	0	0
Calf, - - - -	0	10	6
Per Cow, - - - -	£. 7	18	6

" And I may observe to you, that a farmer at Bad-
dingham, who has forty-eight cows, and has neither
wife nor housekeeper, hired a dairy-maid at 9d. per
firkin of butter and wey of cheese, and her wages came
to 6l. 19s 5d.; the number must therefore have been
186, or very near four per cow.

" In order to secure such products, several circumstances must unite: no cows are to be kept that do not
milk well; they must be fed plentifully; and well
kept in winter, when cabbages are found essentially
useful; but this is a point which I leave to Mr. Chevallier; he can give you better information on it.
Extreme cleanliness in the dairy is an article on which
more depends than is usually conceived; not in quality
only, but even in quantity of produce.

" I have found it a very good way to add, in winter,
hot water to milk directly as it comes from the cow; it
makes it yield the cream better   The trays in which it
is set should also be scalded with hot water, or else
warmed by the fire, before the milk is set in them. All
trays should be of deal, about three inches and an half
deep; they are preferable to lead, which not only blisters
when hot water is poured into them, but are said to be
unwholsome. About twelve square yards of tray will
do for twenty cows, with some spare bowls. And the
churn for such a dairy should contain about fifty gallons,
beer measure. The copper should hold an hundred

gallons. Chaffing dishes of charcoal are kept in dairies
in frost, but the cream does not rise so well. The best
dairy-maids never put the butter in layers in the firkin;
but leave the surface every day rough and broken, in
order to unite better with that of the succeeding churn-
ing : from three and an half to four pints of salt commonly used to a firkin of butter ; but two with good
management are better. The milk after the first skimming is left twelve hours more in the farm house, to
make a second butter, which the poor buy at four-pence
per pound. Another advantage for them is, skim-milk
being constantly sold at three pints for a halfpenny. A
dairy-maid commonly milks seven or eight cows in an
hour ; but Mr. Sad, of Little Stonham, had a maid who
milked for a wager, thirty cows in three hours, and was
followed to see that she milked clean. In your calculations, you must not charge the dairy with all the expence of the dairy-maids ; for they spin usually four-
pence a day (or to the full amount of their wages) either
by hemp for the family use, or wool, the business of the
dairy being over by nine or ten o'clock ; and in all the
calculations of produce in this country, the sale to the
butter-factor is meant, which is exclusive of the family
consumption. Hence the labour of the dairy is reduced
exceedingly.

" In relation to weaning calves, my method, which
has proved very successful, is to take them from the cow
at a fortnight old, and to give them water-gruel and hay,
by which means they are weaned at a very small
expence, and with little skimmed milk.

" If not carefully attended to in the winter following,
they are subject to the garget ; by which distemper I
have known eight lost out of nine. I believe it is nearly
the same as the rheumatism in the human body ; lying
wet, or having only very wet land to be on, will

certainly give it: I know no cure; but being kept
perfectly dry, is an almost sure prevention."

SCOTCH CATTLE.

In those parts of the county where the sheep and
cows do not consume the turnips, the common practice
is, to buy black cattle at fairs, from north country dro-
vers, for that purpose. Some are Irish, and some
Welch; but the greater part are Scotch, of various
breeds; Galloways, Fifes, and Highlanders The system
in which they are grazed, is of two kinds: some farmers
buy in autumn, and give a winter's straw, fattening
them in summer; this takes place where live stock is
wanting to consume the straw. The other method is
practised when the common stock of the farm is sufficient for the straw; then to purchase in autumn, and
put to rouen for seven or eight weeks, and from that to
turnips, to which hay is added; and a few farmers
have finished on oil cake, and other articles of food.
The late Mr. Mure, of Saxham, stall-fed on a very
large scale, upon cabbages and potatoes This is a
branch of the farmer's business, in which *general* details
are nearly useless; it is only by the recital of particular
experiments, that any accurate conclusions can be drawn.

SECT. II.—SHEEP.

THE Norfolk breed of sheep spread over almost every
part of the county; and as the most famous flocks are
about Bury (much more celebrated than any in Norfolk),

it has been observed, that they ought rather to be called
the Suffolk breed. This race is so well known, that it
would be useless to give a particular description of them;
it is, however, proper here, to note their principal excellencies and defects. Among the former is the quality
of the mutton ; it being admitted at Smithfield, that as
long as cool weather lasts, it has, for the table of the
curious, no superior in texture or grain, flavour, quantity and colour of gravy, with fat enough for such tables.
In tallow, they reckon no sheep better. In fatting, at
an early age, they are superior to many breeds, though
said to be not equal to some others. The wool is fine,
being in price, per pound, the third sort in England.
Their activity in bearing hard driving, for the fold, is
much spoken of. In hardiness and success, as nurses,
they are also much esteemed in this county. Such are
their excellencies : the defects with which they are re-
proached, are, a voracity of stomach, which demands
more food, in proportion to their weight, than some
other breeds ; and the consequent circumstances of being
necessarily kept very thin on the ground : a want of
that disposition to fatten, which keeps stock in great
order on middling, and extraordinarily fat on good food:
both circumstances, resulting from an ill-formed carcass,
a ridged back, large bones, a thin chine, and heavy offals:
a restless and unquiet disposition, which makes them
difficult to keep in any other than the largest walks,
commons, or fields : a texture of flesh that will not
keep in hot weather so long as that of South Down,
and consequently said to be inferior in price at that
season : a loose ragged habit of wool, losing if not in
high keep.

These ill qualities have so much foundation in facts,
that other breeds are introducing rapidly into both Suffolk
and Norfolk, and promise speedily to be well established.

It is proper to observe, that of all these objections to the Norfolk breed, there is none more notorious, or more susceptible of direct proof, than the number kept on a given quantity of ground; which, in these two counties, is fewer than is kept on similar land, of some other breeds. This is an object of importance; whatever merit or advantage is attained by keeping 500 sheep on a farm of 750 acres sinks much, if 750 of some other breeds might be kept on the same land. The first and greatest of the national interests, as well as the profit of the individual, is intimately concerned in such a position.*

In the management of their flocks, our farmers have no point so interesting, as the almost entire reliance for the winter support on turnips. In some counties, large flocks are kept without turnips: here they have not an idea of the possibility of such a conduct. The late Mr. Macro, and the present Duke of Grafton, have given most particular and accurate details of their respective flocks;† and the former allowed eighty acres of turnips for thirty-six score ewes; besides twenty acres of winter tares, twenty acres of rye, and sixteen tons of hay. The latter, for forty-seven score of ewes, one hundred acres of turnips, fifty of rye, twenty-two tons of hay; and I

---

* It is not in my power to controvert what is here advanced by the author. I cannot however, forbear remarking, that each county seems to have a breed of sheep peculiar to the soil. And were there as much pains taken to remedy the defects in our own breed, as there is in crossing the breeds, and in introducing those of other counties, I conceive that the Norfolk breed would be inferior to none. One method of remedying these defects, would be to alter the mode of choosing the lambs for stock. Instead of the largest, which are now universally preferred, we should choose those which are shortest in the leg, and have the broadest loin and shoulder. This would contribute very considerably to improve the shape complained of, and make them more productive in the fleece.—*Note by J. R.*

† Annals, vol. 2. p. 247. vol. 7. p. 1.

find that it may be taken as a common allowance one
hundred acres of turnips for a flock of thirty score of
ewes, which makes six to an acre. But this breadth will
not be sufficient, without some assistance from hay, and
also from rye ; the quantity of both these vary much.
It depends also on the breadth of sheep-walk ; and whether such walk is well stocked with ling or furz, and
kept back in summer, in order for yielding the more
food in time of snow and frost. If these preparatives
are compared with those of most other counties, it will
be found, that our Suffolk flock-masters allow, with
great liberality, for the winter season, and are at an
immense expence to meet it. Whether this does not
partly arise from the breed they are so fond of, demand-
ing great *keep*, deserves inquiry.

This most ample provision of turnips is, however,
attended with one very great inconvenience ; which is,
the excessive distress that results from such a severity of
weather as rots that crop ; the loss of 100 acres, or even
half of it, in the provision of thirty score ewes, can only
be made up by a dreadful expence in hay ; which, in
such severe winters, is usually at a price much beyond
its average value. I have known flock-masters buy hay
for their sheep, at the rate of 5*l.* a day, for weeks together. Such accidents ought certainly to induce them to
vary their provision more, by substituting cabbages,
kale, cole-seed, Swedish turnips, &c. in lieu of a part of
their turnips.*

* From an experience of twenty-three years, in which, upon a farm of
between twelve and fourteen hundred acres of land, two hundred of which
are heath (which is very black and bad), I have maintained with tolerable
success, from forty-five to fifty-five score breeding ewes; and have found,
that much less provision for them is required, than the author seems to
think Fifty loads of hay have not been expended upon them during the
whole time ; and generally, I have had about one hundred and thirty acres
of turnips yearly, which have been appropriated to the use of the flock.—
Note by J. R.

But the provision, of all others, the most important, because the cheapest and most effective, is *rouen*, as it is called in Suffolk, that is, the after-grass of the mowing ground. The value, fed in autumn, rarely excee s 10*s.* or 12*s.* an acre ; but kept till the spring for ewes and lambs, is worth from 20*s.* to 30*s.* an acre.*

For the summer food of sheep our flock-masters de pend altogether on what is called the sheep-walk (a piece of waste land) and the *layers*, artificial grasses, clover, trefoil and ray, which are regularly sown in their course of crops, and which are often double the quantity of the turnips.

Folding is universally and anxiously practised, as the manure upon which the corn principally depends : the value of it is reckoned from 1*s.* 6*d.* to 1*s.* 8*d.* a head of the flock.†

The other circumstances proper to note are, that the rams are turned into the flock about a fortnight after Michaelmas, sometimes later : and in doing this, ten or twelve will be let in promiscuously among 600 ewes, without the least attention or idea of separating the sixty best ewes to put to the best ram, in order that some part of the flock might be improving ; on the contrary, the worst ewes may, in the common method, have the best ram ; and the best ewes the worst ram. With such con- duct, a farmer has good luck, if his flock is not in a state of degradation. The lambs are born pretty well woolled. They are weaned immediately preceeding Ipswich fair (August 22), perhaps a month too late ; nor is it

* The method of feeding here recommended, would be certainly attended with profit, but in most flock farms there is a great scarcity of meadow, or pasture land.—*Note by J. R.*

† The method of valuation of folding, is generally per acre ; and for thirty score sheep folded within six dozen hurdles, from 7*s.* 6*d.* to 10*s.* 6*d.* per acre. But, in, my opinion, on an improved soil, it is worth much more. —*Note by J. R.*

uncommon to see the lambs drawing the ewes to skeletons, the middle of August, with clover over the hedge in full blussom, *kept for seed*, instead of weaning the lambs in it.*

The following *system*, is the common *flock* management : the wether lambs sold ; and the refuse ewe lambs, after drawing off that number to keep, which supplies the place of the *crones*, sold. The return lamb and wool. Wether lambs of the best flocks sell at from 14*s.* to 15*s.* in good times ; ewes 10*s.* to 11*s.* but the average of all their lambs at Ipswich fair, in a common year, does not exceed 10*s.* 6*d.* The price of flock wool, for seven years, from 1778 to 1784, was 1*l.* 2*s.* 6*d.* the tod of 28lbs. It kept rising till 1789, when it was 29*s.* in 1790 32*s.* in 1791 35*s.* and in 1792 40*s.* In 1796 it sunk to 36*s.* Some flocks sold higher than these prices, but others were lower. It is a point of considerable consequence, to ascertain what is the annual *return* of a sheep in all the breeds of England ; for many curious and important questions, relating not only to the breeds of sheep, but also to the comparison of grass and arable, and of different rotations of crops, depend on it. Mr. Macro's flock returned him 11*s.* 3*d.* a head per annum, for his whole flock of ewes. Prices have risen since ; so that I am inclined to think, that *large* Norfolk sheep like his, which ranked among the finest flocks we had, may be calculated to pay in lamb, wool and fold, 13*s.* a head, which will make just three-pence a week for the year round : but this must not be considered as the average of Suffolk flocks, but beyond it, for great numbers of lambs are sold at Ipswich, Horrenger, Harling, Coolege, and Newmarket fairs, from 6*s.* to 10*s.* each.

* The custom the author here justly ridicules, must not be supposed to be ery prevalent, as there is very little clover-seed grown on flock-farms ; the lands in general not being sufficiently good.—*Note by J. R.*

It is probable, that all the sheep in the county do not pay more than 9s. a head; at least, this is the opinion of various practical farmers, who know the county well. And that it is a matter of serious national concern, to have so great a number of sheep, kept in a county so well adapted to that animal, for so small a return, will, I believe, be admitted by every one.

1803.—Prices having risen greatly since the former edition of this work ; for the three last years the wether lambs of many flocks have reached 20s. and 21s. per head ; and ewe lambs but a few shillings lower ; crones at 15s. and 16s. And wool up to 45s. and even 47s.

There is no other sheep system on a scale large enough to demand particular notice. In the richer parts of the county, most farmers keep a few of a changeable stock, bought and sold every year, either wether lambs kept a year, or a year and a half, and sold to the butcher ; or *crones* bought in autumn ; the lambs sold fat early in summer, and the sheep at the Michaelmas following. Where this is done, it is not common to find them in greater numbers than in the proportion of five acres to a sheep, that is, 20 upon a farm of 100 acres. In all such cases, and speaking not of particular instances, but on a general average, if the farmer doubles his money within the year,* he thinks himself pretty well paid ; if he returns two and a half for one, he is well paid ; but good managers will sometimes treble their money. All such points, however, depend for their merit on the number kept.

Much might easily be added on the subject of shepherds, shearing, mode of folding, distempers, and other interesting objects : but I am giving not a dissertation

* Perhaps the profit is somewhat greater, as the folding, and the feeding of turnips by the flock, is the basis of a good crop on light soils ; indeed, no corn could be grown without this practice on such soils.—*Note by J. R*

on sheep, but the sketch of a county, and wish to confine myself to those points which are somewhat local
and appropriated.

Perhaps it will be admitted that a foreign cross is necessary ; as much so for the profit of the farmer, as for
the interest of the nation. The Norfolk breed certainly
have merit; but merit, purchased at the expence of
keeping only half a fair stock, becomes something very
different from merit. The South Down, and Bakewell's breed, are introduced, and will probably make
their way.

1803.—The efforts which have been made in spreading South Down sheep through this county have been
very successful, even to a full establishment, so that in
several parts of it there are nearly as many of that breed
as of Norfolks, and every year at Ipswich fair the polled
lambs from this cross annually increase, besides a great
and increasing number of the pure blood. In the Appendix, under the article of the Earl of Albemarle's
husbandry, is inserted a most satisfactory and important
comparison of the two breeds on the same farm

In regard to the number of sheep in the whole county,
as it is a point of some importance to approximate to
the truth, I shall calculate thus : that the sand districts
have (which is nearly the fact) one sheep to two acres ;
that the rich and strong loams have one to five acres ;
and that the fen has one to six. Under these proportions,
the numbers will be :

Sand,   270,000 acres,   -   - sheep, 135,000
Loam,   500,000   -   -   -   - 100,000
Fen,   30,000   -   -   -   -   5,000
         ———————   ———————
         800,000   240,000

SECT. III.—HORSES.

THE Suffolk breed of horses, is no less celebrated than the cows. They are found in most perfection, in the district of country that is upon the coast extending to Woodbridge, Debenham, Eye, and Lowestoff. The best of all were found some years ago upon the *Sandlings*, south of Woodbridge and Orford. Amongst the great farmers in that country, there was, forty years ago, a considerable spirit of breeding, and of drawing team against team for large sums of money. Mr. Mays, of Ramsholt-dock, was said to have drawn fifteen horses for 1500 guineas. It is to be regretted, that such a spirit of emulation was lost.—I remember seeing many of the old breed, which were very famous, and, in some respects, an uglier horse could not be viewed ; sorrel colour, very low in the fore-end, a large ill-shaped head, with slouching heavy ears, a great carcass and short legs, but short-backed, and more of the *punch* than the Leicestershire breeders will allow.* These horses could only walk and draw ; they could trot no better than a cow. But their power in drawing was very considerable. Of late years, by aiming at coach-horses, the breed is much changed to a handsomer, lighter, and more active horse. It is yet an excellent breed ; and if the comparison with others, and especially the great black horse of the midland counties, be fairly made, I have no doubt of their beating them in useful draft, that of the cart and the plough. But the fair comparison is this :

* Clean legs and well formed shoulders, are criterions of the true Suffolk horse, points which entitle them to be good movers ; and such they are in general, if used in chaises, and not too long habituated to draw only.— *Note by J. C.*

let a given sum be invested in the purchase of each
breed ; and then, by means of which, will a thousand
ton of earth be moved to a given distance by the smallest
quantity of hay and oats? It is the oats and hay that
are to be compared, not the number or size of the cattle.
The present price of these horses is high ; good geldings,
of five or six years old, selling at thirty to forty guineas.
A spirited and attentive breeder, upon a farm of 1000
or 1500 acres of various soils, that would admit two or
three stallions, and thirty or forty capital mares, might,
by breeding in and in, with close attention to the improvements wanted, advance this breed to a very high perfection, and render it a national object: but then, query,
whether the same expence and attention would not produce a breed of cattle that would, by training, supersede
the use of horses? Of all the branches of live stock,
perhaps nothing is in such an imperfect state as working
oxen ;* in most things that concerns them, we are in
the infancy of agriculture.

The cows and horses of the county are already so
good, that the only attention they want is that of selec-
tion for the purpose of breeding in and in. A skilful
attentive occupier of a large farm, who carried these
breeds to the perfection they admit of, would find his
account greatly in it, and raise the prices of these stock
high enough to excite competition, without which
nothing can be perfected.

In the article *carrots*, I have inserted much information

* I have used for a year past, and continue to use, a pair of oxen to
a plough, harnessed exactly the same as horses, driven with reins, and
the same man drives and ploughs, as done with a pair of Suffolk horses.
I work the pair of oxen but one journey, taking another pair in the
afternoon: by practice, they will walk very fast, and in this way I can
plough from an acre to an acre and a half per day. As they do nothing
but ploughing, and are not used upon the road, they are not shod. —
Note by a Correspondent of the Board.

on the singular method in which Suffolk horses are fed, to which it is necessary here to refer.

Addition.—" In the east district, in winter, horses are never permitted to remain in the stable at night, but about eight o'clock are turned out into a yard, well littered with straw, and have plenty of good sweet oat or barley straw to eat ; but never clover or hay. By this treatment, a horse is never swelled in his legs, or seldom has any ailment about him. Horses in this county, are as good as any in England, and are kept in as fine condition. A horse turned out every night, will hold his work several years longer than one confined in the stable.

" Cutting straw, clover, or hay, and mixing them with the horse-corn and chaff, is a very good way, and is a saving in stover ; but in the county of Kent, where they cut all the provender for their horses, they have a practice which the farmers in Suffolk are not acquainted with, and which I recommend to their notice. It is their custom, in the month of April, or sooner, if the season permits, to cut every day, a small quantity of green rye, and mix with their corn and chaff. Every farmer knows, that in the spring, many horses pine, and take hurt for the want of green food; and if the weather is dry and hot at the time, will see many that will not eat dry meat without its being watered: half an acre sown in the latter end of September, will be sufficient for ten or twelve horses till they go out to grass. Lucern will come in to cut as early as rye, and is preferable. I am convinced that whoever tries this *once,* will never leave off the practice."—*A. Collet, Esq.*

SECT. IV.—HOGS.

OF the hogs of Suffolk I shall only observe, that the short white breed of the cow district has very great merit : well made, thick short noses, small bone, and light offals; but not quite so prolific as some worse made breeds.

SECT. V.—RABBITS.

THERE are many warrens in Suffolk, especially in the western sand district ; but within the twenty last years, great tracts of them have been ploughed up, and converted to the much better use of yielding corn, mutton and wool.* From this circumstance, has arisen the great increase of the price of these furs. Thirty years ago, the skins were at five shillings a dozen ; they gradually rose to twelve shillings ; but, since the commencement of the present war, have fallen to seven shillings, which may be considered ar an event favourable to agriculture ; for improvements will, without question, be the consequence. It is very difficult to gain a satisfactory knowledge of the acreable produce of land, in this application of the soil ; for the warrens are more commonly estimated than measured. There

* I apprehend that the soil of the principal part of the warrens in this county, is so extremely barren, and at so great a distance from lands of superior quality, from whence they might be improved, the present method of farming them with rabbits, produces more profit than any other that could possibly be devised, both to individuals and the public at large.—*Note by J R.*——If so, why have such large tracts been ploughed at a higher rent ?—*A. Y.*

is one near Brandon, which is said to return above forty
thousand rabbits in a year. Estimating the skin at
seven-pence, and the flesh at three-pence (in the country
it sells at four-pence, and five-pence), it makes ten-
pence a head ; and if ten are killed annually, per acre,
the produce is eight shillings and four-pence ; which
may not be far from the fact, on some soils ; but variations are very considerable. The expences are lessened,
since faggots, which the rabbits peel, have been partly
substituted in lieu of much of the hay which was once
thought necessary for them in snows.*

SECT. VI.—POULTRY.

I LET the title of the section stand, to shew that if
any Suffolk farmer has information to communicate, it
will be received with thanks. The county is exceedingly well supplied, and especially with turkeys, for
which it is almost as famous as Norfolk.

SECT. VII.—PIGEONS.

PIGEON houses abound in the open field part of the
county bordering on Cambridgeshire ; but I have had
no communications touching the advantages or disad-
vantages of them.

* The calculation in Lincolnshire is, that an acre of warren should
produce twenty rabbits annually. The carcass is estimated to defray the
rent and expences, and the skins are considered as clear profit. If this
calculation be generally true, there is no mode of occupying such land
as is usually appropriated to warrens, that can compare with it, in point
of profit to the occupier.—*Note by a Correspondent of the Board.*

SECT. VIII.—BEES,

ARE very little attended to, in general ; they would probably, in the neighbourhood of uncultivated lands, admit of a considerable increase.

CHAPTER XIV.

RURAL ECONOMY.

SECT. I.—LABOUR.

THE variations in the price of labour in the county, are not considerable : it may be stated generally (beer included) at 1s. 4d.* in winter, 1s. 6d. in summer, and 2s. 10d. in harvest. Call winter twenty-nine weeks, harvest five, and summer eighteen ; this will make the year's earnings 23l. 18s. A woman earns sixpence, and the wages of men servants rise from 5l. to 10l.

These are prices by the day ; but the great mass of work in this county is done by the *piece*, in which earnings are usually much higher.† With a clay cart, which goes on through winter, the earnings are pretty generally 10s. a week ; and but little work is taken, at

---

* Labour by the day, in the parish of Hoxne, is only one shilling, and beer, from the end of September till new layers are began to be cut: from that time till the end of September, one shilling and four-pence, and beer, except during the harvest: for the harvest month, if the men are not taken into the family, they generally have half-a-crown a day, and two bushels of malt.—*Note by a Correspondent of the Board.*

† The putting out work by the piece is certainly preferable to work by the day, and that which I have always pursued. By this mean, the labourer works with greater satisfaction to himself, and does more for his master ; his earnings being then more than here estimated, in general.—*Note by J. R.*

that season, for less than 9s. In summer, the rates are higher. In regard to the rise in labour, it is considerable. In my own vicinity, I remember it to have risen in twenty to twenty-five years, from 1s. in winter, to 1s. 4d. a day ; and in harvest from 10s. to 12s. and of late to 14s. a week. There are parts of the county, where the rise has not been equally great.

Some rates of labour communicated by correspondents, are : at Brome, from Lady-day to Michaelmas, 1s. 4d. and pint of beer ; the other half year 1s. 2d. and ditto ; at Hopton, 1s. 6d. summer, 1s. 4d. winter ; at Fornham St. Martin, 1s. 5d. no beer ; at Lackford, 9s. a week, and small beer.

1803. The effect which the two scarcities have had in raising the price of labour, united with that of military arrangements, has been very great indeed. The last and present year, with rather a low price of corn, the prices have advanced in such a manner as to threaten the farmers profit most severely. We now pay,

In winter 10s. 6d. a week without beer.

In summer 12s. ditto.

In harvest 7l. 7s. 0d. for 5 weeks, or 29s. 4d. per week, including every thing.

Winter, 29 weeks, at 10s. 6d.	-		15	4	6
Harvest, 5 weeks, at 29s. 4d.	-	-	7	7	0
Summer, 18 weeks, at 12s.	-	-	10	16	0
52			33	7	6
	Before	-	23	18	0
	Increase	-	9	9	6

Or a rise of above 27 per cent.

Suppose the labour of 100 acres of land, at the rent of 20s. an acre, was, under the former case, 100l.

which was nearly the fact, it is now become 127*l.*; and this, with the present price of corn, is a deduction from his former profit of 5*s*. 4*d*. per acre. If to this is added 9*d*. per acre income tax, the rise of poor rates, tithe, and wear and tear, an account will be formed, the effect of which will by and by be felt by landlords in a manner they do not think of at present.

SECT. II.—PROVISIONS.

THROUGHOUT the county, the average of mutton, beef, and veal, to take no *weighing* meat, on contract for the whole year, may be stated at 5*d*. per pound. But mutton usually a halfpenny per pound dearer than beef ; and the coarse joints of the latter, bought *in the afternoon*, may be had in general by poor house-keepers, at 2*d*. or 2½*d*. the pound. Pork 5½*d*. Butter, salt 8½*d*. 9*d*. and 9¼*d*. ; fresh 10*d*.* and to 1*s*. at scarce seasons. Cheese 5*d*. but Suffolk 3½*d*. and 4*d*. The price of all these is risen considerably in twenty years. Bread 1½*d*. and not risen.

1803. The prices of meat, except pork, are at present high.

	s.	*d.*
Beef, mutton, and veal, - - - -	0	8½
Pork, - - - - - -	0	6
Butter, - - - - - -	1	6
Suffolk cheese, - - - -	4*d*. to	6

* At Hoxne, fresh butter is always sold by the pint (a pound and a quarter), and during many weeks of this winter, it hath been sold at one shilling per pint : a very rare circumstance indeed.— *Note by a Correspondent of the Board.*

SECT. III.—FUEL.

THE fuel of the poor is in general wood; but for the last twenty years, coals have been gradually introducing in some cottages; and in the parts of the county joining to heaths, fens, and commons, they burn, as in other countries, heath and peat.

CHAPTER XV.

POLITICAL ECONOMY.

SECT. I. ROADS.

THESE are uncommonly good in every part of the county ; so that a traveller is nearly able to move in a post-chaise by a map, almost sure of finding excellent gravel roads ; many cross ones in most directions equal to turnpikes. The improvements in this respect, in the last twenty years, are almost inconceivable.

SECT. II.—CANALS.

For the following account of the new navigation from Stowmarket to Ipswich, I am indebted to the Rev. Henry Hill, of Buxhall:

It will be a great satisfaction to me, to give you the best intelligence in my power respecting our navigation ; or on any other subject which may assist you in your very useful undertaking. I have, therefore, according to your request, sent you a full statement of the expences, receipts, &c. &c. of the canal from Stowmarket to Ipswich ; the expence of making which, was greatly enhanced by the trustees being forced into a law-suit with the first contractors who had began the work, sometime before they were dismissed; and as their work was began at the lower end, at different places, and could not be settled for till after the law-suit was concluded, the trustees were obliged to begin their works at the upper end, consequently the carriage of many of the heaviest materials, which would have been brought by water-carriage (had the works been finished below first), were brought by land. It is now nearly completed, and of infinite service to the country, and will be still more so, as the Suffolk farmers (who, you know, are not easily put out of the old road), find their way to Stowmarket; and indeed I may take in some part of Norfolk, for I understand we had a great deal of corn brought to Stowmarket from the country round about Thetford, Brandon, &c. last year.

Length.—From Stowmarket to Ipswich, sixteen miles forty rods.

Locks.—Fifteen; each sixty feet long, fourteen feet wide: three built with timber; twelve with brick and stone.

Expence.—The sum of 26,380*l.* taken up at interest, upon the credit of the tolls, which sum was expended in procuring acts of parliament, paying interest to sub-scribers during the carrying on the work, and for making the river navigable; and may be said to have cost 23,000*l.* in making the same.

Tolls.—Each barge pays for twenty-four tons to Ipswich from Stow, 1*l.* 12*s.*; and from Ipswich to Stow 16*s.* each voyage: up and down, 2*l.* 8*s.*; which tolls are intended to be altered from twenty-four ton, and charged at thirty-five ton (agreeable to the act), at the same rates as before, when each voyage will produce

2*l*. 6*s*. 8*d*. down to Ipswich, and up to Stow 1*l*. 3*s*. 4*d*.: up and down, 3*l*. 10*s*.

Revenue.—From September 14, 1793, to July 1794, the tolls amounted to 460*l*.;—from July 1794, to July 1795, to 937*l*. 10*s*. Ten barges were employed the latter part of the year: twelve will be employed by Michaelmas next. In the months of January, February, and March last, from the frost and floods, the earnings were only 103*l*. 19*s*. 6*d*., which would otherwise have been at least 400*l*.

Annual Charges.—The navigation was opened on the 14th of September, 1793, when only from two to four barges were employed from that time to July 1794; and the navigation not being at that time completely finished, the expences cannot be exactly ascertained. From July 1794, to July 1795, it was intended by the trustees to have had the expences accurately ascertained, but from the late floods (the repairing the damages of which cost little short of 1000*l*.), they cannot be accurately made out; but from the best calculation, including surveyors' and clerks' salaries, rent of towing paths, and other annual charges, and repairs, they are estimated at 380*l*.

Effect.—Reducing the price of land-carriage more than one half, and a reduction (of *carriage only*) of four shillings per chaldron on coals, and consequently raising the rent of land considerably.

Tonnage.—The charge, one penny per ton per mile, from Stow to Ipswich; and from Ipswich to Stow-market, one halfpenny per ton per mile.

SECT. III.—FAIRS.

IPSWICH for lambs, Aug. 22 ;—Horringer, for crones, &c. Sept. 4 ;—Woolpit, for cattle and horses, Sept. 20 ;—Bury, for cattle, Dec. 1 ;—Thetford, for wool, in July, but not fixed.

SECT. IV.—COMMERCE.

THE trade of Suffolk does not merit a particular attention, unless there were documents before me which would lead to ascertain the consumption of the county. The imports are the same as in all other maritime counties, and corn the principal export.

At Lowestoff, the principal support of the place is the herring-fishery, in which they have 40 boats, each of 40 ton, which they build themselves, at the expence of about 6*l.* to 7*l.* a ton : to each boat there are two fleets of nets, the price of which are 300*l.* Each boat requires eleven men. They catch from 10 to 40 last of herrings per boat ; average 20 ; and the mean price 12*l.* a last, rising from 6*l.* to 20*l.* A last requires 5 cwt. of salt. The men are paid wages, except the master, mate, and one other ; these by the last. To four herring-smacks, there are two boats employed in landing the herrings ; they are carried immediately to the salting-house, washed in fresh water, spitted, and hung up in drying lofts : fires are made under them ; the fuel, oak, elm, or ash-billet, cut out of the arms of timber-trees ; other wood not so good ; when dried, they are packed

up in barrels and shipped for the Mediterranean. The
nets and casks are all made in town.—The boats are
laid up all the year, except from September 22 to
November 22, which is the season. If built larger than
40 ton, they are not so well for the fishery.

Both this town and Yarmouth have as many smacks
as ever ; yet the trade is much declined in the three or
four last years ; owing not to a want of fish or demand,
but to the expences of all sorts rising. Dr. Campbell,
in his account of Lowestoff, in the *Political Survey of
Britain*, takes no notice of this almost only branch of
trade ; but speaks of a lobster-fishery here, which has
no existence.

SECT. VI.—MANUFACTURES.

THE principal fabric of the county, is the spinning
and combing of wool, which is spread throughout the
greatest part of it ; except in the hemp district marked
in the map, where hemp is spun and wrought into
linen.

At Sudbury, they have a manufacture of *says*. A
weaver of *says* earns 10*s*. a week, if a good hand, but
many less. Wool-combers 14*s*. The *says* are made in
pieces of 27, 30, and 42 yards; one of 27 yards, at 2*s*.
a yard, will cost about 3*d*. a yard weaving. The same
master-manufacturers here conduct the combing, spinning, and weaving branches. Others buy the spun wool
to employ the weavers. They have also a small silk
manufactory here, established by the London mercers
about twenty years ago, on account of the dearness of
labour in Spitalfields ; these men earn more than the
say-weavers. No baize made here. Calamancoes at
Lavenham.

The following satisfactory account of the woollen fabric, was drawn up in 1784, by James Oakes, Esq. of Bury.

" Account of the number of journeymen and spinners at this time supposed to be employed in the county of Suffolk, with the computed amount of their annual earnings:

We imagine there are at this time, including all degrees, about 120 yarn-makers: but our following calculations are entirely founded upon the number of journeymen wool-combers employed by the masters, which think may be fairly stated at 1200.

We say, that every one of these journeymen-combers deliver in to their respective masters, weekly, upon the average, 33lbs. of tear or tops, and that this is full employ for thirty spinners, including women and children of all ages.

First, as to numbers:

1200	combers,
30	spinners each,

36,000	spinners,
1200	combers,
300 {	journey-men, apprentices, riders, sorters, &c. &c.

37,500

Second, their earnings:

Combers and journeymen,   1500, at 10s. per week.

£. 750 per week.

£. 39,000 per annum.

Deduct 1-12th allowance } 3,250
for harvest month, &c. }

Net earnings of 1500 for } ——— - - - - £. 35,750
eleven months, - -   }

Spinners, including women and children,   - - } 36,000 at 3*d.* a day.

$\pounds$. 2,700 weekly.

$\pounds$. 140,400 per annum.

Deduct 1-12th for harvest, &c. - - - - - } 11,7000

Net earnings of spinners,   - - $\pounds$. 128,700

Amount of all the earnings,   - - $\pounds$. 164,450

In a bad trade, when spinning-wages are particularly low, the earnings must, of course, be less; but think the average, *communibus annis,* may be fairly computed at 150,000*l.*

Estimate of the number of people employed, and the quantities and value of yarn made in the county of Suffolk, solely for the Norwich manufacture:

Combers,   - - -   523
Spinners,   - - -   16,736
Journeymen, &c. - -   100

             17,359
65 packs weekly, at 30*l.* - - - $\pounds$. 1,960
3397 packs—364 ton per annum, - $\pounds$. 101,920

This manufacture is supposed to have declined considerably since that period.

In the year 1775, it was computed that goods were manufactured in Norwich, for America, to the amount of 50,000*l.* per annum; and this was reckoned only one twenty-eighth of their trade: if so, the total of their manufacture in the woollen branch must be 1,400,000*l.* per annum."

SECT. VII.—THE POOR.

THE most singlar circumstance relating to this subject, in the county of Suffolk, is the incorporation of
various hundreds, for erecting and supporting *houses of
industry*. Thomas Ruggles, Esq. a friend of mine, having examined these, with great attention, is so kind as
to communicate the result of his inquiries in the following memoir, which I insert, as the most satisfactory
mode of introducing them in this report.

" The local inconvenience and distress arising from
the number of the poor, and the expences of maintaining them, had occasioned may districts within the county
Suffolk to apply to parliament for the power of incorporating themselves, and of regulating the employment
and maintenance of their poor, by certain rules not
authorized by the existing poor laws ; in consequence,
several acts of parliament passed, incorporating those
districts ; the poor have been governed and maintained
within those districts, according to the power given by
such acts ; and the conveniences and inconveniences,
the benefit and the disadvantage, experienced from the
execution of those acts of parliament, will be explained
and elucidated by the best information obtained from the
districts thus incorporated.

That this might be performed with accuracy and certainty, I determined to visit all or most of the houses of
industry within the county of Suffolk, that I might be
able, from actual inspection and personal inquiry, to
state the facts which have been experienced respecting
these institutions ; the conduct of them, together with
the consequences which have arisen to the public from
them ; and to make also some observations on those
facts and consequences.

The middle of the summer was the time when the excursion was made ; and the houses were visited and inspected as suited convenience, from the morning to the evening. The notices taken on the spot, and the informations received since by letter, shall be stated according to the priority, in point of time, of the acts of parliament incorporating the districts, and the erection of the respective houses.

The following questions were put to all the governors of the houses of industry, and their answers to them minuted, when answered satisfactorily ; and the information obtained is incorporated with the general account ; except when the governor or attendant could not answer them immediately, but engaged to do it by letter :

1. How many poor men, women, and children, have been admitted since the building of the house, annually?

2. How many have died since the same time in the house ?

3. Has any, and how much of the debt contracted by authority of parliament, been paid ?

4. Have the poor-rates in the districts incorporated, been increased or diminished ?

5. What are the manufactures in which the poor are employed ?

6. Is the sale of any of these manufactures, and which of them, diminished by the war ?

7. Are the poor, or any of them, and how many, employed in agriculture ?

8. Is any particular disease epidemic, or more prevalent than another, and what is the nature of such disease ?

These questions were calculated with a view to form some judgment, whether these institutions tended to increase the chance of human life ; to diminish the poor-rates in time of peace and war ; and also to form a comparison of the probable profits arising from the manufactures of wool and hemp, in houses of industry.

Colness and Carlford hundreds were incorporated by act of parliament, in the twenty ninth year of his late Majesty's reign ; and their house of industry in the parish of Nacton, was built in 1757, and first inhabited in 1758.

The information which could be obtained on the spot, was not of the best authority ; the governor and his wife being from home when the visit was made, which was about six o'clock in the evening of the committee day.

Manufactures in this house—cordage, sacks, plough-lines, spinning wool for Norwich.

Boys spin hemp, stinted at six-pence a day, one with another.

Girls spin wool ; great girls stinted at six-pence a day, but receive for their work only half.

In the dormitory for men and boys, two men are usually put into a bed, and three or four boys ; certainly too many : one man, or two boys, is the proper number; probably it arose from this circumstance, that the dormitory was neither neat nor sweet; dining-hall very neat.

The poor are allowed more liberty without the walls at present, than they used to have, and are more healthy.

Five acres of land are occupied by the house ; two cows are kept.

Only one man out at work in agriculture ; no boys.

The highest poor-rate in any of the parishes when incorporated, was four-pence or five-pence, quarterly.

What follows, is the answer to the foregoing questions, transmitted to me by Mr. John Enefer, the governor of Nacton house of industry, by the order of Philip B. Brooke, Esq. one of the directors.

NACTON HOUSE OF INDUSTRY.

The poor are employed in wool-spinning, home spin-ning, and making sacks, &c. the neat profits of which, upon an average, for the last seven years, amount to 277*l.* 13*s.* 6*d.* per annum.

The poor-rates were at first 1,487*l.* 13*s.* per ann. but advanced at Midsummer 1790, to 2,603*l.* 7*s.* per annum.

The expenditure, upon an average, for the last seven years, 2,367*l.* 8*s.* 8*d.*

The original debt was 4,800*l.* is now 4,400*l.* and will be reduced 500*l.* more at Michaelmas 1793.

The men and women able to work, earn from two-pence to six-pence a day.

The children are stinted according to their abilities, and not according to age, from one half-penny to six-pence a day.

Very few hands are employed in agriculture.

The number of poor admitted into the house, for the last fourteen years, amounts to 2017.

The number of deaths, for the last fourteen years, amounts to 389.

The most prevalent diseases in the house, have been the small-pox, measles, hooping-cough, and fever.

BLYTHING.

The hundred of Blything was incorporated in the year 1764; and the house of industry built on a rising ground, in the parish of Balcam, about a mile from Blithburgh.

The manufactures are woollen and linen, for the use of the house, shoes, stockings, and all their clothes;

linen is made in this house, up to the value of three shillings and six-pence a yard ; nothing is sold.

The house also spins for the Norwich woollen manufactures, and has earned 400*l.* a year.

Forty-six parishes were incorporated.

The average number of poor admitted the first five years, amounted to about 203, annually.

There are now in the summer generally about 250, in winter about 300 in the house.

The number of men, women, and children admitted into Balcamp house since the institution, Oct. 13, 1766, total 5207.

The number of men, women, and children, who have died since the same time, total 1381.

These totals were taken from a list of admissions and deaths, transmitted to me by Sir John Rous, Bart.

Many children are admitted without their parents.

Near 800*l.* a year is paid to out-pensioners.

The sum borrowed was 12,000*l.* half of which was paid off in 1780; the whole in 1791.

The average of the poor-rates annually, at the first incorporating the hundred, was not above one shilling in the pound ; this rate was diminished one eighth in 1780, when half the debt was paid.

None of the poor are at present employed in agriculture.

In 1781, a putrid fever broke out in the neighbourhood ; this house lost by it one hundred and thirty of its inhabitants ; the town of Blithburgh one-third of its inhabitants.

Twenty-five acres of land belong to the house, which, together with thirty-one acres hired, are occupied, some for the plough, some pasture and garden.

MUTFORD AND LOTHINGLAND.

The hundreds of Mutford and Lothingland were in-corporated in 1764. The house of industry is in the parish of Oulton, near Lowestoff, and has been built twenty-seven years.

The number of parishes incorporated is twenty-four.

Yearly income about 1,200*l.* of this near 200*l.* arises from the earnings of the poor.

Sum borrowed, 6,200*l.* Expences in building the house about 3000*l.* It is erected on a frugal plan, and will contain about 200 poor.

Not more than 100 were admitted annually for the first seven years ; the number now amounts to about 150.

1,700*l.* of the original debt has been paid ; besides 300*l.* a debt contracted when the house was under bad management.

The poor-rates were advanced, in 1781, ten per cent. on the original assessment, and have not been diminished; but the debt continues diminishing at the rate of 300*l.* annually.

The register of deaths has not been regularly kept during the first years of the institution ; but the average number during the last six years, has been eleven annually.

The manufactures are, making nets for the herring fishery. The merchants furnish the twine, and it is braided by the yard.

The hemp which they grow is also manufactured in the house ; but lately the weaving has been put out.

Woollen yarn is also spun, but the trade is at present bad ; therefore only such are employed in spinning wool as can do nothing else.

A child's stint, either for braiding nets, spinning yarn

or hemp, is four-pence a day. Several children not above seven years of age, were employed in braiding.

Sometimes some of the poor are let out to work in husbandry at six-pence a day : their employment chiefly weeding.

The weekly earnings of the house, on an average 4*l.*

Out-allowances were, last year, 55*l.* and are increasing, but supposed to be injurious to the establishment.

Land in occupation twelve acres, all arable; two yearly sown with hemp. No cows kept; their butter and milk bought.

WANGFORD.

The hundred of Wangford incorporated 1764.

Shipmeadow house of industry, between Harleston and Beccles, has been built twenty-six years.

The number of parishes incorporated, twenty-seven.

Annual income for their rates, 1,750*l.*

Annual amount of labour, about 156*l.*

Number of paupers in the house, about 200.

Deaths in a year, about 20.

There is no manufactory in this house ; but their employment is spinning for the Norwich manufactures.

Out-allowances about 80*l.* a year.

Children are taken into the house from large families, instead of relieving those families by out-allowances.

Original debt 8,500*l.* of which 4000*l.* is paid off.

Land, forty-five acres, of which twenty-seven are arable ; five cows are kept.

The house has no chapel ; but they attend the parish-church.*

---

* Oulton and Shipmeadow houses of industry were visited, and the notices of them taken by a friend who accompanied me to the other houses of industry in the county.

LOES AND WILFORD.

Loes and Wilford hundreds, incorporated in 1765.

The house of industry in the parish of Melton, erected the same year, is on a more extended and expensive scale than any of those which have hitherto been examined.— Their dining-hall is very spacious and neat ; as are the dormitories. There are apartments appropriated to the surgeon. The governor's apartments are large and convenient. The cellars are excellent. There are good rooms for the boys and girls schools ; and there are also apartments fitted up and appropriated as penitentiary lodgings for refractory people, and those who may be guilty of offences requiring solitary restraint, under authority of the act of parliament which passed in 1790, enabling the incorporated hundreds to borrow an additional sum of money.

The manufactures are linen and woollen : the first principally for their own use ; the last is considerably affected by the war.

The number of poor in the house is from 230 to 240.

The average number of deaths, for the last three years, is about sixteen annually. The governor could not give any information, in this respect, farther back, not having been there longer.

The out-allowances are large ; and, by the last rules and orders drawn up for the regulating the proceedings of the directors and acting guardians, printed in 1792, although they seem to have limited the sums to be allowed, with prudence, they do not seem to have been equally careful, that the number of paupers who receive out-allowances shall be reduced, by obliging them to come into the house. These out-allowances are the cause of the increase of expence, and tend to the old system, to avoid which was the occasion of erecting these houses. By a letter I was favoured with from the Rev. Dr. Frank, of Alderton, it appears, that the original debt of these hundreds was 9,200*l.*—The present debt is 10,050*l.* That the maximum of the poor-rates, in the incorporated hundreds, was not more, including Marshalsea-money, &c. than fifteen-pence in the pound annually, estimating at rack-rents, when the hundreds were incorporated, and that they remain the same. A surgeon and schoolmaster reside in the house.

There were between thirty and forty in the sick-wards, mostly confined by the infirmities natural to age; but sore legs were the prevailing complaint among them.

The poor children were taught different trades in the house, besides the manufacture; such as making clothes, shoes, &c. Three poor men were employed in agriculture.

Quantity of acres belonging to the house, about thirty. Three acres of hemp are grown annually, and manufactured; about an acre and a half of garden; the rest pasture. Six cows are kept.

The late governor considerably injured the revenue of this house by his management of the manufactures.

SAMFORD.

Samford hundred, incorporated 1765.

The house of industry erected 1766, in the parish of Tattingstone, and opened for the reception of the poor at Michaelmas in the same year.

The original sum borrowed was 8,250*l.* of which 2,450*l.* has been paid.

The number of parishes incorporated is twenty-five.

The yearly assessments 2,262*l*. 18*s*. 6*d*.

The rates were settled in 1766, at 2*s*. 8*d*. in the pound by the year, and remain the same.

The average number of poor in the house, and the number of deaths for the same years:

	POOR IN THE HOUSE.	DEATHS.
In 1786,	280	47
1787,	251	12
1788,	262	26
1789,	262	32

The average number of poor admitted from 1766, annually, could not be exactly ascertained, but is about 260. The average number of deaths from the same year, annually, is 37 and a fraction; but the small-pox, attended, or rather followed, by a putrid fever, has been in the house three years, viz. in 1780, 1781, 1791, when the number of deaths each year was 76, 81, 56.

The poor are principally employed in spinning for Norwich; the profit on which was,

	£.	s.	d.
In 1786,	514	9	11
1787,	509	0	3
1788,	407	18	9
1789,	401	16	7

	£.	s.	d.		£.	s.	d.
Out-allowances the same years,	186	6	4½	—	240	17	10
	320	4	9	—	294	19	9

Income and expenditure the same years:

	INCOME.				EXPENDITURE.		
	£.	s.	d.		£.	s.	d.
In 1786,	2838	12	4	-	2575	18	6
1787,	2857	5	5	-	2722	14	4
1788,	2737	2	9	-	2938	3	3
1789,	2721	2	9	-	2907	12	4

There are at present eleven packs of top-work, value about 300*l.* left unsold on account of the stagnation of the Norwich trade.

Only two men and three boys are at present employed in agriculture.

The officers of the house are, a governor, surgeon, chaplain, matron.

In the dormitories, which are large, there are two or three windows in each, opposite to the general range of windows; these have a great effect in keeping the rooms airy and sweet.

There were no sick in the infirmary.

The land belonging to the house is thirty-six acres.

BOSMERE AND CLAYDON.

The hundreds of Bosmere and Claydon were incorporated in 1765.

The house of industry was erected in 1766, in the parish of Barnham, and opened for the reception of the poor in the month of October in the same year.

The original sum borrowed was 9,994*l.* of which 7,294*l.* has been paid off.

The number of parishes incorporated is thirty-five.

The yearly assessments 2,561*l.* 4*s.* 10*d.*

The poor-rates remain the same.

The average number of poor in the house, and the number of deaths for the same years:

	POOR.	DEATHS.
In the year 1787,	200	34
1788,	246	35
1789,	247	32
1790,	247	55
1791,	213	72
1792,	197	25

The small-pox was the occasion of the increased number of deaths in the years 1790 and 1791.

The information received on this head was, that the poor in general were very averse to inoculation ; therefore, when the pest-house (one of which each house of industry has) is full, there were no means to prevent the disease going through the house of industry itself ; the consequence has been a considerable mortality, but probably not greater than when the same disease has attacked the village poor, and its fatal effects have not been prevented by inoculation. The Barham house has now two pest-houses at a little distance from it.

The poor are principally employed in spinning for Norwich. Their profit has been, on an average, about 200*l.* annually ; but for the half-year ending at Midsummer 1793, only 72*l.* 1*s.* 8*d.*

	£.	s.	d.
Out-allowances, 1786,	323	3	8
1787,	308	3	2
1788,	357	3	10
1789,	377	6	10

Income and expenditure for seven years :

	INCOME.			EXPENDITURE.		
	£.	s.	d.	£.	s.	d.
1786,	2959	12	0	2380	13	0
1787,	2905	2	0	2175	8	6
1788,	2857	14	6	2574	7	0
1789,	2876	8	0	2587	5	0
1790,	2908	16	11	2622	10	2
1791,	2890	10	0	2529	18	10
1792,	2920	13	6	2810	10	3
Total,	£.20,318	16	11	17,680	12	9

Profit to the house in seven years, ending in 1792, 2,638*l*. 4*s*. 2*d*.

There were more women between the ages of twenty and thirty years in this house, than in any of the other houses of industry.

Seventeen aged and infirm people were in the sick-wards.

Land belonging to this house, twenty acres, of which two acres were garden ; six cows were kept.

COSFORD.

The hundred of Cosford and the parish of Polsted incorporated in the nineteenth year of the present reign.

The house of industry is situated in the parish of Semer, and was erected in 1780.

The original debt was 8000*l*.—is now reduced to 180*l*. and an annuity of 20*l*. payable to a person upwards of sixty years of age.

The poor-rates have been reduced three-eighths ; and a considerable fund remains in hand.

The poor in the house are employed in spinning wool, which is washed and combed in the house ; and the yarn is sold at Norwich by commission ; but the sale has been considerably affected by the war : a considerable quantity now remains in hand.

The poor, who are able, are employed in agriculture, when an opportunity offers.

The average number of paupers generally in the house, is about one hundred and eighty.

The average number of burials annually, since the institution, is about twenty-six ; the much greater proportion died the first two years after the house was inhabited, which was attributed to too much meat diet being allowed to the paupers after their first coming into the house, after having suffered extreme poverty : this cause has been since guarded against, and the burials have considerably decreased.

The house has been free from any epidemic disease, since it has been inhabited ; when the small-pox has been prevalent in the country, there have been two general inoculations in the house, with great success each time.

When I visited this house of industry, the governor was from home ; as was the Rev. Mr. Cook, the son of that worthy magistrate who from the first institution of the house to the time of his death, regulated the management of it with so much attention, as to make it productive, in the shortest space of time, of more beneficial effects than any other in the county of Suffolk. It was from an answer to a letter I took the liberty of writing to this gentleman, that the foregoing account has been extracted ; the information obtained, and observations made on the spot, shall follow from my own notes.

The chief employment is spinning yarn for Norwich ; but some of the top-work is wove into serge for the women's jackets.

Coarse thickset is bought at Norwich for cloathing ; linen cloth for shirts and shifts, at the market town of the hundred.

Poor in the house, July 25, 1793 ; men 27, women 42, children 22, between the ages of 12 and 20 ; under the age of 12 years, 74 ; in all 165.

No men are out at day labour ; four boys are scaring birds at the wages they can earn by spinning, which is five-pence a day. Girls at the age of thirteen are put to service ; boys at the age of fourteen.

Twenty-two packs of yarn remained unsold, valued at about 600*l.* Land belonging to the house, about twelve acres; of which two are garden, ten meadow and pasture.

HARTSMERE, HOXNE, AND THREADING.

Hartsmere, Hoxne, and Threading hundreds, incorporated in the 19th of the present reign.

There is no house of industry erected.* Owing chiefly to the difficulty, at the time of incorporating the hundreds, of borrowing money, several parishes in the hundreds have erected workhouses for setting to work and maintaining the poor; and, in general, it is supposed by the incoporated hundreds, that this plan is equally, if not more beneficial to the respective parishes, than if they had built a house of industry, as they were empowered to do by the act of parliament incorporating them. For this information, I am obliged to a letter from the Rev. Mr. Chevallier of Aspal.

---

* Sixteen thousand pounds was the sum wanted; 500*l.* was only offered; it was borrowed, and repaid by a contribution among the several landlords within the hundreds, when it was found impossible to put the act of parliament into execution. It was said the district was too large to be well managed. This occasioned the difficulty in raising the money wanted, though it is well known that the large hundred of Blything was much better conducted † than any of the smaller ones.— *Note by a Correspondent of the Board.*

† If, by "better conducted," the author of this note means more successfully as to *profit*, I agree; but there is great doubt as to the other part of good conduct. By having been very profuse in their out-door allowances, they have wonderfully increased the wants and demands. They have done well from having a very large income, and only one town, for Southwell can scarcely be termed a town.—*Additional Note by another Correspondent.*

Stow.

The hundred of Stow, incorporated in the 20th of his present Majesty's reign. The house of industry in the parish of One-house, opened for the reception of paupers Oct. 11th, 1781.

The sum first borrowed was only 8000*l.* but the expence of building the house so much exceeded the sum intended to be laid out for that purpose, that an additional debt of 4,150*l.* was afterwards incurred; and the rates were increased one fourth, by common consent, for three years: they remain now the same as they were at first. Fifteen hundred pounds have been paid of the debt.

The poor are employed in spinning top work for Norwich; the wool is bought by the house; and the cloathing for the use of the house, is made from the refuse of the wool, and such spinning as is unfit for the Norwich manufactory; their best rugs are also made from these materials: no part of their cloathing is put out to be made except stockings.

The sale of their spinning is considerably affected by the war; twelve packs were left in the house unsold the latter end of July, the value of which is about 24*l.* a pack.

None are employed in agriculture at present; only two men are in the house, who can do harvest work; some children are sometimes employed in weeding; all who are able are employed in hop-picking; but it is conceived that nothing is saved by such employment.

The average number of paupers in the house, about two hundred.

The number of burials since October 11, 1780, to August 1, 1793, as follows:

Oct. 11, 1780, to Jan. 1, 1781,   8
   In the years   1781,   25
                           1782,   51 a putrid fever.
                           1783,   61 a putrid fever.
                           1784,   51 a putrid fever.
                           1785,   14
                           1786,   2
                           1787,   17
                           1788,   15
                           1789,   11
                           1790,   13
                           1791,   19
                           1792,   18
To August 1,   -   1793,   17

These form, taking the fractions of a year in 1780 and 1793, as one year, an average of twenty-four and two-thirteenths yearly; or omitting the three years when the putrid fever prevailed, the average of the remaining ten years is only fifteen and one-tenth.

Annual income from rates, 1,987*l.* Ditto from labour, manufactures, &c. 350*l.* or thereabouts, for the last ten or eleven years; but the last half year has amounted only to 104*l.* owing to the stagnation of the Norwich manufactory.

The out-allowances arise from 250*l.* to 300*l.* annually, and are increasing, and likely to continue so during the stagnation of the Norwich manufactory.

There has been no fever or epidemic disorder in the house since 1784, although there has been much sickness in the hundred; nor were there in the house at the time these notices were taken any of the poor so ill as be confined to their beds.

The number of acres belonging to the house is twenty-four; of these, three and a half are arable, one acre garden, the rest pasture.

Four cows are kept, and two horses.

A schoolmaster to teach the children to read, and a mistress to teach the little children, are constantly in the house.

Relief is given to large families, by taking those children into the house which are a burden to their parents; the same method is also practised by all the houses of industry; consequently the children are taken very young.

In this house, the spinning-rooms and working-rooms are divided by partitions, in such a manner that few spin or work together; the dormitories are also divided in the same manner. This is an improvement not observable in any other of the houses of industry, and tends much to the preservation of health and order.

*　*　*

In the incorporated hundred, the houses of industry strike one in a different light from the cottages of the poor; they are all of them built in as dry, healthy, and pleasant situations, as the vicinity affords; the offices, such as the kitchen, brewhouse, bakehouse, buttery, laundry, larder, cellars, are all large, convenient, and kept exceeding neat; the work rooms are large, well aired; and the sexes are kept apart, both in hours of work and recreation.

The dormitories are also large, airy, and convenienly disposed; separate rooms for children of each sex, adults and aged: the married have each a separate apartment to themselves; mothers with nurse children are also by themselves.

The infirmaries are large, convenient, airy, and comfortable; none without fire places.

All the houses have a proper room for the necessary dispensary, and most of them a surgeon's room
besides.

The halls, in all, are large, convenient, well venti-
lated, with two, or more fire places in them, and calculated, with respect to room, for the reception of full
as many as the other conveniencies of the house can
contain.

The chapels are all sufficiently large, neat, and plain.
Several of them rather tending to grandeur and elegance ;
there were two houses which had no chapel ; one of
them made use of a room ample enough for the con-
gregation, properly fitted up, and kept very neat ; the
other house attended the parish church.

The apartments for the governor were in all the houses
large, and conveniently disposed ; in one or two of the
houses of industry, these apartments were rather more
spacious and elegant than necessary ; there are also
convenient storehouses and warehouses, for keeping the
manufacture of the house ; the raw materials and the
cloathing, &c. for the use of the inhabitants.

The land about the houses belonging to them, particularly the gardens, are all calculated for producing a
sufficient quantity of vegetable diet ; so necessary to
the health, as well as agreeable to the palate of the
inhabitants.

In general, the appearance of all the houses of industry, in the approach to them, somewhat resembles
what we may suppose of the hospitable large mansions
of our ancestors, in those times when the gentry of the
country spent their rents among their neighbours.

The interior of these houses must occasion a most
agreeable surprize to all those who have not before seen
poverty, but in its miserable cottage, or more miserable
workhouse.

In looking over my notes, I find that the affirmative neatness which prevailed from the cellar to the garret, in all the houses, with very few exceptions in particular departments, occasioned not only a memorandum of the fact, but gave rise to a conception, which possibly lies more in imagination than in reality ; that where a deficiency in this respect is observable in any domicile, a concomitant deficiency is also observable in the healthy looks of the inhabitants.

This neatness, which had so pleasing an effect on the eye, was the cause also, that the other senses were not disgusted by that constant attendant on collected filth and foul air, a noisome stench ; as deleterious to human life, as it is in general nauseating to those who accidentally breathe such an atmosphere.

The practice of frequently white-washing, does much in preserving the air of these houses wholesome and sweet : but the constant attention of those who perform the offices of the house, is absolutely necessary ; and even that is insufficient, unless the halls, working rooms and dormitories, have the external air admitted through the windows, whenever it can be done with safety to the inhabitants, with respect to catching cold. This practice of keeping the windows open, cannot be trusted to the paupers themselves ; for, strange to tell ! the general complaint against them was, that they would, not only, not attend to keeping them open, but if the adults and aged had their choice, such depravity arises from habit, that they would live in that atmosphere of putrid air, which would undoubtedly produce contagion.

The neatness and *proprieté* which prevailed in their halls at the hour of refection, were also laudably observable ; most of these houses of industry being visited at the hours of breakfast, dinner, or supper. At times I

have felt disgust, when requested to take some refreshment which has been offered me in a cottage ; a disgust
arising from the absence of that neatness which attends
the tables of those among whom it has been my lot to
live ; but no want of neatness in these houses created
disgust : a breakfast, dinner, or supper, might have
been ate at their tables with a keen appetite.

Their bread was, in all the houses, particularly pleasant ; it was good brown bread, made from the flour
deprived of the coarsest of its bran : white bread was
also baked, for the infirm, the convalescent, and young
children.

Their cheese was in general good, although frequently
the cheese of the country. In one house they bought
Dutch cheese, which was stronger in its taste; and consequently, to some palates not so pleasant. The small
beer was also pleasant ; no wonder, they bought the
best malt and hops, brewed a large quantity at a time,
and kept it in excellent cellars. Ale was also brewed
in inferior quantities, and given to the convalescent, and
to those whom the governor thought proper, either as a
necessary refreshment, or as a reward ; and it was also
distributed at stated times to the whole house.

It did not occur to me to take minutes of the bill of
diet in any of the houses, because no doubt has been
suggested that it is not wholesome and sufficient.
That, in some instances, it has been too abundant,
may be suspected, as well from the relicts which were
seen after their meals, as from the idea thrown out
by one of the directors, in a letter which has been
alluded to.*

The application of these facts, which have been

---

* See the extract from Mr. Cook's letter respecting the Semer house of
industry.

stated as well upon the credit of personal inspection, and information from those whose duty it certainly was, and whose inclination it appeared to be, to give true and full information upon the subject, as from those gentlemen also who obligingly communicated any information by letter, now remains to be made to three important queries.

1. Have these institutions amended the morals of the poor ?

2. Have they tended to diminish the burthen of expence to society attending their relief and maintenance ?

2. Have they increased, or do they tend to decrease the chance of human life ?

With respect to the first question, it may be answered in the affirmative, without a possibility of contradiction.*

They have amended the morals of the lower orders of people ; if the proportional few instances of indictments at the quarter-sessions, for actions of inferior criminality, which lead to greater crimes, will prove the fact.

If the general good order and regulation the labouring poor are kept in, throughout the incorporated districts, which good order is evidenced by their general conduct and conversation, and by their observation of those laws, the breach of which may tend to endanger the lives and diminish the safety and comfort of his Majesty's subjects in general ; such as drivers riding on their waggons,

---

* I wish the proofs of this had been more satisfactory. The following observations scarcely afford the shadow of a probability. Even granting that the morals of the children brought up in these houses, were bettered by the education there received, which is very questionable, their numbers are too inconsiderable to have produced any visible effect in the district at large.—*Note by the Rev, Mr. Howlett.*

tipling in ale-houses, and the smaller immoralities and improprieties of conduct—if such attention to the orders of society proves the fact: if the respectful and civil behaviour of the poor to their superiors, the very rare instances of children being seduced to steal wood, tur-nips, &c. and to the commission of other small thefts; —if these, and similar proofs of good morals, unfor-tunately not prevalent in those districts within the county, where these houses are not instituted—if such instances prove the fact, experience tells us these insti-tutions have tended to reform the morals of the poor.*

And the prophetic spirit of theory had before-hand informed those who wished to form a judgment on the subject, that the effect could not be otherwise.

A large building, calculated for the reception of the poor of the district, situated in the most healthy situation, with convenient offices of all kinds, the inhabitants of which are under the regulation of well-chosen officers, subject to excellent rules, all of them calculated to promote regularity, industry, morality, and a religious sentiment. The hours of work, refreshment, and sleep, uniform and regular.

The children, from the earliest age, on leaving their mother's arms, are under the care of proper dames, who

* From whom this information was procured, I cannot tell. I myself, in the summer and autumn of 1789, visited nearly *all* the houses of industry both in Suffolk and Norfolk, and I travelled over the districts in which they are respectively situate; and the accounts I uniformly received, were of a very different complexion; except only from such persons as were zealous promoters of these institutions. By others, I was constantly assured that hedge-breaking, turnip and wood stealing, &c. were much more common since the opening of these houses than before; and this appeared to me extremely probable, as their temptations had been increased by the dimi-nution of parochial allowance. But supposing it otherwise, it could not possibly have been owing to these houses, but to some other cause; pro-bably in some measure to the increased vigilance of the magistrates, &c.; but the vigilant exertion of magistrates is totally independent of these houses.—*Note by the Rev. Mr. Howlett.*

teach them obedience, and give them the habits of attention.

When more advanced in years, schoolmasters teach them to read ; and the superintendants of the working-rooms, some industrious employment, and take care that their hours of work shall not be passed in idleness. Here they are generally stinted, so that greater industry is rewarded with greater leisure.

The duties of religion are expected to be regularly attended by all the poor of all ages, no excuse being admitted but illness.

It required no prophetic spirit to foretel, that these duties, and this system of regularity, being persevered in, the best effects must of consequence ensue to the morals of the poor of all ages, and to those of the rising generation in particular.*

To determine the second question with certainty, recourse must be had to the notices taken respecting the fact, in the different incorporations ; and it will be found, that, in some, the poor-rates have been diminished ; in others, they remain the same as at the time of the institution ; and, in a few, the rates have been increased : the different instances shall be pointed out, and some observations made on the facts as they have been stated.

Blything hundred, Bulcamp house of industry : the whole debt, 12,000*l.* has been paid off ; the rates were

* The inhabitants of a house of industry are seldom above a fortieth, or perhaps even a fiftieth, of the population of the district they belong to. Of this fortieth or fiftieth, scarcely one half are children ; of course, not more than an eightieth of the district can receive the benefit of the education afforded in the house. These, when sent to their respective parishes, will they become such efficacious preachers of righteousness in word or deed, as to convert the great bulk of the people around them, or even any part of them ? No, no ; on the contrary, they will soon sink to the common level of morals and behaviour.—*Note by the Rev. Mr. Howlett.*

diminished one-eighth in 1780 : and as they were not, on an average, above one shilling in the pound annually, when first incorporated, they are now inconsiderable.

The hundred of Cosford, and the parish of Polsted ; the house of industry at Semer : the whole debt, 8000*l.* has been paid off, except an annuity of 20*l.* a year, and 180*l.* but they have stock more than sufficient to discharge these remaining demands ; the poor-rates have been diminished three-eighths ; and the rates were very moderate when the hundred was incorporated.

Wangford hundred ; house of industry at Shipmeadow : original debt 8,500*l.* of which 4000*l.* is paid. Rates remain the same.

The hundred of Sampford ; the house of industry at Tattingstone : the original sum borrowed 8,250*l.* of which 2,450*l.* have been paid. The rates were settled at 2*s.* 8*d.* in the pound annually, and remain the same.

Hundreds of Bosmere and Claydon ; the house of industry at Barham : the original sum borrowed 9,994*l.* of which 7,294*l.* have been paid. The rates remain the same.

Stow hundred ; the house of industry at One-house, near Stowmarket : the original sum borrowed 12,150*l.* of which 1,500*l.* have been paid. The rates remain the same.

Hundreds of Colness and Carlford ; the house of industry at Nacton : the original debt was 4,800*l.* is now 3,900*l.* The rates were increased at Midsummer 1790, from 1,487*l.* 13*s.* 4*d.* annually, to 2,367*l.* 8*s.* 8*d.* But from information it appears, that the rates were not more than sixteen or eighteen-pence, annually, when the average was fixed ; and the revenue of the house has exceeded its expenditure, on an average of the last seven years, 513*l.* 11*s.* 10*d.* annually.

Hundreds of Mutford and Lothingland ; the house of industry at Oulton : the original debt 6,500*l.* of which 2000*l.* has been paid off. The poor-rates are advanced ten per cent. ; but 300*l.* of the debt is annually paid off.

Hundreds of Loes and Wilford ; the house of industry at Melton : their original debt was 9,200*l.* their present debt is 10,050*l.* Their poor-rates, together with their county-rates, do not now exceed 15*d.* in the pound, at rack rent.

By this recapitulation it appears, that, at two of the houses of industry, the rates have been considerably diminished, and the original debt annihilated.

At four, the rates remain ; but a considerable part of the original debt has been paid.

At two, the rates have been increased, and the debt diminished. At the last house of industry, the debt has been increased, and the rates remain the same.

The question, whether houses of industry tend to diminish the expence of the relief and maintenance of the poor is therefore answered in the affirmative ;* since

---

* How this question can be answered in the affirmative, I cannot conceive. Not a circumstance here mentioned can enable us to form any judgment of the matter. It only appears, that in some of the districts in which houses of industry have been erected, the rates have been diminished, and in others increased. But what is this to the purpose? Had it been even proved, that the rates not only in a *few*, but in *all* these districts had been diminished, and that not a *little* but a *great deal*, still it would have really been no proof at all of these institutions tending, in themselves alone, to the diminution of the expences of the poor, till several other points were fairly ascertained : but especially till we know how much the paupers in these houses cost yearly a head. If that amounted to less than what the possible earnings of the bulk of labourers can afford for the maintenance of the individuals of their families, the scheme is useful for the purpose in question ; if not, the contrary. Now the expences annually of the paupers in these houses, per head, are upon an average above 8*l.*; which is nearly double the greatest possible earnings of the labourers in the districts where these houses are, can produce for the maintenance of the

in two, the rates are diminished, the debt is paid; in
four, the debt has been considerably diminished, consequently the annual balances in their favour might
have been applied to the purpose of diminishing the
rates, *pari passu*, with the debt: in two of the others,
the balances have been applied hitherto to diminish the
debt only, and the rates have increased: in one, the debt
is somewhat increased, and the rates remain the same,
at the low average of fifteen-pence in the pound annually.

When the average at which these parishes settled
their rates at the time they were incorporated, and the
number of years which have elapsed since that average
was settled, are considered; in some, being between thirty
and forty years, and in none less than twelve or fourteen, and compared with the proportion the rates then
bore to a pound, and the proportion they would now
bear, had there been no house of industry, taking the
advance of the poor-rates in other parishes throughout
the kingdom in general, and in Suffolk in particular, as
they are proved to be by the returns of the overseers to
the inquiries made by parliament in the years 1776, and
1783, 4, and 5; as the rule of computation, and no
better can be obtained, in which returns it appears, that,

several individuals of their respective families. If, therefore, the aggregate
expences of the several districts have been diminished since the opening of
these houses, it cannot have been owing to their management and frugal
economy, but must have arisen from some other cause or causes. And other
causes readily present themselves in abundance; such as the negligence
and extravagance of parish officers previous to these institutions; the exorbitant orders of magistrates for the relief of paupers applying to them;
the increased numbers of deaths of such paupers, who chuse rather to
perish than submit to the imprisonment of these houses; the increased
mortality in these houses; and the greater *private* relief which is afforded
to many individuals, &c. I regret very much, that the narrowness of the
margin does not allow me to enlarge upon these causes, and illustrate their
operation by well-authenticated facts.—*Note by the Rev. Mr. Howlett.*

in the two contiguous hundreds in Suffolk, not incorporated, Risbridge and Babergh, the *nett expences* of the
poor alone had advanced from 11,023*l.* 7*s.* 11*d.* to
13,840*l.* 3*s.* 9*d.* being a difference of 2,817*l.* or thereabouts, in the course of eight years ; or above 25*l.* 9*d.*
per cent. ; an advance that brings forward the most un-
thrifty management of any of the houses of industry into
a state of positive prosperity and reduction of expence.
It will therefore be found, that not only where the rates
have been stationary, but where they have advanced,
and in the instance where the debt has increased, the
poor-rates have been very much decreased from what
they would have been, had the poor been managed according to the old and common system ; we may therefore, with certainty, apply the old adage, *non progredi
est regredi*, with respect to the expences of the poor in
all the incorporated houses of industry.

On the whole, although, in an instance or two, origi-
nating from an improvident mode of building the houses
of industry at first, more subsequent expences have been
incurred than were at that time foreseen, and consequently a larger revenue became necessary to pay the
interest of the additional sum they were obliged to borrow, and to support the expences of the house, than was
at first thought sufficient ; and, in another instance,
the dishonesty or profusion of the then governor, has so
disarranged the affairs of the house, as to render a new
loan, and consequently an increased rate, convenient ;
yet on the whole, it is conceived, that not the least shadow of doubt can be raised, but that, even in these
instances, the revenue of the houses are increasing beyond the disbursements ; the debt is diminishing, and
the rates will fall even beneath that low medium they
have hitherto preserved ; and which rates, had there

been no house of industry, would probably have risen twenty-five, or even fifty per cent. above their present amount.

The other question, whether the houses of industry have increased the chance of human life? involves in it such complicated considerations, is a question of such uncertainty of proof; a comparison with the state of population in county villages, and with the chance of human life of people of particular ages, and particular situations only, and not with human life in general, being to be taken into consideration; and there being no data with which the comparison of the facts can be made, the tables of the chance of human life being of too general a nature; and the facts themselves, as to deaths, in the houses of industry, not being sufficiently particularized, as to age and state of patients' health when admitted, to give an exact result, that some general observations on the deaths which have happened in these houses, compared with the numbers admitted, is all that shall be attempted; leaving the reader to make up his own mind, as well as he is able, from the imperfect sketch of the question it is in my power to offer; to which I shall very humbly add my opinion, without presuming to dictate any positive conclusion to his judgment.

And first, it will be proper to pay some attention to the situation of the poor and their families, before they take refuge from the misery of extreme poverty in a house of industry; what are at that time their expectations of health and life?

They are so reduced by poverty as not to be able to maintain themselves and their families, and therefore they become inmates of a house of industry, consequently the constitution, both of parents and children, must

have been debilitated,* by want of necessary food, raiment, and shelter, that none can be said to be admitted
in sound health ; † no estimate can, therefore, be made
of their chance of life, in comparison with the inhabitants of villages, towns, or cities in general.

They are afflicted with disease, either parents or children, and therefore they are sent by the parish-officers
to a house of industry : the chance of life with such is
still decreasing.

Children are born, and, at the earliest age at which
they can leave their mothers, are received in these
houses, and are kept in them through that period when
the chance of human life is least; and much the greatest
number in all the houses is composed of children.

The other considerable class is composed of the aged,
and the infirm, either from age or accident. The
chance of life, in this class, is small indeed.

Such are the different situations of the inmates in a
house of industry. Very few poor, between the age of
fifteen and fifty, are seen there, except diseases, accidents, infirmities, or particular irregularities of life have
occasioned them to be sent there.

The chance of life, to people in these situations, and
of the ages, under these pressure of penury, although not

---

* This is a presumptive confirmation of what I have hinted above,
that the number of deaths are increased by means of these houses, both
before and after admission; I mean that many actually perish rather
than enter them, and that many are so debilitated by want of necessary
food, raiment, and shelter, that their lives become very precarious after
their entrance; both the one and the other are fairly to be imputed to
these houses; and indeed, every observation in the above paragraphs,
tend to establish the fact, that houses of industry increase the mortality
of the poor.—*Note by the Rev. Mr. Howlett.*

† This is certainly a mistake; no inconsiderable proportion of the
children admitted, are orphans in perfect health.—*Note by the Rev. Mr.
Howlett.*

absolutely chilled by the cold hand of extreme poverty,
would, in their miserable cottages be small indeed. Is
that chance diminished or increased by going into a
house of industry ?

Is the chance of human life increased or diminished,
by being brought from an unwholesome starving diet to
wholesome moderate plenty ? from nakedness to cloathing ? from filth to cleanliness ? from cold to warmth ?
from the noisome contagion of a filthy cottage, or parish
work-house, to a healthy air, free from noxious effluvia?
Surely the answer to these questions would at once determine the point, did it depend on theory only.*

But it may be said, the question has been tried by the
touchstone of experience ; one single page of which,
honestly recorded, goes farther towards proof-positive,
than volumes of theoretic reasoning ; we must therefore
have recourse to this best of demonstration.†

* The questions in this paragraph are totally foreign from the purpose.
—*Note by the Rev. Mr. Howlett.*

† We now pass from speculation to facts ; but unfortunately the facts
here stated are rendered, by this writer's preceding observations, totally
unfit to assist our judgment. But there are facts which might have been
selected, that would have led to pretty satisfactory conclusions. For although the aggregate body in a house of industry be in a very different predicament respecting healthiness, from that in parishes at large, yet there
are particular descriptions of *individuals* in them whose condition, independent of the influence of these houses, is altogether as advantageous
as that of persons of the same description in the parishes at large :
these descriptions are children in the houses under fourteen or fifteen
years of age; and children born in the house, and under a month old.
With regard to the children in the houses under fourteen or fifteen
years of age, it is to be observed, that not *half* of them were born there ;
and of *that* half, far the greater part at least were probably orphans in
perfect health, between the ages of five and fourteen years ; past the
peculiar perils of infancy, and now in the least mortal period of human
life. All these circumstances duly considered, the proportion of deaths
among these children ought to be less than in the parishes at large. But
what is the fact? The mortality in the houses, of children of this description, is annually about one in eight or nine; in parishes at large, not one
in forty ; in my parish of Dunmow, on an average of eleven years, it is
scarcely one in forty-five. But the second description, that is, the proportion

The solidity of this observation must be allowed, were the facts produced of mortality in houses of industry, capable of being compared with the deaths of people under similar circumstances, and of similar ages, at large.

In Nacton house of industry, the number of poor admitted the last fourteen years, are 2017 ; the number of deaths 384. The annual average of inhabitants is therefore 144 ; of deaths 27.

In Bulcamp house of industry,* the number admitted since the institution in 1766 to 1793, twenty-seven years, 5207 ; the number of deaths in that time, 1381 ; but in the year 1781 and 1782, a putrid fever carried off one third of the inhabitants of Blithburgh, and 217 of the inhabitants of this house ; therefore, those two years should be omitted in the comparative statement. The numbers then will stand : of inhabitants admitted in twenty-five years, 4725 ; of deaths, 1064 ; or annually, inhabitants, 189 ; deaths 42.

Oulton house of industry ; number of inhabitants on an average, annually, about 150, the last six years ; of deaths for the same period, annually, 11.

of children dying within the first month after birth, is still more satisfactory : their mothers, and consequently the children themselves, with very few exceptions indeed, are in the same predicament in point of healthiness as the poor in the parishes at large ! Now this proportion, in all the houses in which I could procure the requisite data, I found to be one in about six of all the children born there. In the London workhouses, it is about one in five ; a difference one would naturally expect to find. In my parish of Dunmow, on an average of eleven years, it is but about one in twenty-three. The facts of comparative mortality being established with regard to these descriptions of persons, they may be applied by analogy to others. The aged and infirm, who are past work, have to encounter the effects of a sudden and total change of habit and situation, added to the horrors of confinement and banishment, which doubtless occasion horrible slaughter. —*Note by the Rev. Mr. Howlett.*

* Of the children born in this house, one in about five and a half die in the first month : of the children in the house, nearly one in two annually die of those under two years of age.

Shipmeadow house of industry; number of poor about 200 annually; number of deaths about 20 in a year.

Melton house of industry; number of poor in the house from 230 to 240; the number of deaths for the last three years about 16 annually.

Tattingstone house of industry; average number of poor in the the house annually for 23 years, 260; average number of deaths annually for the same time, 33. In this computation the three years are omitted when the small-pox and putrid fever prevailed; the deaths, in the three years when these contagious distempers were so fatal, bring the average number of deaths up to 37 9-13ths, as has been stated in the notices respecting the houses.

Barham house of industry; average number of poor inhabitants annually for five years, as appears by the notice, 222; average number of deaths, 42. In this house also, the small-pox prevailed for two years, and destroyed 127 of the inhabitants; the average of deaths otherwise would not have been so high.

Semer house of industry; average number of poor inhabitants in the house annually, from its institution, 180; annual number of deaths 26.

Stow house of industry; annual average number of poor inhabitants in the house, about 200; of deaths annually, 24; but in this house a putrid fever prevailed three years, and was fatal to 163 people; the average, omitting these three years,* and taking for ten years only, is 15 in a year.

In the nine houses of industry which have been the objects of our attention, there are constantly, one year with another, 1780 poor inhabitants, men, women, and children.

In the same houses there happen annually two hundred

* But the three putrid years ought not to be omitted.

and forty-five deaths, as the number appears by the averages taken.

The number of deaths to the number of inhabitants annually, in all the houses of industry in Suffolk, is therefore as one to seven and one-third, or nearly one-seventh of the number dies every year.

It should be recalled to the reader's mind, that the inhabitants are composed of children from birth to the ages of 12, 13, or 14, when they are bound apprentices or get services. The chance of life in this early age is such, as in the healthiest towns not half the number is alive at the age of 13,* as appears from the tables in Dr. Price's Supplement to his Observations on Reversionary Payments ; of old people whose work is done ; and of poor of all ages, who from sickness and infirmity are unable to maintain themselves ; such being the description of paupers admitted into these houses of industry. It must again be observed, that no comparison can be made between the chance of life of such inhabitants, and of those inhabiting in cities, towns, or villages in general ; because, in the first instance are comprised only the very young, the very old, and the infirm and diseased ; and these are also poor, and of impoverished blood, and constitutions weakened by the effects of poverty ; whereas the tables in Dr. Price's Supplement to his Reversionary Payments, and in the publications of other political arithmeticians, comprehend people of all ranks, orders, and situations in life, as well the healthy and robust, as the infirm and the diseased ; as well people of all classes, at those periods when the chance of human life is greatest, as at those when it is the least.

* In my parish, almost half the number is alive at forty.—*Note by the Rev. Mr. Howlett.*

The question of the comparative chance of human
life, in these houses, must, therefore, be left undetermined
by any comparison with such chance in general ; and
probably the question would be more fairly tried, could
a comparison be made between the mortality in the
parishes incorporated, before such incorporation took
place ; and such mortality since ; taking into account
the number of the poor of each parish who have died in
the houses of industry.*

The effect these institutions have had with respect to
population, might also, by means of such comparative
researches, be more accurately ascertained, were it likely
that such inquiries would be attended by certain information ; which probably might be the case with respect
to the comparative number of deaths, by means of the
parish registers, and the books of the respective houses ;
but that part of the question which respects comparative
population, could not, by any direct inquiry, be ascertained ; and can only be computed from the births and
burials in the parishes, which would afford by no means
an exact result.

On the whole, this question must be left in doubt for
the present. To judge from every appearance attending
the interior of the houses of industry, no one could
hesitate to declare, that they must tend to increase the
chance of human life, and to increase the population of
the districts : the same judgment must be deduced from

* This kind of comparison I attempted to make more than seven
years ago ; but I was unable to procure the proposed data, not having
been favoured with a fifth part of the Parochial Registers. But perhaps the result would not have been at all satisfactory, on account of the
small proportion of the numbers both in and out of these houses, whose
health can be influenced by those institutions, to the total population of
the district. An occasional fever in the district, the change in the number
of inhabitants, and many other causes, would defeat the purpose.—*Note
by the Rev. Mr. Howlett.*

all theoretic proofs ; reasoning from probable, nay, almost necessary consequences. But when the comparative number of the living to the dead, taken annually, appears to be only as seven and one-third to an unit ; or in other words that the chance of life in a house of industry is not equal to eight years, the fact strikes strongly, and occasions the judgment upon the question to remain suspended.

But still two great points are determined in their favour ; they certainly tend to meliorate the morals of the poor, and they also tend to diminish the burthen of the expence attending their maintenance. That the other point is not on experience determined in their favour also, arises from the difficulty of acquiring every information necessary to its investigation ; and from the inability of the writer to apply with precision and certainty of proof, such facts as he had obtained. He still believes that this point will, whenever it falls under the pen of a more accurate inquirer, and able political arithmetician, conduce also to the recommendation of district incorporated houses of industry, as tending to increase the chance of life and population.

I cannot take leave of this subject,* without animadverting upon some information received, respecting the

* After a pretty full and minute investigation of the subject of houses of industry, I have not been able to discover any useful tendency in them, but in two respects ; first, the general aversion of the poor from entering those houses, as it were, compels them to do their utmost, and even to submit to great hardships, rather than apply for parochial relief ; and, secondly, that the business being in some measure collected to a point by means of them, is more easily transacted. I may add, that they may also, in some instances, prevent impositions from counterfeit distress. Though these are advantages, I am doubtful whether they might not be obtained without these institutions ; nay, it would be no difficult matter to prove that it certainly might, though perhaps attended with more trouble both to the gentlemen and the farmers.—*Note by the Rev. Mr. Howlett.*

dissatisfaction of the poor at the first erection of houses
of industry; which broke out in riotous proceedings,
and in some instances, occasioned a great additional
expence to the incorporated hundreds; the spirit of riot
having proceeded so far as to pull down the buildings
erected, and to commit other flagrant acts of outrage.
It is a well known fact, proved by long experience, that
the class of people constituting what is called a mob, is
never collected and excited to mischief but at the instigation of an individual, or some few individuals, who
poison the minds of their uninformed but well-meaning
neighbours; these are men generally of a class a little
superior to the mob itself; they are men who mix in
conversation with them at the ale-houses, at the shopkeepers', and at the barbers' shops; are in general interested cunning people, who, under the mask of great
humanity, tender affection, and kind regard for their
poor neighbours, instigate them to these and similar acts
of outrage. Examine the situations in life, the habits,
the connexions of these people, when their secret machi-
nations are discovered, by the effects of open riot and
mischief, and they stand the confessed encouragers of
the mob. It must strike every inhabitant upon the spot,
that a trifling degree of attention to the conduct of this
description of people, would have demonstrated before
the fact, that those very individuals would be guilty of
that clandestine incitement of the mob of the neighbourhood, to the very deed of riot which has been committed;
and consequently, it would be proper, in a district
where such an incorporation is intended, to be watch-
ful of the conduct and conversation of that description of
men whose interests will be most injured by a plan of this
nature; and to oppose the effect of their conversations
on the minds of the poor, by every means which prudence can devise and the laws will sanction.

Was any additional inducement wanting to recommend district houses of industry, the particular situation and temper of the times would be that inducement. The lower orders of the kingdom are now pressing on the next; and the toe of the peasant truly galls the kibe of the courtier. That relief which formerly was, and still ought to be petitioned for as a favour, is now frequently demanded as a right; that idleness and intemperance which formerly feared to be observed, now obtrusively presses forward to sight; the pauper is no longer satisfied with his allowance, nor the labourer with his hire; the faint rumour of distant atrocities, which disgrace human nature, reaches the ear of the multitude cleansed from the blood and carnage, and assumes to them the pleasing shape of liberty and property. The only class of men who have the power to calm the rising storm, are those in the middling ranks of life; and they are as much interested to preserve things as they are, as any other rank in the state. Property is the only solid bulwark of the nation; for, those who possess it have a natural desire to preserve it, and our laws and our constitution must stand or fall with it; besides, the danger lies immediately beneath this description of people. District houses of industry consolidate all the men of property resident in the county in the same laudable plan; the preservation of industry, good order, and a religious sentiment among the million. The few gentlemen of fortune who reside in the county, meritoriously take an active part in all the incorporated houses; the beneficed clergy resident there, also do the same; and it does them honour, for it is equally their duty as their interest; so also do the more opulent yeomanry of the country, a body of men of the first consequence to the preservation of peace and order. Permit, therefore, an individual who thus freely

declares his sentiments on a subject not generally understood, to assert, without the imputation of presumption
or arrogance, that equally the duty as the interests of
government, call on them to encourage these institutions,
by every mode in their power.*

* *How the two last paragraphs are applicable to houses of industry, or
how such houses are calculated to prevent riot and sedition, and preserve public order and tranquillity, I am not clear-sighted enough to discern.*—The fact
with which they are introduced, proves either the strong aversion of the
poor from these houses (which is certainly universal), or that they were
stirred up to the outrage committed, by some ill-disposed seditious
persons of superior rank. How can houses of industry remedy either
of these evils? The paupers, while confined *in* these houses, can have
no influence at all upon the conduct of those who are *out*. Their won-
derful benefits are to be produced, I suppose, by the youths issuing from
these seminaries of industry, wisdom, and virtue. These, being about
an eightieth part of the total number of their poor neighbours, would
doubtless, by their wise exhortations, and exemplary conduct, not only
give them a quiet, peaceable, contented disposition, but effectually baffle all
the insidious attempts of certain wicked superiors to corrupt and poison
their minds.—Upon the whole, of the three points proposed to be
established, the great utility of these institutions for reduction of
expence, preservation of health, and improvement of morals, not one,
as it appears to me, has been rendered in the smallest degree probable.
As to the two first, reduction of expence, and preservation of health,
the requisite facts or data to enable us to judge, have not been given;
though facts and data might have been adduced, which would either
have proved the contrary, or rendered it highly probable. With regard
to the last, the improvement of morals, it is, perhaps, from the very
nature of the thing, incapable of decisive satisfactory evidence on either
side; though a very suspicious circumstance, is the general dislike to
receive servants out of workhouses and houses of industry; convincing
proofs of this I met with in my tour through Norfolk and Suffolk, and
in the isle of Wight. In the latter, a very striking instance of this kind
occurred: in looking over the accounts of the house established there, I
observed, that refusal of servants from thence was very common; and
in one particular year, not less than 50*l.* were paid by five persons by
way of fine, for not receiving them in their turn. This does not seem,
that the estimation of servants brought up in these houses is very high.
—*Note by the Rev. Mr. Howlett.*

Letter from Mr. Ruggles.—" You were so kind as to give me an opportunity of seeing Mr. Howlett's notes on the information respecting the houses of industry in Suffolk, which was printed in the statistical account of the county of Suffolk drawn up by order of the Board of Agriculture, and which you received from me, which account, together with my reflections on the subject, I thought proper to introduce into the first edition of my History of the Poor, and shall also into the second, which is now in the press.

" I shall be obliged to you, if you see no impropriety in it, that you would, in the corrected report of the county of Suffolk add this letter, as the only observations I think it incumbent on me to make on those notes by Mr. Howlett.

" As there seems to be a disposition to invalidate the truth of the notices contained in the account alluded to, it becomes me to assert, that I visited the houses to obtain information, not to support an argument; that I began my inquiry rather with a prejudice *against* houses of industry, than with a determination to become an advocate for them; that ocular demonstration, intelligence received from various people on the spot and in the districts; and information afterwards received from very respectable names by letter and otherwise, altered my pre-conceived opinions, obliterated my prejudice, and occasioned that *limited* recommendation of them which I sent you, and afterwards printed in my History of the Poor.

" Therefore, if we are to issue upon facts, I may appeal to common opinion, which facts are best substantiated, mine, or his; but I forget; he gives none, or supports none he gives, but he contradicts mine; and he does not deny that the information was given as I state it to be: that would be going too far; but

he says I must have received the information only
from such persons as are zealous promoters of these
institutions.

" Your report of the county, and the publication I
have alluded to, inform the public from whom the
information was collected; the validity of it cannot,
by any thing I can add, remain on a surer and more
respectable basis.

" Now I will add a word as to our application of
the facts. The conclusion I deduce from the whole of
the evidence I have collected, viz. ocular observation
information *viva voce,* and by letter, and comparison of
the number of indictments for trifling as well as capital
offences, in that part of the county where these houses
are instituted, with that part where they have not been
introduced, is, that houses of industry within the county
of Suffolk, have tended to meliorate the morals of the
poor.

" Mr. Howlett, first, doubting the validity of my
notices, in this respect, afterwards, supposing them to
be true accounts for them on other principles—the increased vigilance of the magistracy in that part of the
county. The fact must be proved before it is argued
from; and when proved, if it can be proved, it does not
redound to *our credit* as magistrates, where these institutions are not introduced; but it redounds to the sub-
stantial commendation of the management and discipline
of the poor where the districts are incorporated.

" With respect to the deductions I have made from
the information obtained, as to the expences of maintaining the poor in the incorporated districts, I must
request Mr. Howlett again to read over the two paragraphs marked with an asterisk in page 88 of the report;
(see pages, 259, 260 *of this work)* I will then ask him,
whether it is not logically and *arithmetically* proved, that

those houses of industry have tended to diminish the expence attending the relief and maintenance of the poor? bearing in his mind the mode in which that proof is laid before the public, viz. this expence is supported by the poor's-rate: some of the houses have diminished that rate; some have applied their favourable balances to pay off the great debt contracted by building; in no district is that rate increased in the proportion it is in the rest of the county. But he afterwards allows it to be a fact, and acknowledges the inference I deduced from it; as they have tended, *he says*, " *to prevent the extravagance of parish officers previous to these institutions, and the exorbitant orders of magistrates*"—these are his own words. As to what he says about increased mortality in the *parishes* incorporated, at present, it is *gratis dictum*. I hope and believe on examination, it would not be found supported by proof.

" In page 90 *(see note in page* 268 *in this work)*—to this remark I will only ask, how any person's observations on facts, can render those facts totally unfit to assist the judgment? The facts remain on paper the same after I have observed on them, equally clear, to assist his, or any person's judgment.

" Mr. Howlett having denied most of the facts on which I have attempted to account for the number of deaths in a house of industry, and it not being my disposition to re-echo contradiction, I will only add, that I have already received intelligence from five of the incorporated districts, from the same gentlemen who gave me information in 1792, to whom I have lately written, requesting to know their belief as to the state of population in those districts; informing me population increases—not one answer yet received says otherwise.

" Before I conclude; one of the assertions made by Mr. Howlett ought to be taken notice of; to be *doubted;*

but not to be *contradicted*—he says, " *the inhabitants in a house of industry are seldom above a fortieth, or perhaps a fiftieth of the population of the district they belong to; and of this proportion scarcely one half are children* " If he is right, the population of the districts in Suffolk where houses of industry are instituted, is very near a hundred thousand—a great population for such a proportion of the county ; and the proportion of children to the other inhabitants in the only house I happened to notice the fact, is as three to two nearly. *(See Semer house of industry)*.

" What is contained in the margin of page 92 of the report *(see note in page 269 of this work)*, is on the whole so favourable to houses of industry, that it astonishes me much, a sensible man should fancy himself inimical to these institutions: was I a slave of system, in the management of the poor, and were houses of industry the key-stone of that system, I think the observations I have here had occasion to comment upon, in my own defence, would more strongly rivet my fetters to my favourite system ; but as it is, I am only sorry to differ so much in opinion, both as to allowed facts, and intended deductions from them, with a man whose ability and industry I respect.

" I visited the houses of industry in Suffolk to inform myself and the public, from my own observation, and such information as I could obtain on the spot, and from the neighbouring gentlemen who had attended to them, by personal conversation and by letter, as to three points which I thought material, and of importance to the subject I was then investigating—Whether houses of industry tended to a diminution of the poor's-rate ?— Whether they tended to improve the morals of the poor ?—Whether they tended to increase the chance of human life ?—I was convinced they manifestly tended

to the two first purposes, to diminish the poor's-rate,
and to improve the morals of the poor. I was *then* in
doubt as to the third point, or rather was of opinion,
from the evidence I had collected, that they did not tend
to increase the chance of human life; but confessed my
inability to apply the facts to the subject with that
precision of argument which carries conviction : I am
now of a different opinion as to the third point, and
believe they tend to increase the chance of human life
in the districts where they have been instituted, because
I find it to be the general opinion, that population
increases within those districts in Suffolk; and it is not
allowed to be a fact by those political arithmeticians
who see through such sombrous optics as the late Dr.
Price did, that population increases throughout England
in general, these districts therefore must have something
particular in the management of the bulk of the people
resident within them; that bulk is the poor, and the
particularity is, houses of industry. Did I want a
sanction to my opinion, as to all the three points, by
extending my observations to those two large houses of
industry of which Sir F. M. Eden has given the public,
in his History of the Poor, so ample a detail, that near
Newport, in the Isle of Wight, and that at Shrewsbury,
I am confident, data would not be wanting to sanction
me in saying, those houses of industry tend to diminish
the poor's-rate, to increase the chance of human life,
and to amend the morals of the poor; the last good
effect, the more inimical a writer is to the institution,
the more liable his argument is to admit—*the strong
aversion of the poor to them; and about an eightieth of the
population in them*. I will take their argument, and reply
" *ut metus ad omnes, pœna ad paucos perveniat*," an
excellent police ! But what is the dreaded *pœna ?*
Wholesome provisions, cleanliness, regularity, morality,

industry, a regular discharge of the religious duties, a certain degree of confinement while an inmate of the house ; not the confinement of a prison, but of a well-regulated society ; these are the horrors of a house of industry—the apprehension of these concomitants of parochial relief, may have its effect, although only an *eightieth of the population* are subject to them, upon the morals and industry of the rest of the poor of the district within which they are established."

Some notes received from correspondents, mention, that,

At Hopton, the additional assistance given on occasion of the late scarcity, and independent of regular collections and occasional relief, was six-pence a week per head for every child in a family.

At West Stowe, rye was sold at four shillings a bushel ; and at Lackford the poor were allowed a mixed flour, two parts wheat, one rye, at one shilling and six-pence a stone, at half a stone per head per week.

At Stoke, by Nayland, Mr. Parlby observes, that " with respect to the poor, strange as it may appear, their condition seems to have grown worse, in proportion as agriculture has been improved. There are at present forty-three persons, young and old, maintained in the parish workhouse, besides several who, from age or infirmities, receive a constant weekly allowance. One hundred and seventy-seven families and single persons, at present receive an extraordinary allowance of sixpence per head to the smaller ; nine-pence to the larger families ; and this added to their wages, about eighteen-pence per day to the peasantry, is barely sufficient to furnish them with bread only ; nor does any other mode of relief seem likely to prove effectual to the lower orders, except a rise of the labourer's wages proportioned to the price of corn, so that a peasant might earn the value of a peck, or at least three quarters of a peck of flour, by a day's labour."*

HOUSE OF INDUSTRY AT MELTON.

	Baptized.	Buried.		Baptized.	Buried.
1776,	13	16	1786,	5	41
1777,	9	15	1787,	17	9
1778,	9	23	1788,	15	19
1779,	4	14	1789,	15	18
1780,	7	52	1790,	12	25
1781,	10	35	1791,	12	26
1782,	10	67	1792,	16	15
1783,	12	42	1793,	13	13
1784,	20	54	1794,	11	29
1785,	17	29	1795,	13	48

Number of paupers in the house February 29, 1796, three hundred and seventy seven.

JOHN BLACK, Chaplain.

The following valuable communication is from Mr. Brand. of Wickham Skeith:

" The number of baptisms in the ten years from 1776 to 1785, the lowest in the century. There were at that time four or five cottages, in which spirituous

---

* Much of the present distress certainly arises from the monopoly of farms, which is an increasing evil to the community, as this parish experiences with others, for here

One farmer holds three farms,
One ditto   ditto ditto,
One ditto   ditto ditto,
One ditto   five ditto,
One ditto   two ditto,
One ditto   two ditto.

On these farms, eighteen families were formerly brought up above the condition of mere peasantry; now they are in six opulent hands. Very few cows are now kept, whereas, forty years ago, every one of these farms had a dairy, and grew pigs and poultry for the supply of the neighbourhood.

liquors were sold without licence; which in part accounts for it. I believe this nuisance to have been very extensive at that time in this county, and that the returns of births from many parishes will be found too low on that account.

"Again, the number of births for the second ten years is the greatest in the century: the last year should be omitted, as anomalous; and the births will a little exceed those of the ten years beginning in 1730 and 1740, *i. e.* in the proportion of 1055 to 1020. Hence I conclude the number of inhabitants to have been nearly constant.

"This parish is five miles distant from Thorndon: the longevity in the latter is mentioned somewhere by Mr. Howlett, to be at least equal to that of Holy-cross, near Shrewsbury, particularly adverted to by Dr. Price. After the beginning of 1784, the ages of the persons buried in this parish were entered in a column in the register. In twelve years there were seventy burials; and the sum of the ages of the persons was 2550 years, or the mean age 36-42 years. This is the expectation of life here of an infant at its birth: in the parish of Holy-cross, that expectation is 33-9 only (Price's Revertionary Payments, vol. i. p. 365). The fact from Mr. Howlett is quoted from memory.

"The history of the manners of the lower classes is combined with that of the poor-rates. Their increase has been attributed to an increase of immorality in those classes; and the fact has been denied. The proof on either side ought to have been sought in parochial registers: the following table gives a melancholy presumption on which the truth lies.

" Baptisms for ten years, beginning with the year.

Years.	Total.	Illegitimate	Years.	Total.	Illegitimate	Years.	Total.	Illegitimate	Years.	Total.	Illegitimate	Years.	Total.	Illegitimate
1690	95	1	1710	84	3	1730	102	5	1750	98	7	1770	86	7
1700	86	1	1720	73	3	1740	102	10	1760	73	4	1780	77	12

Avr. 20 yrs.	Legitimate			Legitimate				Legitimate			Legitimate			Legitimate	
89.5	1		75	5	3	0		94.5	7.5		80.0	5.5		7.20	9.5
Suppose Legitm. Children	100,000		100,000				100,000				100,000			100,000	
Base born will be	1,117		3,973				7,936				6,875			13,194	

" These are averages of twenty years each, for a complete century, ending 1789; the third deserves consideration.

" It may be taken for granted, that the price of labour in husbandry had been increasing during the first half of the century; particularly, as the demand for it increased greatly to supply the great exportation of corn, then arrived at its highest point. Let this circumstance be compared with the price of provisions.

" Dr. A. Smith has given the price of the best wheat in Windsor market, per quarter of nine bushels, for the years here to be considered; whence it appears the average price of forty years, ending with 1730, was 1l. 9d. per coomb, and it is evident by inspection, that the average of the first twenty years of that term exceeded that of the second; that of ten years, beginning in 1731, was 16s. 6¼d. and of the following ten years, 15s. 0¼d.

" The next article is the price of beef, or butcher's meat: contrary to the common opinion, this had greatly fallen : before 1612 it amounted to three-pence eight-tenths of a penny per pound weight of the whole carcass. (Wealth of Nations, vol. i. p. 236, 1784); in 1710 Davenant stated it at one-penny seven-tenths only, (Sinclair Hist. Rev. p. 3, p. 201, 1770).

" This increase of wages, and great decrease of the price of food, must have had much effect on the manner of living of the labourers in agriculture ; they became greater consumers, and of more expensive articles. The decrease of prices continued so long, that a new set of commodities were now called their necessaries of life, and believed so to be. Wheat slowly re-attained the price it sold for at the beginning of the century ; meat has risen greatly above it ; and as wages have not risen in the same proportion since 1740, the whole class is involved in great distress, on account of the habits of living which had then become established. This I take to be the leading cause of the accelerated rise of the rates since that time.

" The great cheapness of corn from 1740 to 1750, seems to have had a pernicious effect upon the morals of the lower classes : severe economy was almost unnecessary ; and a relaxation of economy was followed by that of morality. The illegitimate births of these ten years were double those of the preceding periods, though the latter greatly exceeded those births in the four former equal terms.

" There however existed then one circumstance, to preserve economy among the labourers, which is now of greatly less force, or we may say, lost. There was a multitude of small farms, for which such economy could in time lay up a capital : there is but little probability any such use can be made of such hoards now ; therefore, they are not made. A labourer will not hoard to spare the parish : every thing he can expect, is given him by law, wages, and parish allowance ; therefore the cause of subordination is gone. For the favour of his superiors is always a great step to a man's obtaining an establishment. The ruling classes have thus lost a great part of their physical strength in society : if they have made some yearly gain by it, they pay its price, in a part of the increase of the poor-rates.

" It may be doubtful, whether the abolition of small farms has made an addition to the national stock of provisions, or not : it is dearly paid for, by the degeneracy of the common people, and being obliged to watch against the violences which may spring from it : and it is the same in towns ; there are fewer manufactures than formerly, in which small capitals can find employment.

" I add only the measure of the increase of the irregularity of the common people in the twenty years beginning with 1776 ; there are 187 baptisms registered in this parish, of which twenty-nine were of illegitimate children, or the proportion of children born in wedlock, to those which are base-born, was at the end of 1785 as 100,000 to 18,354. In the beginning of the century their numbers were respectively as 100,000 and 1,117. Therefore, from the beginning of the century to the middle of the last twenty years, in the tables, that is, to the end of 1785, the illegitimate births have increased in the proportion of 18,354 to 1,117 ; or of 16 2-5ths to unity. This proportion is deduced from a parish whose inhabitants do not exceed 400 : the basis is too narrow to conclude that it ought to be held general ; but Dr. Price has founded three tables on the registers of a parish containing 1,113 inhabitants in 1780, and refers to it repeatedly (Holy-cross). The regularity of the series of illegitimate births for a century, gives

the result much confirmation. It is shewn not to be
shaken by an excess in the third term, as that is ac-
counted for.

" But although the near approach of this result to the
truth must be accidental, yet thus much clearly appears,
that the increase of these births is too serious not to call
for examination ; and the account is perhaps an example
of one of those modes in which materials, adequately
full, may be digested, in order to attaining a proper
knowledge on this very important business.

" In the last ten years we see a high price of corn and
a great multiplication of births : this admits of a solution, as the labourer has no advancement to hope, for
the spirit of hoarding will not make him afraid of having
a family ; he is now not ashamed of applying to a parish
in his youth, and is sure of a sordid sufficiency, with a
family of any magnitude. In these circumstances population will increase, but the people will become debased
—industry and frugality have lost much of the hope of
independence ; laziness and profligacy of the shame of
coming to a parish, or the fear of wanting absolute
necessaries.—The further evils these things may gene-
rate in the character of that numerous class, the labourers, are beyond all estimate,

" The births during the first fifty years of the second
table, were 430 ; of the next fifty years 436 ; but an
allowance being made for the anomalous year 1789, they
are to be taken as equal, and the population of the century stationary.

INCREASE OF POOR-RATES IN THE SAME PARISH.

" There is much disorder in the books of the parish in question : the average of seven years, the middle term of which was Michaelmas 1748, was 66*l.* 9*s.* 6*d.* That of four years and a half, beginning October 1789, the middle term of which was the first day in 1792, was 211*l.* 8*s.* 8*d.* The charge, therefore, had increased in forty-three years and a quarter, in the proportion of 3·1,808 to unity ; and if it had increased at an equal rate per cent. every year,* that rate would have been 2.71*l.* per cent. ; but the celerity of increase, is certain, was less in the beginning, and much greater at the end of the term. Nothing ought to be inferred on the general celerity of advance from the accounts following that time : they contain the charges of furnishing a workhouse, and all the effects of singular mismanagement, and the late prices of corn.

" When from two given amounts of this charge at distant periods, in one place, or larger district, the annual rate of advance per cent. is found, the account is reduced to a proper form for comparison with any other, so treated. In 1776 I obtained the rates of ten parishes in Suffolk, at two periods, twenty-two years distant : their first amount was 800*l.* ; the second 1.345*l.* ; the rate of advance was 2.30*l.* per cent. yearly. There is a tolerable coincidence of this rate with that of Wickham.

" Secondly, about the year 1775, the hundreds of Mitford and Laundilch were incorporated. The average payment of each parish was taken from the last seven

---

* All supposition, that the rates of parishes in general increase only equal sums in equal times, must be rejected as contrary to the nature of hings.

years ; in the first of which the charge was 3,411*l.* ; in the last, 4,462*l.* The annual increase of this charge was, therefore, 4.58*l.* per cent. for seven years. In ten years, ending with 1775, the poor-rates of the hundred of Forehoe, in Norfolk, (exclusive of three parishes) increased from 2,030*l.* to 2,972. : the rate of increase was therefore 3.885*l.* per cent. If in these latter instances the comparisons had been made for longer terms, as thirty or forty years, the rate of advance found, would not probably have so much exceeded that of Wickham and the twenty-two parishes.

Twaite average years, 1785, 6, 7, 8, 9, £. 103 18 0
Six following years,   -   -   107 9 8
Advance in this parish in five years and a half, 3.41*l.* per cent. and the annual rate of advance is 0.61*l.* per cent. which is to be regarded comparatively as very small.— Register of ten years from 1775 imperfect."

BOX CLUBS.

This admirable institution has flourished considerably in Suffolk, as may be seen by the following list of them in the office of the clerk of the peace for the county :

No. not to exceed		No. not to exceed	
1 Ipswich, -	61	8 Yoxford, -	31
2 Sproughton, -	61	9 Kersey, -	31
3 Lavenham, -	—	10 Boxford, -	51
4 Ditto, -	—	11 Stoke, -	—
5 Ditto. -	31	12 Groton, -	41
6 G. Bradley, -	—	13 Stoke, - -	51
7 Bungay, -	41	14 Lavenham, -	31

	No. not to exceed			No. not to exceed
15 Melford,	— —		50 Ipswich,	— 61
16 Bures,	— — 50		51 Eye,	— — —
17 Bures,	— —		52 Stonham,	— —
18 Melford,	— —		53 Stratford,	— 41
19 Ditto,	— —		54 Stowmarket,	— 61
20 Bealings,	— 61		55 Somersham,	— 41
21 Rushmere,	— 45		56 Stowmarket,	— 31
22 Alderton,	— 41		57 Chelmondiston,	45
23 Framlingham,	— 81		58 Ipswich,	— 61
24 Coddenham,	— 61		59 Westerfield,	— 61
25 Ipswich,	— 61		60 Ipswich,	— 61
26 Needham,	— 51		61 Bramford,	— 61
27 Crowfield,	— 41		62 Stowmarket,	— 41
28 Hintlesham,	— 61		63 Ipswich,	— 61
29 Ditto,	— 51		64 Onehouse,	— 61
30 E. Stonham,	— 43		65 Ipswich,	— 61
31 Stowmarket,	— 31		66 Sproughton,	— 51
32 Coddenham,	— 61		67 Ipswich,	— —
33 Stowmarket,	— 41		68 Riskinghall,	— 41
34 Needham,	— 50		69 Ipswich,	— 61
35 Willisham,	— 45		70 Stonham,	— 43
36 Stowmarket,	— 61		71 Stowmarket,	— —
37 Gosbesh,	— 51		72 Ixworth,	— 35
38 Ipswich,	— 61		73 Kessingland,	— 41
39 Ditto,	— — 61		74 Ditto,	— — 41
40 Ditto,	— 61		75 Benacre,	— 61
41 Shitton,	— 51		76 Walton,	— 51
42 Belstead,	— 51		77 Alderton,	— 51
43 Ipswich	— —		78 Saxmundham,	— 51
44 Ditto,	— — —		79 Walton,	— 51
45 Ditto,	— — 61		80 Woodbridge,	— 51
46 Needham,	— —		81 Wilnesham,	— 51
47 E. Bergholt,	— 61		82 Framlingham,	— 65
48 Eye,	— 51		83 Earlsoham,	— 61
49 Blakenham,	— 41		84 Framlingham,	— 61

	No. not to exceed			No. not to exceed
85 Saxmundham,	51		120 Hintlesham,	—
86 Ditto,	—		121 Higham,	31
87 Framlingham,	—		122 Bramford,	61
88 Sudborn,	41		123 Lowestoff,	—
89 Nacton,	61		124 Hopton,	—
90 Needham,	42		125 Lowestoff,	41
91 Swilland,	—		126 Ditto,	41
92 Claydon,	51		127 Ditto,	61
93 Barham,	41		128 Ditto,	31
94 Ipswich,	61		129 Ditto,	31
95 Freston,	45		130 Ditto,	41
96 Lawshall,	—		131 Ditto,	31
97 Nayland,	—		132 Ditto,	41
98 Weststow,	41		133 Ditto,	31
99 Lawshall,	—		134 Ditto,	31
100 Melford,	—		135 Hopton,	31
101 Cockfield,	—		136 Huntingford,	41
102 Nayland,	—		137 Blunderstone,	31
103 Halesworth,	—		138 Woodbridge,	40
104 Ditto,	—		139 Ditto,	61
105 Peasenhall,	61		140 Ditto,	61
106 Wangford,	—		141 Ditto,	51
107 Framsden,	41		142 Melton,	36
108 Woodbridge,	61		143 Alderton,	41
109 Levington,	41		144 Walton,	45
110 Saxmundham,	61		145 Framlingham,	61
111 Trimley,	51		146 Brantham,	45
112 Woodbridge,	61		147 Holton,	41
113 Ditto,	41		148 Gislingham,	41
114 Ditto,	61		149 Withersdale,	—
115 Trimley,	51		150 Erwarton,	61
116 E. Bergholt,	61		151 Haughley,	51
117 Tattingstone,	45		152 Yaxley,	41
118 Capel,	51		153 Stowmarket,	31
119 Ditto,	51		154 Ditto,	31

	No. not to exceed			No. not to exceed
155 Haughley,	- 31	188 Hadleigh,	-	31
156 Wishambro',	- —	189 Stradishall,	-	—
157 Hadleigh,	- 31	190 Bury,	-	- 41
158 Bayton,	- 31	191 Newmarket,	-	40
159 Layham,	- 31	192 Ditto,	-	- 51
160 Ditto,	- - 31	193 Stoke,	-	- —
161 Lavenham,	- —	194 Ditto,	-	- 60
162 Glemsford,	- —	195 Nayland,	-	—
163 Woolpit,	- 31	196 Bury,	-	- —
164 Hinderslay,	- 41	197 Polstead,	-	41
165 Clare,	- - —	198 Waldingfield,	-	31
166 Norton,	- 41	199 Newton,	-	31
167 Cavendish,	- 61	200 Thelnetham,	-	41
168 Ditto,	- - —	201 Haverhill,	-	61
169 Glemsford,	- —	202 Barnby,	-	41
170 Haverhill,	- 61	203 Hessett,	-	41
171 Bury,	- - —	204 Sproughton,	-	61
172 Ditto,	- - —	205 Wortham,	-	45
173 Ditto,	- - —	206 Stradbrooke,	-	61
174 Ditto,	- - 31	207 Worlington,	-	42
175 Medical Society,	—	208 Haughley,	-	31
176 Bury,	- - —	209 Hadleigh,	-	31
177 Ditto,	- - 25	210 Swefling,	-	61
178 Ditto,	- - —	211 Monk Ely	-	—
179 Ditto,	- - —	212 Sapiston,	-	35
180 Ditto,	- - 31	213 Oulton,	-	31
181 Barrow,	- —	214 Gazeley,	-	- —
182 Fornham,	- 31	215 Fornham,	-	31
183 Hessett,	- 31	216 Homersfield,	-	31
184 Thurlow,	- - —	217 Ipswich,	-	61
185 Cornard,	- —	218 Barrow,	-	31
186 Eriswell,	- 31	219 Peasenhall,	-	61
187 Shimpling	- —			

Number of Clubs, 219—7709 members; average of members, 35 in each Club.

From this account it appears, that these societies flourish very considerably in Suffolk.

Of the parishes in the county (in all 443*) 232 are in the incorporated hundreds. Now, deducting 29 friendly societies at Ipswich and Bury, where there are particular acts of parliament for the management of the poor, somewhat resembling those corporations, there remain 190 of these societies in the county. In order to see whether houses of industry have the beneficial effect of driving, by a species of apprehension, the poor into such societies, or on the contrary, to discover whether they prove by the number of societies in the incorporated parishes, that the poor have no such a terror of them as thus to be induced to become members, let us compare the number of societies in and out of those hundreds:

There are in the incorporated hundreds,   - 103
In the non-incorporated ones,   -   -   87

Thus, there ought to be in the non-incorporated hundreds 93 clubs; which is so near the fact, that it may be called an equality. From which it appears, they have no such effect; and it should therefore seem, that there results no conclusions to be drawn in favour of the houses, as an encouragement to societies; but very much in favour of their treatment of the poor; for if the fear of entering them was as great as some have represented, assuredly we should have found a greater proportion of these societies in the incorporated hundreds than out of them, of all other measures, they being the most effective to remedy such apprehension.

* By Mr. Hodskinson's map.

SECT VIII.—STATISTICAL DIVISION OF THE PRODUCE OF LAND IN SUFFOLK.

I HAVE often reflected on the most simple method of bringing into the shortest compass possible, a view of the gross produce of the soil, diffusing itself through the variety of classes most nearly concerned in the culture, receipt, and consumption, of the earth's products. What may be called, without impropriety, political agriculture, depends altogether on this division being clearly understood. Volumes have been written diffusely upon the subject, and have perhaps failed in utility in proportion to their bulk ; but if tables, on a plain and simple plan, could be constructed, which would present the leading facts in a clear view, the road to this branch of knowledge, so unquestionably important, would be greatly shortened. Inquiries, however of this nature, must be long pursued, and by many persons, before any thing near perfection is to be attained. I present the following sketch to the Board, as an attempt which may in time be ameliorated, in more able hands, into a general view of the kingdom, which shall contain, in a very small space, abundance of useful information.

SUFFOLK RICH LOAM.

STATISTICAL DIVISION OF THE PRODUCE OF AN ACRE OF WELL-MANAGED ARABLE LAND.

Rent, 15s.
Farmer's capital, 5l. per acre:

Course of crops :

        1. Turnips,
        2. Barley,
        3. Clover,
        4. Wheat.

GROSS PRODUCE.

	£.	s.	d.
1. Turnips, keeping, 6¼ sheep 26 weeks, at 3d.	2	0	0
2. Barley, 4 qrs. at 21s.* -	4	4	0
3. Clover, 7 sheep 26 weeks, at 3d. -	2	5	6
4. Wheat, 3 qrs. 42s. - -	6	6	0
Divide by 4 years, -	14	15	6
Per annum, - - £.	3	13	10

THE ABOVE DIVIDED AMONG

The landlord,	-	0	12	0	net rent,
The state,	-	0	2	6	land-tax,
Artizans,	-	0	0	6	repairs,
		0	15	0	gross rent,

* For the price of wheat and barley in Suffolk, see Annals of Agriculture, vol. xv. p. 83.

	£.	s.	d.	
Industrious poor,	1	1	0	labour,
Indigent poor,	0	3	6	poor-rates,
Artizans, and sundries,	0	0	6	other rates,
Artizans,	0	2	0	wear and tear,
The church,	0	4	0	tythe,
The farm,	0	7	0	seed,
Ditto,	0	10	0	team of 4 horses, at 12*l*. 10*s*. per 100 acres.
The farmer,	0	10	10	
	£. 3	13	10	

Produce,	£. 3	13	10

DEDUCT.

Seed,	0	7	0	
Team,	0	10	0	
Half wear and tear,	0	1	0	
Five-sixths of labour,	0	17	6	
Three-fourths of poor-rates,	0	2	6	
				1 18 0

For market,	£. 1	15	10

In order to form such a table as this, it is necessary to simplify the business, more than it admits in every case, in fact. The clover is supposed to be the food of sheep alone; but in common practice, the horses, hogs, cows, and, in general, all the stock of a farm consume it; but for the great objects of such an inquiry, to substitute sheep does not affect the principles of the calculation.

To discover what portion of the produce comes free

to market is always an inquiry of considerable import-
tance ; for if the subject was thoroughly analyzed, it
would probably be found, that that system of rural economy, whether respecting the size of farms or the
conduct of the soil, would be found politically best,
which sent the largest *surplus* to market   In order to
discover what this is, deductions should be made of that
portion of the produce consumed by the necessary neighbours of the farmer in the village, including a very large
portion of the labour, a smaller proportion of poor-
rates, and a still smaller one of the wear and tear ; all
the seed, and (but not with positive accuracy) the team.
The farmer's personal consumption should also be deducted ; but this is more difficult to estimate. When
the consumption of these several classes is deducted, the
remainder forms that portion of the produce which may
be said to go *free* to market, and forms the great basis
which supports towns and manufactures.

STRONG LOAM.

STATISTICAL DIVISION OF THE PRODUCE OF AN ACRE OF ARABLE LAND IN COMMON MANAGEMENT.

Rent 15s.
Farmer's capital, 5l. an acre.

Course of crops :

    1 Fallow dunged for,
    2. Wheat,

3. Barley,
4. Clover,
5. Wheat.

GROSS PRODUCE.

	£.	s.	d.
2. Wheat, 3qrs. at 42*s.* - -	6	6	0
3. Barley, 3½ qrs. at 21*s.* ◦ -	3	13	6
4. Clover, 6 sheep 26 weeks, at 3*d.* -	1	19	6
5. Wheat, 2¾ qrs. at 42*s.* - -	5	15	6
Divide by 5 years, -	17	14	6
Per annum, - -	£. 3	10	10

THE ABOVE DIVIDED AMONG

The landlord, -	0	12	0	net rent,
The state, -	0	2	6	land tax,
Artizans, -	0	0	6	repairs,
	0	15	0	gross rent,
Industrious poor, -	0	18	0	labour,
Indigent poor, -	0	3	6	poor rates,
Artizans, and sundries,	0	0	6	other rates,
Artizans, -	0	2	0	wear and tear,
The church, -	0	4	0	tythe,
The farm, -	0	8	3	seed,
Ditto, - -	0	12	0	team.
The farmer, -	0	7	7	
	£. 3	10	10	
Produce, - - - -	3	10	10

DEDUCT AS BEFORE,

	£. s. d.
Seed, team, five-sixths labour, three-fourths poor-rates, and one half wear and tear, }	1 18 10
For market, - - - £.	1 12 0

This table explains the circumstance to which I have already adverted, the profit of cultivating dry soils on comparison with wet ones; and it shews, that while fallows are retained, neither the produce for the public, nor the profit for the farmer, can be carried to the heighth they are capable of. If, instead of this fallow course, a different one be substituted, such as, 1. cabbages; 2. oats; 3. clover; 4. beans; 5. wheat; the produce and advantage would probably be found to become greater.

SAND.

STATISTICAL DIVISION OF THE PRODUCE OF AN ACRE OF POOR ARABLE.

Rent, 5s.
Farmer's capital, 3l. 10s. an acre.

   Course of crops:

         1. Turnips,
         2. Barley,
         3. and 4. Trefoil and ray,
         5.   Ditto, and bastard fallow.
         6. Rye.

GROSS PRODUCE.

		£.	s.	d.
1. Turnips, 4 sheep 24 weeks, at 3*d.* -		1	4	0
2. Barley, 2½ qrs. at 21*s.* - -		2	12	6
3. Clover, 3 sheep 26 weeks, at 3*d.* -		0	19	6
4. Ditto, 2 ditto ditto, - -		0	13	0
5. Ditto, 2 ditto, 12 ditto ditto, -		0	6	0
6. Rye, 1½ qr. at 11*s.* - -		1	13	0
Divide by 6 years, -		7	8	0
Per annum, - -		1	4	8

THE ABOVE DIVIDED AMONG

		s.	d.	
The landlord, -	0	4	4	net rent,
The state, -	0	0	6	land tax,
Artizans, - -	0	0	2	repairs,
	0	5	0	gross rent,
Industrious poor, -	0	4	0	labourer,
Indigent poor, -	0	0	10	poor-rates,
Artizans, and sundries,	0	0	2	other rates,
Artizans, - -	0	0	9	wear and tear.
The church, -	0	1	0	tythe,
The farm, - -	0	2	6	seed,
Ditto, - -	0	2	0	team.
The farmer, -	0	8	5	
	1	4	8	
Produce, - - - -	1	4	8	

DEDUCT AS BEFORE,

	£.	s.	d.
Seed, team, proportion of labour, rates, and wear and tear, - - }	0	8	10
For market, - - -	0	15	10

It is proper to explain here, and the observation is applicable to all these estimates, that the proportion assigned to the farmer concerns no farm in general, but merely land precisely thus managed. If any of the expences run higher, or the products lower, that proportion is of course affected. The general profit of his business has no place in this enquiry, which is confined merely to such fields as are cultivated in the course assigned, and under the circumstances minuted. It is, however, of high importance, that his interests should flourish ; which in very many cases, they do not sufficiently, either from his expences being too high, or his products too low.

GRASS APPLIED TO COWS.

STATISTICAL DIVISION OF THE PRODUCE OF AN ACRE OF GRASS LAND.

Rent, 16*s.*
Farmer's capital, 5*l.* an acre.
Three acres supposed to carry a cow through the year.

GROSS PRODUCE.

	£.	s.	d.
Of a cow, - - - -	8	5	0
Divide by three years, -	£. 2	15	0

THE ABOVE DIVIDED AMONG

	£.	s.	d.	
The landlord, - -	0	13	0	net rent,
The state, - -	0	2	9	land tax,
Artizans, - -	0	0	3	repairs,
	0	16	0	gross rent,

			£.	s.	d.	
Three years,	-	-	2	8	0	gross rent,
Industrious poor,	-	-	1	0	0	labour,
Indigent poor,	-	-	0	10	6	poor-rates,
Artizans,	-	-	0	1	6	other rates,
Ditto,	-	-	0	4	0	wear and tear,
The church,	-	-	0	12	0	tythe,
The farm,	-	-	0	8	0	fuel,
Ditto,	-	-	0	18	0	{ renovation of stock,
Ditto,	-	-	0	5	0	team,
The farmer,	-	-	1	18	0	

		£.	8	5	0
Ditto on 3 acres,	-		1	18	0
Per acre,	-	£.	0	12	8
Produce,	- - - - -	£.	8	5	0

DEDUCT AS BEFORE,

Team renovation and fuel, $\frac{5}{6}$ of labour, $\frac{3}{4}$ } poor-rates, and $\frac{1}{2}$ wear and tear, -   2 17 6

Divide by three years,   -   £. 5 8 6

For market,   - - - -   £. 1 16 2

I am inclined to believe, that no calculation of grass land can be made on any data, tolerably fair, that will not shew, as this does, the benefit to the public, of land being under grass; here is a larger produce free for market, than in any of the preceding estimates.

SHEEP-WALK.

STATISTICAL DIVISION OF THE PRODUCE ON AN ACRE OF SHEEP-WALK.

Rent, 2s. 6d.
Farmer's capital, 10s. per acre.

It is extremely difficult to calculate with accuracy, the produce of land which is never managed or kept distinct from the rest of the farm. In such cases, all that is possible to be done is, to approximate as near the truth as a variety of information, not founded on experiment, will allow. From such circumstances, I am inclined to believe, that the average produce of such sheep-walks in Suffolk, as let for 2s. 6d. an acre, land-lord's rent, do not produce gross more than 5s. which may be called the keeping of one sheep twenty weeks, at 3d. a week. This sum may be thus divided :

	£.	s.	d.	
Landlord, -	0	2	3	net rent,
The state, - -	0	0	3	land tax,
	0	2	6	gross rent.
Indigent poor, -	0	0	3	rates,
Industrious poor,	0	0	2	labour,
The church, -	0	0	4	tythe.
	0	3	3	
The farmer, -	0	1	9	
	£. 0	5	0	

If this estimate approaches the truth, it explains the reason why such immense tracts remain in a state disgraceful to the kingdom. It is evidently the farmer's interest to make a large return on a small capital. Were such lands improved, he would receive a smaller return from a much larger investment. Hence arises the fact, that all land lords, when they let such wastes, should take care to fix on them a very high rent as an inducement to the tenant to cultivate them. If favour is shewn in rent, let it be in any other part of the farm.

The real produce of such lands will never be known till inclosures are made, and sheep confined to them without folding, through the year. The question might be ascertained in that manner, with great ease.

GOOD GRASS LAND APPLIED TO SHEEP.

STATISTICAL DIVISION OF THE PRODUCE OF AN ACRE OF GOOD GRASS LAND.

Rent 15*s.*
Farmer's capital, 6*l.* per acre.

It is proper to observe, that there is very little land in this county thus applied ; and I insert the estimate merely by way of query, to bring to light such observations as individuals may have made on sheep-feeding good land, without the stock being folded from it.

GROSS PRODUCE.

	£.	s.	d.
Seven sheep, 26 weeks in summer, at 3*d*.	2	5	6
Winter, half a sheep per acre, 20 weeks, at 3*d*.	0	2	6
	£.2	8	0

DIVIDED AMONG.

		£.	s.	d.	
The landlord,	-	0	12	0	net rent,
The state,	-	0	2	9	land-tax.
Artizans,	-	0	0	3	repairs,
		0	15	0	gross rent,
Industrious poor,		0	2	6	labour,
Indigent poor,	-	0	3	6	poor-rates,
Artizans, &c.	-	0	0	6	other rates,
The Church,	-	0	4	0	tythe.
The farmer,	-	1	2	6	
		£.2	8	0	

Produce,	-	-	-	-	-	£.2	8	0
Deduct 5-6ths labour, and 3-4ths poor-rates,						0	4	8
For market,	-	-	-	-		£.2	3	4

RECAPITULATION.

	Rent.			In market.			Gross produce.		
	£.	s.	d.	£.	s.	d.	£.	s.	d.
Arable good dry loam,	0	15	0	1	15	10	3	13	10
Ditto, strong loam,	0	15	0	1	12	0	3	10	10
Ditto, sand,	0	5	0	0	15	10	1	4	8
Grass,* cows, -	0	16	0	1	16	2	2	15	0
Sheep-walk, -	0	2	6	0	0	0	0	5	0
Grass, sheep, -	0	15	0	2	3	4	2	8	0
				8	3	2	†13	12	4

If in future, a greater light should be thrown on these inquiries, it will probably be found, that an apprehension, very common with some persons, of grass land being, on comparison with arable, injurious to the public interests, is extremely ill-founded, and that, on the contrary, the support of great cities and flourishing manufactures very intimately depends on a large proportion of the soil being thus employed.

Comparing the sum total of the gross produce with the portion free in the market, it should appear, that the latter exceeds considerably the half of the former.

* It may be presumed, that if the rich loams were occupied in grass, the clear profits to the tenant, the landlord, and the public, would increase.—Note by H.

† Without including 5s. sheep-walk.

SECT. IX—POPULATION.

THIS object, so highly interesting in the statistics of a kingdom, demands a much closer inspection than it has yet received. I took the only step that could give me a better knowledge of it in Suffolk ; which was that of writing to all the rectors and vicars of the county, requesting the births and burials from their registers for the last twenty years, with an enumeration of the houses and people.* To above four hundred letters I had two hundred and sixty answers, which enable me to form the following very satisfactory table.

* The two latter queries were not in my first letters, or more return would have been made in all probability.

TABLE.

Parish.	Births 1776 to 1785.	Births 1786 to 1795.	Increase of births.	Decrease of births.	Burials 1776 to 1785.	Burials 1786 to 1795.	Increase of burials.	Decrease of burials.	Number of houses.	Number of souls.	Souls per house.	Proportion of births to the number of souls in last period.	Proportion of deaths to the number of souls.
			3	4	5	6	7	8	9	10	11		
Stowlangtoft	32	58	26	—	19	39	20	—					
Braesworth	36	19	—	17	21	16	—	5	19	111	5¾	1 in 55	1 in 74
Pettaugh -	31	64	33	—	27	24	—	3	30	157	5¼	1 in 96	1 in 78
Helmingham	55	53	—	2	30	20	—	10	26	226	8½	1 in 45	1 in 113
Wickhamskeith	69	118	49	—	59	63	4	—	63	399	6½	1 in 33	1 in 66
Hartest -	206	171	—	35	151	137	—	14					
Brockley -	94	55	—	39	45	34	—	11					
Boxted -	39	54	15	—	28	20	—	8					
Honington -	42	62	20	—	38	40	2	—					
ThorpbyIxworth	40	30	—	10	27	19	—	8					
Fakenham M.	63	54	—	9	39	28	—	11					
Chevely -	129	108	—	21	89	80	—	9					
Frotenden -	79	78	—	1	55	29	—	26	26	245	9¼	1 in 32	1 in 81
Felsham -	108	74	—	34	79	58	—	21	45	273	6	39	48
Gedding -	28	23	—	5	22	19	—	3	18	110	6	55	55
Onehouse -	40	40	—	—	39	33	—	6	23	158	6¾	39	52
Brentely -	68	77	9	—	40	46	6	—	44	232	5¼	30	50
Monksely -	120	195	75	—	105	144	39	—	111	474	4¼	23	33
Preston -	85	94	9	—	83	34	—	49	40	313	7¾	34	104
Lavenham -	593	626	33	—	514	456	—	58	344	*1741	5	28	38
Whepstead -	131	116	—	15	127	86	—	41	99	465	4¾	42	54
Westthorpe -	77	59	—	18	35	30	—	5	24	180	7½	30	60
Beighton -	61	58	—	3	52	37	—	15					
Uggeshall -	66	109	43	—	61	58	—	3	33	236	7	21	39
Sotherton -	63	61	—	2	31	21	—	10	28	171	6	28	85
Knattishall -	11	8	—	3	9	2	—	7					
Polsted -	199	237	38	—	126	117	—	9					
Chellesworth	54	59	5	—	43	46	3	—					
Grundisburgh	156	163	7	—	93	79	—	14	78	486	6¼	30	60
Bentley -	96	107	11	—	97	58	—	39	47	286	6	26	47
St.Steph.Ipswich	77	100	23	—	120	113	—	7	70	337	4¾	33	30
Wherstead -	47	44	—	3	36	43	7	—	30	196	6½	49	49
St.Marg. Ipswich	470	553	83	—	486	481	—	5					
Tudenham	83	77	—	6	34	53	19	—					
Rickinghall	95	142	47	—	78	83	5	—	83	421	5	30	52
Bradfield St.Geo	110	113	3	—	78	75	—	3					

* In 1778 the houses in 1796.

Parish.	1	2	3	4	5	6	7	8	9	10	11		
Poslingford -	78	94	16	—	49	55	6	—					
Rattlesden -	246	236	—	10	165	149	—	16					
Hunston .	33	44	11	—	30	35	5	—					
Wartham -	268	282	14	—	175	175	—	—	100	700	7	1 in 25	1 in 41
Burgate -	104	107	3	—	84	39	—	45	36	289	8	28	72
Stuston -	59	52	—	7	46	35	—	11	36	187	5	37	52
Thrandeston -	85	100	15	—	91	75	—	16	40	277	6¾	27	36
Palgrave -	154	171	17	—	128	109	—	19	81	564	6¾	33	51
Chilton -	12	19	7	—	15	5	—	10					
Corneath .	102	107	5	—	111	85	—	26					
Thornham Mag.	80	99	19	—	56	58	2	—	43	299	6¾	29	49
Thornham Parv	36	36	—	—	23	18	—	5	18	117	6½	32	58
Semer -	59	65	6	—	38	50	12	—					
CretingSt.Peter's	42	59	17	—	26	20	—	6	14	*151	10¾	25	75
Brandiston -	86	90	4	—	42	53	11	—	55	335	6	36	67
Cavendish -	311	272	—	39	236	220	—	16					
Kelsale -	280	288	8	—	158	180	22	—					
St. Mary Ipswich	98	118	20	—	104	113	9	—	61	301	4¾	27	27
Aldham -	67	49	—	18	39	15	—	24	30	170	5¾	34	112
Fornham St. M.	43	43	—	—	31	24	—	7					
Fornham All Sts.	74	48	—	26	42	32	—	10	41	220	5¼	48	73
Westley -	26	16	—	10	19	14	—	5	14	50	3¾	32	32
Mellis -	160	102	—	58	71	51	—	20	48	†339	7	33	66
Little Saxham	75	64	—	11	42	38	—	4	18	157	8¾	26	39
Finningham -	127	99	—	28	70	60	—	10	50	300	6	30	50
Welnetham Parv.	40	57	17	—	34	33	—	1					
Staningfield -	77	65	—	12	59	54	—	5					
Lawshall -	259	254	—	5	209	167	—	42					
Stoke by Nayland	316	3[illegible]9	—	7	291	244	—	47					
Assington -	139	151	12	—	129	114	—	6					
Milding -	36	41	5	—	31	20	—	11					
FornhamSt.Gen.	20	27	7	—	19	10	—	9	19	98	5¼	38	49
Ousden -	61	86	25	—	53	70	17	—					
Kersey -	192	144	—	48	149	93	—	56					
Lindsey -	42	37	—	5	38	33	—	5					
Henley -	61	103	42	—	43	46	3	—	30	204	6¾	20	44
Stratford St.Mar.	140	153	13	—	96	92	—	4					
Wetherden -	115	103	—	12	104	78	—	26	50	292	5¾	29	38
Coddenham -	177	254	77	—	119	146	27	—	124	820	6½	32	58
Westerfield -	65	67	2	—	32	22	—	10	24	130	5¼	20	65
Exning -	197	228	31	—	168	150	—	18					
Huntingfield -	76	115	39	—	50	54	4	—					
Ashboking -	40	54	14	—	19	18	—	1	26	150	5¾	30	75
Bucklesham -	63	64	1	—	41	23	—	8	26	165	6¼	27	82
Wetheringset	285	228	—	57	192	118	—	72					
Newbourn -	39	48	9	—	7	30	23	—	18	104	5¾	22	34

* In 1788, souls 118. † Families 70.

Parish.	1	2	3	4	5	6	7	8	9	10	11		
Hawkdon -	52	66	14	—	49	62	13	—					
Somerton -	34	29	—	5	32	20	—	6					
Stradishall -	100	137	37	—	83	67	—	16					
Hoxne -	283	269	—	14	204	164	—	40	150	932	6	1 in 35	1 in 58
Rickinghall -	148	181	33	—	128	93	—	35		474		26	52
Mendlesham -	326	377	51	—	237	200	—	37		850			
Stuston -	64	54	—	10	51	37	—	14	35	187	5¼	37	52
Mendham -	230	233	3	—	134	118	—	10					
Weybread -	184	227	43	—	136	120	—	16					
St. Mary Stoke Ipswich	92	108	16	—	134	97	—	37	63	368	5¾	36	36
Stansfield -	127	122	—	5	72	85	13	—					
Denston -	108	84	—	24	69	48	—	21					
Kirkton -	138	170	32	—	107	94	—	13	44	390	8¾	22	43
Falkenham -	76	81	5	—	58	47	—	11	27	224	8	28	48
Easton -	140	91	—	47	90	58	—	32	40	233	5½	25	38
Boyton -	63	66	3	—	66	46	—	20	†20	170	8½	26	36
Bailham -	78	85	7	—	62	44	—	18					
Hemingston -	49	76	27	—	*	41	30	—	35	237	6¾	30	59
Halesworth -	412	494	82	—	308	271	—	37	400	‖1500	3¾	30	55
Chediston -	92	104	12	—	70	54	—	16					
Eye -	—	—	—	—	—	—	—	—	—	1769			
Brome -	69	76	7	—	61	56	—	5	29	233	8	30	42
Rushbroke -	38	33	—	5	31	25	—	6					
Barham -	77	105	28	—	53	57	4	—	‡45	323	7	32	58
Hawleigh -	172	203	31	—	124	100	—	24	115	440	3¾	22	44
Chillesford -	126	139	13	—	43	53	10	—	44	382	8½	27	76
Mitfield -	217	255	38	—	141	131	—	10	72	623	8½	24	47
Fressingfield -	355	356	1	—	244	165	—	79	112	976	8½	27	60
Wethersdale	24	42	18	—	22	15	—	7	15	97	6½	24	64
Syleham -	83	70	—	13	59	61	2	—	40	288	7	41	48
Copdock -	69	79	10	—	72	54	—	18					
Washbrook	62	73	11	—	40	35	—	5					
Culpho -	10	16	6	—	10	5	—	5	9	69	7½	46	138
Monewden -	48	35	—	13	27	24	—	3	22	130	5¾	36	65
Worlingham -	61	67	6	—	65	40	—	25	24	169	7	26	42
Brampton -	75	93	18	—	43	38	—	5	23	235	10	26	58
Acton -	105	169	64	—	110	86	—	24					
Harkstead -	69	79	10	—	47	50	3	—	33	238	7	29	47
Belstead -	60	78	18	—	42	26	—	16	§38	200	5¼	25	80
Mettingham -	94	93	—	1	48	36	—	12	30	150	5	26	42
Cowling -	112	204	92	—	125	91	—	34					
Lidgate -	109	101	—	8	99	49	—	50					
Thorpe -	77	69	—	8	56	46	—	10					
Great Bradley	92	102	10	—	61	64	3	—					
Barnidiston -	53	51	—	2	51	17	—	34					

* Register lost.—† Forty tenements.—‡ Sixty-five tenements.—§ Tenements reckoned as houses.—‖ In the year 1790.

Parish.	1	2	3	4	5	6	7	8	9	10	11		
Chevington	134	164	30	—	96	86	—	10					
Hargrave	115	98	—	17	59	55	—	4					
Euston	38	44	6	—	39	20	—	19					
Barnham	101	100	—	1	66	55	—	11					
Little Thurlow	80	108	28	—	77	66	—	11					
Lakenheath	206	225	19	—	168	139	—	29					
Flempton	79	86	7	—	42	57	15	—					
Culford	61	84	23	—	49	37	—	12					
Kedington	161	165	4	—	139	143	4	—					
Wickhambrook	288	320	32	—	182	174	—	8					
Hepworth	143	169	26	—	80	105	25	—					
Clare	305	338	53	—	251	245	—	6					
Timworth	28	52	24	—	30	24	—	6		169	1 in 33		1 in 84
Ingham	53	40	—	13	21	21	—	—		135	33		67
Ampton	7	16	9	—	9	10	1	—		97	64		97
Thurston	110	107	—	3	87	57	—	30					
Ashfield Magna	94	119	25	—	48	62	14	—					
Wood Ditton	164	169	5	—	125	114	—	11					
Great Livermere	112	85	—	27	55	50	—	5					
Little Livermere	31	20	—	11	14	17	3	—					
St. Mary Newmt.	377	446	69	—	319	*332	87	—					
Melford	577	610	33	—	478	468	—	10					
Barningham	85	109	24	—	71	63	—	8					
West Stowe	56	33	—	23	37	21	—	16					
Lackford	48	52	—	4	26	11	—	15					
Kentford	33	41	8	—	24	15	—	9					
Norton	161	173	12	—	151	99	—	52					
Great Wratting	62	65	3	—	62	61	—	1					
Hundon	184	271	87	—	175	160	—	15					
Bildeston	165	169	4	—	132	127	—	5					
Mildenhall	573	682	109	—	565	406	—	159					
Gazeley	159	165	6	—	82	78	—	4					
Elden	53	31	—	22	21	19	—	2					
Elmset	85	114	29	—	61	65	4	—					
Ixworth	228	243	15	—	140	119	—	21					
Wethersfield	126	141	15	—	97	85	—	12					
Laxham	187	150	—	37	141	99	—	50					
Downham	4	11	7	—	8	10	2	—					
Gt. Waldingfield	174	205	31	—	159	107	—	52					
Burwell	339	373	34	—	346	324	—	22					
Ubbeston	59	79	20	—	21	24	3	—	23	200	8¾	25	80
Hemstead	130	119	—	11	75	53	—	22					
St. Matt. Ipswich	314	323	9	—	303	290	—	13	207	927	4½	29	31
Playford	62	57	—	5	39	24	—	15	22	209	9½	38	82
Hemley	18	25	7	—	28	22	—	6	9	57	6	22	28
Covehithe	70	96	26	—	40	52	12	—	26	185	7	20	37

* In 1792 and 1793 great ravages by the small-pox.

Parish.	1	2	3	4	5	6	7	8	9	10	11		
Benacre -	57	57	—	—	34	36	2	—	19	159	8	1 in 28	1 in 44
Ringsfield -	27	50	23	—	23	27	4	—	18	165	9	33	66
Baudsey -	87	129	42	—	93	69	—	24	57	296	5	22	42
Holton St. Mary	57	54	—	3	41	27	—	14	25	159	6	31	62
S.Marg.Ilketshal	93	101	8	—	57	43	—	14	38	284	7¼	28	62
St. Lawrence do.	36	26	—	10	16	5	—	11					
Tunstall -	159	218	59	—	105	75	—	30					
Iken -	54	82	28	—	54	45	—	9					
Bardwell -	122	175	53	—	106	90	—	16	90	483	5⅓	28	53
Sapiston -	68	67	—	1	49	48	—	1	41	200	5	28	40
Cratfield -	18:	176	—	4	118	*86	—	32	63	555	8¾	32	64
Laxfield -	322	339	17	—	185	201	16	—	120	800	6½	24	40
Rougham -	188	175	—	13	125	86	—	39					
Stradbrook -	323	449	126	—	184	216	32	—					
Beccles -	669	702	33	—	520	491	—	29	571	2440	4¼	34	50
Brantham -	89	102	13	—	69	52	—	17	50	250	5	25	50
Great Wenham	58	52	—	6	40	21	—	19	22	154	7	30	77
East Bergholt	326	324	—	2	227	239	12	—	190	1000	5	31	43
Heveningham -	69	70	1	—	51	65	14	—	38	273	7	39	40
Farnham -	50	62	12	—	31	24	—	7	23	190	8	31	76
Tattingstone -	59	118	59	—	77	†97	20	—					
Gosbeck -	83	115	32	—	37	41	4	—	35	281	8	25	70
Stonham -		154				61	—	—	107	552	5	36	92
S.Peter's South }Elmham	30	41	11	—	24	20	—	4	16	120	7½	30	60
St. Marg. S. do.	53	58	5	—	22	19	—	3	22	179	8	29	89
Aspal -	25	21	—	4	13	10	—	3	14	86	6	43	86
Cransford -	55	52	—	3	25	21	—	4	36	201	5½	40	100
Badingham -	181	215	34	—	95	100	5	—	59	439	7¼	20	43
Bedingfield -	91	124	13	—	49	54	5	—	30	250	8	25	44
Kenton -	72	82	10	—	37	40	3	—	26	219	8¼	27	54
Mickfield -	52	63	11	—	26	44	18	—	22	173	7¾	28	38
Holton -	83	114	31	—	74	45	—	29	51	263	4¾	23	58
Witnesham -	111	131	20	—	62	50	—	8	76	338	5¼	26	67
Mutford -	70	61	—	9	54	41	—	13	40	280	7	46	70
Chedburgh -	67	68	1	—	58	33	—	25	—				
Depden -	29	53	24	—	20	30	10	—					
Kesgrave -	20	27	7	—	11	14	3	—	13	70	5½	28	46
Stutton -	117	105	—	12	80	68	—	12	66	140	2	14	20
TudenhamS.Ma.	108	101	—	7	82	75	—	7					
Ashby -	8	18	10	—	—	3	3	—	4	38	9½	24	120
Butley and Capel	142	151	9	—	129	103	—	26	84	392	4½	26	39
Brightwell and }Foxhall	80	81	1	—	39	‡41	2	—	27	200	7¼	25	50
Martlesham -	43	84	41	—	52	‡44	—	8	48	245	5	28	56
Chillesford -	13	26	13	—	19	16	—	3	24	120	5	18	88

* Many die in the house of industry.——† Including thirty from the hundred house.
‡ House of industry, Nacton.

Parish.	1	2	3	4	5	6	7	8	9	10	11		
Oakley -	134	94	9	—	53	64	11	—	40	298	7¼	1 in 33	1 in 44
Sutton -	104	131	—	3	57	66	9	—	58	372	6¼	28	56
Ilketshall St. And	105	105	1	—	65	62	—	3	43	370	8½	37	61
AllSts.St Nich } S. Elmham	56	85	—	20	30	31	1	—	37	283	7½	32	94
Freckenham	93	71	15	—	48	61	13	—					
Hopton -	101	167	74	—	88	103	15	—					
Hesset -	185	91	—	10	51	60	9	—					
East Stonham	153	197	12	—	119	115	—	4	68	387	5½	20	35
Worlingworth	95	186	33	—	73	77	4	—					
Little Cornearth	248	88	—	7	64	67	3	—					
Debenham -	125	278	30	—	261	260	—	1	185	1161	6¼	43	44
Marlesford -	181	119	—	6	110	60	—	50	46	353	7½	29	58
Thorndon -	56	180	—	1	116	112	—	4					
Chattisham -	37	83	27	—	22	33	11	—	27	179	6½	22	59
St. Michael So. } Elmham	51	41	4	—	5	7	2	—	14	112	8	28	150
Homersfield -	52	65	14	—	42	34	—	8	25	164	6¾	24	46
Sandcroft -	45	60	8	—	38	30	—	8	27	185	6¾	30	61
North Cove -	110	79	34	—	33	29	—	4	28	179	6¼	22	59
Belton -	175	113	3	—	*79	62	—	17					
Bungay Trinity	336	252	77	—	160	173	13	—	} 468	†2340	5	36	58
Bungay St. Mary	70	404	68	—	255	233	—	22					
Botesdale -	48	84	14	—	80	97	17	—					
Shadingfield -	336	54	6	—	24	17	—	7	16	165	10	30	110
Brandon -	19	334	—	2	241	191	—	50	204	1072	5¼	32	55
Wangford -	239	20	1	—	17	2	—	15	10	495	5	24	§245
Barrow -	82	191	—	48	150	124	—	26	115	578	5	30	48
Buxhall -	62	75	—	7	68	33	—	35					
Troston -	47	75	13	—	49	42	—	7	31	237	7¾	30	59
Higham -	156	56	9	—	44	35	—	9	34	178	5	32	50
Middleton -	219	188	32	—	93	85	—	8	70	460	7½	24	72
Werkton -	123	285	66	—	126	114	—	12	75	618	8½	22	56
Blythburgh -	62	143	20	—	115	65	—	50	54	‡310	5¾	22	46
Wallerswick -	138	97	35	—	68	52	—	16	30	212	7	21	42
Alderton -		152	14	—	1c6	88	—	18	82	415	5	27	46
Bradfield Combt.	41	40	—	1	20	28	8	—	21	136	6½	34	45
St.Peter Sudbury	465	473	8	—	365	389	24	—					
St. Gregory ditto	342	306	—	36	389	377	—	12					
Glemsford -	444	496	52	—	385	529	—	56					
Woolpit -	217	158	—	59	180	114	—	66					

* Many from Yarmouth in these ten years.—† Multiplied by five, but probably not an enumeration.—‡ A fire destroyed some houses, and the people went.—§ Besides four hundred in a house of industry.

Total 1st column, being births in the first ten } 29,684
        years, Hemingston deducted, }

Ditto, 2d ditto, deducting Stonham,   154 } 33,011
        and Hemingston,   76 }

Ditto, of 5th ditto, being burials in the first } 22,800
    ten years, -   -   -   -   - }

Ditto of 6th ditto, being ditto in the second }
        ten years, deducting 102 for } 20,259
        Stonham and Hemingston, }

Ditto, of the 9th ditto, being number of }
        houses, 7,767 }
                                 } $5\frac{1}{4}$ per house
Ditto, of the 10th ditto, being number of }
        souls, 44,416 }

      Deducting Rickinghall,   474
               Mendlesham,   850
               Eye,   1769
               Timworth,   169
               Ingham,   135
               Ampton,   97
                               ——
                            3494

On an average of the second period of ten years, one in thirty of the population is born, and one in sixty buried.

    Births in the first ten years,   -   -   29,684
    Deaths in ditto,   -   -   -   22,800
                                       ——
        Difference,   -   -   -   6,884

    Births in the second ten years,   -   33,011
    Deaths in ditto,   -   -   -   20,259
                                       ——
        Difference,   -   -   12,752

It should seem from this comparison, that population must either have increased very greatly in this county, or, that a considerable emigration from it is constantly going forward. The numbers here minuted, are great enough to admit of both these circumstances ; but what proportion is to be assigned to each, does not appear. As, however, the accounts which have been published of other parts of the kingdom, are nearly of the same tenor, the probability is, that population has been rapidly increasing.

An account of the number of houses, servants, horses, dogs, and carriages, in the county of Suffolk in 1796:

	Houses.	Servants.		Horses.		Dogs.		Carriages.	
		for pleasure.	for husbandry.	at 5 shillings.	at 3 shillings.	four-wheels.	two-wheels.		
Under 7 windows, -	8,376								
From 7 to 9 windows incl.	3,607								
10 to 12, ditto,	2,117								
13 to 20, ditto,	1,977								
21 to 24, ditto,	265								
25, and upwards,	602								
	16,944	1,065	4,012	33,474	6,026	4,710	456	440	

An account of the number of inhabited houses, servants, horses and carriages, as assessed to their several duties, in England and Wales in 1796:

	Houses.	Servants.	Horses.		Carriages.	
			for pleasure.	for husbandry.	four-wheels.	two-wheels.
Houses under 6 windows,	354,391					
From 7 to 10 incl.	160,084					
11 to 15 ditto,	61,473					
14 to 19 ditto,	61,356					
20 to 24 ditto,	19,898					
25 and upwards,	31,642					
	688,844	56,850	178,784	900,700	19,070	24,305

For Suffolk to be in proportion to England, it will contain by acres:

Horses in husbandry,	-	-	15,871	
Houses,	-	-	-	12,181
Horses for pleasure,	-	-	3,150	
Servants,	-	-	-	1,001
Carriages, four-wheel,	-	-	336	
Ditto, two wheel,	-	-	428	

Proportion by rent, of 444,000*l.* to 26,000,000*l.*

Horses in husbandry,	-	-	15,381
Houses,	-	-	11,763

POPULATION OF THE COUNTY OF SUFFOLK,

Ascertained in consequence of the Act 41 George III, 1800.

HUNDREDS.	HOUSES.			PERSONS.	OCCUPATIONS.		
	Inhabited.	By how many families occupied	Uninhabited.		Chiefly employed in Agriculture.	In trade, manufactures, or handicraft.	In all other occupations.
Baberg	3147	3944	71	18,685	3804	5393	9588
Blackbourne	1572	2198	28	10,773	3857	1149	5391
Cosford	1250	1615	33	7,384	1715	794	4875
Hartismere	1795	2348	21	12,133	3557	1562	6631
Hoxne	1756	2487	14	13,299	4121	1685	6083
Lackford	1505	2347	31	8,384	1615	1571	5190
Plomsgate	1145	1710	13	8,549	2525	842	4643
Resbridge	1680	2176	32	10,894	4872	1460	3877
Stow	860	1081	15	5,708	1486	1537	1933
Thedwestry	1070	1506	17	7,259	2526	774	3959
Thredling	593	638	2	2,616	436	165	2008
Blything*	2579	3432	25	18,483	7018	3452	8010
Bosmere and Claydon }	1590	†1986	13	10,042	2760	780	5947
Carlford	665	855	4	4,300	1205	239	2013
Colneis	399	619	2	2,946	1273	148	1525
Loes	1661	1992	16	9,578	2209	1664	5362
Mutford and Lothingland }	1670	1913	36	9,409	1666	703	7043
Samford	1089	1487	11	7,457	2462	491	3841
Thingoe	716	973	11	4 982	1510	441	3031
Wangford	1668	1987	41	10,037	2045	1810	6190
Wilford	719	1048	10	5,298	2506	771	1924
Town of Bury	1360	1648	37	7,655	94	4198	3363
Ipswich	2170	2738	51	11,277	448	1810	8733
Sudbury	594	735	18	3,283	34	625	2624
	30,253	43,481	552	210,431	55,744	34,064	113,692

* The last ten hundreds incorporated.
† In the original here is an error; it is entered 1086, but by turning to the detail it appears to be 1986.

Horses for pleasure,   -   -   3,052
Servants,   -   -   -   -   970
Carriages, four-wheel,   -   -   -   325
Ditto, two-wheel,   -   -   -   415

Hence it appears, that this county contains more than the double of its proportion of horses in husbandry; one-fourth more of those kept for pleasure; one-fourth more houses; about its proportion of servants; about a-fourth more four-wheeled carriages; and nearly its proportion of two-wheeled ones. This is on the supposition that the kingdom at large pays correctly.

Let us, on the contrary, suppose that Suffolk is correct, and inquire what ought to be the proportions of the whole kingdom?

Answer. Really paid for.

	33,474 horses in husbandry,		1,978.009	900,000
If 440,000*l.*	4,012 horses for pleasure,	What should	237,072	178,000
rental	16,944 houses,	a rental of	1,001,235	688,000
maintains	1,065 servants,	26 millions	62,931	56,000
	456 4-wheel carriages,	maintain?	26,945	19,000
	440 2-wheel ditto		26,000	24,000

CHAPTER XVI.

OBSTACLES TO IMPROVEMENT.

In whatever counties these are found, they will consist of circumstances either generally affecting the whole kingdom, or locally particular counties: the latter I conceive to be the objects that ought more especially to attract the attention of any person who is employed to report the state of a county : in this respect, I am happy to observe that Suffolk labours under no such obstacle.

Those which are general to the whole kingdom, such as the payment of tythe, the existence of commons, and common-fields ; the practice of some individuals not to give leases to their farmers on soils which want improvement ; the rapid increase of poor-rates, and various other evils and deficiencies—these to analyze, would lead rather to general dissertations, which in my opinion ought carefully to be avoided in a local work, than to explanations of any thing essentially necessary to be known for well understanding the husbandry of a county. Among the notes which have been added to my former report by correspondents, I find but one to insert here.*

---

* As to tythes, it is at least a question, whether they are not more imaginary, than real obstacles, to improvements ? If in some parishes where tythes have been constantly gathered, improvements have progressively been carried very high ; if in others, though tythe free, improvements have comparatively stood still; it at least shews that tythes are not the general, though they may sometimes be the partial obstacles to improvements. At any rate, it must be considered, that tythes are estates invested either in the crown, or public bodies of men, or individuals by inheritance or purchase; secured by the same laws as the most antient landed property; and possessed by a body of men who

GAME.

On this subject, Mr. P. Edge, of Ipswich, thus expresses himself :—" An unnecessary consumption of corn is at all times to be carefully avoided. I will therefore take the liberty of informing the Board of Agriculture, that a most alarming quantity of corn is destroyed by game preserved in woods and plantations, in various parts of this kingdom. It is not possible for me to make any calculation as to the quantity destroyed ; but I will beg leave to mention, that in a field of eleven

perform the most essential service to the public, who are precluded from other professions and occupations, and for incomes generally inadequate to their education, and situations in life. The example of France, is perhaps most strikingly, in this instance, a warning to Britain, not to attack a property intimately connected with the constitution, under the fascinating idea of *reform*. The Devonshire society sets out with professing to offer nothing less than an adequate compensation for tythes ; but a corn-rent is extremely fallacious and injurious. The difficulty of first ascertaining the rent, is very great ; and if ascertained, would ultimately act as a modus. Had a corn-rent been substituted a century back, the estates of the church would at this time have been, probably, only half their present value. Let tythes be considered as they really are, a rent in kind, known and experienced both to landlords and tenants, and if they make a fair calculation, such a rent can be no reasonable bar to improvements. The argument that would make it so, might by parity of reasoning be extended to the *landlord's* rent, and to all taxes, and leads directly to the levelling system. And indeed, rents in kind are, in some countries, paid as high as one-fourth or one-third of the produce, with a flourishing agriculture. From various discussions on this subject, land has been fixed upon as the nearest adequate substitute for tythe. This, under new inclosing bills, has taken place to advantage, and may probably be gradually extended. But the difficulty of setting out land in old inclosed parishes, the satisfaction of contending parties, is often insurmountable. And if done, the future increase of dilapidations to the family of a late incumbent, and the necessary increase of a capital, and skill in husbandry, to his successor, are objections formidable and valid, to such commutation in general.—*Note by the Rev Mr. Carter, of Flempton.*

acres of wheat within three miles of this town, the
occupier, from the goodness of the land, from the excellent state of its cultivation, and from the health and
vigour of the plant, had a right to expect from eight to
ten coombs an acre.   His neighbours, men of great
respectability, were of the same opinion. Unfortunately
for the farmer, the field joined a wood full of hares and
pheasants, preserved and fed by the game-keepers; and
such was the havock made by the game, that the produce of the field was only fifteen coombs.

"In this single instance, no less than seventy coombs
of wheat were lost to the tenant, as well as to the public.
What therefore must be the astonishing quantity of
corn destroyed throughout the kingdom by game that is
preserved? I humbly hope the Board of Agriculture
will excuse me in observing, that this evil loudly calls
for the interference of parliament, to adopt some plan to
redress this grievance. Let me thefore stand forth as
the unsolicited advocate of the farmers, and request the
Honourable Board to recommend to the House of Commons to make such alterations in the game laws, as will
in some measure decrease the quantity of preserved game.

" I have no doubt but the legislature will endeavour
to put a stop to an evil so prejudicial to individuals, and
at the same time so detrimental to the community."

CHAPTER XVII.

MISCELLANEOUS OBSERVATIONS.

SECT I.—AGRICULTURAL SOCIETIES.

THE only society of this sort ever established in Suffolk, is the present existing one, called the Melford Society, which now meets alternately at Bury and Melford. At first, some of the members, according to the design of the institution, read memoirs of experiments, which appeared in the Annals of Agriculture; but for some years this has been discontinued. A few premiums were offered but never claimed; and these have consequently been also discontinued. County societies, however, if well imagined, and tolerably supported, might work very beneficial effects; and it is to be regretted, that so large, opulent, and respectable a province, should not possess an establishment of this kind, on an effective scale. Were such an one instituted, to meet three times a year at Bury, twice at the assizes, and once at the time of Bury fair, when there is a considerable assemblage from every part of the county; with local committees at the chief towns, they might be able to do some good, provided their premiums were few and considerable: and aimed at such objects as would promote the inquiries peculiarly adapted to the agriculture and live stock of the district. But the general failure of such societies, proves that most of them have hitherto adopted improper plans of proceeding. Till a better is established, the present one should continue, as the mere existence of a body to whom other societies may apply for assistance in various respects, is of itself a circumstance of considerable value.

SECT. II.—WEIGHTS AND MEASURES.

UNDER this head, there is nothing peculiar in the county. The Winchester bushel is universally used.

APPENDIX.

STATISTICAL DIVISION OF THE PRODUCE OF THE SOIL.

SIR,

IF, as you suppose, in your " General View of the Agriculture of the County of Suffolk," page 31, " inquiries into the expences and profits of husbandry, are suggested by the Board of Agriculture, with a view to excite a spirit of industry, and to shew the importance of investing in agricultural pursuits a sufficient capital to ensure to the cultivator of the soil a fair return for his exertions and skill ;" it appears to me, that inquiries into the profits on *a part only* of the farmer's process, tend to damp the spirit of industry, and to shew that money cannot be employed to a less beneficial purpose than in the occupation of land; for it is not easy (except indeed to experienced and able farmers) to imagine, when the profits on arable lands, under the best course of crops, and of grass, under different applications, are proved little more than sufficient to pay the outgoings, from what other sources so great a profit can arise, as (to borrow your words, p. 13) to yield " on dry lands very handsome profits, visible in various circumstances, and ascertained at the death of the farmer, and to place on wet soils, numbers very much at their ease." Under these impressions, I am induced to make a few observations on your estimates. You state

	CAPITAL.	RENT.	PROFIT.
On an acre of rich loam	£5 0 0	0 15 0	0 10 10½
strong loam	5 0 0	0 15 0	0 7 7
sand -	3 10 0	0 5 0	0 8 5

	CAPITAL.	RENT.	PROFIT.
On an acre of grass to cows £.5 0 0	-	0 16 0	- 0 12 8
sheep walk 0 10 0	-	0 2 6	- 0 1 9
grass to sheep 6 0 0	-	0 15 0	- 1 2 6

From these profits are to be deducted (for you have not included them in your particulars of outgoings) interest on capital employed, insurance, and loss of stock.* The former, of course, ought to be reckoned at five per cent. and the two others perhaps would not be too high at that rate ; I will however set them at only two and a half per cent. Your estimate will then stand thus:

$£. \quad s. \quad d.$

		£.	s.	d.
Profit on rich loam, - -		0	10	$10\frac{1}{2}$
Deduct $7\frac{1}{2}$ per cent. on 5l. capital -		0	7	6
Neat profit, - - -		0	3	$4\frac{1}{2}$
Profit on strong loam, - -		0	7	$7\frac{3}{4}$
Deduct $7\frac{1}{2}$ per cent. - -		0	7	6
Neat profit, - -		0	0	$1\frac{3}{4}$
Profit on sand, - - -		0	8	5
Deduct $7\frac{1}{2}$ per cent. on 3l. 10s. - -		0	5	3
Neat profit, - -		0	3	2
Profit on grass to cows, - -		0	12	8
Deduct $7\frac{1}{2}$ per cent. on 5l. - -		0	7	6
Neat profit, - -		0	5	2

* Nothing is to be deducted, in any mode of calculation, except interest of capital. Insurance is too trifling an article acreably. Losses on stock are already included.—A. Y.

	£.	s.	d.
Profit on sheep walk, - -	0	1	9
Deduct 7½ per cent. on 10s. -	0	0	9
Neat profit, - -	0	1	0
Profit on grass to sheep, - -	1	2	6
Deduct 7½ per cent. on 6l. - -	0	9	0
Neat profit, - -	0	13	6

It is necessary now to state the *general profits* which a farmer ought to make, that it may be seen how far these *particular* ones contribute to them. Adopting the old opinion, that of the thiee rents* the farmer should be allowed one for his expenditure, there are to be raised, in addition to the profits under the circumstances minuted by you, the following sums per acre :

	£.	s.	d.
On rich loam, - - -	0	11	7½
Strong loam, - - -	0	14	10½
Sand, - - - -	0	1	10
Grass to cows, - -	0	10	10
Sheep walk, - - - -	0	1	6
Grass to sheep, - - -	0	1	6

If you or any of your correspondents would shew from whence these sums (in addition to the profits before stated) are to be raised, it would prevent any erroneous conclusions being drawn from your estimates, and remove the doubt they are likely to create of the expediency of applying either money or attention to the pursuits of agriculture. You say (p. 25,) that "a farmer

---

* But this is a mere vulgar error, and no more a foundation to calculate on, than the number of miles from Bury to London.—*A. Y.*

should make 10 per cent. and in many cases he must make much more." Do you mean he should clear that after paying his house and personal expenditure? * (for many I understand reckon no profit till these are paid,) or do you speak as a merchant, who does not include these in computing the profit on any branch of his trade?

I am, Sir,

Your obedient servant,

Cockfield.   WILLIAM GOOCH.

SIR,   July, 1799.

I BEG to trouble you again on the subject of my last letter; I give you joy on a great agricultural acquisition; your most inveterate enemies, are become your most staunch friends. They who have hitherto denied your merit (I beg not to be included in this *discerning* class) and have thought you would ruin their interest, now begin to allow you possess some knowledge. They who have hitherto ridiculed and rejected all " book farming," now listen with respectful attention to your calculations, giving them their most cordial approbation, and will, I doubt not ring them in the ears of their landlords, instead of the hackneyed string of complaints. They who have hitherto lamented your having opened the eyes (as they express it) of country gentlemen, and your having induced so many of them to farm, now rejoice at your

---

* Certainly not, for that would, in many cases, raise 10 to 40 per cent. *A. Y.*

having *done them justice*, by publishing *their real situa-tion*, which never would have been credited had it come from themselves. Your opinion (Report p. 25) being that the average profit on agriculture is 10 per cent. on the capital employed, permit me to lay before you the consequent situation of farmers in this county. You state (Report, p. 13) the size of farms in Suffolk to be, in strong wet loams, from 20*l.* to 100*l.* and from 150*l.* to 300*l.* and in the sand districts from 300*l.* to 900*l.* a year. Hence, supposing as you do, (p. 267, &c.) that the loams are let at 15*s.* per acre, and that the capital employed on them is 5*l.* per acre : and that the sand districts are let at 5*s.* per acre, and the capital employed on them is 3*l.* 10*s.* per acre (you make no calculation on the maritime district, let, p. 13, at 10*s.*), it follows that

	Rent £.	Containing acres.	Capital employed.	Profit of 10*l.* per cent.		
An occupation of loam of	20	26	130	13	0	0
————————————	100	133	665	66	10	0
————————————	150	200	1000	100	0	0
————————————	300	400	2000	200	0	0
———————————sand of	300	1200	4200	420	0	0
Mr. Howlet's farm of sand of	900	3600	12600	1260	0	0

The half of these profits being what the capital would pay at interest, the other half is what the farmer is paid for his skill and attention. Do you think it adequate ? and do you think the whole consistent with the apparent, and I hope real, situation of the occupiers in this county ?

It appears (unless I have made some egregious error) that any occupation on loam under 300*l.* a year will yield little more than a decent maintenance for a family of an average number, and that saving money in such is impossible. You say (note on my last) that one rent of the three (the old idea) is no foundation to calculate upon; I did not think it was when I adopted it, I only meant to say, that the tenant must gain at least one rent to *live* by farming ; he must gain much more to make a *fortune* by it, excepting indeed in such farms as Mr. Howlett's. You say losses on stock are included in your outgoings; pray in which particular? Having said so much upon your calculations, you might with propriety call upon me to point out wherein I conceive them to be erroneous. Were I put to that task, I confess I should, so far from removing the paradoxical conclusion resulting from them, that I should increase it, by setting the rent and tythe on the loams higher than you do, because I really believe they are so in a great many instances, and lower in a very few. My own occupation is too confined to enable me to offer an estimate worthy notice, or to disprove yours being applicable to the county in general. I would however soon decline all agricultural pursuits if they paid me no better than 10 per cent. Since you say (speaking of your estimates, p. 273,) that the general profit of the farmer has no place in them, I am not without hope that their direct tendency to discourage agriculture will soon be removed by an able and fair calculation of the probable profit, from the whole of the farmer's process ; which I trust will be found to yield, instead of the starving 10 per cent. such as will induce men of abilily, education, and property, to give their attention to it.

I am, Sir,

Your obedient servant,

WILLIAM GOOCH.

P. S. A rent's profit on loams (rent and capital, as stated by you,) is equal to 15*l.* per cent.

A rent's profit on sands (rent and capital, as stated by you,) to near $7\frac{1}{2}$ per cent. and these profits must be raised in addition to the common interest of money, or fortunes cannot be obtained by farming.

DEAR SIR,   Cockfield, Oct. 7th, 1803.

I WISH the following account of my husbandry may be a satisfactory answer to your queries.

Had you only practical farmers for your readers, I would furnish you with the produce from broadcast and drill sowings under similar circumstances ; but, as there are many who give full credit to all statements of large produce, and absolutely discredit those of expences, making use of their knowledge of the former oppressively, and suspecting the latter to be impositions, you must not expect that full and free communication from the tenantry of the country you may wish ; you must be content with being told which mode the farmer has found the best ; indeed this information is all I conceive necessary for public benefit.

My course is turnips, barley, clover, wheat ;
I drill Turnips at 18 inches seed, very fleet,

     Barley or oats at 9 and 12 inches.

     Barley 6 pecks seed.

     Oats $11\frac{1}{2}$ pecks about 2 inches deep.

My clover I sow at the same time I drill the barley, 10lbs. per acre, broadcast.

I drill wheat at 12 inches and 18 inches 6 pecks about 2 inches deep.

When I grow beans and pease, they are in the place of clover.

I drill them at 18 inches. Beans 2 bushels of seed. Pease 9 pecks about 2 inches deep.

I horse-hoe the intervals of my corn, and hand-hoe the rows. I have no doubt of the superiority of drilling over broad-cast; I am warranted in my opinion from the testimony of those on whose correctness and word I can rely, and, from my own experience, of short duration indeed, and on a small scale. I weed my clovers as often as weeds appear.

On my wheat stubbles I sow tares or rye, (and this autumn winter barley also) for sheep feed; then plough, skim, and scarify for turnips till I get a fine clean tilth.

For barley, or oats, I plough only once after turnips, and sometimes not at all, only scarify; I have reason to believe the latter method as good as the former; and as 6 acres can be scarified in the same time that one can be ploughed, it is better.

For wheat, after pease or beans, sometimes plough only once, sometimes only scarify.

For beans or pease, plough once *deep* before winter; scarify at sowing.

I wish to sow early both in spring and autumn. After Christmas I draw my turnips and set them into every other furrow, (an old practice) and plough into them, which secures them as effectually as Mr. Munning's plan, which I tried, I found it more expensive, and that it left the land very uneven.

My grass I appropriate to bullocks and sheep. My plan hitherto has been to buy Galloway Scots between Michaelmas and Christmas, and sell them from August to Michaelmas following; my winter keep of them, grass till about Christmas, then chaff, (viz. hay and straw cut) in a well littered yard, in the *spring a very few* turnips; thus kept they go to grass in excellent condition, and go *immediately* " forward" fast. My sheep (wether lambs bought in about Ipswich fair) I keep the same, and return at the same time as my bullocks.

I believe my bullocks and sheep pay me better than cows pay, except perhaps where the *mistress* does the work, *or sees it done*. I judge from the stated produce per cow, of the finest and best managed dairies, and from the *very great deductions* by expences, which latter statement, however, every farmer is not prepared to make ; he is not in the habit of it ; I never met with one who had ever done it ; get your neighbour Green to furnish you with one ; if you give him a skeleton it will save him a deal of trouble, and remind him of many articles he would otherwise forget.

Don't misunderstand me; I don't mean the difference between the purchase and sale of one of my bullocks, is equal to *the gross produce* of a cow, in the year, I mean the net difference is more. The high price of Scotch beasts, particularly of those of a proper age to fat the succeeding summer, has induced me to change my bullock system, and to adopt an old one, of keeping " three stocks" as it is called. Instead of returning yearly all that my pastures will fat, I mean to return half that quantity only, and I expect the annual profit will be the same, at any rate as much, and that the *same breadth of land* will, winter and summer carry the stock of one process as of the other. For example, if on my first plan

	£.	s.	d.
I bought annually 10 Scots at 12*l.*	120	0	0
Sold them at 21*l.*	210	0	0
Difference	90	0	0

	£.	s.	d.
On my intended plan I shall buy annually } 5 calves, about August 3*l.*	15	0	0
Sell annually 5 home breds at 21*l.*	105	0	0
Difference,	90	0	0

My constant stock then will be 15 head, viz.

> 5 fatting 3 years old off.
> 5 lean   2 ditto.
> 5 ditto   1 ditto.

And on selling the fat ones I replace them by 5 calves.

Of course I must *now* buy of these different ages, to set this scheme immediately on foot.

The advantages I expect from this latter plan, are that the homebreds will, at 3½ years, weigh more than the Scots; that, should I be obliged (from such a drought as we have lately had) to finish any of my stock, the lean ones will take less hurt from it than the fatting ones, *which must be returned* from grass; the money employed after the *first* calves bought are returned, is evidently less, thus

	£.	s.	d.
10 Scots annually at 12*l.*	120	0	0
5 calves, at 3*l.* returned at 3½ years old, viz. } when 15 of them have been bought	45	0	0
Less employed by one system than the other,	75	0	0

When I grow potatoes it is on my summer lands, or in the place of clover.

My wheat this year suffered from the worm and mildew, so much so, that it is worth very little.

I keep a good many hogs (though I have only two cows) ; I think the best plan is to breed and sell lean. I give them while at large, during winter, potatoes ; and, in cold or in wet weather, beans ; I think I shall give beans only, in future ; believing a bushel of beans will go further than a sack of potatoes. I give my sows, while they have pigs on them, pollard, &c. Wishing for the muck, I will try this winter fatting some hogs for market, and will let you have the result.

I could not make corn-grazing bullocks answer, when the lean price was 6s. per stone, on the weight they would fat to, and the fat price 10s. 6d. The price of fatting, barley 10s. and 11s. beans 13s. 14s. and 14s. 6d. I mean I did not get the muck. I wish some communicative corn grazier would let me into his secret of getting money that way ; I hope a medal from Mr. Coke another year will bring it out.

If I have neglected any point on which you wished me to speak, pray say so, and I will communicate as much as any *tenant* should do. Your corresponding landlords will, I am sure, give you the information we *tenants* cannot, without being branded by our brethren, with titles which would not set easy.

I have one piece of strong land on which I mean to grow beans and wheat alternately ; beans at 18 inches, wheat at 18 or 12 inches.—When at 18 inches the barley cup should be used ; this I discovered after I had drilled mine with the usual wheat cup, I had too little plant all the way through, but the ears were remarked for their large size. My neighbours, *anti drillers*, laid it, before the mildew affected it, at 6½ coombs an acre.

DEAR SIR,

FARMING information is a subject *sore* to all concerned. Sheep at corn have *paid nothing*, in many instances known to me, hereabouts. A vast number of beasts are at corn in this neighbourhood; from the information I get, I find they eat about 8*s*. 6*d*. per head per week, at barley-meal and bean-meal; all allow it a losing game.

You have given in your Annals the " day at Ardleigh," correctly indeed. I am afraid the " farm near Saffron Waldon" is too true a statement.

W. G.

SOME PARTICULARS RELATING TO CERTAIN PARISHES.

WOODBRIDGE.

BY MR. ROBERT LODER OF THAT PLACE.

INQUISITION of the inhabitants of Woodbridge, taken in the years 1770, and 1777.

1770.	Of the Established Church,	-	1973
	Independents,	- -	275
	Quakers,	- -	82
	Papist,	- - -	1
			2331

1777.	Of the Established Church,	-	2105
	Independents,	- -	283
	Quakers,	- -	86
			2474

Taken in the years 1760, 1763, and 1781 (no separate distinctions).

1760,	- -	2026	1781, 534 houses.
1763,	- -	2197	591 families.
1781,	- -	2600	

Progressive increase, from 1760 to 1763, - 171
1763 to 1770, - 134
1770 to 1777, - 143
1777 to 1781, - 126

Total increase in 21 years,   -   574

In the year 1666, the plague raged violently in this parish. It appears from the parish register, that in the months of July and August in that year, there were buried no less than 327 persons: whereas the burials in those two months in each of the ten preceding years did not, on an average, exceed the number ef twelve. Tradition says, the dead were buried in the field now called Bearman's Hill.

BARNHAM.

THE parish of Barnham, near Euston, contains 5302 acres, viz.

In 1764.			
Infield arable, inclosed,		-	381
Outfield arable,	-	- -	2626
Meadow and pasture,		-	559
Heath, or sheep-walk,		-	1735
Total,	-	-	5302

And consists of four farms. The whole belongs to his Grace the Duke of Grafton, to whom I am obliged for these particulars. There are 3300 sheep in it, 60 cows, and 43 horses.

Land-tax,	-	-	101*l.* 2*s.*
Poor-rates in 1764,	-	- -	£. 53
1765,	-	- -	41
1767,	-	-	45
1787,	-	-	131
Windows in the assessment,		- -	94
Houses appearing on the duplicates,		-	9

But this number being very small for a village which I recollected had quite another appearance, I counted, and found them to be forty-six.

Hence, whatever examination a political arithmetician could make at the Tax-office, to discover the population of this parish, would give him not more than the number of forty-five souls, at five to a house; but the fact is, there are at that ratio 230, or nine times as many.

PARISH REGISTER.

	Baptisms.	Burials.	Incr.
In 14 years, from 1731 to 1744,	112	92	20
In 14 do. from 1745 to 1758,	76	56	20
In 14 do. from 1759 to 1772,	115	104	11
In 14 do. from 1773 to 1786,	145	98	47

This rapid increase in the fourteen last years, ought to be attributed to some clear and manifest cause: it is very general in this county, but I know not to what peculiarity to assign it.

A vast improvement upon the outfield land of this parish, would be to add a good portion of burnet and chicory to the ray, with which they lay down for four years.

TROSTON.

BY CAPEL LOFT, ESQ. OF TROSTON-HALL, NEAR
BURY.

THIS village consists of twenty-eight houses.

Of the twenty-eight houses, the assessment to window lights is,

					£.	s.	d.
Old duty,	-	-	-	-	13	5	6
New ditto,	-	-	-	17	13	0
The lights are, 1 house	-	-	-			36
1 ditto	-	-	-	-		21
4 ditto between 20 and					10
3 ditto	-	-	-		9
11 ditto	-	-	-		6

20

Seven are excused on account of poverty: one exempted as being the poor-house.

Assessment to the house duty,   -   £. 1 2 0

Only five houses assessed.

			A.	R.	P.
Pasture,	-	-	123	0	0
Arable,	-	-	-	205	0	0
Common field,	-	-	613	0	0
Mixed, pasture and arable,	-	4	2	0
			945	2	0
Common, about	-	-	83	0	19
			1028	2	19

The nine hundred and forty-five acres above specified, stand at the yearly value of 595*l.* as stated in the
assessment to the poor-rates; which appears to be fairly
made to the full rents. But it must be remarked, that
this includes the valuation to tythe and glebe; which
are farmed by an inhabitant, who stands at 110*l.* in the
assessment on that account.

The glebe is fifty-eight acres.

If it stands at 8*s.* per acre, this is 23*l.* 4*s.* say 23*l.*
allowing the remaining 87*l.* for tythes, then the parish
rental will be (by the deduction of 87*l.*) 508*l.* This, to
the number of acres, is as near as is well possible, 10*s.* 9*d.*
per acre.

	£.	s.	d.
The assessment to the poor-rates at 1*d.* in the pound for a single rate, stands	2	9	7½
This at 21 penny rates, as was the case last year, would give - -	52	2	1¼
In 18 years from 1767, the average is 44*l.* with a very small fraction beyond: the total in that time being only -	3	4	11½
Beyond then, it would be at the annual assessment above taken as the average,	795	4	11½
For the first nine years of this period, the average is rather below 39*l.* -	350	3	10
The greatest sum hitherto assessed, was in 1783, by twenty-five rates, on 2*l.* 9*s.* 7*d.* penny rate, - - - -	61	19	7
The least in 1767, by 13 rates of 2*l.* 5*s.* 0½*d.*	29	5	6½
The mean of these two very near exactly, was assessed in 1769, - -	45	0	10
To the land-tax the parish is assessed -	92	8	0

Outgoings, exclusive of non-enumerated taxes, as
servants' tax, horse and wheel tax, &c. are as follow:

	£.	s.	d.
House,	1	2	0
Lights, old duty,	13	5	6
Ditto new,	17	3	0
Poor-rates, on average,	44	0	0
Land-tax,	92	8	0
	167	18	6
Tythe and glebe farmed at 110*l.* value : } set at no more than it is farmed,	110	0	0
	277	18	6

Rents as per assessment,   -   -   £.595   0   0

Number of inhabitants.—I find, by my account, that the inhabitants (exclusive of such servants as are not comprehended under the description of the several families) were, at the end of the year 1784, as follows:

Husbands,	31
Wives,	31
Widowers remaining unmarried,	8
Widows ditto	7

There are, at present, of inhabitants, as before explained,

Males,	92
Females,	89
	181

Add to these, twenty-three servants, not enumerated under other descriptions;

Males and females,	181
Servants,	23
	204

More than seven, on an average, in each house.

There are of freehold, enabling them to exercise the
right of voting at elections, - - 9
    Our quota to the militia was, - - 1
    Births, in 49 years from 1679 to 1727, - 278
    Ditto in 49 years from 1727 to 1776, - 294
    In favour of the last, - - - 16
The greatest number of marriages in these periods,
    is from 1706 to 1713, and from 1734 to 1741,
    in each period, - - - 14
The fewest from 1720 to 1727, and again from
    1748 to 1755, in each, - - 7
The greatest number of births is from 1762 to
    1769, - - - - 51
The least, from 1685 to 1692, - - 29
The least of deaths is the same period at the least
    births, 1685 to 1692, - - 15
The greatest from 1713 to 1720, - 48
    The comparison may be stated another way :

Years.		Births.		Deaths.
1677 to 1685,		36		29
1692,		29		15
1699,	189	43	130	27
1706,		46		24
1713,		35		35
1720,		48		37
1727,		41		30
1734,	203	36	159	35
1741,		41		31
1748,		37		26
1755,		43		31
1762,		41		35
1769,	220	51	163	29
1776,		45		35
1783,		40		33

    Hence we see, that in these periods of thirty-five
years, population has increased very considerably.

EXTRACT FROM THE REGISTER OF THE PARISH OF
TROSTON, FOR 20 YEARS, FROM 1776 TO 1795,
BOTH INCLUSIVE.

	BAPTISMS.		BURIALS.	
	Males.	Fem.	Males.	Fem.
1776, -	2† -	3	2* -	2
1777, -	3* -	7	2 -	5
1778, -	3† -	0	2* -	2
1779, -	4 -	3	2* -	3
1780, -	1† -	4	3† -	6
1781, -	5* -	4	0* -	2
1782, -	0† -	1	2* -	0
1783, -	5 -	2	2* -	3
1784, -	4 -	4	2 -	3
1785, -	4 -	3	3 -	3
1786, -	7* -	3	1* -	2
1787, -	4 -	2	1* -	2
1788, -	6* -	4	2* -	3
1789, -	3* -	6	2* -	2
1790, -	4* -	5	3† -	6
1791, -	3* -	0	3* -	1
1792, -	5 -	2	3* -	1
1793, -	3 -	4	2* -	3
1794, -	5 -	3	1* -	0
1795, -	1 -	5	1* -	3
	72	65	39	52

Diff. of male births　7†　　　Diff. of male burials 13
Diff. in favor of births 46

Gen. total males　-　72　　Gen. total males　39
Gen. total females　-　65　　Gen. total females　52

Whole No. of births 137　　Whole No. of deaths 91

The * to the Baptisms, denotes a year favourable; or in which they
are nine or more.—The † denotes an unfavourable year; or in which
they are five, or under.—For the Burials, these signs are reversed.

OBSERVATIONS.

First Decennium.

Table of Births.—1 year singly favourable; or births above the par taken.

     1 do. doubly; or births above, and burials below the par.

     3 do. singly unfavourable.

     1 do. doubly; where both births below, and deaths above par.

Table of Burials.—5 years singly favourable.

     1 do. doubly.

     1 do. doubly unfavourable.

Second Decennium.

Table of Births.—1 year singly favourable.

     3 do. doubly.

Table of Burials.—6 years singly.

     3 do. doubly favourable; where births above, and deaths below par.

In the first decennium the male and female baptisms were exactly equal. In the second, the males are to the females as 41 to 34, or as 14 to 11 nearly in favour of the females.

In the first decennium, the male burials are to the female as 20 to 29, or as 5 to 7 nearly in favour of the male.

In the second, they are as 19 to 23, or as 6 to 7 nearly in favour of the male.

The whole number of males born in the 20 years (72) to the whole number of females (65) is as 12 to 11 nearly in favour of the male.

The whole number of males dying (39) to the whole number of females dying (52) is as 13 to 14 in favour of the males.

The male births exceed the male burials   -   33

The female births exceed the female burials   -   13

In the 1st decennium the male births exceed ⎱ 11
    the burials by   -   -   ⎰

    The female by   -   -   -   2
                                          —

    Total excess   -   -   13
                                          —

In the 2d, the male births exceed the deaths by 22

    The female by   -   -   -   11
                                          —

    Total excess of male births above deaths ⎱ 33
       in 20 years   -   -   ⎰

    Of female   -   -   -   13
                                          —

    Total excess of births above burials   46

Annual average of births in the 20 years, $6\frac{3}{4}$ nearly.

    Of deaths, $4\frac{1}{2}$ one-twentieth nearly.

GENERAL OBSERVATION.

The excess of births above burials, amounts in the 20 years to one-third, if there had been only one birth more:
$$46 \times 3 = 138.$$

Such an instance of increasing population, if the register is correct, and I know nothing to the contrary, I believe will hardly be paralleled.

Troston has no manufactures, to increase it adventitiously. I think, therefore, such an increase may be taken as evidence of great salubrity in the air and soil; which indeed the former registers and extracts confirm. But as the favourable difference considerably exceeds the former proportions, other favourable circumstances of a more variable nature, such as season, modes of living, modes of nursing, must have been presumably in its favour also.

The latitude of Troston, 50° 18′.

E. longitude 48′. 20″.

The soil dry, and rather sandy, with a gravel or chalk bottom. The country flat and open, abounding in heath and common, in proportion to the size of the parish. A small proportion of the heath put under cultivation within the last ten years.

General level rather high: air, taken in different places very good, by the test of the Eudiometer. No epidemical disorder. About twelve years back, agues had been pretty frequent; rare since. Several rather deep ponds: scarcely any marsh, or bog land. The water moderately good.

Thirty-one houses in Troston. Two added since the year 1790.

In the account you honoured me by inserting,* eleven years back, twenty-eight houses are stated; and two hundred and four inhabitants.

As only two or three persons have migrated from the parish into others, and about as many have come into it from others, the surplus by births within these last eleven years, may be taken in addition to the two hundred and four.

Taking it for ten years, that it may coincide with the period you proposed, the surplus of births above burials is thirty-three.—$33 + 204 = 237$.

Two hundred and thirty-seven to 31 houses, is above $7\frac{3}{4}$ on the average, to each house.

The average of deaths in the last ten years, is four two-tenths annually. The average of births, seven five-tenths.

The deaths, therefore, are about one in fifty, annually; which is one of the lowest rates of mortality.

The births one in thirty yearly, taken on the last ten years. Of these births, three have been twins; or one in ninety nearly.

* Annals, vol. iv. p. 305.

4

2 **APPENDIX.**

FORNHAM ST. MARTIN'S.

BY THE REV. DR. ORD.

THE number of inhabitants in the parish of Fornham
St. Martin's, is at this time (1784) 134. The number
of houses 22 ; of which six are double tenements, and
one is a treble one ; of tenements, therefore, there are
30. Of the 22 houses, there are charged to the window-
tax 13.

I learn from the parish register, that from the
year 1711 to 1733, there were 43 baptisms and 49
burials; from the year 1762 to the year 1784, there
were 76 baptisms and 61 burials.

The annual expence to this parish, for the support of
the poor, was in 1745 - - £. 12
1756 - - - 27
1776 - - - 50
From 1776 to 1783, on an average, - - 59
The parish contains, of arable land, 932 acres.
of grass land, 116
———
1048
There are of commons and roads, 241
———
1289

FORNHAM ST. GENOVEVE.

BY THE REV. DR. ORD.

On examining the register of the parish of Fornham
St. Genoveve, during the same periods as I did that of
Fornham St. Martin, I find that

	Bap.	Bur.
From the year 1711 to 1733, there were	76	96
1762 to 1784,	60	54
Decrease in first period	20	
Increase in second		6

This parish contains, at present, 108 persons, inhabiting eleven houses, five of which are double tenements, and three pay to the window-tax. It consists of
five hundred and eighty acres, of which the average
value is about nine shillings an acre: of these five
hundred and eighty acres, two hundred and seventy have
lately been imparked. The whole parish belongs to
one person.

MOULTON.

BY THE REV. E. WILSON.

THIS parish contains about sixteen hundred acres of arable land, chiefly in open fields, and lying in small pieces. Course, two crops and a fallow.

About one thousand acres of heath, in eight several sheep-walks. Much of this convertible (as appears by experiment on some parts) into good arable.

A small quantity of meadow, pasture and common.

Rental about 750*l.*

Poor-rates about 3*s.* 3*d.* rack rent.

Houses thirty-seven : inhabitants about two hundred and twenty.

Wages, 14*d.* a day with beer. Employment of the women and children, spinning for Norwich.

	Births.	Burials.
In 20 years, ending with 1620 -	132	128
1700 -	113	95
1754 -	148	155
1794 -	147	106

BURY ST. EDMOND'S.

In 1775, there were in Bury St. Edmond's, twelve hundred and ninety-four houses: seven thousand one hundred and thirty-five souls: five per house.

About 4000 paupers.

Land-tax 2080*l.*

Assessed taxes 2540*l.*

BARROW.

BY THE REV. GEORGE ASHBY.

Had your knowing and communicative correspondent, Mr. Macro, been alive, you would perhaps have received a complete account of the agriculture of this parish: from me it will be quite superficial. By a large plan, from a survey taken in 1597, the contents, with roads and wastes, are set down at two thousand five hundred and fifty acres.

Mr. Macro mentions the smut prevailing one year in this and the neighbouring fields. I have known a year when the smut was in the neighbouring fields and not in this.

A grand disadvantage which the open field labours under, is not (as you probably pre-suppose) the tythes: for if they were entirely done away, by allowing the Rector a compensation, the field, I should suppose, would receive no benefit thereby, whilst run over by a flock of seven or eight hundred sheep belonging to one farm. This is an hardship of the worst kind, as it prevents a single turnip being grown, except by one tenant, and the whole system, to the disgrace of a more enlightened age, effectually prevents him, and all the rest of the farmers, from adopting the improved course of, 1. turnips ; 2. barley ; 3. clover ; 4. wheat ; instead of the rotation most of our common fields in East England are bound to, by the thraldom of *common rights ;* which might more properly be called common wrongs, as injurious to the individual and public, in lessening by fallows, once in three years, the produce, instead of a fallowing crop of turnips, beans, peas, or grasses, that would feed many animals.

We have no waste, or common.

The well at the rectory is deep, probably the same as at St. Edmond's Hill, Ickworth, and Higham, all which are one hundred and thirty feet nearly. Ours is probably for this reason neglected, and we content ourselves with a pump set down in land springs, which lie very little below the surface. If we go lower, there is no water till the former depth is reached.

Baptisms from 1774 to 1794, one hundred and seventy-one more than deaths.

Average of baptisms,   - -   21 two-thirds.
deaths,   - -   13 one-half.
marriages,   - -   4 one-third.

Of the persons buried, the following were aged seventy, or upwards :

70	4	76	1	81	2	86	3
71	1	77	2	82	2	88	1
72	2	78	3	83	1	89	1
73	1	79	2	84	1	90	1
74	2	80	6	85	2	91	1

In the baptisms, twenty, or one a year nearly, should

be deducted, as not belonging to the parish, but brought
from the neighbouring ones (where no minister resides)
to be named. So of the burials, twelve seem not to have
been parishioners, and three that were, may have been
carried away ; which, upon the whole, may lessen the
burials one in two years. So it appears that one in forty-
two died annually.

This place may therefore boast of a desirable degree of
salubrity, compared with many other places ; but which
is nothing in respect of your Bradfield, perched on a
raised ridge of earth full two hundred feet above the
level of the water coming out of Bury. In Manchester,
one in twenty-eight die, and in the country immediately
surrounding it, only one in fifty-six.

	£.	s.	d.
Poor rates, 1774, at 2s. in the pound, -	94	17	1
1784, at 2s. 3d. - -	161	5	2¼
1724, at 2s. 9d. - -	213	14	8

Against this latter period the rents were raised.
Land-tax 180l.

Four or five houses at least have been built within
these twelve years. Cottages much wanted.

In the twenty first years of my constant residence, I
have known of no prevailing distemper. Inoculation
has been little practised, so that the number liable to the
distemper is great.

On the 13th of April, 1714, there were, 108 houses,
144 men, 143 women, 131 boys, 120 girls, 14 men
servants, 17 women servants ; in all 569 persons.

On the 13th of April, 1789, there were, 115 houses,
134 men, 147 women, 146 boys, 119 girls, 18 men
servants, 14 women servants ; in all 578 persons.

Our town stands high, and exposed to north winds,
coming over a vast tract of bald and bare country ; yet
I know of no particular mischief done, except on the

last day of 1778, or first of 1779, in blowing down a
large new barn that I had just built : when no other
harm was done here ; but in Ickworth park the storm
blew down, or disbranched, many large trees.

WELNETHAM.

BY THE REV. R. PHILLIPS.

THE air at Welnetham is very keen, being a high
spot.

No. of burials, 1784, 3—1 at 45, 1 at 75, and an
infant.

        1785, 1—aged 85.

        1786, 5—1 at 86, 1 at 30, 1 at 22,
and 2 infants.

        1787, 1—an infant.

        1788, 3—1 at 86, and 2 infants.

The daily wages of the labourers, during the winter,
is 1s. 4d. a day without beer ; with beer 1s. 2d.

Of thirty-one labouring families, five contain three
children ; five ditto, four ; three ditto, five ; and one
ditto, six children.

It is not usual, in this neighbourhood, to board the
harvest-men ; their wages are twelve shillings a week,
for five weeks, and allowed three bushels of malt in lieu
of beer.

Number of labourers in the prime of life, viz. from
25 to 45 years of age, 19 ; 9 from 45 to 60 ; 2 between
60 and 70 ; and 1 of 79.

Number of inhabitants:

Farmers, wives, children, and servants,	113
Labourers,	31
———— wives and children,	109
Widows,	6
Total,	259

I believe 27 of the above mentioned labourers earn, upon an average, upwards of 20*l.* a year per head, and those that *take work* considerably more. The earnings of the remaining three must be small, as they are very infirm, and receive something weekly from the parish.

I believe the average earnings of the wives and children, in each of the thirty-one families, exceed 2*s.* a week, though spinning is at this time very bad ; we have many children that in autumn earn 4*d.* a day in dropping wheat.

Number of houses charged in the parochial duplicate to the window tax at 3*s.* house duty, 23.

The net annual average expence of the poor, for the last four years is 100*l.* (1792).

THE DRILL HUSBANDRY.

IT has for some years been generally known that the drill husbandry has made a considerable progress in several of the counties of this kingdom, but on examining the various accounts which have been published of the experiments registered, the soil in most of the cases will be found dry and light ; or at least sound land on which the difficulties in the management are not great. Every practical farmer knows that the ease of introducing such new methods has usually been the greatest on dry land. Wet, strong, tenacious soils, that are apt to poach if not tilled with much care and attention, are difficult to manage, and have been thought peculiarly unfavourable to drilling. Of the truth of this remark Norfolk affords a striking instance : drilling has made a rapid and very extensive progress on sand ; but in going through that county lately I found but one decided case of its introduction for white corn on clay. In such a state of the public knowledge relative to this interesting object, it will, I conceive, be particularly satisfactory to the agricultural reader to find that a district exists in which the drill husbandry for all sorts of crops has been very generally introduced on a strong, wet, difficult, tenacious soil, utterly unprofitable to farm without careful draining. Till I made a re-examination of the heavy-land district of Suffolk, I had not met with any such case in general practice.

The soil is a strong loam, wet, adhesive, tending to clay, upon a clay marl bottom, much too wet for turnips, though some are found on it ; dries into impenetrable clods, and moistens into mud, but is vastly improved by hollow draining; yet in its best state turnips are consumed or removed with difficulty. In order to examine the state of drilling on this land, which has usually been held so unfit for it, I made three journies through various parts of the district ; my former Report for the County of Suffolk having been drawn up at a period when the practice was but slowly creeping in on the farms of only a few individuals : I shall now register the observations made on various farms, which, I trust, will be sufficient to shew that drilling is thoroughly established in this district.

MR. SIMPSON, of *Witnesham*, five miles from Ipswich, has been in the drill husbandry fourteen years ; he came into it gradually till the whole of his two farms (the total amount of which is about 700 acres) was under this new culture. For many years all his white corn was at nine inches equally distant ; but he has for a few years past changed it to 12 inches, which he thinks preferable, and all his present crop is at that distance ; but his beans at 18.

Drilling has of late years spread through all the neighbourhood ; labourers buy drill machines (Cook's) with which they go out drilling at 2s. an acre, and some of them earn from 10l. to 20l. a year, and some more, by this practice ; and the husbandry much increases in estimation.

But on these wet soils Mr. Simpson justly remarks that the drill system is intimately connected with another object, from which respecting profit it can scarcely be separated ; and this is that of avoiding as much as possible all spring ploughing. To introduce the drill generally on a wet-land farm without practically comprehending the importance of putting crops in *upon a stale* furrow, will probably turn out a difficult, embarrassing, and perhaps a failing attempt ; and he conceives that this is the circumstance which has occasioned in various districts so many failures on heavy soils.

The spring crops are barley or oats, and beans. The barley after fallow, tares, beans, or turnips ; and the beans after barley, oats, or wheat. The management is this : whatever crop or fallow the white spring corn succeeds the land is ploughed into the intended form before the winter frosts. Mr. Simpson's *stitches* are 5 feet 3 inches broad for one movement of the drill machine ; some farmers 9 or 10 feet for a *bout*, or two movements of it. In either case the horses go only in the furrows. Whatever the preparation by tillage, whether many ploughings in a fallow, two or three after tares, or one after beans ; the same conduct as pursued in the last being before the frosts, that nothing may be wanting in the spring but to scuffle and harrow, and then drill in the seed. And beans are managed on the same principles ; the only difficulty is on turnip land, when the consumption of the crop is after the frosts ; whether they have been fed on the land, or carted off, the surface is probably left in a trodden state. This has induced Mr. Simpson to clear all his turnips and cabbages, if possible, by the beginning of March, and to plough as quickly as possible for the chance of late frosts to gain a friable surface, which once got he never ploughs it down again, according to the old practice, for the sake of more tillage, but when in the right temper scuffles and drills. Some farmers have found their account, when the season has been favourable, in only scarifying, and scuffling, and harrowing the turnip land, and drilling the barley or oats without any plough-ing ; but season must govern for such a practice, which however proves the great idea they have of the im-portance of avoiding spring ploughings as much as possible.

I was anxious to discover the origin of this practice, which is, to all appearance, of so much importance. Mr. Simpson informs me that, as far as his knowledge extends, Mr. Edwards, of Ash, was the first person who harrowed in broadcast barley on a stale autumnal furrow upon fallow ; and his success was such that he not only continued it himself, but was presently followed by some his neighbours. This was about twenty years ago. The next step taken in the system was to put in beans on a stale furrow, in which the success was still greater, and became a most important improvement. The common husbandry at that time was the course of 1. Fallow, and generally a very bad one. 2. Wheat. 3. Barley or oats. When barley was sown with a great certainty by avoiding spring tillage, it became generally substituted for wheat, which brought another improvement of no less consequence, that of clover with it ; and the wheat on this preparation instead of fallow ; and though oats followed, yet the management was decidedly improved. In proportion as spring ploughing was rejected the crops were greater. Drilling was soon introduced, and extended every year from its first introduction in this neighbourhood by Mr. Simpson, to the present time ; when it may be said to occupy the fields of every farmer noted for good management.

It is obvious from this account, that all depends in drilling these soils on their being constantly kept in stitches of the exact breadth requisite for drilling ; no successive care or attention will remedy any neglect in this point. Mr. Simpson prefers such as admit only one movement of the drill, because the horse-hoeing is performed with more certainty than when the junction of a *bout* is to be made, which is liable to inequality of space, if a most minute attention be not paid to the operation. His drill (Cook's) is made to sow five rows at 11¼ inches; there are consequently four spaces between them, occupying 45 inches, and he leaves a furrow between each stitch of 18, that is 9 on each side; thus the whole stitch is 63 inches.

In regard to the success that has attended the practice of this husbandry, Mr. Simpson is well satisfied; of the superiority of it to the broad cast management, he has entire conviction. His crops have been much better from the drill than ever they were in the old method. This point he conceives is not to be ascertained by the comparison of two pieces, the one drilled and the other broad cast; but from a comparison of two fields during a period that should shew the effect of the superior cleanness resulting from the continued use of the horse-hoe. Mr. Simpson horse hoes all his crops; which was one great inducement for preferring 11¼ to 9 inch rows; he horse-hoed the latter; but it is more effectually performed in the former.

His quantities of seed, wheat one bushel; barley 6 to 7 pecks; oats 2 bushels; pease, at 18 inches, 2 bushels; and beans, at the same distance, 6 to 7 pecks.

Course:

1. Turnips or cabbages,
2. Barley,
3. Clover,
4. Wheat,
5. Winter tares,
6. Barley,
7. Beans,
8. Wheat. A double four shift.

He has been in what he calls the five shift husbandry of

1. Turnips,
2. Barley,
3. Clover,

4. Wheat,
5. Beans,
6. Tares,
7. Barley,
8. Clover,
9. Wheat,
10. Beans,

but has changed it for the above mentioned much superior system.

I ventured to recommend a variation:

1. Cabbages,
2. Barley,
3. Clover,
4. Beans,
5. Wheat,
6. Tares,
7. Barley,
8. Clover,
9. Beans,
10. Wheat.

A very material objec on a wet land farm is to have a power, twice in a year, of carting dung without damaging the land; this is effected by putting in the beans upon the clover lay, which offers a valuable opportunity, and for a crop which pays better for dung than perhaps any other.

Mr. Simpson's cabbage husbandry is to sow the drum head and tallow loaf sorts in February, on land manured with 14 loads an acre of dung from the fatting stalls, and to plant the middle of June, one row on his stitches of 5 feet 3 inches; 2 feet from plant to plant; and he has had cabbages in this way that were 6 feet across. On the same lands he drills 2 rows of turnips at 2 feet asunder. Both crops are removed in one-horse quartercarts; the horse and wheels going only in the

furrows; by which poaching the stitches is entirely
avoided.

The consumption of the cabbages and turnips is for
fatting bullocks; and Mr. Simpson, from much experience, being convinced that the only reason why many
farmers have left off the cabbage culture, has been their
remaining too long on the land, consumes both these and
turnips early ; but as this leaves a considerable period in
the spring unprovided, he applies great quantities of his
beans (even to 200 qrs. in a season) ground into meal
and mixed with bran, to the purpose of finishing his
beasts. He reckons that 8 combs of beans will feed a
bullock of 40 or 50 stone, or even more, 16 weeks, in
which time 16 loads of excellent dung are made, so that
if he loses 3s. a comb in the price of the beans, still he
gets 16 loads of dung for 24s. which far more than re-
pays him. In general he reckons that a comb of beans
will give 2 stones (at 14lbs.) of beef. However, he admits, that of all animals none give so much flesh for
food as hogs, especially if of a good breed; he has very
often had 3 stones of pork for every comb of beans
given. In grazing he has been very successful with the
calves of heifers ; he had last year four which weighed
from 36 to 46 stones each, at 14 months old. They ran
with their mothers for 10 months, who weighed not
more than 36 or 40 stone at 2 years and an half old.
The breed Suffolk, and the system remarkably profitable.

Eating straw by any sort of stock Mr. Simpson thinks
very bad management ; *it is good for land but bad for
stock* ; he therefore consumes at home as many of his
beans as possible, to tread the straw into dung.

All his manuring is with one-horse carts; and he
approves their use so much, that at his Ottley farm,
where the implements are new, he has nothing else.

I saw on his farm several heaps of burnt earth ; all borders, hills, and corners, that are in common management dug up for composts, he burns into ashes ; they prove a valuable manure, as well as operate mechanically on these stiff soils.

Mr. Simpson watches every opportunity to save ploughing ; remarking a very fine crop of winter tares in a year when they generally were weak, I found that they had been drilled on an oat stubble without any ploughing ; this could not have been done on a broad cast stubble, unless in most singular order and after repeated and severe scuffling.

In the culture of beans, he is not convinced that 18 inches is the right distance for the rows. He cropped a ten acred field two years running with beans ; the first at 18 inches, and the second at 24 equidistant ; both crops were very good, and produced exactly the same quantity.

He is now in the third year of an interesting experiment on wheat. Having met with Mr. Tull's book of horse-hoeing husbandry, he thought the details interesting enough to induce him to make trial of his system in a six acred field. He began with a short fallow, and drilled it 2 rows at 9 inches on 5 feet ridges. In the spring he passed a fixed harrow through the intervals, and in the space between the rows ; then horse-hoed with three shares ; and also the narrow spaces ploughed two furrows from the plants, hand-hoed the spaces, and ploughed back the earth. After harvest, reversed the ridges, and drilled again in the same manner. The first and second year the produce was 6 combs per acre ; the present crop promises, in his opinion, to be better.

An observation in one of his barley fields after turnips, confirms a remark I have often made, that thin sown or drilled corn ripens later than thick sown; by mistake his men drilled two stitches twice over, and these were forwarder than any other part of the field.

In hollow draining (a husbandry in which he has made great exertions) Mr. Simpson has a singular practice; it is the general method of the county to strike them diagonally *across* the slope of a hill; on the contrary, he draws them *with* the slope, and he contends that the water has a less distance to percolate to get at his drains than if they were in the usual direction. If they are marked a rod asunder he observes that some of the water, in common, has a rod to flow before it reaches the drain; but in his method none more than half a rod, as it percolates laterally in any direction in which the depth of the drain gives a fall. The idea is new, and the fact is that no fields can be better drained, he asserts, than his own, in this method.

The mole plough he has used with good success on grass lands, and his method is excellent. He first ploughs a furrow with a double coultered plough, then the mole passes, and the first furrow being turned back and rolled down, keeps the frost out of the slit, which is apt, by mouldering the earth, to stop the pipes. His common drains are 16 to 18 feet asunder, and 26 to 30 inches deep, and filled with straw. When straw has been wanting he has made some without materials for filling, by drawing a deal planed to the shape along the bottom of the drain, ramming in the earth, and if any sand *gauls* are met with claying them, these have lasted as well as any. Mr. Simpson remarks that the water from his drains runs out clear, bringing with it no particles of earth, which he thinks a proof that the greater steepness which his direction with the slope occasions, is not an evil from an increased velocity in the current.

The rouen of dry pastures Mr. Simpson keeps for winter and spring use of sheep, &c. and finds it of very great use.

To return to drilling, for a concluding remark. Mr· Simpson contends that the broad cast husbandry demands rather more horses than the drill system, chiefly because in that a dead year of fallow must occur every four or five years, as the land will not be clean enough to avoid it, which is the case of drilled fields. He keeps 5 horses to every 100 acres arable, but has much grass.

I quitted with regret this very sensible and intelligent farmer, who has made great and laudable exertions in his business.

HIS GRACE THE DUKE OF GRAFTON, at Euston, has been for two years in the drill culture upon his very extensive sand farm, and found it so beneficial that his Grace ordered a new drill machine to be procured while I had the honour of viewing his crops. All his barley was this year (1803) drilled, except one close; half his wheat was dibbled, and half of it drilled ; and the latter answered best. The distance of rows for all corn 9 inches, and the depth 3. Seed barley 10 to 12 pecks ; wheat 8 to 9 pecks. Pease are dibbled 8 pecks, and oats put in with the Norfolk drill roller, 4 bushels. Last year his Grace had some drilled turnips which did well. The crops vary of course with the soil, for on part of the farm it is much better than on the rest. The average crop of barley on bad land 5 combs ; on better $8\frac{1}{2}$. Oats on the former produce 6 combs, on the latter 10. Wheat 5. Last year the oats were 14 combs round, and I viewed, in 1802, one of the finest crops I ever saw after turnips sowed on paring and burning, which turned out 20 combs and a fraction per acre. Last year the peas yielded 10 combs an acre, and this year full as much ; both dibbled on a layer.

His Grace is a good farmer in many other particulars besides drilling. He is claying a great breadth of land, which is done by contract at o*d.* a cubical yard, the Duke finding tumbrils and every tool except shovels for spreading. He supplies the man with oats at 8*s.* a comb, and straw for the dung. On newly broken up heath he spreads 100 cubical yards an acre; and on cultivated land 60. He has lately done 100 acres of the former, and 110 of the latter, which though cultivated before were very poor. He prefers spreading it on a layer to any other method; and leaves a year, or a year and a half, and even two years, by which it mixes with and assimilates to the soil much better than if it was tilled sooner. At Sappiston his Grace has let a farm under condition that it should be clayed; it was 3*s.* an acre, and is now worth 15*s.*

The Duke is a very successful cultivator of sainfoin. He sows 4 bushels an acre. Last year, and this also, he has had 2 tons an acre at 5*l.* per ton, and this on land not worth above 5*s.* per acre, (to be kept in constant culture,) and the after-grass well worth 20*s.* an an acre for lambs. Such a plant ought to be esteemed as the utmost point of perfection in the cultivation of these sands on a chalk or marle bottom.

Carrots his Grace has cultivated many years, and has now 8 acres. They are put in on turnip land, on one ploughing, as deep as a pair of horses can turn a furrow. The products have been various, and the success sufficient to induce a continuance in the practice. They are given to horses.

The Duke's course of crops:
1. Turnips,
2. Barley,
3. Seeds; ray grass, trefoil, and white clover,
4. Ditto,

5. Pease,

6. Wheat, &c.

On bad land :

1. Turnips,

2. Barley,

3. Seeds,

4. Ditto,

5. Ditto, finishing with a bastard fallow,

6. Rye or oats.

Land in his Grace's hands :

Arable, - -	786 acres.
Heath sheep walk, - -	305
Grass, - - - -	489
Woods and young plantations,	227
Park, - - - -	1450
	3257

Fakenham wood, of 314 acres, contiguous to the park, is lately let. Of the park 80 acres are always in tillage in a very profitable system, by means of great hurdles as a fence against the deer. It is that of breaking up and taking one or two crops of turnips, and then one of oats, and laid down again with those oats. Mown the first year, fed with sheep the second, and then thrown out to park, and another piece that wants tillage managed in the same manner.

His Grace's flock consists of 41 score, exclusive of 6 score in the park.

Farm horses, - -	22 to 26
Ditto the stud, about - -	20
Cows, - - - -	12
Young cattle, - - -	29
Fatting beasts, - - -	80
Hogs, - - - -	50

The Rev. HENRY HILL, at Buxhall, near Stow-market, has been a very steady driller for many years. Early in his career I viewed his farm, and some parts of his practice appearing extraordinary, I waited till a more confirmed experience should have been gained before I examined more particularly the operations. The circumstance which struck me as the most singular, was the practice of drilling wheat in rows at 18 inches, equidistant; but Mr. Hill having continued this husbandry to the present time, and with much success, it certainly deserves an inquiry into those objects of soil and culture which enable him to procure an ample produce in a method I believe very rarely pursued by any other person.

His wheat, drilled at 18 inches, has produced as high as 4 quarters per acre in very favourable seasons; in general it has produced equally with other crops at 12 and 9 inches; but I remarked that he chooses his best fields for the wider intervals; this undoubtedly is wise, as wheat will tiller in proportion to the richness of the soil. I found crops on his farm at all the three distances, and he seems to proportion those distances to the fertility of the land. The crops are all very fine and clean, and do credit to his husbandry.

His motive for using such wide rows is the power they give for more complete horse and hand hoeing, which give considerable tillage to the land, and prepare it so much the better for whatever crops may follow; so that a field which is thus treated will be gradually accumulating a larger stock of fertility than another in which narrower intervals are used, and as the freedom from weeds will be in proportion also to this power of giving tillage while the crop is on the ground, continued superior cleanness during a course of years will also add to the productive powers of the soil. From these principles he regulates his system in every field, to have the intervals as wide as the goodness of the land will admit ; his best soil does well at 18 inches, and therefore he prefers that distance.* The soil is a rich strong loam on a clay marl bottom, throws out great crops of every thing, but under the common broad cast husbandry and quantity of seed, was extremely liable to have the wheat crops *laid*, that is, beaten down by slight rains, and greatly injured both in quantity of produce and value of sample. The drilled crops, however luxuriant, are never laid, the straw is stronger, the free current of air being far more effective than can possibly take place in common crops. At the same time, it should be remarked, that to the eye the field is well covered by its produce of straw, which is longer than common ; and Mr. Hill assures me that he has made comparative experiments on the weight of the straw, and that the drilled crops, at 18 inches, have yielded a greater weight than broadcast crops :—in the same field, I conclude, or the observation would not be relevant.

I enquired particularly into the circumstance of the mildew, of which distemper I should be greatly apprehensive with such wide spaces ; Mr. Hill's crops have very rarely been in the least subject to it ; he has had none for many years. It is certain that light and more friable soils, of a freer but less stable luxuriance of vegetation, are more liable to mildew than these stronger loams, peculiarly calculated for wheat. And Mr. Hill remarks, that he has generally observed that a thin plant of wheat, *from thick sowing*, is very subject to it ; this he attributes to the land not suiting the crop ; but from sowing thin, on good land, he never saw the mildew

---

* He has however so drilled in all or most of his fields.

take place more than in thick crops. The circumstance certainly deserves attention.

Barley and oats Mr. Hill drills at 9 inches, equidistant, and rarely fails of having very great crops, 4, 5, 6, and 7 quarters an acre of barley, and as high as 9 of oats, which great produce he has had for three successive years, and after wheat too!!—I can only say, good as his management is in other respects, he gained in these fields more than he deserved.*

That drilling upon the whole exceeds the broadcast husbandry, and to a material degree of superiority, he is, and has been long completely convinced. And putting the question to his bailiff, who has a small farm under him, and drills the whole, his answer was, " I would not take 100 acres at present to rent at all, if I was precluded the use of the drill."

For many years the neighbouring farmers held out, condemning the practice ; they are now converted, and the husbandry spreads rapidly. One of the best crops of wheat in the county is on a field of Mr. Cooper's, at Halston, drilled double rows at 9 inches, on 3 feet ridges ; a form of laying land which in Suffolk is considered as essential to its being dry. Should this plan be found to give full crops, of which I have great doubt, except on land as rich as the best of Mr. Hill's, it will at least secure a dry bed for the seed. Double rows with 27 inch intervals, form the same system in point of rows to space, as equidistant at 18 inches. Mr. Hill prefers the latter, as every row then admits horse hoeing on both sides ; it deserves attention however, that with two horses, one walking in each furrow, and consequently moving with great regularity and steadiness ;

* Not in succession however on the same land ; only oats once after wheat.

the space of 9 inches might certainly be scarified ; one scarifier in the center of the beam for the 9 inch space, and 2 scuffling shares for the intervals, thus,

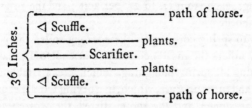

His time of drilling is the first showers after harvest is finished : depth, as deep as usual with farmers on summer land ; but on clover leys 2 or 3 inches. Quantity of seed, 5 pecks at 18 inches, 6½ at 12 inches, and 8½ at 9 inches ; for some years he used less seed, but found the necessity of this increase.

Culture.

The great, and perhaps of all others, the most material object in the use of the drill plough is to put in the crops with as little ploughing as possible ; this point is good for wheat, but essential for spring corn. Mr. Hill has for several years been in the practice of drilling, in certain cases, *without any ploughing at all*, and has succeeded by this means greatly. He has this year a field of 14 acres of wheat at 18 inches, which he offered to bet would produce 4 quarters an acre, that was ploughed in November 1800, and scarified in the spring of 1801 for drilled beans, which produced 6½ quarters an acre : he only scarified the bean stubble, and drilled the wheat now growing : and he is clear that the less tillage which is given for wheat nine times in ten the better.

Mr. Hill's culture, while growing for wheat, is to

horse-hoe it, as soon as dry, in the spring, with a double shared scuffle, one moving on each side of the 18 inch row, earthing up with an additional iron, and 2 hand-hoeings, each from 1s. to 2s. per acre ; and the rows are hand-hoed.

As to spring corn, upon these strong soils, the point of all others the most necessary to attend to is that of avoiding all spring ploughing, which loses a friable surface, and turns up *liver*, which, in a drying wind, becomes hard as stone ; and the more stirred the worse ; time and expence lost in clods or mud. This, united with sowing as early as possible, he has found the surest system to command great crops. He drills barley and oats so early as February, if the weather permit. All turnips, cabbages, &c. are cleared off the land time enough for them ; and potatoe land, bean, or pea stubble, if designed for spring corn, are all laid in autumn on to the requisite lands, so as to scarify and drill in the spring, the horses going only in the furrows.

For beans the land is also laid on to the form proper for the crop in autumn, if ploughed at all, and scarified and drilled early in the spring ; no horse going any where but in furrows ; they are at 18 inches equidistant, and kept quite clean and earthed up by horse and hand-work. The crops great.

Mr. Wooton and Mr. Rout, of Stowmarket, tried dibbling beans against drilling, and acknowledged that the drilled were more regular. I remarked, however, many gaps in Mr. Hill's crops, fine as they are, nor have I any conception that the drill yet exists which will deliver them with a true regularity.

Tares are a favourite crop with him for soiling his horses, cows, &c. As fast as mown, the land is ploughed and turnips drilled in at 18 inches, which succeed extremely well ; he has had them grow so luxuriantly as to prevent his horse-hoeing ; but with cabbages after tares has had no success. Cabbages he has also tried to drill in the spring in order to remain, but always failed ; all eaten by the fly.

Sowing radish seed, as a guard against the fly, he tried 8 or 9 years ago, but failed : his crop was eaten.

Course.

Mr. Hill has chiefly pursued the following rotations.
1. Turnips or cabbages,
2. Barley,
3. Clover,
4. Wheat,
1. Turnips,
2. Barley,
3. Clover,
4. Wheat,
5. Beans,
6. Wheat,
and in some cases of extraordinary fertility, oats after wheat.
1. Turnips and tares,
2. Barley,
3. Clover,
4. Wheat,
5. Potatoes,
6. Barley,
7. Clover,
8. Wheat,
and, on his old farm, has not had a summer fallow (esteemed by most of his neighbours absolutely necessary on very strong wet land) these 14 years past.

But on taking a new farm into his hands in very bad order a few years since,

1. Summer fallow,
2. Barley,
3. Clover,
4. Wheat,
1. Summer fallow,
2. Barley,
3. Beans,
4. Wheat,

and no more fallows after.

Mr. Hill's bailiff, Mr. Wallinger, has made various alterations, which he and his master consider as material improvements, in Mr. Cook's drill; instead of the iron lever for regulating the position of the seed box, he does it by a screw to any degree desired, and very quickly. The wheels are also varied; one higher than the other, for carrying the seed on the same level when drilling on one side of an arched land; this, he says, is absolutely necessary when drilling at 18 inches. He could not drill at that distance with the machine as commonly made; and has made larger cups for the same purpose; he has also added in the tin receivers two sets of cross wires, in order to break the fall of the seed, and make the delivery more equal.

An extremely useful implement on Mr. Hill's farm is a roller in two divisions; the two ends of which, that meet in the middle, turn in an iron which admits being elevated or depressed by means of a screw, so that the horse walking in the furrow, each of the rollers act on the side of a land, by being sunk to its pitch, or section. He does not know who invented it. The thought had much merit.

Remark.

The practice for which Mr. Hill's farm deserves much attention, is the system of putting in certain crops without ploughing the land. He has been in the practice some years: it is, on clay land, novel,* and of vast importance. Those who have had much to do with heavy strong soils; and know, consequently, that they can be ploughed in the spring, only when the land is dry on the surface, and that having turned the friable surface down, and brought up a soil in no such order, which being livery, dries into hard compact clods, or with rain becomes so wet, that much time must be lost before a tool can stir on it, must be sensible that very favourable weather, scarcely to be looked for, must occur, or the farmer is in difficulties; he has a train of them in succession; very often a bad crop the consequence. To make use of the original friable surface, which once lost is not to be regained, and thereby secure not only a favourable matrix for the seed, but an early sowing, is an object which cannot be valued too highly.

The common culture of wheat is not liable to equal difficulties; yet, even with that plant, to save the ploughings usually given, is a matter of importance; and when it is considered that many crops are damaged by being *root fallen*, arising merely from that part of the furrow which is at bottom being too loose, and that by only scuffling the surface, a firmness is left beneath to aid the natural tendency of the roots, it will, in many cases, be found a very beneficial practice.

Mr. Hill's successful culture of wheat at 18 inches

* Ducket practised it on sand.

is a great singularity; but as it holds chiefly on the quality of the soil, and by no means generally applicable; it should every where be tried in small, before it is ventured on a large scale.

MR. PRESS, of *Wetheringset*, drills all his crops; turnips at 18 inches, beans at 12 and 18, barley at 7 and 9, and wheat at 9. He horse-hoes beans twice, and white corn once. He makes his stitches 9 feet 6 inches wide, on which he drills 11 rows of wheat and 12 of spring corn. His success has been great; has had 10 combs an acre of wheat, and 15 of barley. He makes it a rule not to plough in the spring for any crop, and has had very good barley after turnips with only scuffling: but he does not approve of turnips on these heavy lands; last year he had only 8 acres on a farm that employs 12 horses. It is a crop here which does more harm to the land than good to stock. Mr. Lyng, of Thorndon, has put in wheat after beans without any ploughing.

Mr. Press's course:

 1. Fallow,
 2. Barley,
 3. Clover,
 4. Wheat,
 5. Beans,

and, if the land is quite clean, adds

 6. Wheat.

Mr. Press has one of Asbey's thrashing mills, which works with three horses, and thrashes every sort of corn (barley as well as the rest) to his satisfaction. To work it requires two men and three boys; 20 combs of corn an easy day's work. The feeding board 4 feet wide, and 11 beaters on the drum wheel. It does not dress; but he has a chaff cutter worked by it.

Had Mr. Press been at home, this intelligence (given by his bailiff) would have been more complete.

MR. BALLS, of *Wenhaston*, has for some years drilled much wheat and barley at 6 inches; and the practice extends fast through all the vicinity. Drills 7 pecks of wheat per acre at $1\frac{1}{2}$ inch deep. Of barley 10 pecks, 2 inches deep. Some farmers horse-hoe; all hand-hoe.

MR. COOK, of *Halesworth*, makes a variation of his namesake's patent drill machine, in which every share is independent of the rest, for sinking or rising as inequalities of surface may demand; they drill from 8 to 16 rows at a time; the price of the latter 34*l*. he has been 12 years in the trade, and has made above one hundred of these machines. He has in the seasons from two to four always at work drilling for the farmers by the acre. The husbandry, he says, increases rapidly around Halesworth. Some farmers horse-hoe; all hand-hoe. Many beans have been drilled the three last seasons at 10 and 12 inches. He thinks the best depths are $2\frac{1}{2}$ inches for wheat, and 2 for barley.

MR. SPALDING, at *Halesworth*, has drilled much for a few years past, and thinks the husbandry more advantageous on wet heavy land than on light soils; but that success depends much on the system of avoiding spring ploughings as much as possible; none are given for barley on summer fallow, nor any for beans: a *stale furrow* all in all. He admits however that dibbling, *if well done*, will beat drilling for a wheat crop.

MR. FILLPOT, of *Walpole*, drills his wheat at 9 inches, and intends to do the same with his barley. The husbandry increases much. Some horse-hoe, all hand-hoe. He finds both crop and sample better from drilled than from broad-cast corn. He has a thrashing mill erected by Mr. Asbey, which fully answers his expectations; it thrashes barley better than any flail.

MR. WELLS, of *Laxfield*, drills largely, and with much success; the country round is almost all drilled or dibbled, very little sown broad cast; the soil strong, wet, and heavy, on a clay marle bottom. Many beans are cultivated all through this country, and the crops are sometimes great, though certainly drilled too close; at 12 inches. Drilled wheat equals dibbled, and is done much cheaper. All hand-hoed at 2*s*. 6*d*. to 5*s*. an acre. Beans produce sometimes from 12 to 16 combs an acre; Mr. Aldridge had last year (1802) 12 combs of wheat an acre after beans. The advantage of a stale furrow well understood. Mr. Wells burns much earth at 7*d*. a load.

MR. MOORE, of *Crow Hall, Debenham*, drills on a large scale in the following course of crops:

1. Fallow,
2. Barley,
3. Clover or beans,
4. Wheat,
5. Beans or oats.

Wheat, barley, and oats, at 9 inches, pease and beans at 12, turnips at 18. His farm was drilled for 8 or 9 years before he came to it. Seed barley 9 to $10\frac{1}{2}$ pecks, wheat 7, oats 12. He thinks dibbling beans a good practice, but hands not to be had for a large scale; this year he has 74 acres of that plant drilled. His crops of all drilled corn have been great. He horse-hoes to cover the clover seed. I remarked to him a complaint of clover failing; he replied that it had failed in many cases, but not at all owing to that mode of covering the seed but from the greatness of the corn crops killing it. The husbandry of drilling on a stale furrow is almost universal, and has his entire approbation. He makes his stitches 8 feet 10 inches broad; but 9 feet more general in the country; horses, whatever the operation, whether of drilling or of hoeing, walk only in the furrows. I viewed several of his wheat crops and found them very fine and clean, they had been horse-hoed twice, and looked over besides in hand work. When charlock comes in barley, he harrows very boldly, and does not regard burying much of the blade; he treated a field in this manner at Swilling, till his neighbours thought he had destroyed the crop, but it proved a very fine one.

Mr. Moore considers Debenham as nearly the centre of Suffolk drilling on strong land. It extends every way around that place for many miles. Mr. Dove, of Euston Hall, 12 or 14 years ago, practised this husbandry, beginning with a wheel-barrow drill, then one with spiked wheels, which did well; but these were discarded on Mr. Cook's drill coming in. Mr. Dove is a capital driller on a large farm, which he keeps in high order.

MR. FREEMAN, of *Aspal*, near Debenham, was, if not the first driller on strong land in Suffolk, certainly among the very first who attempted the husbandry on a respectable scale. He has been in it about 15 years. His son now manages the farm, and another at Occold

Course:

1. Fallow,
2. Barley at 9 inches,
3. Clover,
4. Wheat dibbled,
5. Beans at 16 inches,
6. Wheat or barley.

If beans follow barley, then wheat always after the beans.

To avoid all spring ploughings on these heavy soils,

he considers as the greatest improvement that has been introduced for many years past. He lays the surface into 9 feet stitches, going a *bout* with the machine on each, the horse both in drilling and horse-hoeing, or scuffling, or scarifying, or harrowing, never moving on the stitches, and consequently all poaching avoided, of so much consequence on these soils. Of barley he drills from 8 to 10 pecks an acre, as shallow as possible, which is about an inch ; clover he sows with the barley, and therefore does not hoe ; but if no seeds, horse hoes it. Wheat he dibbles on clover, because he finds it troublesome to get the layer in order for drilling, and the rows are liable to come up in the seams, which is bad; but drills after beans and other crops, 5 to 7 pecks an acre, and 1 inch deep. His beans at 16 inches demand from 8 to 10 pecks per acre ; he horse-hoes them several times, so as to be kept quite clean. For this crop the manure is ploughed in by the autumnal earth.

Here is no mention made of turnips ; but he has a few at 18 inches ; he thinks it very bad husbandry on these heavy lands, and cabbages also.

It was with pleasure that I viewed some of his wheat crops, put in for this year on bean stubbles, without any ploughing ; the surface only worked with scuffles and harrows ; the crops extremely fine, and quite clean. And at Occold he has barley this year after turnips carted off, drilled without ploughing, and the crop as good as any in the common management.

By drilling, Mr. Freeman is clear that a farm will be kept as clean with a summer fallow once in six years, as in the broadcast husbandry, fallowed every fourth year.

He has this year a clover crop sown amongst barley, and hoed in ; but failing in patches, and too thin in general, he dibbled in tares in all the vacancies as soon as his wheat sowing was finished, and the mixed crop of clover and tares a very fine one.

CAPTAIN WOOTTON, of *Rattlesden*, has been a driller on strong wet land for 12 or 14 years.

His course :

1. Summer fallow, potatoes or turnips,
2. Barley,
3. Clover or beans alternately,
4. Wheat.

In all cropping he is attentive to vary the plants as much as possible, and even in different sorts of the same plant ; for instance, if a field had *red* wheat when last under that grain, he sows *white* the next round ; having observed that some farmers have continued one sort till they complained of failures, and changed too late. In sowing spring corn also, he puts barley in where oats grew last, and *vice versa*. And in fallow crops, turnips, tares, beans, &c. varied on the same principle.

He has tried many experiments on the distance of the rows in drilling ; and is inclined, upon the whole, to prefer 18 inches for wheat, having on an average had rather better success at that distance than at any other ; and his bailiff is of the same opinion. This year (1803) this mode of drilling in the crops I viewed on his farm made a very bad figure indeed, though well conducted ; for having lost plant much in the winter and spring, these wide rows became singularly exposed to the mildew, which made immense ravages every where, but in proportion to the distance of the rows, or thinness of the crop, from other causes, as I was well convinced from the numerous crops at various distances which I viewed this season in Suffolk. Mr. Wootton's was scarcely worth reaping. Yet the crops thus drilled in

1802 yielded 2 combs an acre more than others at 12 inches. The crop being 8 combs 2 bushels and 3 pecks per acre, ascertained by 1 rood and 21 perch, producing 3 combs 1 bushel and 1 peck; the comb weighing 18 stone 7lb.

This year (1803) he has a field occupied with comparisons of the modes of putting in wheat.

No. 1. *Half set*, being one row dibbled on a flag or furrow.

2. *Three quarters set*, being the same as No. 1. but double rows on the outside flags.

3. Drilled at 12 inches.

4. Drilled at 9 inches.

5. Drilled at 18 inches.

The whole on clover land, and on alternate stitches. Such experiments demand a thrashing mill, that the corn may not go into a barn. Seed wheat generally 5 pecks.

He tried Mr. Finch's pickled wheat in every crop he had last year; it came up, but no benefit was manifest; on the contrary, where any difference was perceptible, it was against the prepared wheat.

In taking wheat after clover he has had two combs an acre more after twice mowing, than after feeding through the summer; soil, time, seed, culture, and every other circumstance being similar.

The soil, though strong land at 20s. on a clay or clay marle bottom, and well drained, he does not think that it answers so well for wheat as for oats; such land however must be well adapted to wide intervals, if any where proper. He horse-hoes them thrice; first with a narrow hoe, then with a wider one, and lastly earths up. These operations should be given early.

In 1802 his barley drilled at 12 inches produced 14 combs an acre. He has this year 2¼ acres of 6 rowed winter barley, which, though not sown till December, fed 127 sheep for 5 days in the beginning of May, and then produced a crop of corn which he estimates at 20 combs an acre; the stubble apparently justifies the expectation; part is at 18 inches, and part at 12. He had the seed from Melton, where ¾ of an acre produced that crop.

On being thrashed, he found that 1 rood 17 perches of the 18 inch rows gave 6 combs 2 bushels, or 18 combs 3¾ pecks per acre, weighed 13 stone 4lbs. the comb; 1 rood 19 perch of the 12 inch rows gave 6 combs 3 bushels, or 18 combs 1 bushel ¾ of a peck per acre; but the 12 inch had the better land. Weight 13 stone 3lbs. the comb.

Beans Mr. Wootton drills on 5½ feet stitches, putting in 3 rows at 18 inches; horse-hoes them thrice, the third earthing up; and hand-hoes twice; he has generally ploughed the stubbles for wheat, but last year, in one field only, scarified, and succeeded well. Seed beans near 3 bushel per acre.

There is no point in the management of arable land, in which he is more convinced, than of the necessity of avoiding spring ploughings on these heavy soils; for barley or oats on fallowed or on tare land, he never ploughs in the spring; nor for beans, whatever they may follow. This he considers as a point of great importance, and is alone a most capital modern improvement; and in making a summer fallow, he thinks it is best done by one deep autumnal ploughing, and the following work to be only scarifying and scuffling.

He has tried the mixture of the turnip and bean culture in this manner, on 10 feet stitches. He drilled two rows of beans at 3 feet, one row on each side of the stitch furrow, leaving 7 feet of stitch for turnips; this space was well worked with the scarifiers for that crop, and drilled with 3 rows at 18 inches. The crop therefore consisted of 3 rows of turnips and 2 of beans, instead of 6 of turnips, which the stitches would otherwise have had. For comparison, he ploughed part and scarified the rest for the turnips; and the latter were much better than the ploughed part. Another circumstance he remarked which deserves noting; the two outside rows of the turnips next the beans were much better than the centre row, which he attributed to the shade of the beans being a preservation from the fly. But I remarked in 1803, that where three rows were drilled on a stitch, the two outside ones came pretty well, and the centre failed very generally; this was properly attributed to the land having been very dry when the stitches were reversed, and the centre row on the new stitch being over the old and dried furrow. Mr. Wootton's centre rows might have been affected in like manner; 1802 (the year of the trial) having experienced a drought, though nothing like that of 1803.

Wet as Mr. Wootton's soil naturally is, yet he is much in favour of feeding his turnips where they are raised, by sheep. This cannot be done without a certain degree of poaching, which he disregards, provided it be done early enough for frost to follow: but on lighter land he feeds till April; he finds the difference in the barley to be very great between that which follows feeding, and that which succeeds drawn crops. In 1802 he drew part of a field, and fed part; and in part he drew 2 rows in 6, and fed the rest. To the division which had been drawn, 30 loads an acre of border compost (the dung from the yards) were spread for the barley; this crop I viewed, and without doubt the part that had been fed was superior: he has practised this turnip husbandry two years. I ought not however to let the fact pass without remarking, that though Mr. Wootton's wethers did to his satisfaction, and paid him well, yet both years were on the whole uncommonly dry, so that in a wet spring, if the same husbandry was practised, the result would probably be very different, both to the barley and the sheep.

Potatoes this gentleman has cultivated repeatedly. The best crop he ever gained, was one of 100 sacks per acre, or 300 bushels; he always sows barley or oats after them, and gets as good crops as after tares. He sells all he can at above 3s. a sack, but if he can get on more than that price, uses them at home for bullocks and hogs. He has great doubt, however, of their profit for bullocks; for he has had some beasts scour so much as to become quite rotten ; they had straw with the potatoes.

Nothing has answered better with him in fattening beasts, than beans soaked in water.

Mr. Wootton has done much hollow draining, by drawing on a prepared pole after ramming in the earth upon it ; he has also used the mole plough successfully; both ways have stood well for three years, and promise to be durable.

Crops in 1798.

	C.	B.	P.
White wheat, average produce per acre	7	3	$1\frac{1}{4}$
Red ditto,	7	0	0
Barley,	11	3	$3\frac{1}{2}$
Tick beans,	5	2	$2\frac{1}{2}$
White pease,	6	1	3
Oats,	8	1	$3\frac{1}{4}$
Potatoes,	96 sacks.		

The largest crops he has had are,

Wheat, - - - - -	10 combs.
Barley, - - - -	15
Oats, - - - - -	16
Beans, - - - -	15
Pease, - - - -	10
Potatoes, - - -	100 sacks.

In manuring, Mr. Wootton has found very great benefit from sowing soot on grass land; in a field part thus dressed, and part without any, he had a good crop of hay on the former, but the latter scarcely worth mowing.

This gentleman has been very successful as a sheep grazier; at Michaelmas, 1802, he bought 50 wether lambs at 17s. they had nothing but grass, and he sold them at Michaelmas, 1803, at (wool included) 2l. 7s. profit 1l. 10s. per head, which for 52 weeks is 6¾d. per week. He reckons that of this sum 20s. was paid by the summer half year, and 10s. by the winter. They had 35 acres of grass in winter, and 10 in summer: that is 1½ sheep per acre in winter, and 5 per acre in summer; this makes 5l. an acre, summer produce, and 15s. for winter; or 5l. 15s. per acre in all.

SAMUEL FISKE, ESQ. at *Woolpit*, upon his farm of 200 acres, drills wheat at 12 inches, 8 pecks of seed an acre; barley 10 pecks at 9 inches; oats 12 pecks at 12 inches; and pease 10 pecks at 12 inches; all of them as deep as he can make the machine go.

His course:

1. Turnips,
2. Barley,
3. Clover,
4. Wheat.

Also,

    1. Turnips,
    2. Barley,
    3. Pease,
    4. Wheat.

And,

    1. Turnips,
    2. Barley,
    3. Oats,
    4. Beans,
    5. Wheat.

A much inferior course to either of the former. Manures only for turnips.

MR. THOMAS ROUT, of *One-house*, near *Stow-market*, who occupies a very fine farm of about 500 acres, drills with much success, and has by means of this practice got rid of fallowing. He has this year an experiment, comparing 9, 12, and 18 inch rows for wheat, and produced a sample of each from ears fairly gathered; the best sample and crop was from the 9 inches; the next best from 12, and much the worst from 18; but 2 rows dibbled on a flag much better than any of the three. It being a mildew year is not to be forgotten. The grain of broadcast wheat is rarely equal to that of dibbled.

His course:

    1. Fallow crop; turnips, beans, &c. &c.
    2. Barley,
    3. Clover,
    4. Wheat.

Of all husbandry he esteems that of sowing wheat on a summer fallow to be the worst; and it was remarked that in this mildew year, Mr. Fiske's wheat on clover land suffered much less by that distemper than his other crops.

In discourse on the comparative benefit of mowing and feeding clover as a preparation for wheat ; Mr. Rout preferred mowing ; and remarked, that feeding clover with horses was a most wasteful miserable practice, for it would not, so fed, give half the food that it does when mown and soiled in the stable ; adding that he has not had a horse feeding abroad for the five last years.

Seed :

> Wheat, 3 pecks at 12 inches.
> Barley, 3 bushels.
> Oats, 4 ditto.
> Beans, 2 ditto at 12 to 18 inches.

Mr. Rout horse-hoes his wheat, but is particularly careful in doing it, and also that it be not done too late, as he has remarked many crops much injured by it. He intends trying again, on a small scale, wheat at 18 inches for experiment, but is so clearly of opinion against it, that he added, " I would bet dibbling against that practice for sample and crop, ten guineas to five." But in respect to barley and oats, he will *never broadcast another handful.* As to beans, he has some doubts between dibbling and drilling ; not quite decided.

Mr. Rout lays his stitches 9 feet 2 inches broad by a *marker.* This is a useful tool ; it is a small beam about 10 feet long, like the back of a horse rake, with two teeth fixed at the requisite distance, and one going in the mark of the preceding work ; if it begins straight, the whole field is marked in lines ; the plough there opens a furrow, and sets out the intended stitches exactly.

Mr. Rout is, from an attentive experience, a steady friend to the new system (which has, however, for some years been spreading through High Suffolk) of saving many ploughings.

His wheat this year on bean stubbles was put in part with one ploughing, and part with scarifying only ; the crops, to the eye, are quite equal. Beans he always drills on a stale autumnal furrow.

This gentleman is convinced that the drill husbandry, as now practised in this country, demands fewer horses than the broad cast ; since he became a driller he keeps two less, and shall rid himself of two more.

Enquiring Mr. Rout's opinion whether agriculture in the heavy district of Suffolk was improved or not ? he replied, " Greatly, without doubt, but chiefly of late years, and particularly since scarifying and scuffling have been introduced to the saving of so many spring ploughings ; and also scarifying bean stubbles for wheat.

In respect to sheep, this gentleman is not altogether orthodox, for he prefers the Norfolk breed to any other. On his farm of 500 acres, of which 60 are wood and 20 hops, he keeps 280 breeding ewes, selling lambs and crones ; the best lambs last year at 1*l.* 1*s.* 6*d.* and the rest with the crones at 17*s.* He clips 2lbs. of wool per head, which sells at 47*s.* a tod.

In manuring he has often carried fresh dung from the yard for turnips, and got the best crops where he did so; 12 loads an acre a proper quantity ; but for hops, always carts 240 loads from the yard in the spring, which in a twelve month become 120, and this manures his 20 acres of hops annually at 6*s.* per acre ; and the value of this manuring he estimates at 10*s.* a load of 40 bushels.

MR. FREEMAN, of *Buxhall*, has been a a very successful driller for some years on strong wet land, which he has drained well at 5 yards asunder ; but he has some sound and excellent turnip loams; when he was in the broad cast husbandry, he has had broad cast beans that were hand-hoed at the expence of a guinea an acre, and yet yielded only 6 combs; and has had so little as 4 combs dibbled at 9 inches; but by drilling he has had 9 combs an acre of pease at 18 inches. At present he drills all his wheat at 12 inches, and has often had 9 combs an acre. Barley and oats at 9 inches; pease, beans, and turnips at 18; and if he made any change in the latter, it would be to increase the distance to 24. He has at that distance had $17\frac{1}{2}$ combs French ticks per acre. Since he became a driller, he has not had a summer fallow on his farm, and his crops have been regularly better than they were in the old management. At Old Newton he took a farm in bad order, had it 11 years and never made a fallow, and his last wheat crop was 10 combs an acre all round. Instead of fallows, he depends (where turnips are not taken) on tares, pease and beans, or potatoes. The more fallows the less stock, the less dung, and the less corn.

His stitches are 9 feet wide, but at present he is changing them to $5\frac{1}{2}$ feet for one stroke of the drill machine, which he thinks preferable to going a *bout*. The grand object of his husbandry, so far as it respects tillage, is to save ploughings, and especially in the spring, at which season he never ploughs, except turnip land once as fed off; this he considers as a most essential point; and the management is nearly as successful for wheat; all his crop of which grain, except two small pieces, was this year put in without any ploughing, scarifying only; and these are the best crops and the freest from mildew in this great year of that distemper.

His course of crops:

1. Turnips at 18 inches,
2. Barley,
3. Clover or beans,
4. Wheat.

But cabbages form a variation; of these he plants some every year ; he spreads more manure for these than for turnips, and then finds the barley equal, though the crop is all carted off. An acre of cabbages he finds equal on an average to two of turnips.

Potatoes form another exception to the above course; he takes barley or oats after them, as they are not a good preparation for wheat ; he has had 100 sacks an acre ; but on an average 80.

He has always found a very great difference in barley following turnips fed, and those carted ; the former best beyond comparison ; but to feed half the crop on the land is sufficient to secure great barley

Whenever Mr. Freeman has had   eat after clover, part mown twice and part fed th;   h the summer, the crop has been invariably better   mowing than after feeding.

Mr. Freeman is absolutely convinced of the superiority of the drill to the broad cast husbandry ; and that the former requires fewer horses ; but he remarked that in the latter management a farmer might also make a great saving by substituting the scarifyer and scuffler for the plough on many occasions. He mentioned a farmer at Hadley who saved four horses by the drill husbandry.

I was glad to hear that drilling is making a rapid progress through all this country ; and it is much owing to this circumstance, that the district is more productive in corn by 2 combs an acre round, than it was 20 years ago, as well as having one crop more in five, than at that period.

Mr. Freeman has a dairy of 8 very fine Suffolk cows, for 6 of which he has been offered 20 guineas each. He considers the benefit of cows, received in pigs, to amount to more than 30*s.* a cow.

In manuring, Mr. Freeman dunged part of a field with long dung, fresh out of the yard, the rest of it with that carted and prepared in the common manner ; the best turnips were gained from the former.

MR. THOMPSON, at *Culpho,* drills most of his corn; he has both heavy strong land, and also light soils that do well for carrots. He puts in wheat and barley at 6½ inches, 7½, and 9. The barley is best at 6½. Never horse hoes any. If the land is at all foul, he thinks it does mischief ; clean crops he has observed to be most improved by horse-hoeing, but he has not been induced to widen his rows for the sake of this operation ; the wider they are the more the mildew is sure to take place. Beans he dibbles in at a foot ; ploughing for them before Christmas, and carefully avoiding spring ploughings. Scarifying for barley he thinks much superior to ploughing, by which, on stiff land, many crops are lost : but he ploughs the late fed turnip land once.

He has no opinion of fallowing even on the stiffest soils. Wheat on that preparation is full of rubbish, and if mildew is heard of in a year, fallow crops are sure to be ruined.

His quantities of seed in drilling, wheat, 7 pecks ; barley, 2 bushels ; oats, a comb.

Mr. Thompson, as well as most of his neighbours, cultivates carrots largely. He has this year 18 acres of very fine ones. He ploughs once for them at the end of March, about 7 inches deep, and harrows in 4lbs. of seed per acre ; they are hand-hoed thrice at 10*s.* 6*s.* and 5*s.* an acre. The price therefore (by former notes of mine) not risen above 4*s.* an acre in above 20 years. Mr. Ginger, of Great Bealings, tried drilling for them, but it did not answer ; he had not a plant sufficient, and they cost 33*s.* an acre in hoeing. The farmers find the carrots for their labourers to raise the seed at 1*s.* 3*d.* per lb. They are applied in the first place to feeding horses. Last year Mr. Thompson's clover all failed, and he gave his horses one bushel of corn each per week, and as many carrots as they would eat, which he thinks was about a bushel a day ; the saving, a bushel of oats and all the hay. They are extremely useful for hogs ; and he fattens bullocks on them successfully : these eat more carrots than they do of potatoes ; perhaps twice as many. A neighbour, Mr. Sugget, at Bealings, has had bullocks that eat thrice as many carrots as potatoes. They do uncommonly well upon this food, but potatoes are apt to scour at first.

Mr. Thompson thinks a crop of carrots better than a crop of wheat. He pays 1*s.* a load of 40 bushels for taking them up, and 1*s.* 3*d.* to 1*s.* 6*d.* if the roots are small. Barley after them is as good as after turnips fed on the land. But the best barley of all is after tares ; he has had 4 combs an acre more after tares than after turnips sheep fed, ploughing the tare land 3, 4, or 5 times before the frosts, and only scarifying in the spring.

Potatoes he cultivates largely ; he has 12 acres this year ; from which space of land he has had 1100 sacks, and sold none under 7*s.* a sack. He never mucks for them, spreading most on young clover or for beans. He gets better potatoes after clover land wheat than on a fallow. He gives many potatoes to hogs, but has found that they do nothing upon them if confined ; they run about and do well ; but beans are given all through the year, about a peck a day, to 12 hogs of various sizes.

It is the general custom of the country to turn all horses into the yard at night, except when they come home late and hot.

Mr. Thompson prefers muck that is kept till rotten, rather than spreading it in a fresher state.

J. M. THEOBALDS, ESQ. at *Claydon*, has drilled on an extensive scale for five years; much of his farm a strong wet tenacious loam on a clay and marle bottom, but drained at 5 yards asunder. Wheat he has tried at 6, 9, 12, and 18 inches, but prefers 12 to all the rest. Pease and beans also at 12, at which distance he has had 12 combs an acre of the latter. But barley and oats at 6.

On strong land his course is,

    1. Summer fallow,
    2. Barley.
    3. Clover,
    4. Beans drilled or dibbled,
    5. Wheat.

He has also had

    1. Fallow,
    2. Wheat,
    3. Beans,
    4. Wheat,

and intends going on with beans and wheat alternately. I viewed the wheat of the fourth year, and it was remarkably fine.

But on his dryer soils,

    1. Turnips,
    2. Barley,
    3. Clover,
    4. Wheat.

The respective quantities of seed,

    Of Wheat 6 pecks,
      Barley 10,

Oats 12 pecks,
Pease 3 bushels,
Beans 4 ditto,

and the general depth 3½ inches.

To wheat, beans, and pease, he gives two horse and one hand-hoeings.

He prefers the drill method for wheat, but admits that dibbling is an excellent practice on clover lays.

Mr. Theobalds has some loam on chalk, upon which he has cultivated sainfoin; and never found any crop that paid so well; after 7 years he broke it up for turnips, after which barley, but not good; clover with it, then wheat which yielded well. Turnips, barley drilled, and sainfoin again; drilled also between the rows a comb an acre.

He has no doubt of a drilled farm requiring fewer horses than the same in the broad cast husbandry. In his own, of 500 acres arable, he has lessened them five.

Potatoes he cultivates successfully, attending particularly to earthing up, first with the *double Tom* and then with the *long Betty*; the former the Suffolk name for the common double mould board plough; the latter also a double earth board, but which slides out to a greater length and width, rising behind to drive the moulds to the plants.

Bullocks he fattens with ground beans, and barley mixed with malt combs and grains. But sheep pay him better than any thing; he has bought wether lambs of the Duke of Grafton at 21*s.* kept them a year and three quarters, and sold them at 3*l.* Hogs he also finds very profitable; has 18 sows and 300 of all sorts; yet keeps only 3 cows, and buys only 10 combs of grains weekly.

Of the great importance of saving spring ploughings,

Mr. Theobalds is well persuaded ; he sows all that is possible on stale furrows.

He has 10 acres of carrots this year, a very fine and regular crop ; but they cost him (being his first year) 32*l.* in hoeing and weeding.

THE REV. MR. FREELAND, of *Melton*, *near Woodbridge*, drills successfully on strong land, in the following course :

          1. Turnips,
          2. Barley,
          3. Clover,
          4. Wheat,
          5. Beans,
          6. Wheat.

Beans at 18 inches ; wheat at 9 and 12, the latter best ; barley at 9 ; and oats at 12. He horse-hoes all ; thrice for beans, and hand hoes them besides. He is particularly careful to avoid spring ploughings where-ever possible. Barley he put in on a summer fallow only scarifying, and had 3 combs an acre more than a farmer whose land was contiguous, and similar in soil and tillage, except ploughing it in the spring.

Lucerne Mr. Freeland drilled in rows at 2 feet, on a hot gravelly loam, in April, 1802; he hoed out the plants in the rows to the distance of six inches. He keeps it perfectly clean. This year an acre has sup-ported 2 horses from the last week of April to Midsum-mer, and one horse since. He has mown it thrice, and there will be a fourth. Hoeing costs 15*s.* per acre per annum. It has had no manure.

—— STUDD, ESQ. of *Melton*, *near Woodbridge*, drills all his farm ; wheat at 9 inches, barley and oats at 6, and dibbles beans at 12. He horse hoes his wheat twice, taking care to be as early as possible. His average products

Wheat 7 combs,
Barley 10,
Oats 12,
Beans 9,
Pease 5.

His course :

1. Turnips,
2. Barley,
3. Clover, beans, or pease,
4. Wheat.

MR. COTTON, at *Kesgrave*, occupies a large farm on a sandy soil.

His course:

1. Turnips,
2. Barley,
3. }
4. } Layer of trefoil, white clover, &c.
5. Pease or oats.

But on better land :

1. Turnips,
2. Barley,
3. Clover,
4. Wheat.

He drills all corn ; wheat at 9 inches ; barley and oats at 8 or 9 ; pease in double rows, at $3\frac{1}{2}$, and 12 to 13 inches intervals. He horse-hoes all, thinking this the main use of drilling. He has not the smallest doubt of the drill husbandry requiring fewer horses than the broad cast ; but this point depends much on the great object of saving spring ploughings.

Present state of his farm :

100 acres of turnips,
100 barley,
160 layers,

40 acres of pease,
40   wheat,
40   oats, buck-wheat, and rye;
15   potatoes,
16   carrots,
120   sheep-walk.

Carrots are a favourite crop with him. Of all roots, they are by far the most certain crop. Barley after them is as great as after turnips fed on the land; but not if the carrots are kept so long in the ground that the barley is not sown till too late, in that case inferior of course. They succeed best after turnips, and are cleaner for hoeing. Picked, they sell at 1s. a bushel, but others at 6d. But the consumption at home is the grand object, many farmers selling none. Mr. Cotton fattens 10 or 12 bullocks every year on them. He has taken them from oil cake to carrots, with hay cut into chaff, and they went on well till tares were ready. For horses also, they are the most excellent of all food, and preferred by them to all other; they save half the corn, and all the hay. They will do on carrots alone, or on carrots and hay; but hay has been so dear, that it is better to give a bushel of oats per week per horse. Carrot fed horses in better order than on any other food and will do more work.

I was very glad to hear that the culture increases much all through this country: and a gentleman present observed that from Saxmundham to Lowestoff there are ten times as many as there were 20 years ago.

Mr. Cotton has tried sainfoin thrice, but it will not succeed, the sand is to a great depth, without any impediment of chalk or gravel.

This gentleman's flock is of South-down rams on Norfolk ewes; but only for the first cross. Folds constantly.

―― BLISS, ESQ. of *Sutton, near Woodbridge*, in the farm late Mr. Vancouver's,* is making an experiment on hogs ; of which having heard much, I was desirous of viewing. He has now 45 sows, and 230 hogs, of all sorts and sizes ; he has run up with old barrel staves and rough stuff 33 sties around a yard, and has one or two other yards, with troughs for feeding. I am much afraid that this experiment will fail. I saw only the bailiff, who did not seem very well to understand this branch of husbandry ; nor were the conveniencies contrived with any attention to the danger of keeping many hogs (not in a fatting state) crowded in a small space. The whole herd consumed 2 combs of malted barley per diem, but look as if they would eat ten times as much. No clover ; no lucerne ; no chicory : nor for the ensuing winter any other roots than turnips, and no cabbages. The speculation would be profitable after due preparation, by crops for the support of this animal, which bears hard keep worse than any other. Young weaned pigs were doing very badly on barley, which would have done well on oats. 380 Norfolk sheep are also kept on this farm.

MR. FULLER, near *Rushmere Heath, Ipswich*, drills all his corn. Wheat at 9 and 12 inches ; the latter best ; barley and oats at 9 ; beans and turnips at 18. He tried an experiment, comparing 9 and 18 inches for barley, and cutting and weighing 2 rods of each. The latter gave 18 lbs. of straw and a pint and half of barley more than the former. Horse-hoeing wheat he thinks is often practised with a bad effect, by cutting the coronal roots ; the scarifying harrow much better ; and he has invented an iron treble tooth, for stirring the intervals, which on sand or land in fine tilth promises to be useful. His

* See observations on this farm made in 1794. Annals of Agriculture, Vol. XXIII. p. 35.

mechanical abilities have also been exerted in the invention of a drill attached to a common plough for slitting
the flag in the centre, and there delivering one row of
seed, in which manner he has had 11 combs and an half
of wheat per acre. Another machine of his invention
(which he had the goodness to set to work for my seeing)
is a horse gavelling rake for barley and oats, which
with a horse, a man, and a boy, will do 20 acres a day.
He pays from 8*d*. to 1*s*. an acre to women for this
work, who are so engaged in gleaning, that if they begin,
will go on, and if rain comes, there is more trouble with
an acre on the gravel, than with five in the swarth.

Mr. Fuller tried drilling of carrots several times, but
never succeeded well ; they are too thick in the rows, so
that there are more plants standing singly in broad cast
crops ; but to save hoeing, and stir the land the better,
he horse-hoes the crops, cross and cross, with 6 inch
hoes, cutting half and missing half, which has answered,
and reduced the whole expence of cleaning to 9*s*. an
acre. I must however remark, that I observed more
vacancies in his field than in many others I had viewed,
which however might be caused by other circumstances;
but 12*s*. an acre saving in this method is not of very
great consequence in so valuable a crop as carrots. He
has this year 20 acres, sown broad cast the first week in
April, 5lbs. of seed per acre. This field was under carrots also last year, and produced 14 loads an acre, at 40
bushels, most of which were sold at 40*s*. per load ; nor
would he take 30*l*. an acre for his present crop. He fats
many bullocks on them, and finds that carrots, from one
to three bushels a day, according to the size of the bullocks, with the first mowing of clover hay cut into chaff,
will beat every thing he has tried, and he is no stranger
to the use of corn and oil cake. Taking up the crop,
1*s*. 6*d*. per load. No finer barley than after carrots.

Turnips Mr. Fuller cuts out by cross horse-hoeing (the hoes 12 inches,) in like manner as carrots, leaving the rows 18 inches asunder ; and at the proper season buries them with *a double Tom*, the leaf only being left exposed, which sheep eat without getting at the roots ; and when he wants to consume the crop, scuffles across just under the roots, which are thus turned out on a flat surface for the sheep.

But as great a friend as Mr. Fuller is to the principles of the drill husbandry, he admits that seeds (layers) are better with a broad cast than with a drilled crop.

MR. CHAPLIN, of *Nedging*, near *Hadley*, has drilled all his his corn on a strong land farm for three years past, and is very well satisfied with his success. Wheat at 9 inches, barley and oats at 6, beans 5 rows on an 8 feet stitch, and he horse-hoes beans and wheat.

His course :

1. Fallow,
2. Barley,
3. Clover,
4. Wheat,
5. Beans,
6. Wheat.

He has a thrashing mill, the drum wheel about 2 feet diameter, with 6 beaters, which works with 3 horses, 4 men, and 1 boy, and does 30 combs of wheat in 10 hours. It thrashes all grain perfectly clean.

This gentleman has made a very useful sheep yard for 300, behind his barn, with a great length of troughs, roofed against rain, for giving cut straw, and finds the system highly beneficial.

SIR WILLIAM ROWLEY, Bart. at *Tendring Hall*, has been a few years in the drill culture, and at present practices it in great perfection. I walked over a wheat stubble of above 40 acres which was *positively* clean, not a weed to be seen in it. For this grain the distance he drills at is 9 inches; for barley he has tried both 6 and 9, and prefers the former; for tunips 18. He has not the smallest doubt of the superiority of drilling to broad cast sowing; and his tenants are generally in it, whatever their land may be.

His course:

1. Turnips,
2. Barley,
3. Clover,
4. Wheat.

He has tried horse-hoeing, but has not found any benefit from it; no difference resulting in the crop; but hand-hoes with much attention. Trench ploughing he also tried both for wheat and turnips, gaining $2\frac{1}{2}$ inches additional depth, but it was not attended with any perceivable effect. But another experiment, that of cutting wheat earlier than common, answered, and consequently he pursues it * His method of laying land down to grass is after two successive crops of turnips, to sow the seeds of a selected spot of good meadow, kept till ripe, and thrashed in the field. These seeds answer better than any other. Sir William's flock, of about 200 South Down breeding ewes (the whole produce of which he keeps round), are well worth seeing; they are thoroughly bred from Mr. Ellman's stock, and do credit to it; well formed, with fine close fleeces, and, I may add, well fed too. He has now (September) living 218 lambs from 195 ewes. His shearling wethers come to 18 lbs. a quarter, many to more; and two shears to 24; has had them to 30. His teams soiled all the summer; never out. These features of his husbandry are few; but they are good.

* His crop this year estimated at 5 quarters per acre.

I ought to add, that he has good land to work on; there are not many finer soils than the level below the hill.

MR. HOWLETT, of *Westwood*, near *Southwold*, has for the last three or four years tried drilling on his very large sandy farm. Last year he had 40 acres of barley at 6 inches, and was well satisfied with the result; this year his whole crop is drilled, and he never had such a favourable appearance before. He has, in common with the strong land farmers, found the advantage of lessening his tillage; formerly he never gave less than two spring ploughings to turnip land for barley, unless on land late fed; but this year all is on one earth except a single field.

His course:
1. Turnips,
2. Barley,
3. Seeds for 2 or 3 years, ray, trefoil, and white clover; but ray alone is durable,
4. Wheat, or pease, or rye.
in either case turnips follow.

All his wheat and pease have been dibbled every year from the time I was with him before, which is not less than 10 or 12 years; he approves of that husbandry as much as ever.

THE EARL OF ALBEMARLE, at *Elden*, on a farm of 4000 acres, which the tenant had at 2s. 6d. an acre, in general consisting of a blowing sand, has drilled upon a very great scale, and his Lordship's crops at this commencement of his husbandry * have answered his expectation. I viewed large fields under oats, which promise to yield 9 or 10 combs an acre on the land that has been marled. Clean and well managed.

* He took the farm into his own hands at Michaelmas 1801.

Wheat at 12 inches,

Rye at 9,

Barley at 7,

Oats at 9,

Wheat and pease horse-hoed.

The former, in common with all the wheat in the country this year, much mildewed. A comparison in the preparation deserves noting ; part of the field was what the farmers call *tempered* ; that is, the layer broken up in summer, and a bastard fallow given, part left till seed time and drilled on the flag ; the former is certainly the better crop. The experiment must not however be deemed decisive ; for I have, at various times, seen the result very different. Drilled barley Lord Albemarle has not found at all superior to broad cast harrowed in.

Sainfoin the noble farmer has cultivated with uncommon success ; upon $8\frac{1}{4}$ acres, situated very conveniently for this crop, he sowed 4 bushels an acre broad cast in June 1801, without corn, and the land extremely foul with couch and other weeds ; the crop was not expected to be good or durable, but it was done in order to get some hay as soon as possible. It proved however one of the finest crops that has been seen ; in 1802 produced $2\frac{1}{2}$ loads an acre ; and this year the crop forms a stack 15 yards long, 5 broad, and 4 high to the eaves, being fully equal to the former, probably better. But this is not the most remarkable circumstance, it has completely smothered and killed all weeds, couch and all, and the field is now the cleanest on the farm. There is more couch in some of the turnips than in this sainfoin. The profit of sainfoin was never perhaps more clearly manifested than in this case ; for while he consumed this produce, he went some miles and gave 6*l*. per ton for hay to feed his stock. 15*l*. an acre, besides the after grass for lambs, is a produce on land at any rent that can be supposed for this, truly astonishing. In another field his Lordship made a comparison, in April 1802, of drilling one half at 7 inches with three bushels of seed per acre ; and the other half broad cast with 4 bushels per acre. I viewed the stubble of this year's (1803) crop, and found the drilled much cleaner than the broad cast ; and a better plant. The hint is taken, and all that has been put in this spring is drilled at 7 inches *across* drilled barley or oats ; and a bushel of seed per acre saved.

The importance of this grass on such a soil ; a blowing sand on a white or whitish calcareous bottom, which rises in most places near to the surface, can never be too highly estimated. Where there is one acre on the sands of Norfolk and Suffolk there ought to be 100 ; and the experiment of sowing in June on foul land, combined with the Gloucestershire practice noted by Mr. Marshall, deserves attention in all cases where it is of consequence to procure it as early as possible.

Of lucerne his Lordship has 12 acres broad cast ; and though the soil is not rich enough to do the plant justice, yet it is this summer of very great use in soiling, and will probably be much more productive next year.

The course of crops which he proposes to follow, and has begun with, is

1. Turnips,
2. Barley or oats,
3. Seeds,
4. Seeds,
5. Rye or wheat.

400 acres of turnips, 400 of barley or oats, 800 of seeds, and 400 of rye and wheat, in all 2000 ; remaining consequently 200 for sheep walk, sainfoin, lucerne, &c.

Marling Lord Albemarle has carried on from the
first taking his farm with a steady assiduity ; in this
essential business he has the great advantage of a person
who contracts for the work at 8*d*. a cubical yard,
finding horses and carts, and paying all the labour.
He keeps 10 horses constantly employed at it through
the year, carrying 50 yards a day, or 5 for each horse.
His Lordship lays on 70 yards per acre, spreading
it on layers from a year to a year and a half before
ploughing them, which he thinks an essential point in
order for a due incorporation with the soil ; and he has
made an observation on this farm which confirms him
in the opinion. On ploughing a field deeper than common, which had been marled 15 or 16 years ago, but
turned in directly, he ploughed up lumps as large
as a double fist, quite undissolved, and consequently
unincorporated with the soil.

Winter barley and rye for sheep feed have been attentively compared here ; 15 acres of each contiguous ;
the former was put in on two earths, considered as
necessary ; but the rye only on a *ribbling ;* the sheep
preferred the bear greatly, and it lasted much longer
than the rye. Half the bear was on buck-wheat ploughed
in to manure it, but no difference perceptible in the
crop.

In manuring, his Lordship made the following experiment : in 1802 he had a very fine crop of turnips
drilled at 18 inches, which were thus manured for :
the first division, lime 200 bushels per acre. The second, oil cake 16 bushels per acre. The third, lime
100 bushels, the rest sheep folded.

No difference in the turnips. I viewed the drilled
barley which followed ; the difference very little, but I
thought the oil cake had the advantage.

Lord Albemarle has manured a young layer in a barley

stubble with short dung in autumn, without perceiving the smallest benefit from it.

I found him paring and burning a sheep walk at the expence of 45s. an acre, to compare this method of breaking up with the other more common ones; his Lordship had done much that was sown with cole seed for sheep feed, the plant healthy and promising; 70 acres pared and burnt this season. He proposes barley or oats after the cole with seeds, and then to clay : and he will not be disappointed.

In sheep the Earl has been very successful, and made an important and decisive experiment.

At Michaelmas, 1801, the late Duke of Bedford and Mr. Coke advised him to try South Downs, and the Duke sent him 300 ewes; these were put into a flock of Norfolks (of 900, turning out 300 of the worst, to make room for the new comers), and they went together all the year ; their superiority was such as to convince his Lordship ; so that he got rid of the rest of the Norfolks, and made up the flock 900 South Downs. Having another flock of 900 Norfolk ewes, he began the comparison from Michaelmas 1802 of 900 Downs against as many Norfolks. They fared alike in every respect. The 900 Norfolks, reared to the first of June, 732 lambs, the South Downs 826. A difference of 94. And during the lambing time, which was particularly unfavourable, numbers of the Norfolk ewes left their lambs ; from 15 to 20 were put into the herdles *(hobbling or cooping)* daily, to make them own their lambs ; but of the South Downs, from the first to last, not one. Of the Norfolk ewes there died in lambing 18; of the South Downs 4. Of the wool of the Norfolks 15½ fleeces went to the tod of 28lbs ; of the South Down fleeces 11 ; both sold at the same price. Both flocks were equally folded ; but the South Downs

certainly in much better condition than the Norfolks;
as they were also at the time I viewed both. And I
made another observation which could not be denied,
that the Norfolk flock had the advantage in land ; and
though it is asserted that they fared exactly alike, there
was one difference which should also be noted—the
Norfolks ate 20 acres of turnips belonging to the South
Downs.

Upon the whole, the comparison was so decisive in
favour of the new comers, that Lord Albemarle intends
parting with all his Norfolks, and keeping no other than
South Downs.

Nor is it himself only that is convinced. Four neighbouring farmers hearing that he meant to part with his
Norfolk flock, came to Elden and proposed to part each
of them with a lot of South Downs in exchange for
Norfolks. However, before the terms were discussed,
they rode about the farm to examine the two flocks, and
make enquiries, and the result was, that they changed
their minds, and determined to keep their South Downs.

Judging by estimation, and not actual weight, whole-
bred South Down lambs weigh more than whole bred
Norfolk lambs ; or than half-bred ones out of Norfolk
ewes ; but half-bred Leicesters out of Norfolk ewes,
more than either.

His Lordship would not take 20s. a head for his
South Down lambs all round. Last year he sold the
half-breds at 21s. and crones at 19s. 6d. His flock
therefore cannot be estimated (wool being at 52s. 6d.
per tod, 4s. 8d. a head) at less, allowing for losses, than
upwards of a guinea a head:

900 clipped, 826 lambs at 20s.   -   £.826   0   0
900 fleeces, 2½lbs. at 22½d.   4s. 8d. -   210   0   0

                                       £.1036   0   0

Fold   -   -   -   -

The 900 South Downs go over, at some time or other in the year, 726 acres of arable, and 490 of heath, or walk in all 1216 acres.

His Lordship has made three standing folds, inclosed by thick turf walls, 80 yards square, for sheltering his flock at lambing time against driving snows and other very bad weather, surrounded by plantation, except to the south. A shepherd's house is built to each, with a chimney and fire place for heating milk. In the spring the three inclosures were ploughed and planted with potatoes; the crops very promising. These yards are found to be of excellent use, and cannot be too much recommended.

The place for washing sheep at Elden is also well contrived; a portion of a pond is paled off on each side; the sheep go in at one end and out at the other; and being in three temporary divisions, they swim in the first, are forced down by the shepherd's crook (he standing on a longitudinal bridge, which runs along the three divisions on the outside), and soaked in the second; thence they swim to the men in the third, who wash them, and there, feeling their feet on the pavement, quit the pen. The men assert that the water washes them cleaner the second day than the first; they have then formed their own lye and soap suds.

Lord Albemarle promises to be a very active, and experimental farmer; and will, by improving and planting, change the face of the desart that surrounds him.

MR. READ, of *Darsham*, has this year (1803) a field of barley, the best in the parish, drilled at 10 inches on turnip land, after only one scarifying; and another at 7 inches, but not so good as that at 10; he says that scarifying is more sure for a crop than ploughing; and intends, under similar circumstance, never to plough again. He has tried long muck, and says it will not do. He approves of feeding wheat.

MR. MARTIN, of *Darsham*, has been a driller on good loam for 6 years. Wheat he drills at 8 inches, 2 deep, and uses 7 pecks of seed ; barley and oats at 7 inches, 1 deep, and uses 4 bushels of seed oats and 10 pecks of barley ; beans at 14 inches, 2 deep, and 7 pecks of seed ; with all these plants the drill has beat the broad cast ; he horse-hoes all. This gentleman is clear in the rejection of all spring ploughing ; and he has a neighbour of the same opinion, who says that he will never use a plough for barley after turnips.

His course :

1. Turnips dunged,
2. Barley,
3. Clover or beans,
4. Wheat dunged.

When he introduces carrots, which he has done on wheat and bean land,

1. Turnips,
2. Carrots,
3. Carrots,
4. Barley,
5. Clover,
6. Wheat.

He gives one trench ploughing for carrots ; hoes thrice at the expence of 9*s.* 6*s.* and 5*s.* per acre. He finds that horses will not do upon them without oats, and attributes this circumstance to being obliged to wash them, which makes them disagree with the horses; where, as in the sands, they want no washing. He gives his horses beans bruised, and thinks that 5 bushels are equal to 2 combs of oats. Carrots he has given to bullocks, and finds that beasts of 50 stone will eat

5 bushels per diem. In fattening nothing exceeds them.

MR. T. GOOCH, of *Darsham*, has this year (1803) 7 acres of barley on a summer fallow, put in without either spring ploughing or scarifying, by harrowing only, and his brother assures me that he never saw a finer piece of corn ; and with it a capital plant of clover. The adjoining field is under oats also on a summer fallow, half of it put in on one spring ploughing, and half on one scarifying ; both the crops very fine, and to the eye no perceptible difference, but the scarified part was at sowing in much the finer order.

MR. COATES, of *Sutton*, drills much corn and prefers the husbandry to the broad cast. Barley at $7\frac{1}{2}$ inches, $3\frac{1}{2}$ deep, and 5 pecks of seed ; oats at the same distance and depth, and 6 pecks of seed. He does not think drilled wheat more liable to mildew than broad cast crops, and gets as good a sample from it.

He cultivates 20 acres of carrots yearly in the course of

1. Turnips,
2. Barley,
3. Seeds,
4. Wheat or pease dunged,
5. Carrots.

Trench ploughs for them at sowing about lady day ; seed 4lbs. Hoes thrice at a guinea per acre ; but sometimes only twice at 18*s*. Average crop on poor sand 5 or 6 loads. On better land 10 to 18. Barley is better after turnips than after carrots, unless it be on good land in good heart. He applies them to his teams, &c. The culture increases. He has tried long muck for turnips, and approves of it.

This gentleman keeps Norfolk ewes covered by

Leicester rams, and thinks that he can keep a greater stock than if the breed were wholly Norfolk.

He lays down poor sand with broom, which he leaves for sheep feed for 5, 6, or 7 years, and it is the best thing on poor sheep walk sands, which he has tried.

MR. GROSS, of *Sutton*, began the drill husbandry this year on a sand farm ; his barley at 7 inches, 6 pecks an acre ; oats at the same distance, and 8 pecks ; both 2 inches deep. From what he has yet seen of the husbandry he approves it.

He cultivates about 14 acres of carrots annually in this course, on poor land,

   1. Turnips dunged,
   2. Barley,
   3. Seeds,
   4. Carrots,
   5. Pease or oats.

On better land,

   1. Turnips dunged,
   2. Barley,
   3. Clover,
   4. Wheat,
   5. Carrots.

Trench ploughs for them at sowing, seed 4lbs. per acre steeped. The time lady day or a fortnight after. Hoes twice at the expence of 12s. The produce on poor land 8 loads; on better 14. His barley after turnips better than after carrots, and he has an indefinite notion that they injure land. Average selling price a guinea a load. He has given them to bullocks with success as to fattening ; but the expence is too great ; one of 80 stone will eat 6 bushels a day. From the beginning of April he gives them to his horses ; and finds that a bushel is equal to half a bushel of oats ; but they have corn at the same time and cut chaff. Has given them to sheep but they *crone* them early ; that is, break their teeth. The culture increases greatly, and has now even spread on to the strong land at Tunslat. Mr. Gross thinks that long dung would answer for turnips, but he is obliged to make composts, or he could not cover a sufficient number of acres.

MR. T. WALLER, of *Sutton*, has been a driller upon sand for the period of seven years. His distances are, for wheat 9 inches, and uses 1 bushel of seed ; for barley and oats 6 inches ; seed of the former 5 pecks, of the latter 8 ; pease at 9 inches, and 2 bushels of seed. He has tried wheat at 6, but prefers 9 ; and finds the drill more profitable than either broad cast or dibbling. Nor does he find that drilled wheat is more subject to mildew than broad cast.

He cultivates 16 acres of carrots yearly in this course on the better sands.

1. Turnips,
2. Barley,
3. Clover,
4. Wheat mucked,
5. Carrots,
6. Pease mucked.

But on the poorer sand,

1. Turnips.
2. Barley,
3. Seeds,
4. Carrots,
5. Barley,

He trench ploughs for them at sowing ; time about Lady-day, 5lbs. per acre of seed. He hoes thrice at 7s. 6s. and 5s. sometimes to a guinea per acre. The produce on poor land 8 to 10 loads ; on better soils 15 to 20. His barley is as good after carrots as after turnips.

He has found, from long experience that they are worth
20s. a load to give to horses ; these prefer them to corn
so much that they will not eat it for some time after
feeding on this root ; and it is better for them than
corn and hay. He gives 2 loads a week to 6. The
culture increases greatly. He has carried on sand upon
sand for them, and it has answered.

This gentleman once tried long muck for turnips,
but it would not do. On good land he sometimes takes
beans on a layer, and then wheat.

MR. MABSON, of *Shottisham*, has drilled upon
sandy land 3 years, barley at 8 inches, seed 7 pecks ;
oats at 8, seed 2 bushels ; wheat at the same distance,
seed 7 pecks, but prefers dibbling, 2 rows on a flag.
The depth of all 3 inches. For barley and oats the
drilled are better than broad cast crops. Does not horse-
hoe.

Of carrots he has 20 acres annually in the course of
 1. Turnips,
 2. Barley,
 3. Clover,
 4. Wheat mucked,
 5. Carrots,
 6. Barley or pease : mucks for pease.

He trench ploughs for the carrots at the time of sowing ; 5lbs. of seed (steeped) per acre ; hoes thrice, total
expence from 15s. to 21s. an acre. Taking up 1s. 0½d.
a load. Average crop 10 to 15 loads. In feeding
horses one bushel of carrots equals ¾ of a peck of oats.
A horse will eat a bushel daily. It is not good to give
oats and carrots at the same time, they disagree with
the horses ; they prefer carrots to every thing. Bullocks
fatten well on them ; one will eat 3 bushels per diem ;
and large ones will fatten in 5 months if in good condition when put to this food. The culture increases

much. This gentleman prefers long muck for turnips on heavy land.

Mr. Mabson has a heavy land farm at Kelsale, and there all spring ploughing (to use his own expression) *is scouted.*

Mr. Brewer, of Ramsholt, a late pupil of Mr. Mabson, adopts his carrot system, and raises 20 acres annually.

MR. S. LAWRENCE, of *Shottisham,* cultivates 10 acres of carrots annually in this course:

    1. Turnips,

    2. Barley,

    3. Clover,

    4. Wheat mucked,

    5. Carrots,

    6. Péase or barley.

But if the wheat be not on clover, does not sow carrots. He trench ploughs for them at Lady-day and harrows in 5lbs. of seed per acre. He hoes thrice at 7s. 6s. and 5s. per acre. He ships some at 31s. 6d. per load. Freight to London 16s. a load paid by purchaser. He gives to 6 horses 2 loads a week with straw and chaff, but neither hay nor corn; and they are in better order with this food than if they had each 1½ bushels of oats per week and hay. The culture increases.

MR. W. MAHEW, of *Melton,* sows commonly 5 acres of carrots, but this year (1803) has 9 acres; his course for them:

    1. Carrots,

    2. Turnips,

    3. Barley,

    4. Clover,

    5. Wheat mucked,

in which the carrots are taken on a wheat stubble, which he thinks best for them. He gives two or three spring ploughings for them, the last deep, but not trenched. Steeps the seed in water for 48 hours, drains and spreads on a floor to dry, mixing earth for sowing at Lady-day. Seed 4lbs. per acre. Hoes thrice at 7s. 5s. and 4s. per acre. Average crop 10 loads per acre ; he has had 20 ; he estimates the present one at 15. He sells some to London at the medium price of 30s. per load. He finds them an excellent food for all sorts of stock, and will fatten all well. He gives his horses half a bushel of carrots per diem, with chaff and hay ; no oats necessary. Hogs fatten to 10 or 15 stone on them, eating three quarters of a bushel daily, and do wonderfully well. Taking them up 1s. 6d. per load. He finds that barley after turnips fed on the land, is better than after carrots drawn.

The culture increases much.

He carries on all his dung for wheat.

He has not lost a turnip by the fly in eleven years; which he attributes to steeping the seed.

COMMERCE.

THE fisheries at Lowestoff have increased of late years considerably ; the mackarel boats this year (1803) in 6 weeks earned above 10,000*l.* by mackarel, besides the other fish they caught. And last year something more than 30 boats gained 30,000*l.* the price cured, which was more than ever known. This circumstance keeps husbandry labour high ; it is now 12*s.* a week the year round, except in harvest.

I viewed the Life Boat at Lowestoff, and was sorry to find, from conversation with several sailors and fishermen, that they had no confidence in its superiority to their own craft ; it had been tried, and failed. They assert that it may do well elsewhere, but is not proper on their seas ; some men were washed out of it and others jumped over board ; it was found too heavy. The account was not satisfactory, and appeared to me the result of undue prejudice. No lives have been saved by it, yet wrecks have been numerous.

COMPARISON OF TIMES.

LATE in the spring of 1804, the Board of Agriculture received a requisition from the Corn Committee of the House of Commons, to report to the Committee a comparison of the expences on arable land in 1790 and 1803 ; and in order that the information to be given might be as satisfactory as the powers of the Board and the time would allow, a circular letter to their principal correspondents was immediately dispatched, requesting a particular return upon the objects pointed out in the requisition of the Committee. The answers were numerous, and I am permitted by a vote of the Board, to print in this work the contents of such as came from the county of Suffolk.

DAY LABOUR.

COMMUNICATION.	Price in Winter, 1790. Per Week.		Price in Winter, 1804. Per Week.		Price in Summer, 1790. Per Week.		Price in Summer, 1804. Per Week.		Price in Harvest, 1790. Per Week.		Price in Harvest, 1804. Per Week.	
	s.	d.	s.	d.	s.	d.	s.	d.	s.	d.	s.	d.
No. 1. W. Gooch	6	0	9	0	7	0	12	0	12	0	21	0
2. T. Simpson*	6	0	9	0	8	0	12	0	12	0	21	0
3. Ben. Cotton	7	0	8	0	8	0	10	0	12	0	15	0
4. John Sparrow	6	0	8	0	8	0	9	0	10	6	15	6
5. Sam. Kilderbee	7	0	9	0	9	0	12	0	13	6	21	0
6. S. M. Rodwell†	7	0	9	0	8	0	12	0	22	6	34	2
7. Thos. Maynard	7	6	10	0	9	0	12	0	21	0	30	0
8. W. Green	8	0	10	6	9	0	12	0	15	0	24	0
9. James Fowel.	7	0	9	0	9	0	10	0	20	0	30	0
Average	6	10	9	½	8	4	9	2½	15	4½	23	6
Being per cent.	32 2/8				11½				52 13/183			

* Wheat sold at 6s. and 10 bushels of malt in the year.
† Wheat, butter, &c. sold at a reduced price.

PIECE-WORK.

OMMUNICATION.	Reap Wheat, 1790. Per Acre.		Reap Wheat, 1804. Per Acre.		Mow Barley, 1790. Per Acre.		Mow Barley, 1804. Per Acre.		Thrash Wheat, 1790. Per Qr.		Thrash Wheat, 1804. Per Qr.		Thrash Barley, 1790. Per Qr.		Thrash Barley, 1804. Per Qr.		Filling Earth, 1790. Per Yard.		Filling Earth, 1804. Per Yard.		Filling Dung, 1790. Per Load.		Filling Dung, 1804. Per Load.	
	s.	*d.*	*s.*	*d.*	*s.*	*d.*	*s.*	*d.*	*s.*	*d.*	*s.*	*d.*	*s.*	*d.*	*s.*	*d.*	*s.*	*d.*	*s.*	*d.*	*s.*	*d.*	*s.*	*d.*
No. 1	4	6	8	0	1	2	2	0	2	0	3	6	1	2	1	8	0	3	0	4½	0	1½	0	*2¼
2	5	0	7	6	1	3	2	0	2	4	3	6	1	2	2	0	0	0	0	0	0	1½	0	1¾
3	6	6	7	6	1	6	2	0	2	4	3	0	1	2	1	6	0	2½	0	3	0	1½	0	2
4	5	6	7	6	1	2	1	8	2	0	3	4	1	0	1	6	0	2	0	2¼	0	0	0	0
5	5	6	7	6	1	4	2	0	2	4	3	8	1	4	2	4	0	1½	0	2	0	1½	0	2
6	4	6	7	0	1	3	2	0	2	0	4	0	1	0	1	8	0	2½	0	3	0	1½	0	2
7	7	0	10	0	1	6	2	6	2	6	3	2	1	6	2	0	0	3	0	4	0	2	0	3
8	5	0	8	6	1	6	2	6	2	6	4	8	1	4	2	0	0	2½	0	4	0	1	0	1½
9	5	0	8	0	1	3	1	8	1	6	3	0	1	0	1	6	0	2	0	3	0	2	0	3
Average	5	4½	6	10	1	3½	2	¼	2	2	3	5½	1	2	1	9½	0	2¼	0	3	0	1½	0	2¼
Per cent.	$27\frac{22}{120}$				$56\frac{14}{31}$				$59\frac{8}{13}$				$53\frac{4}{7}$				$48\frac{44}{97}$				50			

* The return is 2*s*. 6*d*. to 3*s*. 6*d*. which is in the proportion of 1½ to 1¾

WAGES.

COMMUNI- CATION.	Head Man's Wages, 1790. Per Annum.			Head Man's Wages, 1804. Per Annum.			Second Man's Wages, 1790. Per Annum.			Second Man's Wages, 1804. Per Annum.		
	£.	s.	d.	£.	s.	d.	£.	s.	d.	£.	s.	d.
No. 1	7	0	0	10	10	0	4	0	0	7	0	0
2	9	0	0	12	12	0	6	0	0	9	0	0
3	11	10	0	14	14	0	7	15	0	9	10	0
4	8	8	0	12	12	0	5	0	0	9	0	0
5	9	0	0	12	12	0	6	10	0	9	0	0
6	10	10	0	14	0	0	7	0	0	8	0	0
7	7	0	0	12	0	0	5	0	0	8	0	0
8	8	0	0	10	0	0	5	0	0			
9												
Average	8	16	5¼	12	2	½	0	6	½	8	11	1¼
Per cent.	38			38						42		

(Weekly-pay notes: Head Man's 1790 — 9s. per w.*; Head Man's 1804 — 10s. per w.; Second Man's 1790 — 8s. per w.; Second Man's 1804 — 9s. per w.)

* The pay per week in forming the totals is changed from shillings to pounds for the averages, which are the principal objects of the inquiry.

ARTISANS.

BLACKSMITH.

COMMUNI-CATION.	Tire, 1790. Per lb.		Tire, 1804. Per lb.		Plough-Irons, 1790. Per lb.		Plough-Irons, 1804. Per lb.		Chains, 1790. Per lb.		Chains, 1804. Per lb.		Shoeing, 1790. Per lb.		Shoeing, 1804. Per lb.	
	s.	d.	s.	d.	s.	d.	s.	d.	s.	d.	s.	d.	s.	d.	s.	d.
No. 1	0	$3\frac{3}{4}$	0	$4\frac{3}{4}$	0	5	0	7	0	$5\frac{1}{2}$	0	8	0	*4	0	7
2	0	$3\frac{1}{2}$	0	5	0	0	0	0	0	6	0	9	0	5	0	$8\frac{1}{2}$
3	0	4	0	$4\frac{1}{2}$	0	5	0	6	0	$6\frac{1}{2}$	0	7	0	6	0	7
4	0	$3\frac{1}{2}$	0	$4\frac{1}{4}$	0	0	0	0	0	5	0	8	0	†5	0	$7\frac{1}{4}$
5	0	4	0	$4\frac{1}{2}$	0	5	0	6	0	6	0	8	0	5	0	6
6	0	$3\frac{1}{2}$	0	$5\frac{1}{2}$	0	$4\frac{1}{2}$	0	7	0	5	0	8	0	$4\frac{1}{2}$	0	6
7	0	4	0	4	0	4	0	6	0	5	0	9	0	†4	0	8
8	0	$3\frac{1}{2}$	0	$4\frac{1}{4}$	0	4	0	7	0	4	0	6	0	4	0	6
9	0	$3\frac{1}{2}$	0	$5\frac{1}{2}$	0	4	0		0	6	0	10	0	4	0	7
Average	0	$3\frac{3}{4}$	0	5	0	$4\frac{1}{2}$	0	5	0	$5\frac{1}{4}$	0	8	0	$4\frac{1}{2}$	0	$6\frac{1}{2}$
Per cent.		$33\frac{1}{3}$				$11\frac{1}{9}$				$52\frac{8}{21}$				$44\frac{4}{9}$		

* The return is from 7s. to 12s. per horse per annum. This is in the proportion of 5d. to 8¼d.

† Return 5s. 6d. to 8s. per horse per annum; or as 5d. to 7½d.

‡ Advanced in this proportion.

ARTISANS.

COMMUNICATION	Carpenter. By Day, 1790.		Carpenter. By Day, 1804.		Mason. By Day, 1790.		Mason. By Day, 1804.		Thatcher. By Day, 1790.		Thatcher. By Day, 1804.		Collar-Maker's Work. 1790.		Collar-Maker's Work. 1804.	
	s.	d.	s.	d.	s.	d	s.	d.	s.	d.	s.	a.	s.	d.	s.	d.
No. 1	1	8	2	2	3	4	4	0	1	6	2	0	1	0	1	6
2	1	10	3	0	1	10	3	0	0	0	0	0	0	0	0	0
3	2	0	2	2	1	10	2	0	2	6	2	0	2	4	2	6
4	1	9	2	10	2	0	2	10	2	0	2	9	increased 40 per cent. or 2 | 0		2	9½
5	2	0	3	8	2	0	3	0	2	0	3	6	increased 50 per cent, or 2 | 0		3	0
6	2	0	2	0	2	0	3	0	2	0	2	0	Doubled. or 2 | 0		4	0
7	1	8	3	4	2	0	3	0	2	6	3	6	Doubled, or 2 | 0		4	0
8	2	4	3	3	2	4	3	3	2	4	3	6	increased 5 per cent. or 2 | 0		2	1⅕
9	1	6	2	6	1	6	2	6	2	4	3	6	0	0	2	0
Average	1	10¼	2	8¾	2	1¼	2	11¼	2	1¾	2	10¾	1	9¼	2	10
Per cent.	47 17/89				39 61/101				34 98/103				60			

SUFFOLK.

RENT, TITHE, AND PARISH TAXES.

COMMUNI-CATION.	Rise of Rent, from 1790 to 1804.	Tithe.				Parish Taxes.			
		Per Acre, 1790		Per Acre, 1803.		In the Pound, 1790.		In the Pound, 1803.	
		s.	d.	s.	d.	s.	d	s.	d.
No. 1	{ 12s 6d. to 14s. 9d. or 36⁶⁰₆₅ per c.	2	6	3	0	4	2	6	8¼
*2	{ 14s. to 24s. or 71³⁄₇ per c.	4	0	6	0	2	6	6	0
3	{ 20s. to 22s. or 10 per c.	4	0	5	0	4	0	5	6
4	40 per cent.	4	6	6	0	inc. ⅓ or 3	0	0 4	0 0
5	33 per cent.	3	0	5	6	3	6	6	6
6	33 per cent.	increased 10 per cent. or 3	0	3	3	0	0	0	0
7		3	6	6	0	2	6	5	0
8	50 per cent.	2	6	3	6	5	0	6	0
9	12½ per c.	inc. 12½ per cent or 4	0	4	6	inc. 12½ per cent. or 4	0	4	6
Average		3	1¼	4	9	3	7	5	6¼
Per cent.	35¹¹⁴⁷⁄₁₄₅₆	53³⁄₁₄₉				48¹¹⁄₄₃			

* Last duty on malt, and tax on cart horses, amount to 2s. per acre on all the arable lands

SUFFOLK.
CULTIVATION.

COMMUNI-CATION.	Expence of an Acre of Turnips.						Expence of an Acre of Barley.						Expence of an Acre of Wheat.						Expence of Manure.					
	1790.			1804.			1790.			1804.			1790.			1804.			1790.			1804.		
	£.	s.	d.	£.	s.	d.	£.	s.	d.	£.	s.	d.	£.	s.	d.	£.	s.	d.	£.	s.	d.	£.	s.	d.
No. 1	2	14	0	3	12	0	3	13	6	4	17	4	2	15	4	3	16	6	0	0	0	0	0	0
2	0	0	0	0	0	0	0	0	0	0	0	0	0	0	0	0	0	0	0	0	0	0	0	0
3	1	16	0	2	0	0	1	15	0	1	18	0	1	18	0	2	0	0	0	3	6	0	4	0
4	3	15	11	4	13	5	3	7	6	4	8	10	4	7	6	5	15	0	0	2	6	0	4	0
5	3	11	6	4	14	8	0	19	0	1	2	6	3	10	0	4	3	0	0	2	0	0	3	0
6	3	8	8	4	17	4	0	18	0	1	2	0	0	10	9	8	1	9	0	5	0	0	7	0
7	1	15	0	2	10	0	1	0	0	1	0	0	4	0	0	0	0	0	0	0	0	0	0	0
8	4	0	0	6	0	0	4	0	0	6	0	0	1	7	0	6	0	0	0	0	0	0	0	0
9	1	10	0	1	17	6	0	18	0	1	4	2	3	9	1	1	18	8	0	0	0	0	0	0
Average	2	14	4½	3	15	7¼	2	1	4½	2	14	1¼	3	9	1	4	10	7	0	3	3	0	0	6
Per cent.	30 $\frac{11}{26}$						31						31 $\frac{1}{8}$						38 $\frac{18}{39}$					

Turnips,   30 per cent.
Barley,   31
Wheat,   31
             ———
Average,   30¾

EXTRACTS FROM THE LETTERS ACCOMPANYING THE PRECEDING RETURNS.

COMMUNICATION, No. 1.

Cockfield, April 29, 1804.

OBSERVATIONS ON ANNEXED ANSWERS.

LABOUR, WINTER AND SUMMER.

In 1790.—Also 1 pint of beer in winter and 2 in summer, or 2*d.* in 1*s.* on wages.
1804.—Also 2 ditto   and 3 ditto   or 3*d.* in ditto.

LABOUR AND HARVEST.

1790—Also 4 pints of beer and various treats, equal together to 6*d.* per day more.
1804—Also 5   ditto   ditto   ditto   to 1*s.*   ditto

N. B. Malt and hops are usually given in lieu of beer, *i. e.* 3 bushels of malt and 3 lbs. of hops per man, and the treats often compounded for, at from 10*s.* 6*d.* to 15*s.* much against the inclination of the men.

THRASHING.

In 1790 and 1804—Also 2*d.* in 1*s.* in lieu of beer.   N. B. Prefer Beer.

REAPING, MOWING, AND FILLING.

In 1790—Also beer, 2d. in 1s. ⎫
1804—— Ditto   3d. in 1s. ⎭ Prefer beer.——Very little claying done.

CARPENTER, MASON, AND THRASHER.

In 1790—Also beer, or 3s. in the pound on bill.
1804—— Ditto,   4s.   ditto.

COLLAR-MAKER.

In 1790 and 1804—Also board. *All articles of this tradesman doubled since* 1790.

POOR RATES.

That this comparison might hold good, the same assessment is assumed (viz. that of 1790); the present one is much more.

RENT.

This parish consists of 3400 acres, *profitable land*, and in 1790 the rental by assessment was £.2133, viz. about 12s. 6d. per acre; now (viz. 1804) the rental (also by assessment) is £.2461, viz. 14s. 9d. per acre. N. B. Tithe excluded in both assessments.

PARTICULARS.—TURNIPS.

	1790.			1804.			
	£.	s.	d.		£.	s.	d.
4 earths, at 4s. - - -	0	16	0	at 7s. - -	1	8	0
2 "roves," at 2s. 6d. -	0	5	0	oat 3s. 6d. -	0	7	0
Harrowing and water furrowing -	0	2	0		0	3	6
Seed, a quart, -	0	0	6		0	0	0
Hoeing twice, including beer,	0	7	0		0	9	0
Workmanship, and carting 15 loads of muck, at 6d.	0	7	6	at 9d. -	0	11	3
Rent, -	0	12	6		0	14	9
Rates, -	0	2	0		0	5	0
Tythe, -	0	2	6		0	3	0
Wear and tear, -	0	2	0		0	4	0
	£. 2	17	0		£. 4	5	6

N. B. Not turnip land——The charge of 2s. per acre for wear and tear, is to cover tradesmen's bills. It is supposed by the farmers who assisted in these estimates, that in 1790, 2s. per acre was by these incurred, and that now it is 4s. I believe it much more. *Query.* In 1790 would £10. be sufficient for these charges on a farm of 100 acres arable? and will £20. pay them now (1804) on the like farm?

PARTICULARS.—BARLEY.

N. B. After complete summer land, for such yet exists!!!

	1790.			1804.			
	£.	s.	d.		£.	s.	d.
5 earths at 4s. - - -	1	0	0	at 7s.	1	15	0
Harrowing and water furrowing,	0	1	0		0	1	4
Seed, 3 bushels, at 14s.	0	10	6	at 10s. 6d.	0	7	6
Two years rent, at 12s. 6d.	1	5	0	at 14s. 9d.	1	9	6
Ditto rates, - - -	0	4	0		0	5	0
Ditto tithe, - - -	0	5	0		0	6	0
Harvesting, including horses and labour,	0	6	0		0	9	0
Wear and tear, see note on turnip } estimates,	0	2	0		0	4	0
	£. 3	13	6		£. 4	17	4

PARTICULARS.—WHEAT AFTER CLOVER.

	1790. £ s. d.	1804. £ s. d.
Mucking, viz, workmanship and caring, 24 loads, at 4½d.	0 9 0	0 14 0 at 7d.
One earth	0 5 0	0 7 6
Seed, 2 bushels	0 12 0	0 12 6
Harrowing and water furrowing	0 1 4	0 2 6
Preparing seed	0 0 6	0 0 9
Rent	0 12 6	0 14 9
Rates	0 2 0	0 5 0
Tithe	0 2 6	0 3 0
Hoeing	0 2 0	0 3 0
Harvesting, including horses' labour	0 6 6	0 10 0
Wear and tear, see note on turnip estimate	0 2 0	0 4 0
	£. 2 15 4	£. 3 16 6

MANURES.

Some little muck is bought, and brought from 4 to 6 miles, and costs—1st purchase, 2s. 6d. per tumbril load, and 4s. 6d. expence getting it home ; total, 7s. per load.

The preceding table of cultivation was more satis-factorily returned than in the case of many other coun-ties; various of the correspondents under the heads of that table, returned only the expence of tillage, omit-ting rent, taxes, seed, and labour; others returned the labour only, omitting every other article, insomuch that in many cases no conclusions could be drawn : this in-duced the Board to order a second letter to be written, which requested an answer to this one query; *What are the charges upon 100 acres of arable land under the following distinct heads?*

	1790	1803
Rent,	——	——
Tithe,	——	——
Rates and taxes,	——	——
Wear and tear,	——	——
Labour,	——	——
Seed,	——	——
Manure purchased,	——	——
Team,	——	——
Interest of capital.	——	——

From the answers to this letter from the county of Suffolk, the following tables are constructed.

SUFFOLK.

COMMUNICATION.	Rent. 1790. £. s. d.	Rent. 1803. £. s. d.	Tithe. 1790. £. s. d.	Tithe. 1803. £. s. d	Rates and Taxes. 1790. £. s. d.	Rates and Taxes. 1803. £. s. d.
No. 1. O. Ray.	75 0 0	115 0 0	15 0 0	25 0 0	15 0 0	25 0 0
2. Jon. Carter.	42 10 0	75 0 0	15 0 0	20 0 0	6 10 0	8 0 0
3. Geo. Pung.	70 0 0	105 0 0	20 0 0	30 0 0	15 8 0	35 0 6
4. Wm Gooch.	62 10 0	73 15 0	12 10 0	15 0 0	15 11 0	51 12 6
5. T. Simpson.	70 0 0	100 0 0	20 0 0	30 0 0	11 0 0	24 0 0
6. Ben. Cotton.	90 0 c	100 0 0	25 0 0	30 0 0	24 0 0	37 10 0
Average, - -	68 6 8	94 15 10	17 18 4	25 0 0	14 11 7½	30 3 9
Or per cent. -	38 59/82		39 23/43		107 1/3 *	

* Here all the taxes paid by the farmer are included, which is not the case in the former table.

SUFFOLK.

COMMUNICATION.	Wear and tear.						Labour.						Seed.					
	1790.			1803.			1790.			1803.			1790.			1803.		
	£.	s.	d.	£.	s.	d.	£.	s.	d.	£.	s.	d.	£.	s.	d.	£.	s.	d.
No. 1.	30	0	0	40	0	0	75	0	0	115	0	0	35	0	0	43	0	0
2.	12	0	0	16	0	0	60	0	0	75	0	0	30	0	0	35	0	0
3.	22	0	0	35	0	0	110	0	0	162	0	0	40	0	0	50	0	0
4.	10	0	0	20	0	0	110	0	0	164	16	0	43	1	$9\frac{1}{2}$	42	16	6
5.	20	0	0	35	0	0	133	0	0	188	0	0	43	0	0	46	17	0
6.	14	0	0	18	0	0	70	0	0	90	0	0	31	10	0	35	10	0
Average	18	0	0	27	6	8	93	0	0	132	9	4	37	1	$11\frac{1}{2}$	42	3	11
Per cent.				$51\frac{23}{27}$						$42\frac{122}{279}$						14		

SUFFOLK.

COMMUNICATION.	Manure 1790.			Manure 1803.			Team 1790.			Team 1803.			Interest 1790.			Interest 1803.			Total 1790.			Total 1803.		
	£	s.	d	£	s.	d.	£	s.	d.	£	s.	d.	£	s.	d.	£	s.	d.	£	s.	d.	£	s.	d.
No. 1.	0	0	0	0	0	0	40	0	0	65	0	0	17	10	0	25	0	0	287	10	0	433	0	0
2.	0	0	0	0	0	0	40	0	0	60	0	0	15	0	0	20	0	0	221	0	0	309	0	0
3.	12	10	0	17	10	0	65	0	0	80	10	0	16	0	0	27	10	0	370	10	0	542	10	0
4.	0	0	0	0	0	0	96	16	0	94	17	0	25	0	0	35	0	0	375	6	$6\frac{1}{2}$	497	10	$6\frac{1}{2}$
5.	0	0	0	0	0	0	87	0	0	120	0	0	25	0	0	40	0	0	409	11	0	583	17	0
6.	27	0	0	27	0	0	102	0	0	120	0	0	20	0	0	25	0	0	403	10	0	483	0	0
Average	19	15	0	22	5	0	71	16	0	90	1	2	19	15	0	28	15	0	344	10	3	474	17	4
Per cent.	$12\frac{1}{2}$						$25\frac{925}{2544}$						$47\frac{27}{77}$						38					

RECAPITULATION.

LABOUR.

	per cent.	per cent.
Rise in the price in winter from 1790 to 1803, }	32	
summer -	11	
		21
harvest - -	52	
reaping wheat, -	27	
mowing barley, -	56	
		45
head man's wages,	38	
second man's ditto,	42	
		40
thrashing wheat, -	59	
barley,	53	
		56
filling earth, -	48	
dung, -	50	
		49
		211
Fractions make it		214
Divide by 5 -		42

Being the general rise in husbandry labour.

ARTISANS.

Blacksmith.

	per cent.
Rise in the price of tire from 1790 to 1803,	33
plough irons, - -	11
chains, - - -	52
shoeing - - -	44
Average, -	36

					per cent.
Carpenter,	-	-	-	-	47
Mason,	-	-	-	-	39
Thatcher,	-	-	-	-	34
Collar Maker,		-	-	-	60
Average of artisans,			-	43	

RENT AND TAXES, &c.

Rise of rent from 1790 to 1803,	-	35
tithe - - -		31
rates, - - -		48

MANURE.

Rise from 1790 to 1803,   -   -   38

CULTIVATION OF ARABLE LAND.

Average rise on an acre of turnips, barley, and wheat,   -   -   - $\Big\}$ 30

PER CENT.

Labour,	-	-	-	42
Artisans,	-	-	-	43
Rent,	-	-	-	35
Tithe,	-	-	-	53
Rates,	-	-	-	48
Manure	-	-	38	
Cultivation,	-	-	30	
Average,	-	-	41	

In remarking on these particulars, I am in the first place to note, that the Board is not in the least committed in drawing any of these averages. That Body simply ordered circular letters to be written ; and every reply stands distinctly on the personal authority of the writer ; there ends the authority of the papers as I received them. All that follows in drawing them into one view, I have done for the satisfaction of such readers as might wish to know what the general result would be.

It does not, however, follow, that (supposing the authority of the letters correct) the averages would be the same, when a certain rise per cent. is deduced from them.

In the sketch, for instance, which gives 38 per cent. every one of the seven articles should be of equal importance, which is far from being the case. Artisans count for one as well as labour and rent, but it is of far inferior importance to either.

The same observation is applicable to the particulars from which these sums are drawn. In that of labour, servants wages count with summer and winter labour; and filling earth and dung the same ; but the fact is very different. In the article of artisans, if the particulars be examined, there will be found a still greater disproportion in their importance to the farmer. If these circumstances be not kept in the reader's mind, he must necessarily be deceived.

In order to come nearer to the real fact, by proportioning the several expences as they are found on an average farm, it will be some satisfaction to the reader to take the expences from the answers to the second letter, and calculate the rise of them by reference to the replies to the first.

The average expence per 100 acres in 1790, returned as above, is:

		£.	s.	d.
Rent,	- - -	68	6	8
Tithe,	- • -	17	18	4
Rates,	- - -	14	11	7½
Wear and tear,	- - -	18	0	0
Labour,	- - -	93	0	0
Seed,	- • -	37	1	11½
Manure,	- - -	19	15	0
Team,	- - -	71	16	0
Interest of capital,	- -	19	15	0

$$£. 360 \quad 4 \quad 7$$

Now if the rise of these be estimated from the first series of letters, viz. rent 35 ; tithe 53; rates 48; wear and tear 43; labour 42; manure 38; and taking the advance in the articles seed, team, and interest, from the answers to the second letter (not having place in the first), the result would stand thus:

	1790. £.	rise per cent.	1803. £.
Rent, -	68	35	91
Tithe, -	17	53	27
Rates, -	14	48	20
Wear and tear,	18	43	25
Labour, -	93	42	132
Seed, -	37	14	42
Manure, -	19	38	26
Team, -	71	25	88
Interest, -	19	47	27
	360		478
Average, - -		32	

The general average rise, therefore, thus calculated, is 32 per cent. which I apprehend is as near the truth as these data will permit us to arrive.

Printed by W. Bulmer and Co.
Cleveland Row, St. James's.